P9-CNG-292

THE FAMILY Handyman

Home Improvement

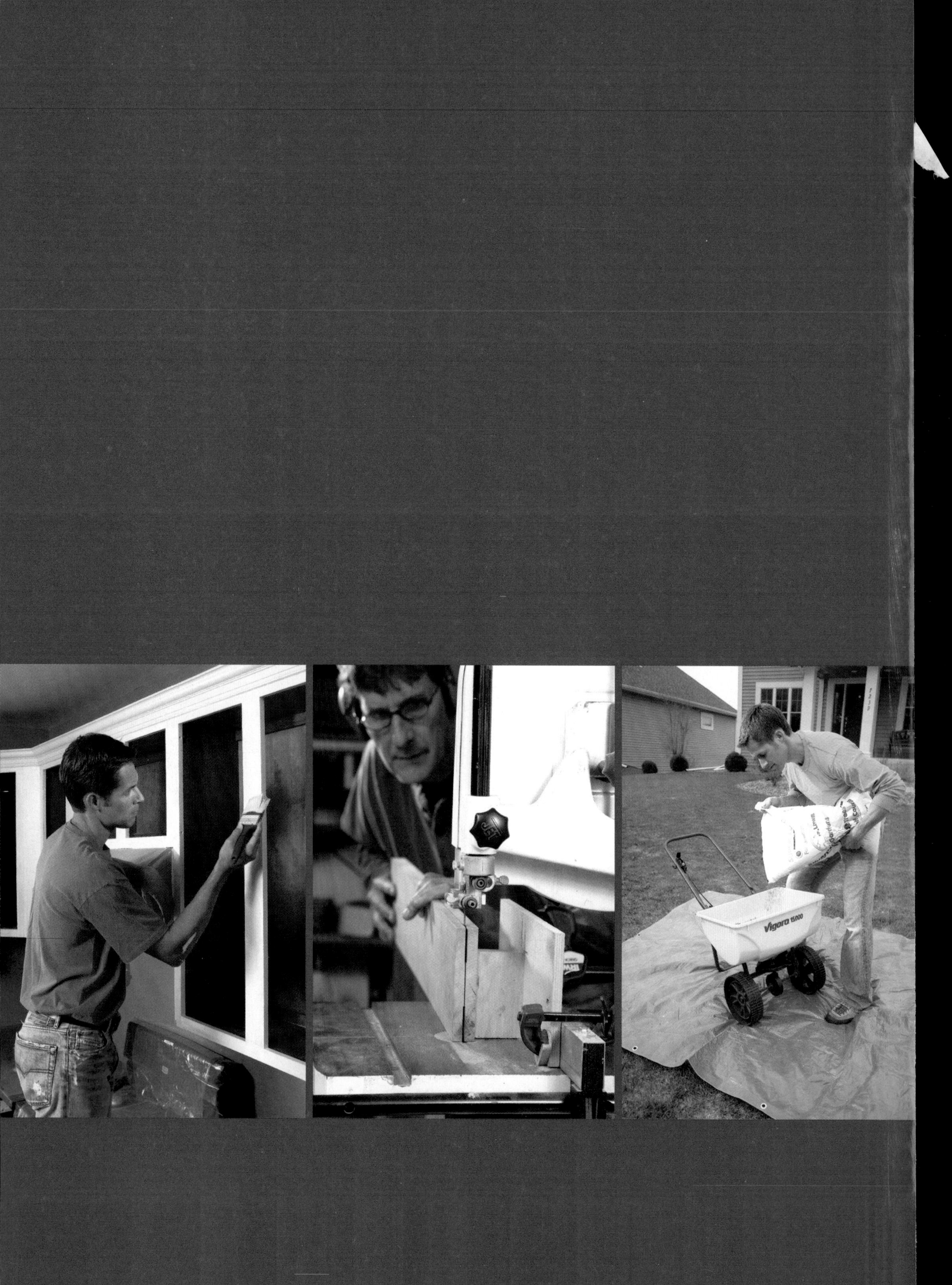
JET
Vigoro 15,000

THE FAMILY Handyman®

Home Improvement

by The Editors of *The Family Handyman* magazine

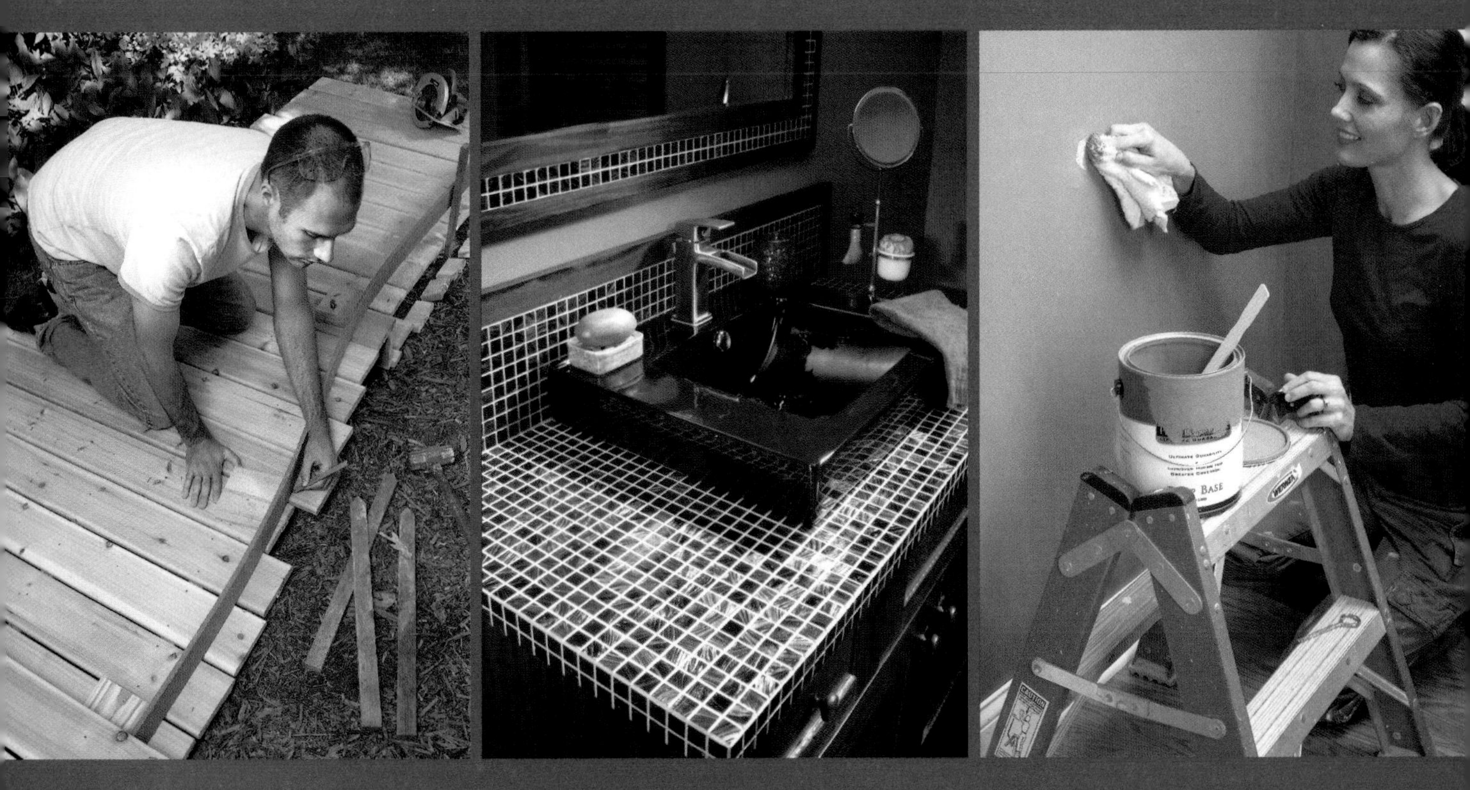

THE FAMILY HANDYMAN HOME IMPROVEMENT
(See page 288 for complete staff listing.)
Editor in Chief: Ken Collier
Project Editor: Mary Flanagan
Contributing Designers: Joel Anderson, Teresa Marrone
Contributing Copy Editors: Donna Bierbach, Peggy Parker
Indexing: Stephanie Reymann

Vice President, Publisher: Lora Gier

The Reader's Digest Association, Inc.
President & Chief Executive Officer: Mary G. Berner
President, North American Affinities and India: Suzanne Grimes
Senior Vice President, Chief Marketing Officer: Amy J. Radin

Warning: *All do-it-yourself activities involve a degree of risk. Skills, materials, tools, and site conditions vary widely. Although the editors have made every effort to ensure accuracy, the reader remains responsible for the selection and use of tools, materials, and methods. Always obey local codes and laws, follow manufacturer's operating instructions, and observe safety precautions.*

ISBN 978-1-60652-322-3   1-60652-322-8

Address any comments about *The Family Handyman Home Improvement* to:
Editor, Home Improvement
2915 Commers Drive, Suite 700
Eagan, MN 55121

To order additional copies of *The Family Handyman Home Improvement* , call 1-800-344-2560.

For more Reader's Digest products and information, visit our Web site at rd.com.
For more about *The Family Handyman* magazine, visit familyhandyman.com.

Printed in the United States of America.
1 3 5 7 9 10 8 6 4 2

INTRODUCTION

"If you only do what you know you can do, you never do very much." —Tom Krause

Home improvement is a process of discovery. First there's the realization that something needs to be fixed, replaced or upgraded. If this project is something you've tackled before, you're likely to feel that your experience is all you need to successfully complete the task again. But what if this is something new? Something you've never done before? Then you'll want some expert advice with step-by-step directions and clear photos and illustrations to help you ensure a fix and not a failure.

That's where *The Family Handyman* comes to the rescue! In *The Family Handyman Home Improvement,* we've collected a year's worth of the most authoritative and up-to-date home improvement content from the pages of our magazine. Whether you're interested in plumbing, tiling, woodworking, lawn care, insulating or trim carpentry, you'll find it inside. Plus, we've included Special Sections on painting cabinets, tools and skills, and storage and organizing. And if you don't have a workbench, there's a top-notch plan starting on p. 266.

During the past year, along with creating all the great content in this book, we also relaunched our Web site, familyhandyman.com. There you'll find hundreds of easily searchable articles, interactive forums, a blog and much more. We encourage you to check it out!

As proud as we are of our new site, rest assured that the core of what we do is still *The Family Handyman* magazine. We continue to deliver the most authoritative, complete and reliable information on home improvement available anywhere. And our editors are committed to making sure that what appears in the magazine, and on the Web site, is nothing but the best.

We hope you enjoy *The Family Handyman Home Improvement.* Best of luck with all your home improvement projects!

—The staff of *The Family Handyman* magazine

Contents

INTERIOR PROJECTS, REPAIRS & REMODELING

ELECTRICAL & HIGH-TECH

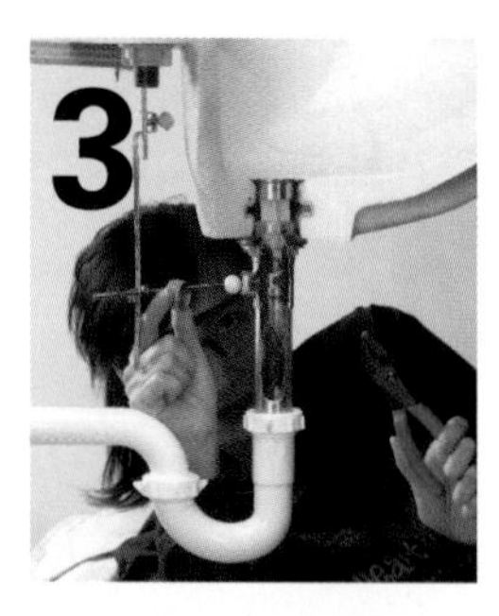

PLUMBING, HEATING & APPLIANCES

WOODWORKING & FURNITURE PROJECTS & TIPS

EXTERIOR MAINTENANCE & REPAIRS

OUTDOOR STRUCTURES, LANDSCAPING & GARDENING

AUTO & GARAGE

BONUS SECTION

SAFETY FIRST–ALWAYS!

Tackling home improvement projects and repairs can be endlessly rewarding. But as most of us know, with the rewards come risks. DIYers use chain saws, climb ladders and tear into walls that can contain big and hazardous surprises.

The good news is, armed with the right knowledge, tools and procedures, homeowners can minimize risk. As you go about your home improvement projects and repairs, stay alert for these hazards:

Aluminum wiring

Aluminum wiring, installed in about 7 million homes between 1965 and 1973, requires special techniques and materials to make safe connections. This wiring is dull gray, not the dull orange characteristic of copper. Hire a licensed electrician certified to work with it. For more information visit inspectny.com/aluminum/aluminum.htm.

Spontaneous combustion

Rags saturated with oil finishes like Danish oil and linseed oil, and oil-based paints and stains can spontaneously combust if left bunched up. Always dry them outdoors, spread out loosely. When the oil has thoroughly dried, you can safely throw them in the trash.

Vision and hearing protection

Safety glasses or goggles should be worn whenever you're working on DIY projects that involve chemicals, dust and anything that could shatter or chip off and hit your eye. Sounds louder than 80 decibels (dB) are considered potentially dangerous. Sound levels from a lawn mower can be 90 dB, and shop tools and chain saws can be 90 to 100 dB.

Lead paint

If your home was built before 1979, it may contain lead paint, which is a serious health hazard, especially for children six and under. Take precautions when you scrape or remove it. Contact your public health department for detailed safety information or call (800) 424-LEAD (5323) to receive an information pamphlet.

Buried utilities

A few days before you dig in your yard, have your underground water, gas and electrical lines marked. Just dial 811 or go to call811.com.

Smoke and carbon monoxide (CO) alarms

Almost two-thirds of home fire deaths from 2003 to 2006 resulted from fires in homes with no smoke alarms or no *working* smoke alarms. Test your smoke alarms every month, replace batteries as necessary and replace units that are more than 10 years old.

As you make your home more energy-efficient and airtight, existing ducts and chimneys can't always successfully vent combustion gases, including potentially deadly carbon monoxide (CO). Install a UL-listed CO detector, and test your CO and smoke alarms at the same time..

Five-gallon buckets and window covering cords

Since 1984, more than 75 children have drowned in 5-gallon buckets. Always store them upside down and store ones containing liquid with the covers securely snapped.

According to Parents for Window Blind Safety, 367 children have died in the United States in the past few decades after becoming entangled in looped window treatment cords. For more information, visit pfwbs.org or cpsc.gov.

Working up high

If you have to get up on your roof to do a repair or installation, always install roof brackets and wear a roof harness.

Asbestos

Texture sprayed on ceilings before 1978, adhesives and tiles for vinyl and asphalt floors before 1980, and vermiculite insulation (with gray granules) all may contain asbestos. Other building materials, made between 1940 and 1980, could also contain asbestos. If you suspect that materials you're removing or working around contain asbestos, contact your health department or visit epa.gov/asbestos for information.

For additional information about home safety, visit homesafetycouncil.com. This site offers helpful information about dozens of home safety issues.

1 Interior Projects, Repairs & Remodeling

IN THIS CHAPTER

SPRAY-TEXTURE A DAMAGED CEILING

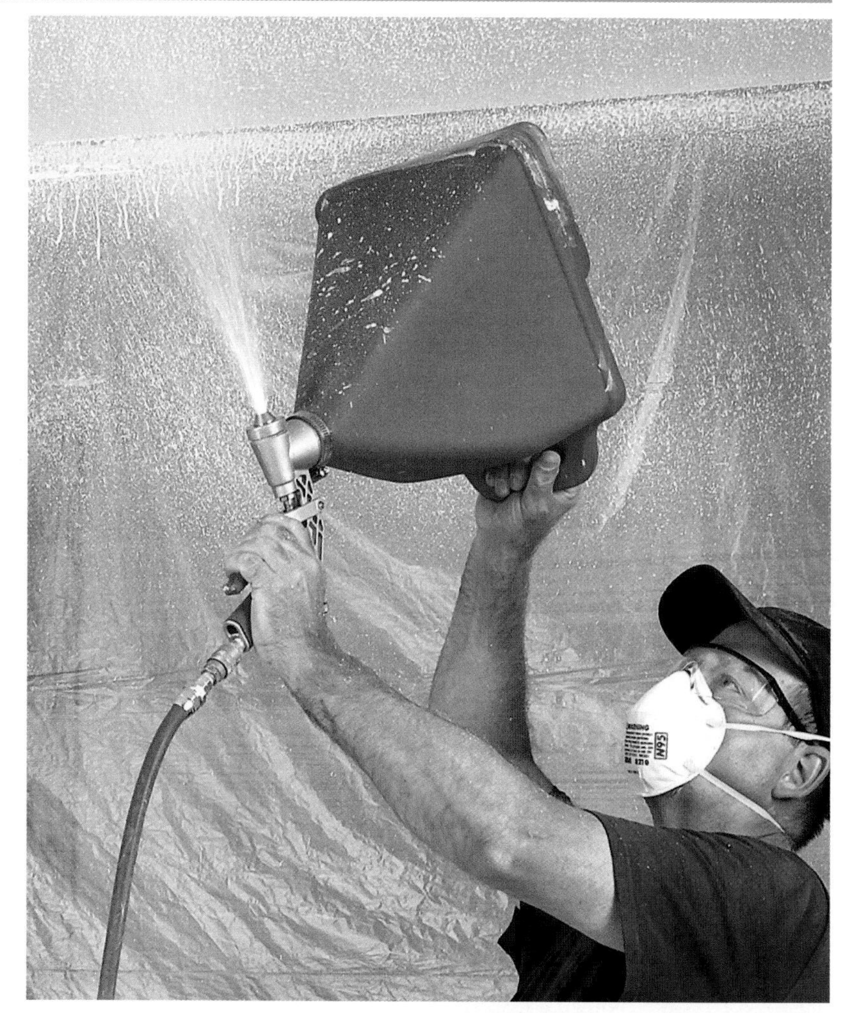

If your spray-textured ceiling is just dingy or stained, you can renew it with a coat each of sealer and paint. But if the texture is falling off or missing in spots, you'll have to reapply texture to fix the problem. For small areas, say less than a foot in diameter, you could try using an aerosol can of repair texture. But the patch is bound to stick out like a sore thumb. For the best results, you're better off respraying the entire ceiling. It's a messy job, but it's not hard to do. In fact, after you spray one room, you'll probably want to keep going. You can spray-texture unsightly plaster or smooth drywall ceilings too. As with most jobs, the key is in the prep work, which is the time-consuming part too. Once the room is masked off, the ceiling prepped and the texture mixed, it'll only take you about 15 minutes to spray the ceiling.

If any of the paper drywall tape is loose or the drywall is soft or damaged, you'll have to repair and sand these areas first. In addition to the putty knives and drywall joint compound for the repairs, you'll need a wide putty or taping knife for scraping, a roll of 1-1/2-in. or wider masking tape, enough painter's plastic to cover the walls, a gallon or two of primer/sealer, a bag of spray texture (enough to cover 300 to 400 sq. ft.), and a compressor and hopper gun. You can buy coarse, medium or fine texture. If you're matching existing ceilings, take a sample of the material with you when you buy the texture and ask for help matching it. Medium is usually the best choice and will match most ceilings. You can rent a compressor and hopper gun for about $30 for a half day or buy a hopper gun for about $70 and connect it to any average-size or larger compressor. If you use a small compressor, you may occasionally have to stop spraying to let the pressure build up. Minimize rental costs by getting all the prep work done before you pick up the compressor and hopper gun.

Start by removing everything you can from the room. If you must leave large furniture in the room, stack it in the center and cover it with plastic. Cover the floor with sheets or a canvas drop cloth. Then cover the walls with thin (1-mil or less) poly sheeting

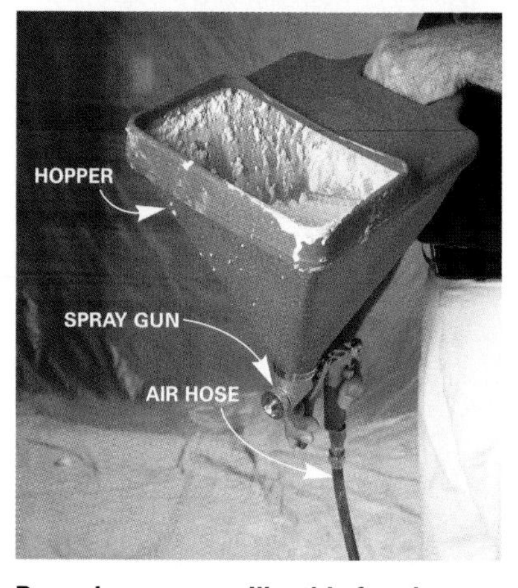

Buy a hopper gun like this for about $70 and connect it to any 2.5-cfm or larger air compressor.

1 **Speed up and simplify your masking job by applying the tape along the ceiling first. Leave the lower edge of the tape loose. Then roll out a length of lightweight poly along the floor, pull one edge up to the ceiling, and stick it to the tape.**

2 **Suit up with goggles, a dust mask and a hat before you start the messy job of scraping texture. Popcorn spray texture comes off easily if it hasn't been painted.**

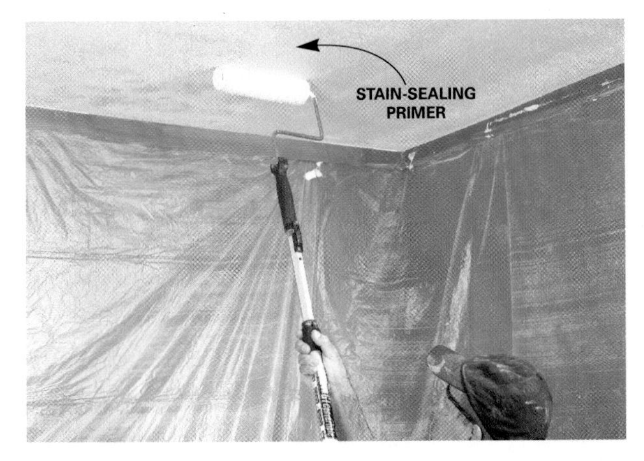

3 **Paint the ceiling with a fast-drying primer/sealer. Let it dry before applying the spray texture.**

CAUTION: If you have ceiling texture applied before 1980, it may contain asbestos. Before you remove any ceiling texture, contact your state's department of environmental protection, department of health or a regional asbestos coordinator for information on asbestos testing and removal. For a list of contacts, go to epa.gov/asbestos/pubs/regioncontact 2.html#reg5. For general information on asbestos, go to epa.gov/asbestos.

(Photo 1). Painter's plastic is very thin and works great. Leave an opening with overlapping poly at the doorway so you can get in and out. Turn off the power to the lights and remove any ceiling fixtures. Don't forget to cap the bare wires with wire connectors. Stuff newspaper into the electrical box to keep out the spray texture.

The next step is to scrape off the old texture (Photo 2), but not before you've had it tested for asbestos. If it hasn't been painted, it'll usually come off easily. So try just scraping it first. If that doesn't work (you'll know right away), try wetting the texture with a pump-up garden sprayer. That might make it easier to scrape, but it'll leave a sticky mess on the floor. If you use this method, cover your drop cloths with 4-mil plastic so you can wad it up and dispose of the wet texture and not track it all over the house. Texture that's been painted over can be a lot harder to remove. Just do the best you can. Try to knock off the high spots and flatten it as much as possible. The ceiling doesn't have to be smooth, but it's easier to get a nice-looking job if most of the old texture has been removed.

When you're done scraping, paint the ceiling with stain-sealing primer (Photo 3). BIN and KILZ are two popular brands. Use an aerosol can of solvent-based sealer such as BIN white shellac to spot-prime severe stains. Then paint the entire ceiling with a water-based primer/sealer.

The key to a successful spray-texture job is mixing the texture to the right consistency. Don't mix it too thick. Use the amount of water recommended on the bag as a starting point. Then adjust the thickness by adding more water or powder. Mix slowly using a mixing paddle mounted in a 1/2-in. drill (Photo 4). Mix thoroughly, adding water until the material reaches the consistency of runny yogurt—or thick paint—with tiny lumps in it. Let the texture sit for 15 minutes, then remix, adding more water if necessary.

There are a few different versions of hopper guns, but they all have a mechanism at the nose that controls the diameter of the pattern, and a trigger control that helps govern the volume of spray. Start by setting both controls to the middle position. Then load the hopper about half full with texture material and practice on a piece of cardboard or drywall scrap (Photo 5). Adjust the spray pattern and trigger until you can get a nice, even pattern without runs or excess buildup. When you're comfortable with the spraying technique, start on the ceiling.

Start by spraying the perimeter (Photo 6). Hold the gun about 18 to 24 in. from the ceiling and aim so that about two-thirds of the spray hits the ceiling and the rest hits the wall. Move quickly around the room, paying special attention to the inside corners where walls meet. Remember, you can make another pass if it's too light. The goal is to cover the ceiling with an even layer of texture. Don't worry if it looks too smooth. The texture will become more pronounced as it dries. Be careful to avoid puddles. If you mess up and get a puddle or just a thick buildup, stop and scrape off *all* the texture with a wide putty knife. Then try again. Move the gun back and forth while backing up across the room. After you've covered the ceiling, turn 90 degrees and apply another light coat at a right angle to the first. Concentrate on filling in light spots to create an even texture.

When you're satisfied with the consistency of the texture, you can clean up the gun, hopper and hose with water and pull down the poly. If your masking job was a little off and there's texture on the wall or flooring, wait for it to dry. Then carefully scrape it off and remove the white residue with a wet sponge.

4 Mix the powdered spray texture and water thoroughly. Lumps will clog the spray tip and could mess up your spray job. Let it rest 15 minutes and remix, adding water if necessary.

5 Practice on cardboard or a piece of drywall to get a feel for spraying. Adjust the gun's tip and trigger until you get a consistent spray pattern that's easy to control.

6 Start by spraying the perimeter, then fill in the middle. Avoid heavy buildup—you can always add more.

1 Remove the sash. Push in on the jamb liner while you pull out on the top corner of the sash. Release the opposite side using the same technique. Then pivot the sash downward and tilt it sideways to remove it.

2 Pry out the jamb liner. Starting at the bottom, wedge a stiff putty knife into the crack between the jamb liner and the window stop. Pry the jamb liner flange out from under the stop. Then slide the putty knife upward to release the jamb liner.

3 Find the information you'll need to order new jamb liners stamped on the metal balance cartridges.

FIX A BROKEN WINDOW JAMB LINER

Modern double-hung windows (the upper and lower window sashes slide up and down past each other) don't use pulleys and sash weights to support the sash (the moving part of the window). Instead they have liners on each side that contain a spring assembly. If your sash won't stay in the raised position, chances are that some part of the jamb liner hardware is broken. You might be able to spot a broken cord or other sign of problem by looking closely as you open and close the window. If you determine that the jamb liner mechanism is broken, you can fix it by replacing both jamb liners.

The first step is to find a source for the new jamb liners. The original manufacturer is the best source of replacement parts. If you don't know what brand your window is and can't find a label, search online for a window repair parts specialist that can help you. Companies like Blaine Window Hardware at blainewindow.com (800-678-1919) can identify the jamb liner and send you new ones. But you may have to remove the jamb liner first and send in a sliver of it. Another option is to scan or photocopy the end profile of the jamb liner and e-mail the image to the parts supplier. Temporarily reinstall the old jamb liner and sash to secure the house while you're waiting for the new parts to arrive.

The photos show how to remove a common type of jamb liner on a Marvin window. **Photo 3** shows where to find the information you'll need to order a new Marvin jamb liner. Start by tilting out the sash (**Photo 1**). Then remove the jamb liner (**Photo 2**). If you're handy and want to save money, you can repair the jamb liner instead of replacing it. To see how, go to familyhandyman.com and search for "window repair."

CURE FOR CURLING VINYL

When water gets under the sheet vinyl along the edge of a shower or tub and the vinyl starts to curl, no amount of caulk can hide the problem. But here's an easy fix that also looks great. Buy a solid-surface threshold strip (Corian is one brand) at a home center or tile shop. They're available in various lengths and thicknesses; the one shown is 1/2 in. thick. The solid-surface material cuts like wood so you can use a handsaw or miter saw to cut the piece to the right length. Photos 1 – 3 show how to complete the repair.

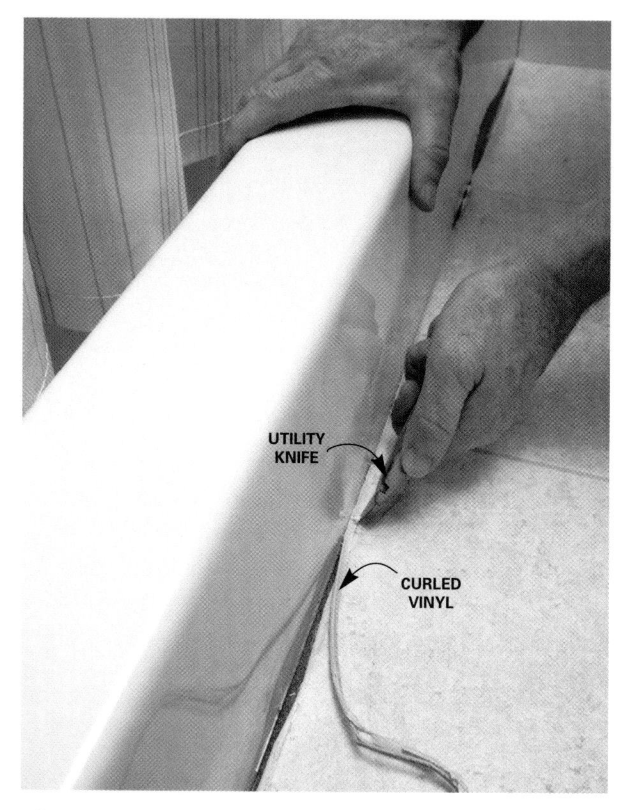

1 Cut out the curled vinyl. Slice alongside the curled edge of vinyl flooring with a utility knife. Then peel off the thin strip of vinyl and clean out any dirt or old caulk.

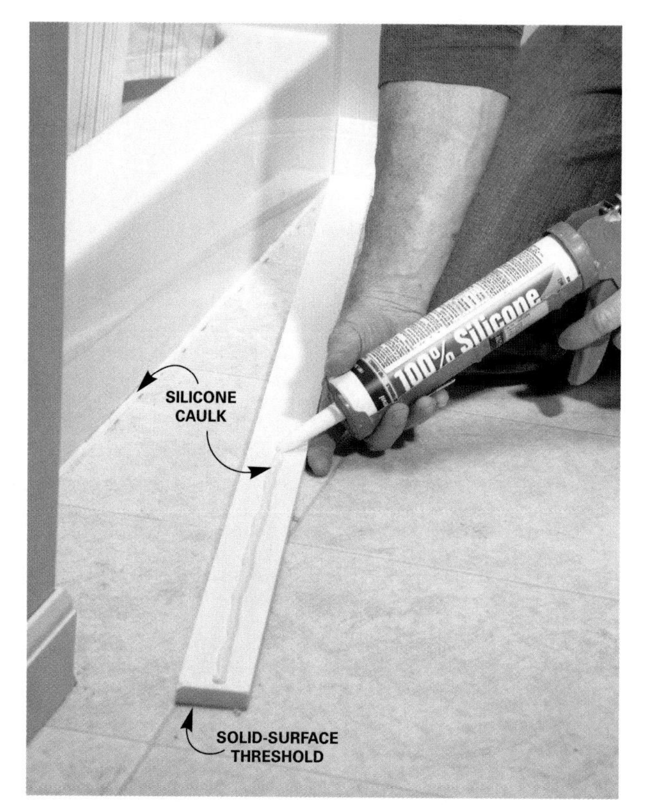

2 Attach a threshold. Spread a bead of silicone caulk on the back of the threshold and along the base of the shower.

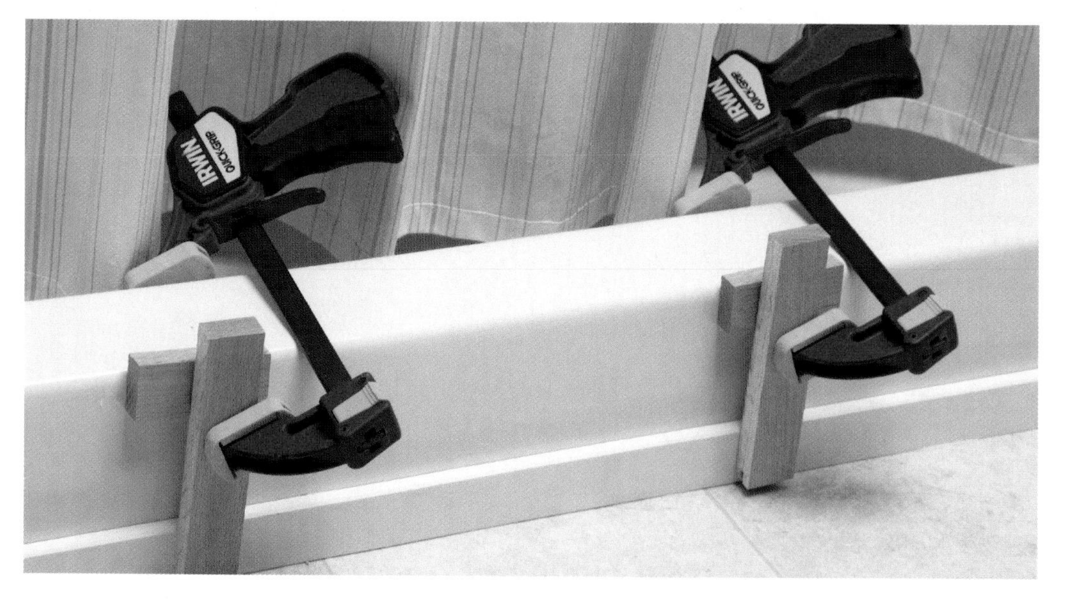

3 Clamp the threshold. Press the threshold against the shower base. If there are gaps, use clamps to hold the threshold tight until the caulk sets.

SUPER-INSULATE **YOUR ATTIC**

Save $1,000 on labor and cut your heating bills

by **Elisa Bernick**

If you need to add insulation in your attic, save big by blowing in cellulose insulation yourself. The pros charge $1,500 to $2,000 to do a 1,200-sq.-ft. house. You can do it yourself for about $500. Blowing attic insulation isn't hard, but it's dusty, sweaty work. To make it easier, grab a helper and set aside two days: one for attic prep and the second to actually blow the insulation. By the end of the weekend you're going to be sore and tired. But saving $1,000 or more will make up for your aching back.

The long-term payoff is impressive too. You could see your energy bills go down by as much as 15 to 25 percent depending on your climate and existing levels of insulation. And you can save an additional 30 percent on the cost of the insulation through the federal stimulus tax credit.

To show you how to do the job right, we asked our expert, Arne Olson, to share his tips for making the job go smoothly and help you avoid the top three attic-insulation mistakes.

DAY 1:

Seal attic bypasses

Leaks from cracks and gaps around lights, plumbing pipes, chimneys, walls and other ceiling penetrations are the equivalent of having a 2-ft.-wide hole in your roof. The worst offenders are open stud and joist cavities and dropped soffits and ceilings in kitchens and baths. We'll show you some basics here (Photo 1), but for complete step-by-step detailed information about how to seal attic bypasses, go to familyhandyman.com and type "sealing attic air leaks" in the search box.

Install or repair vent chutes

"In 95 percent of the homes we work on, the vent chutes are missing or aren't properly installed," says Olson. Without them, you're not getting the most out of your insulation's R-value because air needs to move properly at the eaves to remove moisture in the winter and heat in the summer.

To make sure existing chutes aren't blocked, stand in a dark attic to see whether light from the eaves is filtering through the vents. Replace any chutes that are blocked, damaged or missing. You'll find both plastic and foam vent chutes ($1 each) at home centers. Olson recommends using foam chutes. "They're more rigid and there's less chance of them getting crumpled or compressed when you're installing them." Pull back the existing insulation so you can see out to the edge of the eaves, and install a vent chute in every rafter space (Photo 2).

Dam and insulate the attic access

To keep the insulation from falling through the attic hatch

1 Pull back the existing insulation and use expanding spray foam to seal any gaps around plumbing pipes, ceiling perforations and holes where electrical wires snake through. "Make sure to seal all the way around the pipe," says Olson. For gaps 1/4 in. or less, use caulk rather than expanding foam.

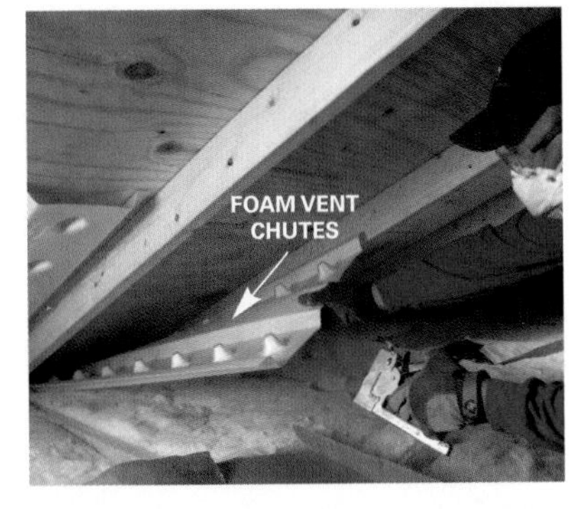

2 Pull the existing insulation away from the roof. Position the new vent chute so the bottom extends 6 in. into the overhang and staple it into place. Olson suggests using a squeeze stapler instead of a hammer stapler. "It's more accurate and there's less chance you'll crumple the chute."

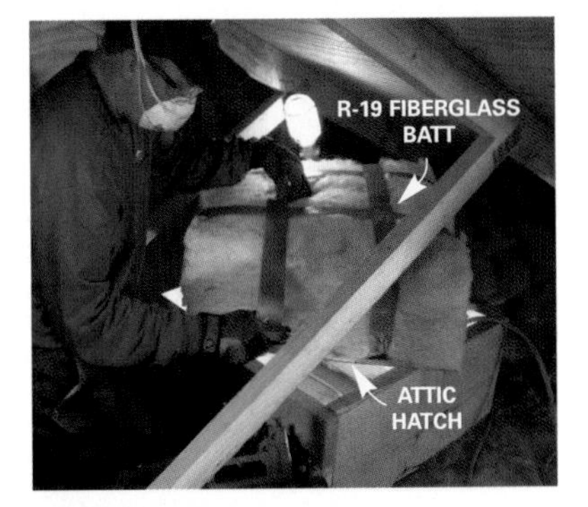

3 Cover the attic hatch with a pillow of fiberglass insulation. "You want a nice, big puffy pillow of insulation to stop any air leaks," says Olson. Cut two layers of R-19 fiberglass batt insulation slightly larger than the hatch and staple duct tape to the hatch edges to secure it in place.

opening, make a 2x12 dam around the hatch perimeter. "Then, to really seal the attic access up tight," says Olson, "lay fiberglass batt insulation on the inside of the hatch or door and wrap it up tight like a Christmas present" (**Photo 3**). You can insulate the hatch door while you're inside the attic or slide the door out and do it more comfortably on a tarp outside.

Mark your final insulation level

When you're blowing insulation, it can get dusty and hard to see whether you've got it deep enough around the entire attic. Mark the desired level on different roof trusses around the attic before you start (**Photo 4**).

4 **Measure up from the ceiling to mark your desired insulation level. Use a permanent marker to mark the level every few trusses so you know you have even coverage around the entire space.**

DAY 2:

Pick up the blower and insulation

Cellulose insulation is a good choice for DIYers. It has a higher R-rating and is less expensive than either blown fiberglass or fiberglass batts. It's an environmentally friendly material made from recycled newspaper, so it's easier on your skin and lungs. And you can blow it easily and quickly into odd-shaped spaces in an attic, where access is limited and dragging up batts is tough.

Most home centers sell bagged cellulose insulation ($6.75 per bag), and many provide the blower for a minimal fee ($20) or free when you buy a certain number of bags (usually 10 or more). You can also rent the blowers from a rental center for about $65 a day. Although rental machines aren't as powerful as the truck-mounted units the pros use, Olson says they work fine for a DIYer.

To determine how many bags you'll need, measure your existing insulation so you know your current R-value and subtract that from the recommended levels (see "Do You Need to Add Insulation?" below for how to find recommended levels for your ZIP code). Check the chart on the insulation bag to determine the number of bags necessary to reach your desired R-value based on the square

5 **Have your assistant crumble the compressed cellulose as he loads the hopper so it doesn't clog the hose. If the cellulose comes out too fast or too slow, adjust the hopper door. The blower machine is loud, and you and your assistant won't be in visual contact. Communicate with each other using a walkie-talkie or cell phone. You can also click the blower control switch on and off several times to get your helper's attention.**

6 **Start at the farthest point from the hatch and sit in the center of the attic. "Don't move around a lot in the attic with the hose," says Olson. "Work from the middle and do three bays at a time." Push the hose out to the eaves and blow those areas first. Then pull the hose back and use a slow, steady sweeping motion until you reach the desired level. Then pivot in place and blow the opposite side of the attic the same way.**

Do you need to add insulation?

The answer depends on where you live, the heating and cooling costs in your area, your existing insulation levels, local codes and more. The first step is to make sure you've sealed your attic bypasses. Then visit eere.energy.gov and go to "Calculators and Software," then "Homes," and the "Zip Code Insulation Tool." Use the insulation calculator to plug in your ZIP code, lifestyle factors, building design, energy costs and budget to get a detailed recommendation.

The recommended insulation level for most attics is R-38 (or about 12 to 15 in. from the drywall, depending on the insulation type). In the coldest climates, insulating up to R-49 is recommended.

footage of your attic. Olson recommends buying more bags than you think you'll need. "You can always return them, and you don't want to stop in the middle of the job because you've run out."

Set up the blower

The blower machine is heavy, so have your partner along to help you load and unload it. Set the blower on a tarp on flat ground near the window or vent opening closest to the attic access. Your helper will feed the insulation into the hopper while you work the hose up in the attic (**Photo 5**).

The blower should include two 50-ft. hoses that you can connect and snake into the attic. If your hoses have to wind their way through the house to reach a scuttle (the attic access) in a hallway or closet, lay down tarps along the way. It keeps things neater during the process and makes cleanup a lot easier.

Connect the hoses with the coupler and then use duct tape over the coupler to secure the connection. "Those metal clamps can vibrate themselves loose," says Olson. "You don't want them to get disconnected and have cellulose sprayed all around your house."

Blow the insulation

Wear eye and hearing protection, a long-sleeve shirt and gloves, and a double-strap mask or particulate respirator. Start as far away from the access panel as possible and blow the eaves and other tight spots first. For hard-to-reach areas, duct tape a length of PVC pipe to the end of the blower hose. As you work back into corners and around eave vents, don't cover any ventilating areas.

You can blow three rafter bays on each side of the attic from one position. Let the hose sit on the drywall to fill the eave areas, giving it a shake to move it from bay to bay. For the center areas, hold the hose level and blow the insulation evenly until you've reached your level lines (**Photo 6**). Then pivot in place and do the same thing to the other side. Move across the attic until you've hit your desired height at every point. Blow the rest of the insulation until the hopper is empty. You'll end up with a clean blower, and the extra inch or two of insulation will settle over the next few months.

Our insulation expert

Arne Olson, the owner of Houle Insulation in Minneapolis (houleinsulation.com), has insulated more than 5,000 homes. "A lot of those homes were insulated by DIYers who didn't know what they were doing," says Olson. "They didn't use enough insulation and they didn't seal up the attic bypasses or put in vent chutes." Olson says it's also common for older insulation to settle over time. "But you can blow cellulose over whatever kind of insulation is already there, and this is a great DIY project for someone who doesn't mind working up a sweat."

THE 3 MOST COMMON DIY INSULATION MISTAKES

Mistake #1:
Not sealing attic air leaks first
"No amount of insulation is going to help if you don't seal your attic properly," says Olson. For detailed step-by-step information about sealing attic air leaks, go to familyhandyman.com and type "seal attic air leaks."

Mistake #2:
Not getting insulation out to the edges
"When you're prepping the attic, use a broom handle or stick to push the existing insulation out to the edges. Then when you blow in the cellulose, make sure you do a good job of getting it way over to the eaves with the hose."

Mistake #3:
Stepping through the ceiling
"It happens all the time," says Olson. "You've got to move around slowly and step from joist to joist." If there's no floor, bring up a 12-in.-wide piece of 3/4-in. plywood and lay it across the ceiling joists to use as a platform to work from. And wear rubber-soled shoes so you can feel the joists through the bottom of your feet.

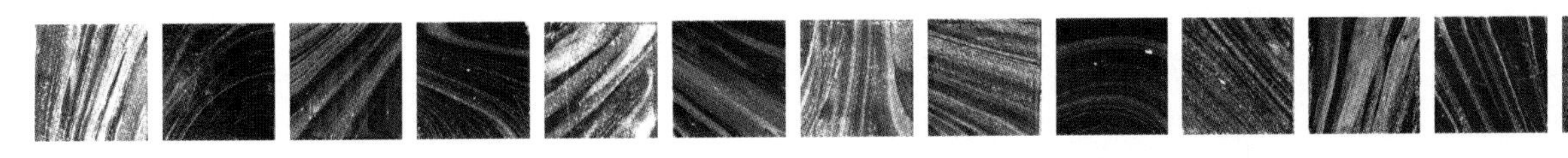

GLASS TILE **VANITY TOP**

A dramatic weekend face-lift

by **Jeff Gorton**

This vanity top would be at home in any luxury bathroom. Even though we chose relatively expensive glass tile, the completed top only cost us a little over $200, less than half the cost of custom granite, marble or solid-surface tops. Glass mosaic tile like we used is perfect for a project like this because you can adjust the size of the top to use only full tiles and avoid cutting. Plus, you can choose from hundreds of colors, textures and patterns to create a look that's perfect for your décor.

You'll be able to finish this project in a weekend using standard carpentry tools and a 3/16-in. V-notch trowel, a grout float and a grouting sponge. A microfiber cloth works better than a cotton rag for cleaning off the grout haze. You can buy them at home centers, hardware stores and most discount retailers. You'll also need buckets for mixing thin-set and grout and for rinse water. Don't forget a pair of rubber, vinyl or latex gloves and safety glasses.

Round up the materials

Start by choosing the tile. (This could be the hardest part!) If your local tile shops or home centers don't have tile you like, shop online like we did. Cooltiles.com is one source that offers an almost unlimited selection and reasonable prices. To duplicate our project, choose a 3/4-in. square mosaic that's 1/8 in. thick and has a mesh backing. Avoid mosaics that are held together with a removable paper face. They're difficult to install.

Plan to spend $7 to $24 per square foot for glass tile. Here's a list of other materials you'll need:

■ **Plywood.** We used two layers of 5/8-in. plywood, which, combined with the 1/4-in. backer board, resulted in a 1-1/2-in.-thick top, a perfect thickness for two courses of our 3/4-in. tile. If your tiles are a different size or you want a different top thickness, adjust the plywood and backer board thicknesses accordingly.

■ **Tile backer board.** We purchased Custom Building Products' EasyBoard (custombuildingproducts.com) from a local tile shop. EasyBoard is a lightweight tile backer board that you can cut with a utility knife. Hardibacker or any similar cement backer board would also work well.

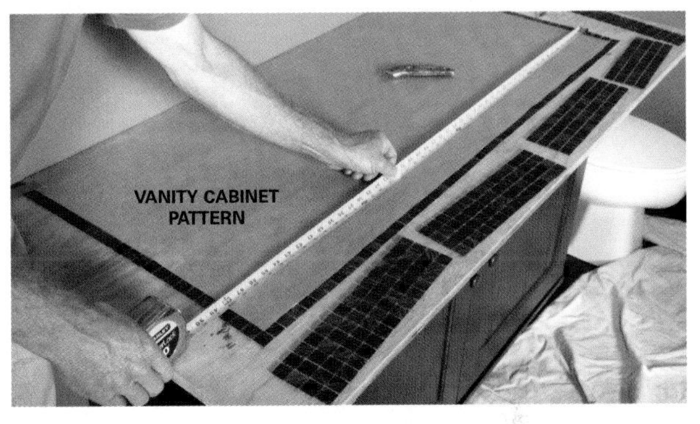

1 Design the top to avoid cutting tile. Cut a paper pattern the size of the vanity cabinet and lay it over the tile. That makes it easy to size the top for full tiles.

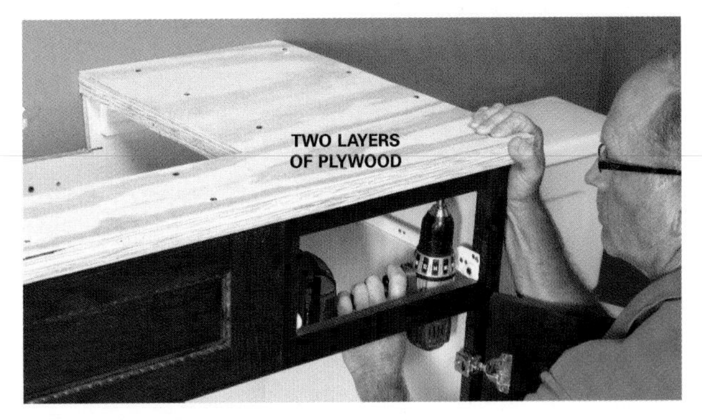

2 Build the plywood base. Two layers of plywood make a stiff, strong base for the tile. Mark and cut the plywood carefully to make sure the top is perfectly square.

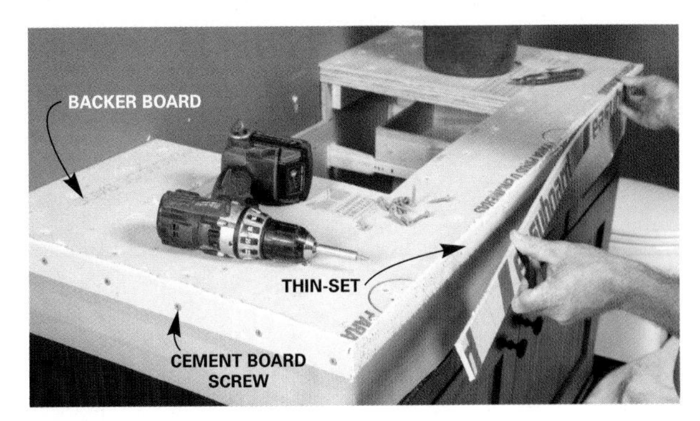

3 Cover the base with backer board. Tile backer board forms a waterproof layer for a long-lasting countertop. Quarter-inch-thick backer is all you need over the strong plywood base.

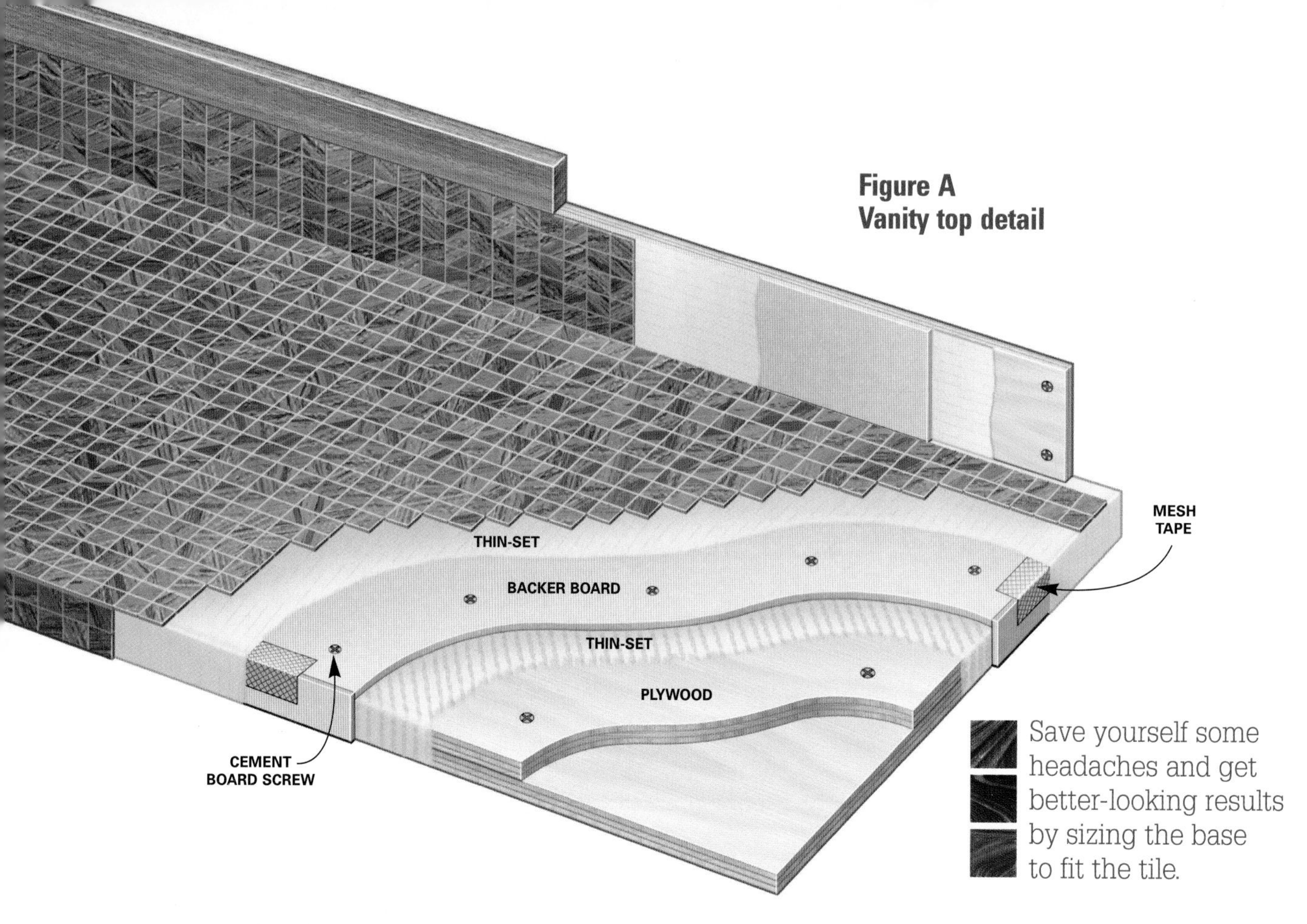

Save yourself some headaches and get better-looking results by sizing the base to fit the tile.

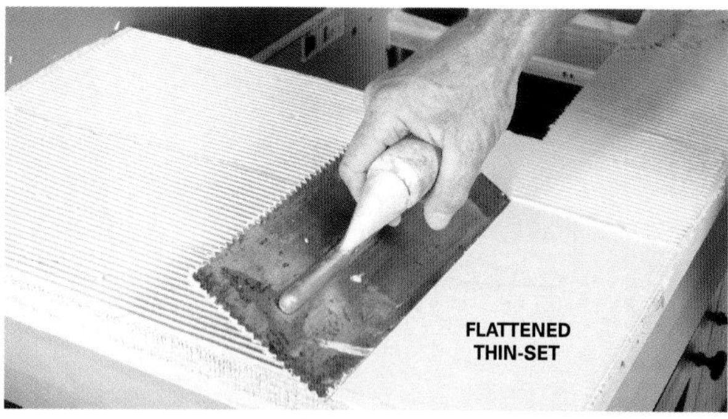

4 Comb out, then flatten the thin-set. Use a 3/16-in. V-notch trowel to spread a layer of thin-set over the backer board. Then flatten it with the straight side of the trowel.

5 Start setting the tile at the corner. For perfectly aligned grout joints, start by setting a strip of tile on the front and side edges, and a full sheet of tile on top. Adjust the tile until the grout lines on the top line up with the grout lines on the front and sides.

- **Thin-set mortar.** Look for special glass tile mortar. It's white and specially formulated to stick well to glass tile. It's available in a powder that you mix with water. Standard modified white thin-set will also work.
- **Cement board screws.** Choose screws that are labeled for use with cement board. They have a special corrosion-resistant coating.
- **Cement board tape.** Check the label—it must be cement board tape so the mesh will hold up to the alkaline cement products.
- **Grout.** We used nonsanded grout because we wanted smooth grout lines. You can also use sanded grout. Make a sample board by gluing a few glass mosaic tiles to a scrap of wood and grouting them to make sure you like the result.

Size the base

Glass tile is a nightmare to cut. Save yourself some headaches and get better-looking results by sizing the base to fit the tile. With the tile in hand, you can figure out exactly what size to build the plywood base. One easy method is to carefully lay out the sheets of mosaic with an equal grout space between the sheets. Make a paper pattern of your vanity cabinet including the thickness of the door or drawer fronts. Arrange the pattern over the sheets of tile and adjust the position until there's an equal-width tile on each side. Use the pattern to determine the overhangs, based on where full tiles occur. Aim for about

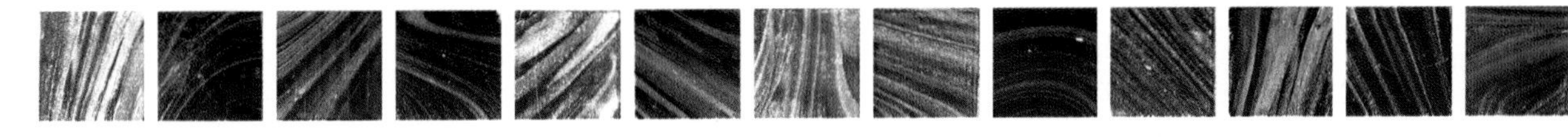

a 1/2-in. overhang on the sides and between 1/2-in. and 1-in. past the drawers on the front. Cut the mesh backing so the sheets of tile are the size of the top. Now carefully measure the width and length of the tiles. This will be the finished size of your countertop after it's tiled.

The plywood base has to be smaller than the size of the finished top to accommodate the backer board, tile and thin-set. To figure the size of the plywood, add the thickness of the tile (1/8 in.), the tile backer board (1/4 in.) and the thin-set (1/16 in.) and subtract this amount from the width (front to back). Deduct twice this amount from the length (side to side). It's critical that you cut the plywood to exactly the right size, so double-check all your math (**Photo 1**).

Build the base

Cut both layers of plywood, being careful to make exact cuts. Then plan the sink location and make the sink cutout. Self-rimming sinks usually include a template that you can use to trace the cutout onto the plywood. Cut the backer board to the same size as the plywood and make the sink cutout. You'll also need strips of backer board to cover the edges.

Screw the two layers of plywood together. Space screws about 8 in. apart. Then screw the plywood to the vanity cabinet, making sure the overhang is even on both sides and that the front edge is parallel to the vanity cabinet (**Photo 2**).

Next, cover the plywood with backer board (**Photo 3**). Cut and test-fit the backer board first. Then mix powdered thin-set mortar with water to about the consistency of peanut butter. Spread it onto the plywood with a 3/16-in. V-notch trowel. Finally, screw the backer board to the plywood, placing screws about 8 in. apart.

The last step before tiling is to wrap the corners of the backer board with cement board tape. Start by vacuuming and then wiping the top and edges with a clean cloth to remove dust. Wrap the adhesive-backed tape around the corners and press it down. Then cover the tape with a thin layer of thin-set mortar. After the thin-set hardens, scrape off any lumps and dust off the top again to prepare it for tiling.

6 Embed the tile with a wood block. Tap the top of the mosaic tile with a flat block of wood to level the surface and ensure a secure bond with the thin-set.

7 Grout the tile. Work the grout back and forth in different directions to completely fill the joints and eliminate voids. Well-packed joints are the key to a lasting grout job.

Glass tile mirror

The mirror frame is made from a 3/4-in. x 4-1/2-in. oak board with a 1-5/8-in.-wide dado on the face to accommodate a band of tile and a 3/8-in. rabbet on the back to hold the mirror. We cut the dado with dado blades mounted on a table saw. A router would also work. We sized the frame so we wouldn't have to cut tiles at the corners. After mitering the parts and staining the frame, we set the tile strips in a thin bead of construction adhesive. Then we finished it off by masking the wood and grouting the tile.

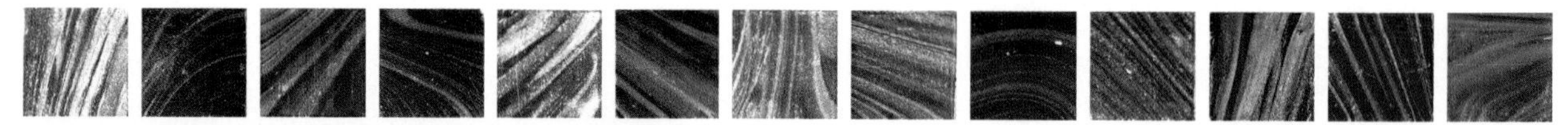

8 **"Tool" the grout with a damp sponge. Wait until the grout starts to set up before tooling. Wring out the sponge until it's just damp. Then rub it over the tile in a circular motion to smooth and shape the grout and fill tiny voids and pinholes.**

9 **Buff off the grout film. Wait until the grout is hard before buffing it. Then polish it with a microfiber cloth to remove the haze.**

Buyer's Guide

- **TILE: HotGlass Aventurine blended 3/4-in. glass tile in Tiger's Eye Blend on mesh-backed sheet. $19 per sheet (HAK-34313). Available online from cooltiles.com.**
- **SINK: Elements of Design, Mission Bathroom Sink (EDV9620-black), $280. Available online at everyvesselsink.com.**
- **FAUCET: Price Pfister Kenzo single-center faucet (T42-DF0), $195. Available online at everyvesselsink.com.**

Tile the countertop

Photos 4 – 6 show how to spread the mortar and embed the tile. Before you start, cut the mesh backing to form strips of tile for the edges and make the sink cutout. Trim the mesh tight to the tile so you don't have any mesh whiskers sticking out. Then arrange the tile in the shape of the vanity and within easy reach of the vanity top so you can easily reach it after spreading the thin-set.

Mix and spread the thin-set. Pay close attention to Photo 4; it shows an important tip. Flattening the mortar after you spread it with the notched trowel prevents thin-set from filling the grout spaces when you embed the tile. Any thin-set that gets into the grout spaces has to be cleaned out before you can grout the tile, so this tip will save you a lot of time and effort.

Set the tiles on the top and edges as quickly and accurately as possible (Photo 5). You need to work fast so you can make slight adjustments to the tile before the thin-set starts to set up. When you're satisfied that the tile top and edges are perfectly aligned, embed the tile (Photo 6). Let the thin-set harden overnight before grouting.

Grout the tile

Photos 7 – 9 show how to grout the tile. Start by mixing the grout according to the directions on the package. Let it rest for about 10 minutes—this is called "slaking." Then mix it again. It'll often thicken a bit after slaking and require a bit more water. The grout should be the consistency of mayonnaise.

Here are some grouting tips:

- Work the grout from all angles with the float to completely fill the joints (Photo 7).
- Scrape off the excess before it starts to set.
- Wait until the grout starts to harden before cleaning it with a sponge. If you can't make a fingerprint, it's hard enough.
- Keep the rinse water clear and wring all the water out of the sponge when you're cleaning the grout. Use a clean side of the sponge for each cleaning stroke.
- Use a damp sponge to tool the grout after it sets up (Photo 8). Wait about 15 minutes after cleaning before tooling the tile.
- Coat the grout with a grout sealer to help prevent staining and make it more water-resistant. Wait two or three days before sealing.

Finishing touches

We added a backsplash before setting the sink. A backsplash could be as simple as tiles attached to the wall with thin-set, or something more elaborate. We screwed 3/8-in. plywood to the wall, covered it with 1/4-in. backer board and surrounded it with 3/4-in.-thick oak trim. Then we tiled over the backer board, grouted the tile and caulked the seam between the countertop and the backsplash with a fine bead of clear silicone caulk.

Do's & Don'ts

TIPS FOR **TIGHT MITERS**

There are perfect miters—and then there are miters that have been tweaked to look perfect. You can learn how to do both with the right tools, a few pro tips and a good dose of patience. We can't help you with the patience, but we can show you tips and techniques for cutting, fitting and joining perfect miters, along with a few tricks for making those less-than-perfect miters look their best.

Make sure your blade is sharp

Choosing the right blade for your miter saw, and making sure it's sharp, are crucial for cutting tight-fitting miters. You can't cut perfect miters with a dull blade, one with too few teeth or one that's designed for ripping. Check your blade for sharpness by cutting a 45-degree miter on a 1x3 or larger piece of oak or other hardwood (**photo below**). If the blade cuts smoothly with very little pressure and leaves a clean, almost shiny cut with no burn marks, it's sharp enough to cut good miters.

When you check your blade or shop for a new one, here's what to look for. First, it should be labeled as a "trim" or "fine crosscutting" blade. A 10-in. blade should have at least 40 teeth, a 12-in. blade at least 60. If the blade is for a sliding miter saw, be sure the teeth have a hook angle of zero to negative five degrees. Teeth with a neutral or negative hook angle are less aggressive and safer for sliding miter saws. Expect to spend at least $50 for a carbide-tipped blade that'll perform well and last.

SHARP BLADE

DULL BLADE

If the cut end of the miter looks scorched, rough or chipped, have the blade sharpened or buy a new one.

Guess and test

There are all kinds of ways to find odd angles, but most carpenters simply make a guess and then cut a pair of test pieces to see how lucky they are. The angle of these two walls looks to be less than 45 degrees. A good guess would be about 30 degrees. Divide 30 by two to arrive at the miter angle, and cut a couple of scraps at 15 degrees. Here there's a gap in front, so we need to increase the angle slightly and recut the scraps at 16 degrees. When you've zeroed in on the correct angle, the scraps will fit perfectly, and you can then cut the actual moldings.

Cut test pieces to check the angle of the miter.

Do's & Don'ts

Tweak the cut

Even on perfectly square corners, 45-degree angles won't always yield perfect miters. Wall corners can be built up with corner bead and compound, and window and door frames can slightly protrude or be recessed behind surrounding drywall. That's when you have to start fiddling with the angles to get a tight fit.

In most cases, you'll be making adjustments as small as a quarter of a degree. If the gap is small (about 1/16 in.), recut one side of the miter (**Photo 2**). If the gap is larger, you'll have to recut both boards or the trim profiles won't line up. For more tips, go to familyhandyman.com and type "tight miters" into the search box.

1 **Cut the moldings at a 45-degree angle. Hold the miter together to see how it fits. If there's a gap, estimate how much you'll have to trim off to close the gap, and make a mark where the moldings touch.**

2 **Push the trim tight to the blade and adjust the angle of the saw until the gap equals the amount you need to trim off the miter.**

Burnish the corner

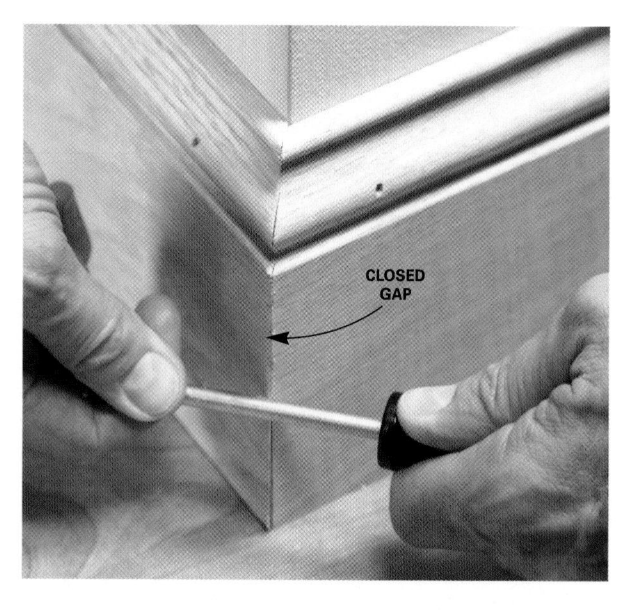

You can make less-than-perfect miters on outside corners look their best with this tip. If your baseboard or crown molding has a slight gap in the outside corner miter, you can hide it by rubbing the tip of the miter with the shank of a screwdriver or nail set. The bent fibers will disguise the gap, and the slightly rounded corner will be less likely to get chipped or damaged.

The best way to prevent this problem is to cut your outside corner miters about 1 degree sharper than the actual angle so the tips of the miters touch. This will leave a tiny gap at the back of the miter where it's barely noticeable.

Hide a slight gap in an outside corner miter by rubbing it with the shank of a screwdriver or nail set. This will bend the wood fibers in and slightly round the corner.

Fit one miter at a time

Whether you're edge-banding a tabletop as we're showing here, trimming out a window or door, or installing baseboard, it's always best to fit one miter at a time whenever possible. Start with a scrap of molding with a miter cut on it as a test piece (**Photo 1**). When you have the first miter fitting perfectly, mark the next one (**Photo 2**). Then cut and fit the adjoining miter before you nail either piece. For edge banding, work your way around the project using the same process for each edge piece.

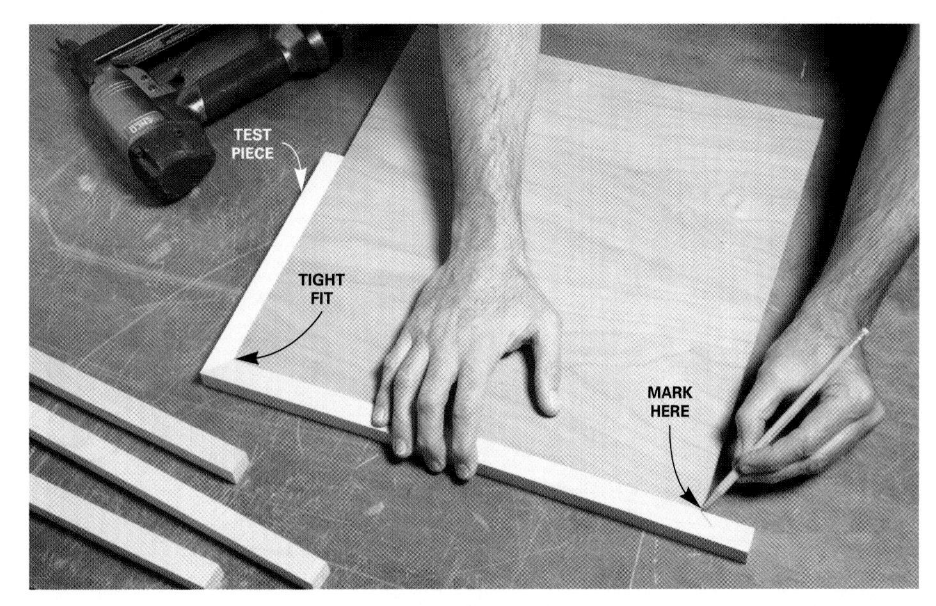

Tack a mitered scrap of edging to one side. Use it to hold the first edging piece in position. Hold the mitered end tight to the mitered scrap while you mark for the opposite miter.

Glue and sand for a seamless fit

Here's a trick to make miters look great, but it only works if you're installing raw trim that will get finished after installation. It's easy. Glue the joint, then sand it smooth.

The sawdust from sanding will mix with the glue to fill any small gaps. Sanding the miter will also even out any slight level differences and make the job look more professional. Don't try to fill large gaps, especially in trim that'll be stained. Glue-filled gaps absorb stain differently than the surrounding wood and will stick out like a sore thumb.

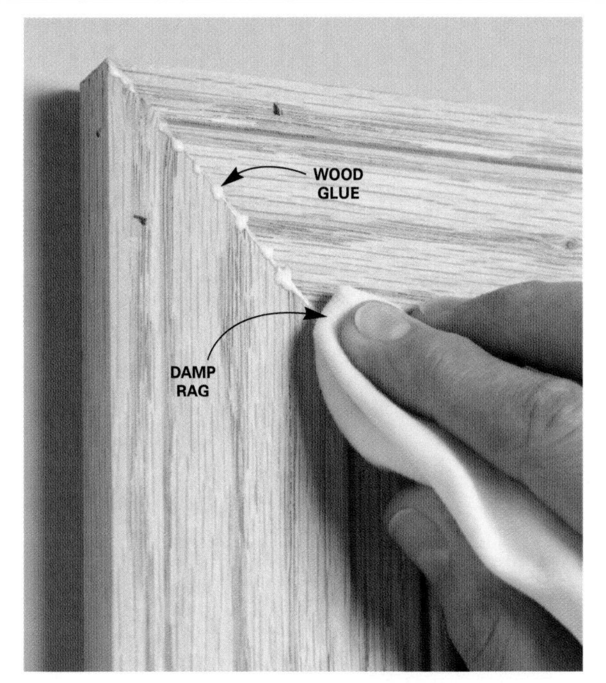

1 Apply a thin layer of wood glue to the end grain of each piece before you assemble them. Use a damp (not wet) cloth to remove excess glue from the joint.

2 Sand over the miter with a small piece of 120-grit sandpaper. Sand across the joint and finish up by carefully sanding out any cross-grain sanding marks by moving the paper with the grain from both directions.

Question&Comment

HOW TO SAVE A FLOODED BASEMENT

My basement flooded and I've got wet carpet. Is it possible to save it?

Rent a commercial extractor or a carpet cleaner to suck out as much moisture as possible. Move slowly and do several passes in different directions.

You didn't give us much info to go on, so you'll have to go by these rules: If the floodwater was clean (broken pipe, burst washing machine supply hose or a foundation leak), you can probably save the carpet (the pad is "iffy"). But you've got to act fast. If the carpet isn't dry within 72 hours, it'll start to grow mold. However, if the floodwater was dirty (sewer back-up or washing machine drain water), you need to call in the pros (see "Call in the Pros," p. 27).

We'll assume the basement was flooded with clean water, the water is now shut off and the cost of the carpet is less than your insurance deductible (or that you simply want to do it yourself to avoid a claim). Before you set one boot on that squishy carpet, heed this warning: You must turn off the power to the basement. If you're not positive which breakers power the basement receptacles, flip the main circuit breaker in the garage panel. If your electrical panel is in the basement, *call an electrician to turn off the power.*

Next, remove any extension cords and power strips from the floor and unplug or switch off all electrical appliances (washer, dryer, HVAC). Ask the electrician (if you hired one) to repower the upstairs (to keep the fridge going) and inspect the basement receptacles to determine whether it's safe to repower them. If not, you'll have to buy several GFCI-equipped extension cords and run power from upstairs receptacles.

Then it's time to extract the water from the carpet. Don't waste your time with a wet/dry shop vacuum—it simply doesn't have enough power. Instead, rent an extractor (if available) or carpet cleaner (shown; $65 per day), an air mover fan or two ($42 per day) and a large commercial

Save your stuff

Most people leave their valuable items in the basement while they dry out the carpet. Big mistake. The longer your items sit in the basement, the more moisture they'll soak up. And that means mold. So get them out of the basement fast!

- **Move all electronic gear upstairs (high humidity can corrode electronic components.)**
- **Take photos and artwork off the walls and move them to a dry location.**
- **Place valuable wet books in your freezer until the "freeze-drying" effect removes all the water from the pages.**
- **If you can't move furniture out of the basement, place aluminum foil under the legs.**

Rent a commercial dehumidifier and air mover fan ASAP. Position the machines on opposite sides of the room to pick up and remove most of the moisture.

dehumidifier ($100 per day; see p. 26). Rent the largest dehumidifier available. The big ones can remove up to 30 gallons per day, compared with 4 gallons for the largest home units.

Extraction is 1,200 times more effective than dehumidification. You'll want to move the extractor slowly across the carpet to suck up as much water as possible. Don't rush this step! Once the water is out, peel back the carpeting (watch out for those rusted sharp nails on the tackless stripping) and remove the wet pad. Cut the pad into strips, roll it up and haul it outside. If the weather is hot, dry and sunny, you can try drying it yourself by rolling it out on your driveway. If that works, you can reinstall it by taping it back together. Just be aware that new carpet pad is cheap, so don't waste a lot of time trying to dry the old stuff.

Lay the carpet back on the floor and fire up the air movers and rental dehumidifier. Keep the basement temperature at or below 75 degrees F. You might think hotter is better because it will dry everything faster. But a higher temp will accelerate bacterial growth and turn your basement into a petri dish.

While the carpet is drying, check the condition of the wall insulation. If you don't have insulation and you dry out the basement quickly, you don't have to replace the drywall. But if the insulation is wet, it's gotta go (wet insulation cannot be saved). Snap a chalk line, cut the drywall with a recip saw and toss the wet stuff. Replace the insulation and install new drywall.

Finally, if your appliances or furnace was under water, call in appliance and HVAC specialists before plugging any of them back in.

Call in the pros

If you had a sewer backup, washing machine drain water spill or river flood, you need professional help. Pros are the only ones with the proper equipment to get your basement dry and disinfected in the shortest possible time.

To find a certified water restoration professional, check the yellow pages under "Water Damage Restoration" or search online. Look for IICRC (Institute of Inspection, Cleaning and Restoration Certification) credentials in the company's description (Servicemaster is one company that is fully certified). Or, go to iicrc.org and click on "Locate a Pro."

Be aware that pros can give you a rough price estimate (the average cost of a basement cleanup is $2,500), but the final cost depends on how long it takes them to dry out your basement. There are just too many variables beyond their control (inside and outside temperature and humidity levels) to give you a set price up front. Be wary of any company that gives you a set price over the phone.

MATCH CAULK TO GROUT COLOR

I tiled and grouted my bathtub walls and went to the home center to buy caulk for the inside corners and tub ledge. I couldn't find anything that matched the sanded grout texture or color. Can I order it somewhere? Help!

Don't look in the caulk department; look for sanded caulk near the grout in the tile department. You'll find caulk that matches most grout colors, both sanded and unsanded. If the store doesn't carry it, or you have an unusual color, you can custom mix your own (**Photo 1**). You'll have to use a makeshift applicator (**Photo 2**) and it will be messy—so tape off the gap. Practice squeezing the bag on a piece of cardboard until you get a feel for how much comes out. Then squeeze out the caulk/grout mix and smooth with your finger.

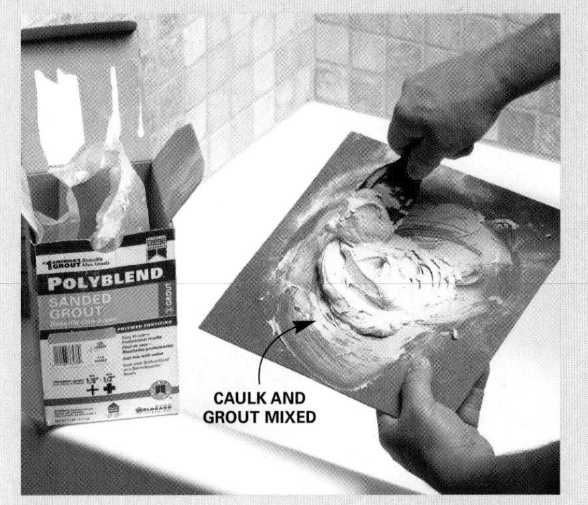

1 **You can color the caulk with grout. Squeeze caulk onto a mixing board, making sure you use enough to complete the entire job (it'll be hard to match if you have to add more later). Then add colored grout to the caulk and mix thoroughly with a 3-in. putty knife.**

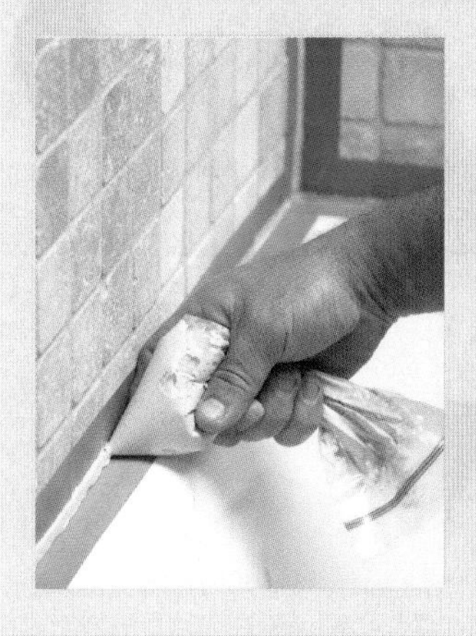

2 **It's like decorating a cake. Scoop a hefty portion into a zip-top freezer bag. Zip the top shut and snip off one bottom corner. Then apply the caulk/grout bead to your tub and tool the joint with a plastic spoon or wet finger. Then pull the tape free before the caulk sets up.**

Question&Comment

SEAL EXPANSION GAPS ON LAMINATE FLOORING IN WET AREAS

I bought AC3-rated laminate flooring for my bathroom because it's a wet area. But now I'm confused about the expansion gap. The instructions say to leave a 1/4-in. gap along the wall. Won't water get in there and defeat the whole purpose of buying water-resistant flooring?

Anytime you install laminate flooring in a bath, laundry room or kitchen, you should fill gaps at flooring ends with 100 percent silicone caulk. It stays flexible, allowing the floor to expand, and in the event of a spill, prevents water from soaking into the laminate core. Filling the gaps can use up a lot of caulk, so buy more than you think you'll need.

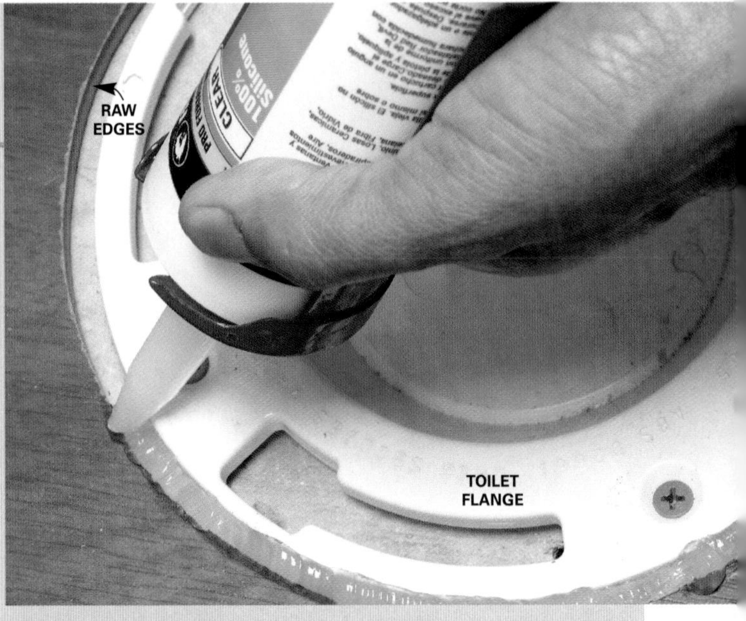

Hold off on setting the toilet and the baseboard molding until you've filled the expansion gaps around room perimeters and the toilet flange with 100 percent silicone caulk.

CEILING FAN REMOTE RETROFIT

I have an old ceiling fan and light that operates via pull chains. Can I retrofit it with a remote control?

Probably. There are many "universal" remote kits on the market ($20 to $80). All of them feature on/off and fan speed control. Others also offer light-dimming and thermostatic control capabilities. But whether you can use a kit depends on the amount of free space inside the fan canopy.

Many "ceiling hugger"–style fans have enough free space for the receiver. But "down-rod" styles may not. Shut off the circuit breaker to the fan and lower the canopy (use a voltage sniffer to make sure the power is really off). Check the fit of the receiver before you commit to wiring it in permanently. Keep your receipt just in case.

With the power off, connect the hot and neutral wires to the "AC-in" wires on the receiver. Then connect the three remaining wires to the fan and light (they're labeled by the manufacturer).

If you have neighbors nearby, you may have to change the frequency on the transmitter and receiver to prevent you or your neighbors from controlling one another's fans (see Photo 2).

1 Slide the receiver into the space above the down rod. If it doesn't fit, try other locations inside the canopy.

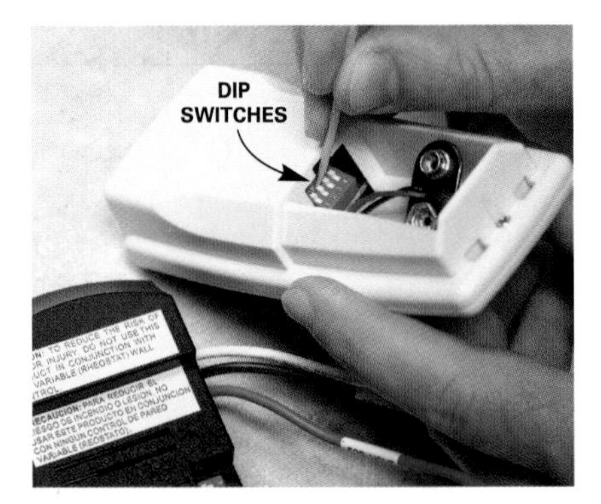

2 Flip the DIP switches to change the transmitter frequency if you have problems with interference. The switch positions on both units must match.

DIY SOLID-SURFACE COUNTERTOPS?

I'm pretty handy, and I'd like to install a solid-surface countertop myself and hopefully save a boatload of money—if that's possible. Is this a DIY project and where would I buy the stuff?

Yes, it's possible and there are sources that will sell to DIYers. But only if you're talking about the acrylic material (like Wilsonart, Avonite and Meganite), rather than "engineered stone" (quartz/resin) products like Cambria and Silestone. Engineered stone materials are only available through authorized dealers and are custom made for each job.

DIYers can buy solid-surface materials at wholesale prices from solidsurface.com. It sells surplus and discontinued sheets from several major manufacturers. Full-sheet sizes vary but are usually 30 in. x 144 in. x 1/2 in. (partial sheets are half that size). The square-foot prices vary by pattern and manufacturer, ranging from $10 to $20 per sq. ft. plus shipping ($150 to $300, depending on your location). The total is about one-third of what you'd pay an authorized dealer if it would even sell to you. Solidsurface.com also carries the special adhesives you'll need for the joinery. And you'll have to spend about $250 for special tools and materials (see photo).

It's possible to do the installation yourself if you've built a cabinet or two or are an intermediate woodworker. Solid-surface materials can be cut and routed just like wood. Use sharp, carbide-tipped bits and blades so they cut cleanly through the material instead of heating it up and melting it.

The supplier provides great instructions on its Web site, but here's the routine in a nutshell. Simply rip the sheets with a table saw or circular saw and straightedge to get the 4-in. backsplash and the 1-in. front lip. Then apply the adhesive to the front lip and clamp the pieces together for 30 minutes. Use the special router bit (with a nylon bearing) to rout a decorative edge. Then lay down 3/4-in. plywood over your existing cabinets and install the new countertop. Glue the backsplash and seams and sand them with the special discs.

Besides your countertop material, you'll need a two-part adhesive gun, adhesive, router bits and abrasives to fit an orbital sander. Then use your regular woodworking tools to rip and crosscut the solid-surface material.

Question&Comment

PREP CONCRETE FOR TILE

The vinyl tile in my basement is in bad shape, and I want to replace it with either ceramic or porcelain. How do I get the old tile off and prep the concrete for new tile?

1 Scrape off as much of the adhesive residue as possible with a razor scraper. If any leftover adhesive is sticky, loosen it with a chemical adhesive remover.

2 Vacuum the area around cracks and apply a "peel-and-stick" primer with a roller or paint pad.

3 Apply a layer of crack isolation membrane over cracks to prevent cracks from appearing later in the overlying tile.

Popping off the old tile is fairly easy—just use a heavy scraper and elbow grease. Then attack the adhesive with a razor scraper (Photo 1). Scrape up as much adhesive as possible, keeping the blade sharp with a sharpening stone as you go. If the adhesive is hard and brittle, use a chopping motion to break it up. Then scrape again. Even then, some of that old adhesive may be impossible to remove. If you can't get it all off, don't worry. Newer latex-modified thin-set can be applied right over the small amount that remains.

After you scrape off the adhesive, touch the floor to see if there are any sticky areas. Use a chemical adhesive remover on those parts. Find one in the flooring department at home centers.

Next, locate all the cracks. You'll have to prime those areas and cover them with a peel-and-stick crack prevention mat (also called anti-fracture or crack isolation membrane; Photo 3) before you lay the new tile (Crack Buster Pro is one brand; a 12-in. x 25-ft. roll is $30). Skip this step and we guarantee your new tile

CAUTION: Most floor tiles made from the 1920s to the 1960s contain asbestos and require special procedures for removal. If you're unsure about yours, remove a tile and send it to a local asbestos abatement firm for testing. If it tests positive, follow these asbestos abatement procedures. Seal off the area with poly sheeting. Wear an asbestos-rated respirator. Change clothes before moving into a "clean" area. Clean the entire room with a damp cloth before removing the sheeting. Follow your local environmental codes for disposal. For more information, search the Internet for "removing asbestos tiles."

will crack right over the cracks in the concrete.

Cut the membrane so it's 1-1/2 times the width of your tiles. Then prime the concrete (see Photo 2) with the recommended solution (consult the membrane manufacturer's literature). Let the primer dry, and then apply the membrane (Photos 3 and 4).

With the cracks patched, apply a latex-modified, crack-resistant thinset (MegaLite is one brand). Then move on to the fun part, the tile setting (see Photo 5). To find a dealer for Crack Buster Pro and MegaLite, go to custombuildingproducts.com (800-272-8786).

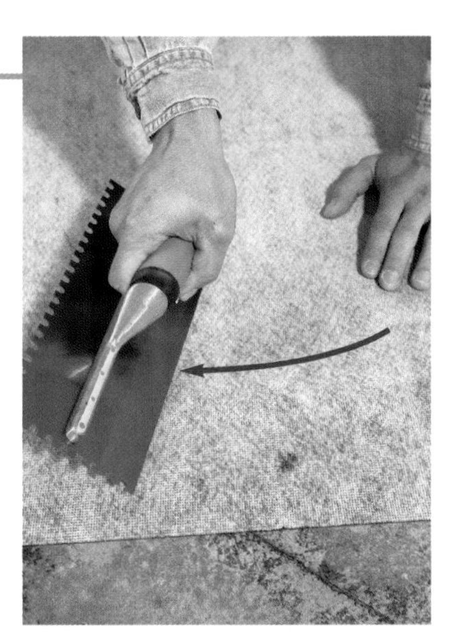

4 Push air bubbles out to the edge with a J-roller or the edge of a grout float. Then apply pressure to the entire membrane to complete the bond.

5 Force a thin layer of thin-set into the membrane fibers with the flat edge of the trowel just before combing on the thicker layer for setting the tile.

DOES NATURAL GAS REALLY DESTROY COPPER?

Previously, we showed readers how to connect natural gas appliances using copper tubing. Barely a week passed before the angry letters poured in. Each was more vehement than the one before, telling us we had committed a life-threatening error by recommending copper hookups. The letters, which came from plumbers and gas company employees, maintained that natural gas should never be run in copper pipe—it must be run in steel (black pipe). They warned us that the corrosive components of natural gas can lead to leaks, explosions and, at the very least, appliance failure.

Their claims had some basis in fact 50 years ago when gas utilities drew their supplies from local wells and piped gas untreated into homes and businesses. But today, almost all natural gas in the United States and Canada is obtained from large pipeline networks. The gas in those pipelines has been treated at the wellhead or at the refinery to remove the corrosive hydrogen sulfide. This gas does NOT present a safety risk when used with copper tubing, yet the terrifying legend lives on. TFH readers should know that copper tubing is approved for gas by the National Fuel Gas Code (NFPA 54), Uniform Plumbing Code, Uniform Mechanical Code, and the International Association of Plumbing and Mechanical Officials. It has been in use in many states for more than 35 years with no safety issues.

Despite all the evidence to the contrary, some state and local building codes continue to ban the use of copper as a material for gas. Because local codes always trump national and international codes, you must obey them. Meanwhile, it's time for the 50-year-old myths and legends to die.

MOLDING **MAGIC**

Extraordinary results with ordinary moldings

by **Jeff Gorton**

I've installed miles of trim over the years, most of it in old houses, where I've encountered every conceivable shape, size and combination of molding. I've learned a lot in the process, but I'm still discovering new tools and techniques that make trim work faster, easier and better. Here are a few tips—some classic techniques and some with a modern twist—that'll help you do a better job on your next trim project.

Combine moldings for extra drama

I love looking around old houses to see how moldings are combined to create baseboards, casings and cornices. I've even been surprised when removing old moldings to discover more layers than I originally noticed. The builders knew the advantages of combining small moldings. In addition to allowing endless possibilities for customization, smaller moldings are easier to cut and install than large moldings, and allow more flexibility on wavy or irregular walls. Plus, you can often achieve a great effect for less money by combining small moldings. I made the decorative ceiling cornice shown below using moldings I found at a home center.

The best way to plan molding combinations is to get your hands on some short lengths of molding and play around with them. Many full-service lumberyards have molding samples available. At home centers, you may have to purchase short lengths of each molding you're considering, or ask for scraps.

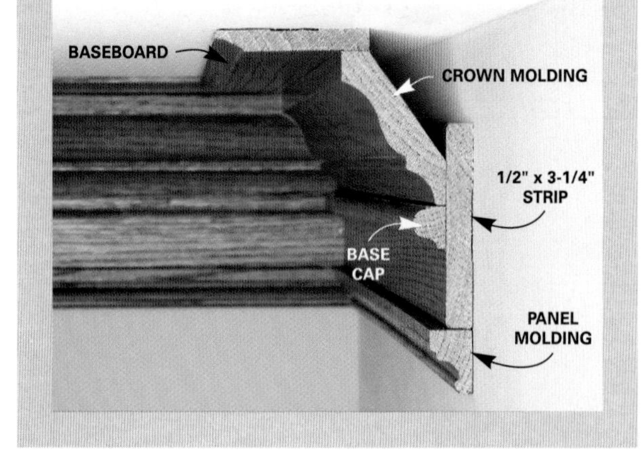

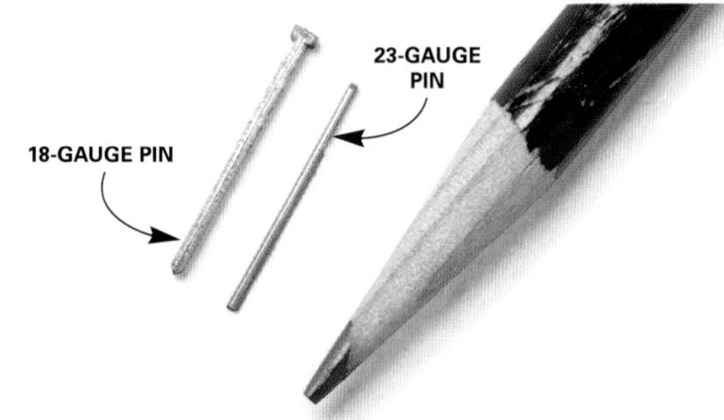

Nearly invisible nails

I was talking to John Frost, a local cabinetmaker, about how he installs moldings. After giving me a bunch of good tips, he said, "And of course you know about micro pinners." Actually, I didn't. John explained that a micro pinner is a finish nail gun that shoots super-thin 23-gauge pins. He uses a micro pinner because the small-diameter pins leave smaller holes that are almost invisible after you fill them. Plus, the tiny pins allow him to nail very small parts without splitting them as thicker pins might.

There are several brands of micro pinners ranging in cost from $120 to $330. The more expensive models drive pins up to 2 in. long. You'll find micro pinners at home centers and online.

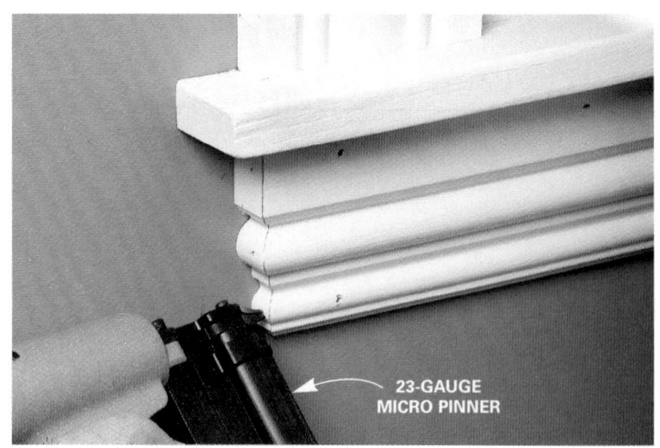

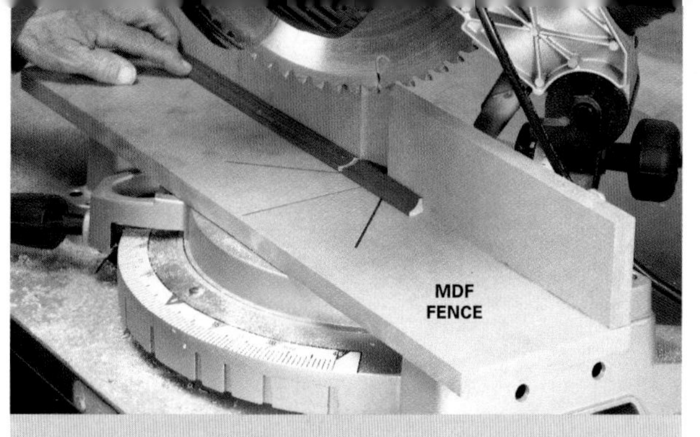

Add an auxiliary fence

I asked a cabinetmaker friend if he ever adds a fence to his miter saw, and he said, "Absolutely, always." An auxiliary fence has several advantages. It reduces the gap under and behind the molding to only what's needed for the blade to fit through. The small gap helps prevent splintering on the back of the board and keeps small cutoffs from dropping through the fence and getting flung by the blade. You can also use the saw kerfs in the fence to help you line up your cut.

An auxiliary fence needs to be accurate but not fancy. I like to build fences from MDF because it's straight, stable and inexpensive. Another good choice is 3/4-in. plywood. Make the back of the fence as tall as possible without letting it interfere with the motor housing or blade guard. If you need several short pieces cut to the same length, make the fence long enough so you can attach a stop. Be sure the bottom and back are exactly perpendicular and that you don't put fasteners where the blade will cut. If you own a plate joiner, use glue and biscuits to join the back and bottom—no need to worry about hitting fasteners. Attach the auxiliary fence with screws through your miter saw fence.

Inspect before you buy

Moldings can vary quite a bit in looks and quality, so it pays to examine them closely when you're picking them out. It's not as critical if you're installing trim that will be painted, but for stained moldings, there are several things to watch for. Make sure moldings that will be close to each other have a similar grain pattern and that the wood is about the same tone. Chatter from shaper blades is another common problem to pay attention to. Although you can't avoid chatter marks entirely, choosing moldings carefully can keep them to a minimum and significantly reduce your sanding time. Also watch out for "snipe," gouge cuts near the end of the molding that are caused by the molding machine. That 10-ft. stick of molding you need may not give you a full 10 ft. of usable molding.

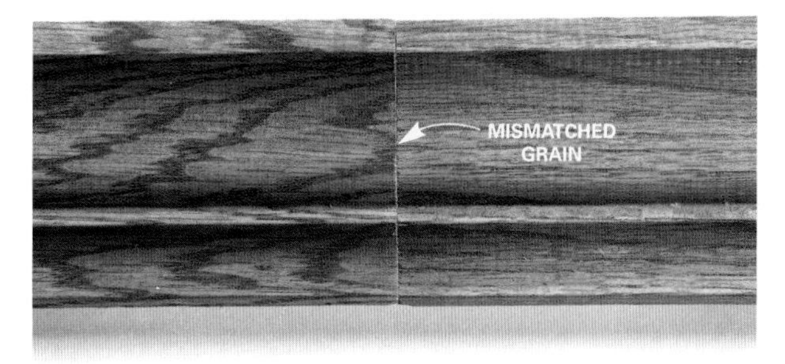

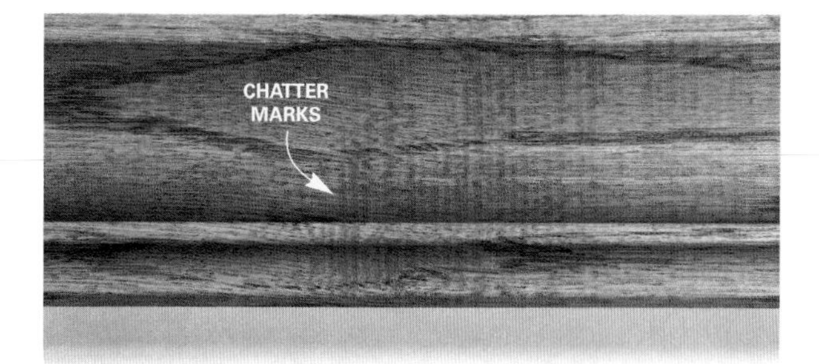

Put the pinch on miter joints

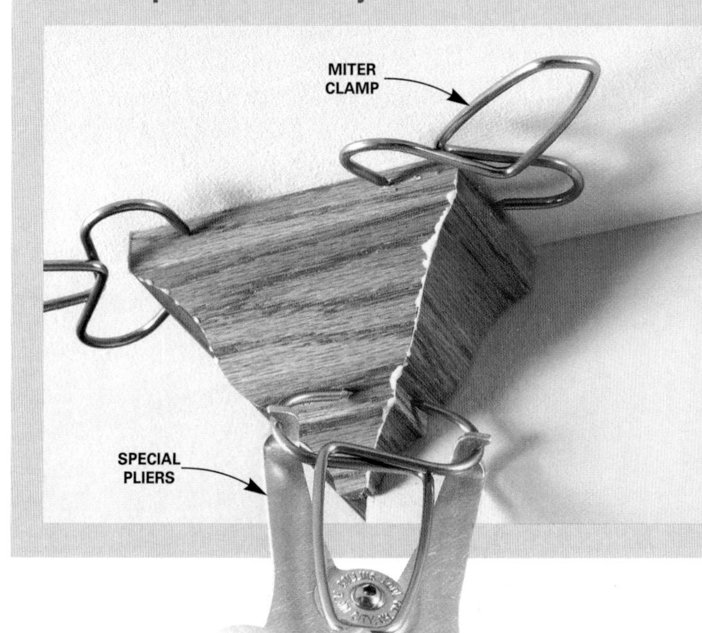

I recently ordered four miter clamps and a special pliers-type tool to install them and am amazed at how well they work. These handy little clamps are basically bent spring steel with sharp points that grab the moldings and squeeze them together. They're perfect for holding small pieces of mitered trim together while the glue dries and for clamping crown molding miters while you pin them together. They're also great for picture frame assembly. Our clamps are from Collins Tool Co. (collinstool.com; 888-838-8988; $29 for the four clamps and special pliers), but other brands are available. Search online for "miter clamps."

Spice up your project with reveals

Like every other rule, this one has many exceptions. But in general, when I'm combining moldings, or adding moldings to plain boards, I offset the parts so that the edges aren't perfectly aligned. The exposed band of molding or board is called a "reveal." Creating reveals has two big advantages. First, it allows a bit of flexibility, since the two edges don't have to be perfectly aligned. Second, reveals look better in most situations.

The typical method of creating a reveal is to set back the edge of the molding from the edge of the board as shown here. However, an equally effective method is to allow the molding to protrude. Some reveals are set by tradition. Door and window casings, for example, are usually moved about 3/16 in. from the edge of the jamb. In other cases, you'll have to trust your eye to determine the right amount.

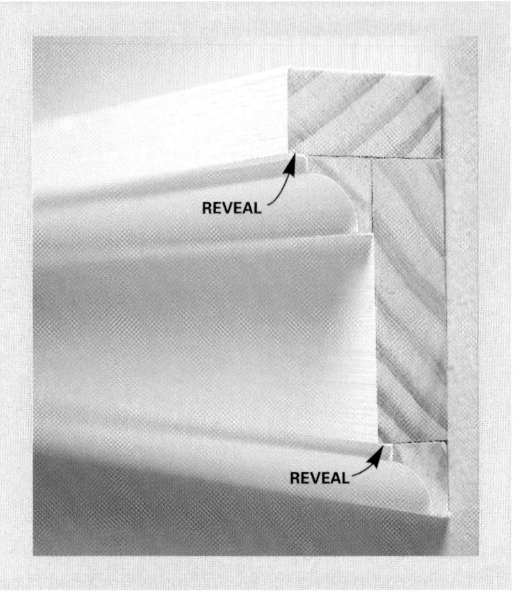

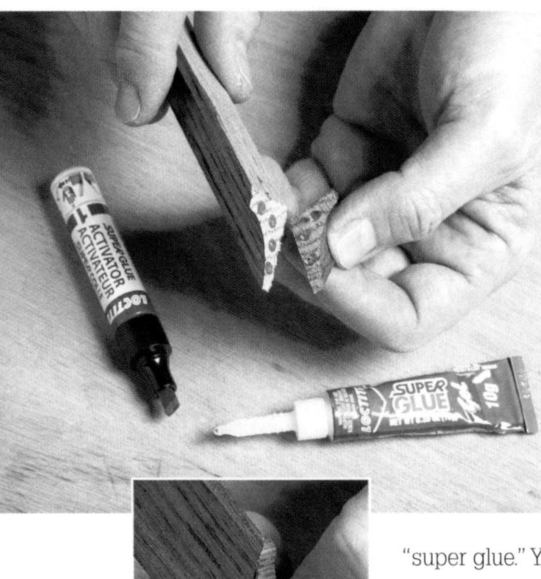

Attach small parts with super glue

Mitered returns are tough to attach. They're usually too small to nail unless you have a micro pinner. I've tried attaching small parts with wood glue, but often the moisture from the glue causes the thinnest part of the trim to warp before the glue dries. Here's a tip I learned from a trim carpenter. Get some cyanoacrylate adhesive (CA) and activator, also known as "super glue." You may be able to find a kit of CA that contains an activator at home centers, but a sure source is a woodworking store like Rockler. Go to rockler.com and search for "super glue" to find a wide variety. I like the medium-body CA. Spread a thin layer of CA on one piece of the molding and activator on the other. Then just press and hold for a few seconds. It works like magic, forming a strong bond unbelievably fast.

No framing—no problem

Once in a while, you may need to attach moldings where there's no framing behind the drywall to nail into. For example, if you're making frames on your wall out of moldings, it's likely that one of the vertical moldings won't have a stud behind it. The solution is to apply a thin bead of panel adhesive or construction adhesive and then tack the molding to the wall with a nail gun. For a better grip, shoot a pair of nails next to each other and at opposite angles so they form a wedge. If nails alone won't hold the molding, press it tight with 1x2s wedged against the opposite wall or the ceiling to hold it until the adhesive dries.

DIY Success Story

I built a new mantel and surround for the fireplace in my den. I decided to combine a number of different design ideas and customize it exactly as I wanted it. I used marble tile, various size pine boards and several types of molding, all from my local home center. The total cost was less than $500. FYI, I'm not a professional woodworker or builder.

—Allan Shaw

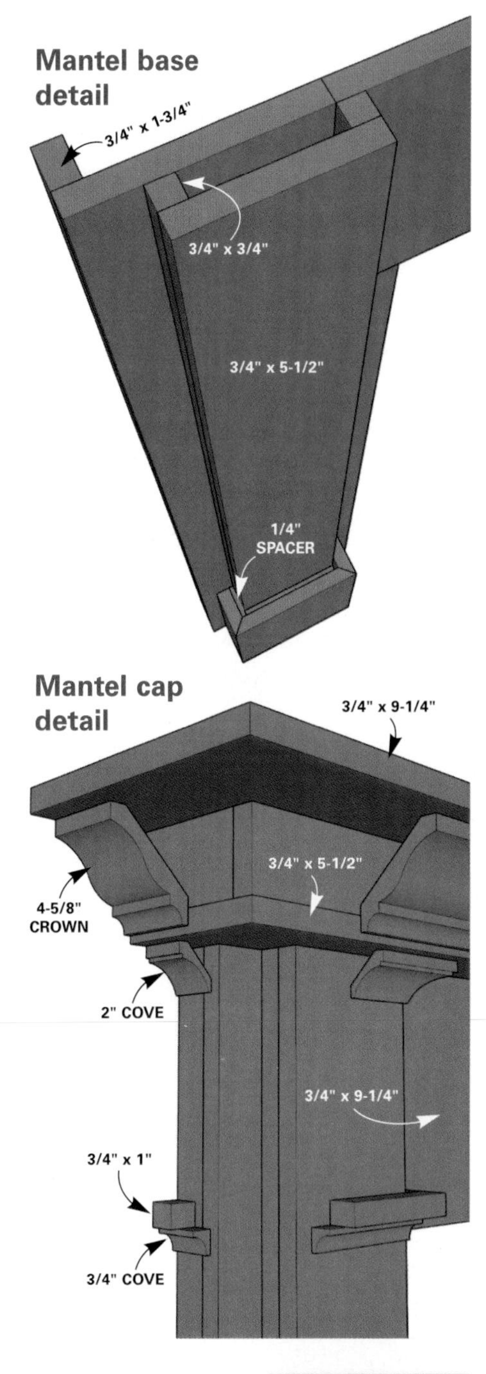

Fireplace mantel and wainscot design with SketchUp

For this article, I worked on SketchUp, a drawing program from Google, to design a fireplace mantel and simple wainscot and window trim. I used moldings that I found at a home center and a local full-service lumberyard. The SketchUp model and some of the building details are shown here. I've been dabbling in SketchUp for a few years but still have plenty to learn. What I like best about this versatile 3-D drawing program is how quickly you can learn the basics and create useful drawings. You'll be drawing 3-D shapes in minutes, and be able to draw a simple bookcase with a few hours' practice. I use SketchUp routinely to design sheds, build bookcases or just work out a tricky building detail.

Get a copy of SketchUp by going to sketchup.google.com. Then click on "Download Google SketchUp."

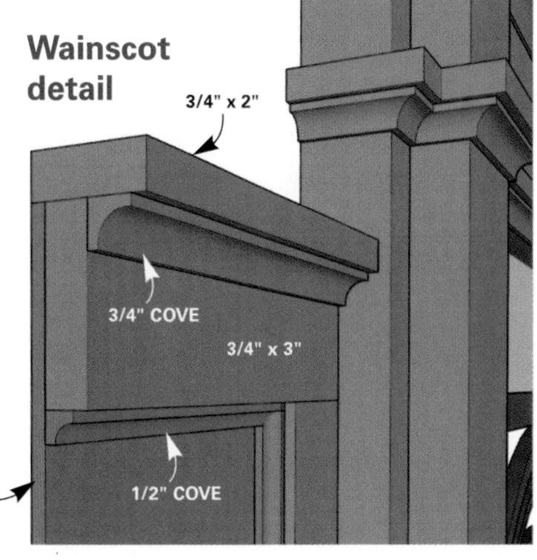

14 CABINET REPAIRS UNDER $14

Quick solutions to the most common cabinet problems

by **Brett Martin**

Some cabinet fixes are tough, even for pros. But the most common problems are easy peasy lemon squeezy, as the kindergartners like to say. Hit the hardware store in the morning to pick up supplies, then come home, get to work and you'll be done in time to feed your crew.

These fixes won't help with major problems like split panels on doors, but they will solve the little problems that bug you daily. Your cabinets will look and operate better—and sometimes a little satisfaction goes a long way.

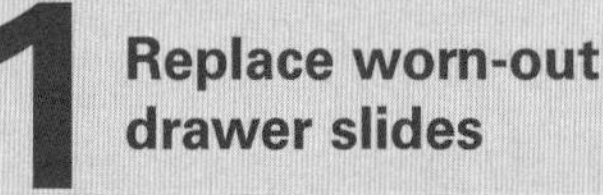

1 Replace worn-out drawer slides

Lubricants won't fix damaged drawer slides. They have to be replaced. This is a common problem on silverware drawers and other drawers that carry a lot of weight. Buy new slides that are the same, or nearly the same, as your old ones. Then it's just a matter of swapping them out. You'll find a limited selection of drawer slides at home centers, but there are dozens of online sources. Three sites are drawerslides.com, thehardware-hut.com and usacabinethardware.com. These sites also sell the plastic mounting sockets that attach to the back of the cabinet to hold the slides in place.

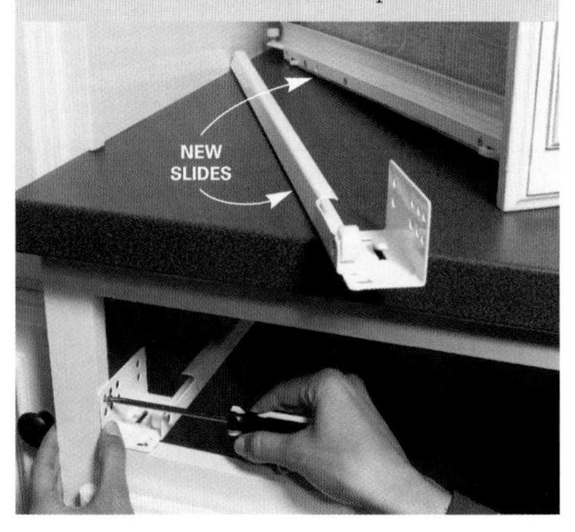

2 Adjust Euro hinges

Adjusting cabinet doors with European hinges is as easy as turning a screw or two. Hinges like this one adjust in three directions; others adjust in two. If your door is crooked—not square with the cabinet—fix that first, then raise or lower it to the same height as adjacent doors.

For crooked doors, adjust the side screw on one hinge, which moves the door from side to side. It's a trial-and-error process. Make a small adjustment, then close the door to check its position. If the door is higher or lower than adjacent doors, loosen the mounting screws on both hinges, raise or lower the door, then tighten the screws. Place a straightedge across the door top or bottom to make sure it's level with neighboring doors.

If the door sticks out too far from the cabinet or the hinge side brushes against the cabinet when you open the door, adjust the depth screw. Some hinges move the door as you turn the depth screw; others require you to tap the door in or out and then tighten the screw.

Door adjustments aren't as easy if you have traditional hinges. If your doors are sagging, first try tightening the screws. If the hinges are bent, replace them if you can find a match.

3 Build a shelf that won't sag

3/4" PLYWOOD

1x2 LUMBER

Don't bother replacing a sagging shelf with another 1/2-in.-thick shelf or it'll end up sagging too. Instead, cut a new shelf from 3/4-in. plywood. Make it the same length and 1-1/2 in. narrower (so you can add rails). Then glue and brad nail (or clamp) 1x2 rails along the front and back of the shelf, flush with the ends. The rails give the shelf additional support so it won't sag, even if you load it up with heavy cookware. Apply a polyurethane (or other) finish to match your other shelves.

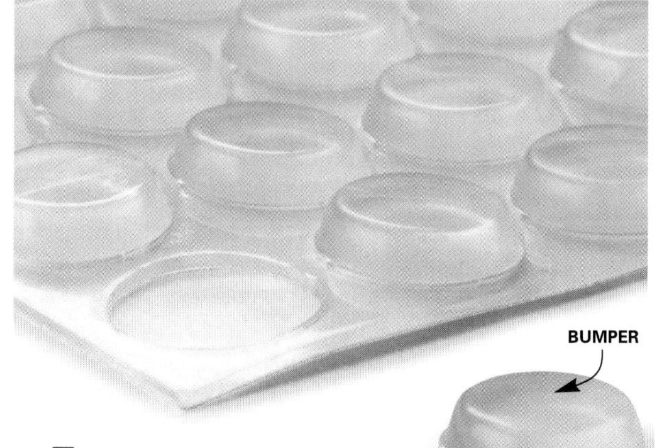

4 Silence banging doors with bumpers

Doors and drawers slam loudly when wood smacks against wood. That's why most have "bumpers" near the interior corners to cushion the impact and reduce the noise. But the bumpers sometimes fall off (or kids pick them off). Get new ones at home centers ($2 for a 16-pack). Peel off the backing and stick the bumpers in place. They're available clear or with felt, and in different thicknesses. Use bumpers the same thickness as those on adjacent doors.

5 Beef up wimpy drawer bottoms

The thin plywood used for drawer bottoms sometimes gets wavy. Stiffen up the bottoms with 1/4-in. or 3/8-in. plywood. Cut the plywood to fit over the drawer bottom, leaving about a 1/4-in. gap on each side. Apply wood glue on the drawer bottom and set the plywood over it. Set a gallon or two of paint over the plywood to hold it in place until the glue dries.

6 Fill in stripped screw holes

When the screws in your hinges or drawer slides turn but don't tighten, the screw hole is stripped. That can prevent doors and drawers from closing properly. Fix the problem with glue and toothpicks. Start by removing the hardware. Then apply a drop of wood glue to the ends of toothpicks and cram as many as will fit into the hole (maybe only two or three). Wipe away any glue that drips out. Let the glue dry, then use a utility knife to cut the toothpicks flush with the cabinet or drawer. Reinstall the hardware, driving the screw through the filled hole.

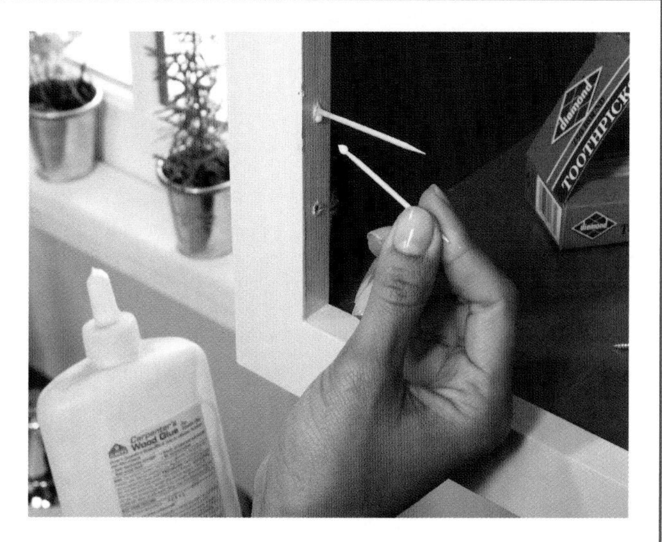

7 Repair busted drawers

Some drawers are held together by only a few drops of glue or short brad nails. When you first notice a drawer corner coming apart, take out the drawer and fix it. And if one corner is failing, others probably will too. Save yourself future hassles by repairing all the weak corners now. Place a piece of scrap wood against a corner and lightly rap it once with a hammer. If the corner comes apart, fix it. If not, it should hold up.

To fix the corner, first remove the drawer front, if possible. Most fronts are attached by screws driven from inside the drawer. Remove any fasteners from the corner, then scrape away the old glue with a utility knife. Reglue the corner, tap the sides back together and clamp the drawer until the glue dries.

8 Renew the shine

Grease splatters and smoke can leave a film on your cabinets, dulling the finish. Wash the cabinets with a wood cleaner to bring back the luster. Murphy Oil Soap is one type of cleaner ($4 for 32 oz.).

Use a sponge to rub the cleaner onto the cabinets. Cleaners like Murphy's don't need to be rinsed off, which cuts your cleaning time. For stubborn grease spots, scrub lightly with the cleaner using a No. 0000 steel wool pad. Cleaning the cabinets once a year keeps them shiny and protects the finish.

MAGNETIC CATCH

PLATE

9 Silence banging doors with bumpers

Sure, this trick is as old as Benny Hill jokes, but it still works. When your cabinet door is warped and won't fully close, simply install a magnetic catch (starting at $1.10 at home centers) at the problem area. Screw the magnetic catch to the cabinet rail or stile and the plate to the door. The magnet pulls the door closed. For powerful magnets, visit rockler.com and search for "magnetic catch."

10 Glue loose knobs

Once knobs fall off your cabinets, twisting them back on won't solve the problem. They'll just keep coming loose. Use a dab of thread adhesive to keep them in place (Loctite 242 is one brand; $6 at home centers). Apply the adhesive to the screw, then attach the knob. If you decide to replace the knob later, don't worry. You can remove it with a screwdriver.

THREAD ADHESIVE

11 Add back plates to cover worn areas

Years of opening doors and drawers can wear away the finish near cabinet knobs. Instead of undertaking the time-consuming task of refinishing the cabinets, try this quick fix: Install back plates under the knobs or handles. Simply unscrew the knob or handle, slide the back plate under it, then reattach the knob or handle. Back plates start at $2 and are available in a wide range of styles. You can special-order them at home centers or buy them online.

BACK PLATE

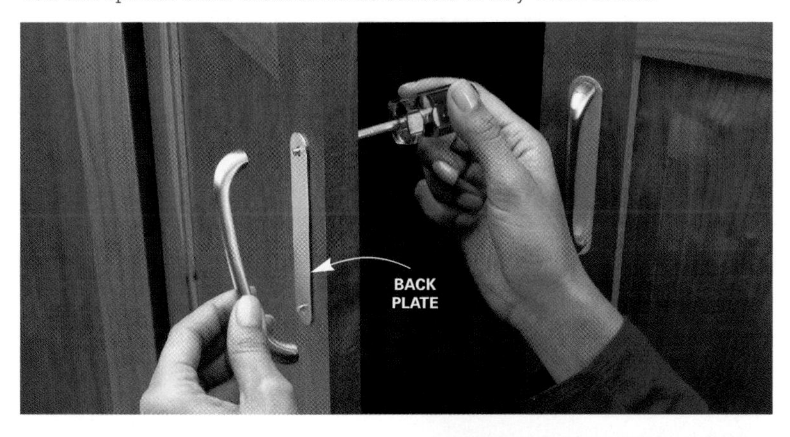

12 Replace bad latches

Older cabinets sometimes have "roller catches" that hold the doors closed. If you have these and your door won't close or stay closed, loosen the screws to slide the catch forward or backward on the cabinet frame. Or replace it if it's broken. The catches are available at home centers for less than $1.

13 Fill in scratches

Use a wood fill stick ($3.50) to make scratches less visible. The stick fills in and colors over the scratch. Soften the stick with a hair dryer to make the application easier. Then run the stick over the scratch and wipe away any excess with a cloth. The fill probably won't be an exact match with the surrounding cabinet, but it'll be close. The sticks work on shallow and deep scratches. They're available at home centers and amazon.com.

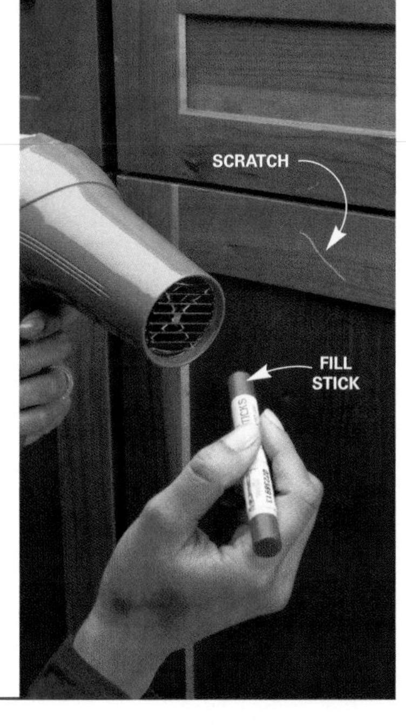

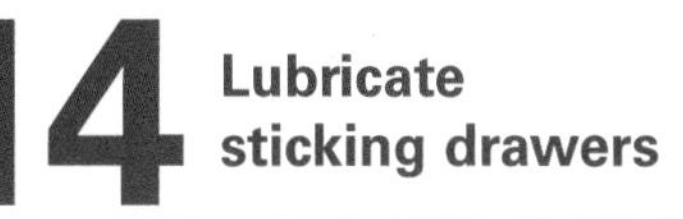

14 Lubricate sticking drawers

The fix for sticking drawers is easy. First remove the drawer. Wipe the drawer slides and the cabinet track with a clean cloth to remove any debris. Then spray a dry lubricant directly on the drawer slides. An 11-oz. can costs $5 at home centers; it'll say "dry lubricant" on the label. Replace the drawer and slide it in and out of the cabinet several times until it glides easily. If the drawer is still hard to open, replace the drawer slides (see p. 36).

Dry lubricants won't leave an oily residue that attracts dirt and dust. The lubricants also work great on squeaky hinges.

DIY Success Story

We replaced our sagging shelves with the white wire shelves typically used in closets. The shelves hold up well, they're inexpensive and I can see through them—which is great when I'm searching for a specific pan, plate or coffee mug in my cabinets. You just cut the shelves to size with a hacksaw or a metal blade in a jigsaw and stick them in place.

— Maureen Riegger

DEAN'S TILE TIPS

by **Jeff Gorton**

Most pros in any trade are creatures of habit. When something works, we stick with it. But during the 15 years we've worked with Dean Sorem, our tiling consultant, he's been constantly researching his trade, trying new products and looking for a better way. So we asked Dean to show us the methods and materials he's using these days. Whether you're a tile setter or a remodeler who occasionally tackles a tile job, you're sure to find at least a few tips here that'll come in handy on your next tiling project.

Back-butter for a better bond

After returning to a floor tile job the other day to reset a loose tile, Dean decided he would make it standard procedure to back-butter every large tile he and his crew install. As bigger tiles have become more common, so has the problem of loose tiles in a finished tile job. It's harder to get a good bond with a large surface. Big tiles require a special technique: You need to trowel a thin layer of thin-set on the back of each tile before you set it. Set the loaded trowel near the center of the tile and spread a thin layer of thin-set to the edge. Then rotate the tile a quarter turn and repeat until the back is evenly covered.

Don't wash the grout too soon

Dean says one of the biggest mistakes you can make on a grout job is to start cleaning up the grout too soon. Wiping the grout before it's hardened a bit allows too much water to penetrate the surface. That means blotchy-looking grout or, worse, hairline cracking and grout that falls out. To avoid these problems, be sure the grout is very firm, about like a wine cork, before you start cleaning it. Press your fingertip into the grout to test it. If it dents easily, wait.

Use a self-feeding screw gun

Screwing down backer board is monotonous and time-consuming, so when Dean discovered that cement board screws were available for self-feeding screw guns and that they didn't cost any more than loose screws, he bought a self-feeding screw gun and left his old screw gun at the shop. The Senco Duraspin tool shown is available at some home centers. If you need help locating a dealer, go to senco.com.

Corded versions of self-feeding screw guns sell for about $100 and cordless for $150. Dean actually prefers the corded version because it always offers full power and he doesn't have to worry about keeping batteries charged. With different screws, you can use the self-feeding screw gun to hang drywall or install decking, too.

Plan layouts with a laser level

Laser levels save time and increase accuracy. Dean uses a self-leveling laser to help plan the tile layout. He projects a level line around the room and measures from it to determine the size of the cut tiles along the edges. Then, after figuring out an ideal layout, he uses the laser as a guide to chalk layout lines. The laser saves time by eliminating the fussy job of extending level lines around the room with a 4-ft. level.

Dean uses the Stanley FatMax Cross Line Laser (about $100) which is self-leveling and projects level and plumb lines. Self-leveling lasers reduce setup time and can be swiveled without readjustment. Mount the laser on an inexpensive ($25) camera tripod for maximum versatility. More-expensive lasers project perpendicular lines on the floor that you can use to plan floor layouts.

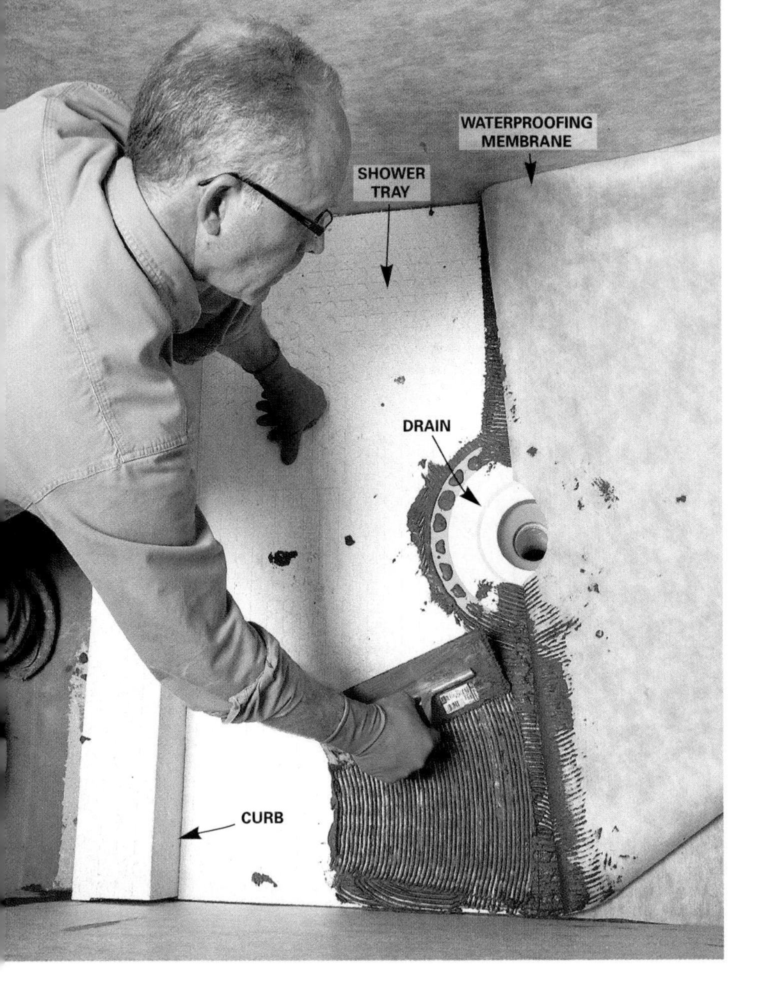

Use a Schluter system for a leakproof shower

Dean loves the simplicity and security offered by the Schluter shower system. Before, he had to pour a sloped mortar bed, cover it with a waterproof membrane and then pour another layer of mortar over that. This traditional method is tricky and time-consuming, and the shower will leak if it's not perfectly executed.

The Schluter system eliminates all these hassles by providing the tile setter with a preformed shower base and curb, a special drain and a waterproofing membrane. Schluter even includes preformed inside and outside corner pieces to seal these tricky spots. All you need to provide is unmodified thin-set and some tools.

The complete system for a 48-in. square shower costs about $400. Dean likes feeling confident that his showers won't leak and being able to start tiling right away without waiting for mortar to set up. For information on where to buy the Schluter system and how to install it, go to schluter.com (800-472-4588).

Instructions are included with the kit, but here's an overview. You embed the foam base and curb in thin-set. Then you install the special drain assembly, embedding it in thin-set as you attach it to the drainpipe. Finally, you'll embed the waterproof membrane in a layer of unmodified thin-set and tile over it. The membrane and corner pieces can be installed in any order.

Polish stone edges

To save money and get a better-looking job, Dean prefers to make his own trim pieces for marble, granite and other stone tile jobs. Take the top of a shower curb, for example. You would have to buy enough bullnose trim to cover both edges, and you'd end up with a grout joint down the center where the two rows of bullnose meet. Dean covers the curb with one piece of stone, polished on both edges.

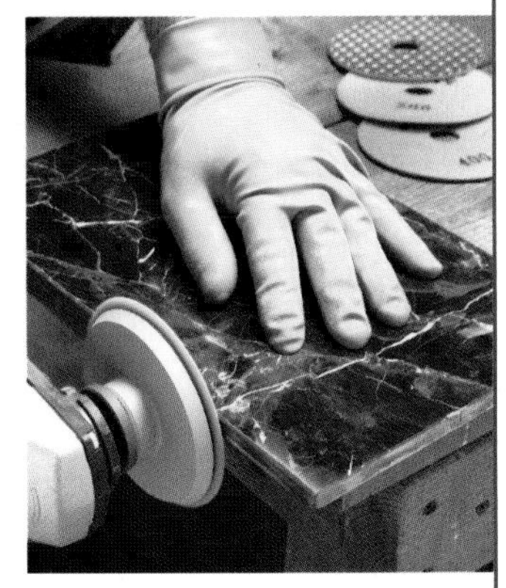

Dean prefers the honeycomb-style dry diamond polishing pads with hook-and-loop fasteners. They allow him to quickly run through a series of grits from 60 to 800 or higher without wasting a lot of time changing pads. One caveat, though. This type of disc requires a variable-speed grinder because the maximum allowable rpm is about 4,000. If you own a single-speed grinder that runs at 10,000 rpm, you'll need a set of PVA Marble Edge Polisher discs that are safe to run at high speed (they polish all kinds of stone). One source for both types of discs is Benfer Blade & Saw (benfertool.com; 952-888-1448), or search online for "marble polishing discs."

Polishing stone is a dusty operation, so work outside. Start by using the coarsest grit to remove the saw marks from all the edges. Then progress through the grits until you reach the level of sheen you desire. Use light pressure to avoid overheating the disc and wearing it out prematurely. You'll have to progress through the finest grit to create a glossy surface.

Waterproof wet areas

It's a surprise to most people that a tiled wall or floor isn't waterproof. Some types of tile are porous, and most grout isn't waterproof either. Water can seep through tile and grout and leak into cracks at corners and other intersections. The only sure way to keep water from reaching the backer board is to waterproof all areas that may be exposed to water. That's easy with the new waterproofing coatings. Dean uses the RedGuard brand, but there are others. Dean says, "If in doubt, coat it with waterproofing."

Follow the application instructions on the container. Dean applies the RedGuard with an inexpensive paint pad, which he prefers to a brush or roller because it works like a trowel, allowing him to quickly spread a thick, even layer over the surface.

Flatten walls with shims

Modern tile backer board beats a traditional mortar bed—unless you're trying to flatten a crooked wall. In the old days, a skillful tile setter could float mortar over the waviest framing and end up with a perfectly flat surface. Nowadays most tilers use some type of tile backer board. But if you screw backer boards to crooked framing, you'll get a wavy surface that makes it tough to do a nice tile job.

The solution is to flatten the walls before you screw the board to them. Dean chooses the longest level or straight screed board that will fit across a wall and uses it to see if any studs are bowed in or out. If a stud is really bowed out (1/4 in. or more) Dean saws a kerf about two-thirds through the stud at its midpoint and pushes it back. Then he'll screw a straight stud alongside to hold it in place. In most cases, though, shimming the studs with thin strips of cardboard to get them into alignment is enough. You can buy long, thin strips of cardboard for shimming at some home centers, but any strips of thin material will work. Leftover vinyl flooring cut into 1-1/2-in. strips is a good alternative.

TRIPLE YOUR **CLOSET SPACE**

FOR ANY SIZE CLOSET!

by **Brett Martin**

If you have to dig through a mountain of clothes to find your favorite sweatshirt, it's time to take on that messy closet. This simple-to-build system organizes your closet with shelf, drawer and hanging space for your clothes, shoes and accessories. Buying a closet system like this would cost you at least $500, but you can build this one for about half that.

Our system is really just four plywood boxes outfitted with shelf standards, closet rods or drawers. We built it for an 8-ft.-wide closet with an 8-ft. ceiling, but it'll work in any reach-in closet that's at least 6 ft. wide if you adjust the shelf width between the boxes or change the box dimensions.

Three times the storage—and more!

Three times the storage in the same space may sound impossible, but just look at the numbers:

STORAGE SPACE COMPARISON FOR 8-FT. CLOSET

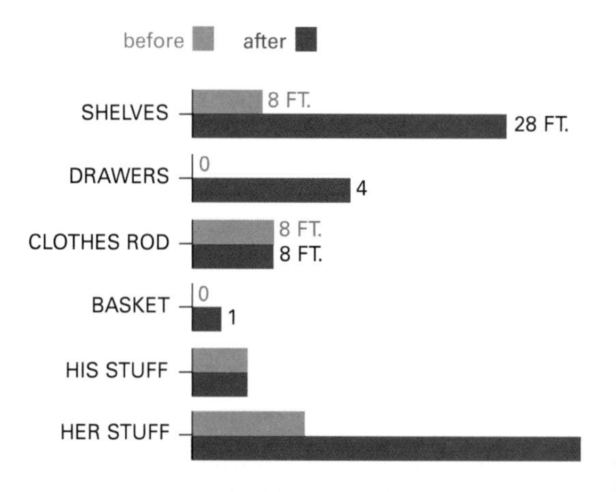

Time, money and materials

You can complete this project in a weekend. Spend Saturday cutting the lumber, ironing on the edge banding and applying the finish. Use your Saturday date night to clean everything out of the closet. That leaves you Sunday to build and install the new system.

We built the entire system with birch plywood ($40 per sheet). The total cost, including the hardware for the drawers, shelves and closet rods, was about $250 (see Shopping List, p. 49). You could use MDF ($30) or oak plywood ($40) instead of birch. Everything you need for this project is available at home centers.

Cut and prefinish the parts

Start by cutting all the parts to size following **Figure C** on p. 49 and the Cutting List on p. 46. The corner box sides are slightly narrower than 12 in., so you can cut off dings and dents and still cut four sides from a sheet of plywood.

You won't be able to cut the shelves that fit between the boxes to length until the boxes are installed (the shelves need to be cut to fit), but you can rip plywood to 11-7/8 in. and cut the shelves to length later.

Once the parts are cut, apply edge banding (iron-on veneer) to all the edges that will be exposed after the boxes are assembled (**Figure A**). Build a jig to hold the parts upright. Place a part in the jig. Then cut the edge banding so it overhangs

DIY Success Story

"Years ago, I built a closet storage system. I made two mistakes. First, I didn't have enough drawers. You can never have too many drawers. But my biggest mistake was using cheap plastic holders for the closet rods. When the first one broke and dumped heaps of clothing on the floor—which had to be ironed again—I bit the bullet and replaced them all. I used the beefy, more expensive metal holders—I could hang suits of armor on them and they wouldn't break."

— Mike O'Brien

1 Finish now, save time later. **Prefinishing gives you a faster, neater finish because you'll have fewer corners to mess with. Apply two coats of polyurethane quickly and smoothly with a disposable paint pad.**

2 Preinstall drawer slides. **Attaching slides is a lot easier before the boxes are assembled. Position the slides using reference lines and a spacer. Remember that there are left- and right-hand slides, usually marked "CL" and "CR."**

3 Gang-cut the standards. **Cutting 16 standards one by one with a hacksaw would take hours. Instead, bundle two or more together with tape and cut them with a jigsaw.**

Figure A
Closet storage system

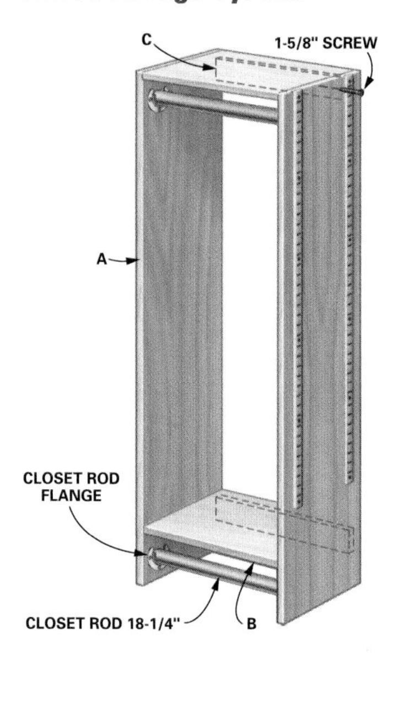

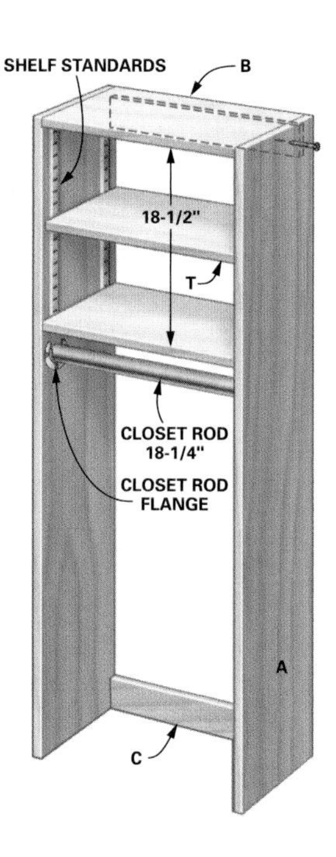

Figure B
Drawer Construction

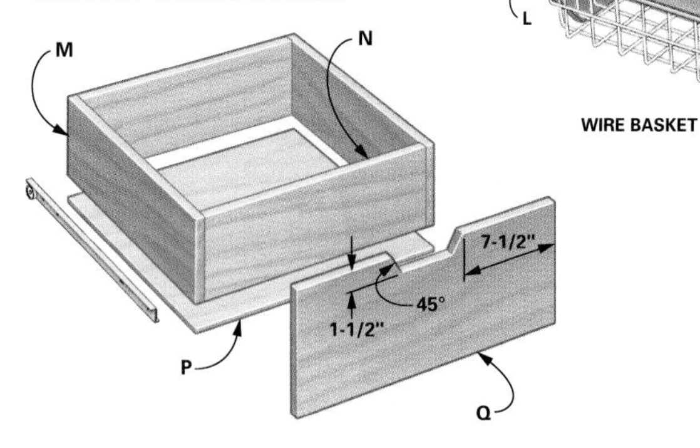

each end of the plywood by 1/2 in. Run an iron (on the cotton setting) slowly over the edge banding. Then press a scrap piece of wood over the edge banding to make sure it's fully adhered. Trim the edges with a veneer edge trimmer ($10).

Lightly sand the wood and your closet rod with 120-grit sandpaper. Wipe away the dust with a tack cloth, then use a paint pad to apply a coat of polyurethane ($6 per half pint) on everything except the drawer parts (**Photo 1**). This $2 pad will let you finish each part in about 20 seconds. Let the finish dry, then apply a second coat.

Attach the hardware

It's easier to install the drawer slides and the shelf standards that go inside the boxes before you assemble the boxes. Use a framing square to draw reference lines on the drawer unit sides for your drawer slides (see **Figure A**). The slides are spaced 8 in. apart, centered 8-3/4 in.

CUTTING LIST

KEY	QTY.	SIZE & DESCRIPTION
A	4	3/4" x 11-7/8" x 52" corner box sides
B	4	3/4" x 11-7/8" x 18-1/2" corner box tops and bottom
C	4	3/4" x 2-1/2" x 18-1/2" corner box screw strips
D	2	3/4" x 13-7/8" x 34" shelf unit sides
E	1	3/4" x 13-7/8" x 22-1/2" shelf unit top
F	1	3/4" x 21" x 24" shelf unit bottom
G	2	3/4" x 2-1/2" x 22-1/2" shelf unit screw strips
H	2	3/4" x 20-3/4" x 44" drawer unit sides
J	1	3/4" x 20-3/4" x 22-1/2" drawer unit top
K	1	1/4" x 24" x 44" drawer unit back
L	1	3/4" x 2" x 22-1/2" drawer unit cleat
M	8	1/2" x 6" x 20" drawer sides
N	8	1/2" x 6" x 20-1/2" drawer fronts and backs
P	4	1/4" x 20" x 21-1/2" drawer bottoms
Q	4	3/4" x 8" x 22-1/4" drawer face
R	8	3/4" x 11-7/8" adjustable shelves, cut to length (not shown)
S	2	3/4" x 13-7/8" x 22" adjustable shelves for shelf unit
T	1	3/4" x 11-7/8" x 18" right corner box adjustable shelf
U	1	3/4" x 14-1/4" x 96" top shelf (not shown)

down from the top of the box. Keep the slides 3/4 in. from the front edge (this is where the drawer faces will go). Use a 7/64-in. self-centering drill bit ($9) to drill pilot holes and screw the slides into place (Photo 2).

You'll need to have your wire basket now (they're available at home centers). Attach the glides for the basket 3 in. below the drawer slides. If your basket is narrower than 22-1/2 in., screw a cleat to the box side so the basket will fit.

Now attach the shelf standards. You can cut them with a hacksaw, but an easier way is to use a metal blade in a jigsaw. Place two or more standards together so the numbers are oriented the same way and the standards are aligned at the ends. Tape the standards together where you're going to make the cut, then gang-cut them with your jigsaw (Photo 3).

Screw the standards to the inside of the box sides, 1 in. from the edges. Keep the standards 3/4 in. from the top (that's where the box tops go). Be sure the numbers on the standards are facing the same way when you install them—this ensures the shelves will be level.

Assemble the boxes

Use a brad nailer to tack the boxes together following Figure A and Photo 4. If you don't have a brad nailer, use clamps. Then screw the boxes together. We used 1-5/8-in. trim screws ($5 for a 1-lb. box) because the screw heads are small and unobtrusive (we left the screw heads exposed). Here are some tips for assembling the boxes:

- Attach the screw strips to the box tops first, then add one side, then the bottom shelf, and then the second side.
- Drill 1/8-in. pilot holes to prevent splitting. Stay 1 in. from edges.
- If your cuts are slightly off and the top, bottom and sides aren't exactly the same width, align the front edges.
- The boxes will be slightly wobbly until they're installed in the closet, so handle them with care.

4 Nail first, then screw. If you have a brad nailer, tack the boxes together to hold the parts in position. Then add screws for strength.

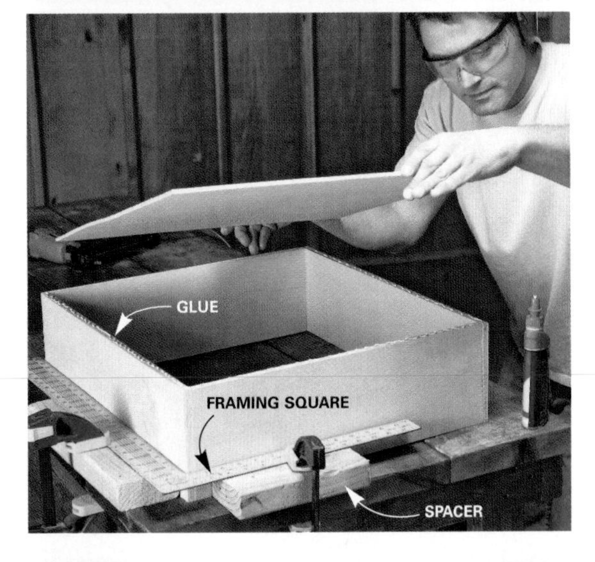

5 Square the drawer boxes. If the boxes aren't square, the drawers won't fit right or glide smoothly. Drawers take a beating, so assemble them with nails and glue.

6 Center the drawer faces perfectly. Stick the faces to the boxes with double-sided tape. Then pull out the drawer and drive screws from inside the box.

- The middle bottom box has a back. Square the box with the back, then glue and tack the back in place.
- After the corner boxes are assembled, screw shelf standards to the side that doesn't abut the wall (it's easier to install the standards before the boxes are installed).

Build the drawers

Cut the drawer sides and bottoms (see Cutting List, p. 49). Assemble the sides with glue and 1-in. screws. To square the drawers, set adjacent sides against a framing square that's clamped to your work surface. Glue and tack the drawer bottom into place (**Photo 5**). Then set the drawer slides on the drawers, drill pilot holes and screw the slides into place.

Install the drawers in the box. Getting the drawer faces in their perfect position is tricky business. If the faces are even slightly off-center, the drawer won't close properly. To align them, place double-sided tape over the drawer front. Starting with the top drawer, center the drawer face in the opening (**Photo 6**). You should have about a 1/8-in. gap on both sides and the top. Press the face into the tape. Take out the drawer and clamp the face to the drawer to keep it stationary. Drive two 1-in. screws through the inside of the drawer into the face.

Hang the boxes in the closet

Now install the boxes. Start by drawing a level line in the closet, 11 in. down from the ceiling. This will give you just over 10 in. of storage space above the closet system after the top shelf is installed. Then mark the stud locations on the wall with tape.

Don't assume your closet walls are plumb—they're probably not. So you can't just place a box in a corner without checking for alignment. Hanging the boxes is a two-person job, so get a helper. Start with the corner boxes. Align the top of the box with your level line on the wall. Have your helper plumb the box with a level while you drive 2-1/2-in. screws through the screw strip into the wall at the stud locations (**Photo 7**). Attach the other corner box the same way.

Find the center of the wall, then make a mark 12 in. on one side of the center mark. That's where your shelf unit will go. Again, have your helper plumb the box while you align it with your marks and screw it to the wall.

Prop up the drawer unit on spacers so it's tight against the shelf unit. Align the edges, then clamp the boxes and screw them together (**Photo 8**). Drive screws through the screw strip into the wall.

Then place the top shelf over the boxes. We could just barely fit our shelf into the closet to lift it into place. If yours won't fit, you'll have to cut it and install it as two pieces. Make the cut near one end, over a corner box, so it's not noticeable. Screw the shelf to the box tops with 1-1/4-in. screws.

Then attach shelf standards along the sides of the shelf and drawer units (**Figure A**). Cut the adjustable shelves to length to fit between the corner boxes and the middle boxes. Finally, screw the closet rod flanges into place, cut the closet rod to size and install the rods.

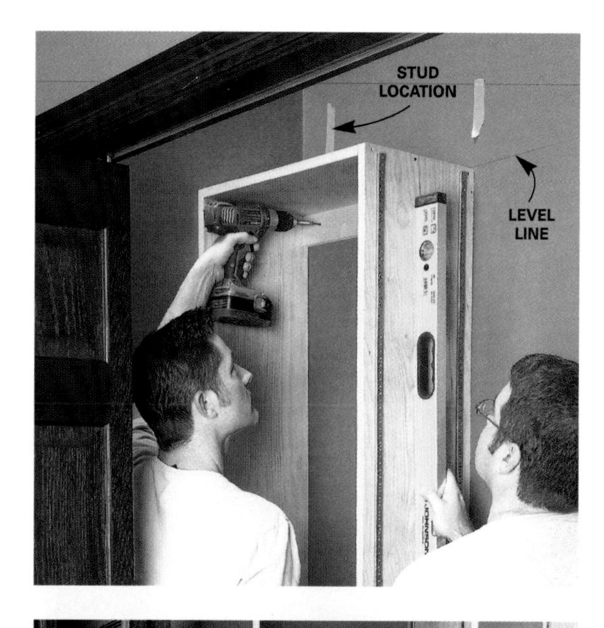

7 Plumb the shelf boxes. The corners of your closet may not be plumb, so check the box with a level before you screw it to the studs. Mark stud locations with masking tape.

8 Install the center unit in two parts. The center unit is big and clumsy, so install the shelf unit first, then prop up the drawer unit with spacers and screw it to the shelf.

Figure C Closet storage cutting diagrams

We're showing only the 3/4-in. plywood here. The 1/2-in. and 1/4-in. plywood sheets are for the drawers and back.

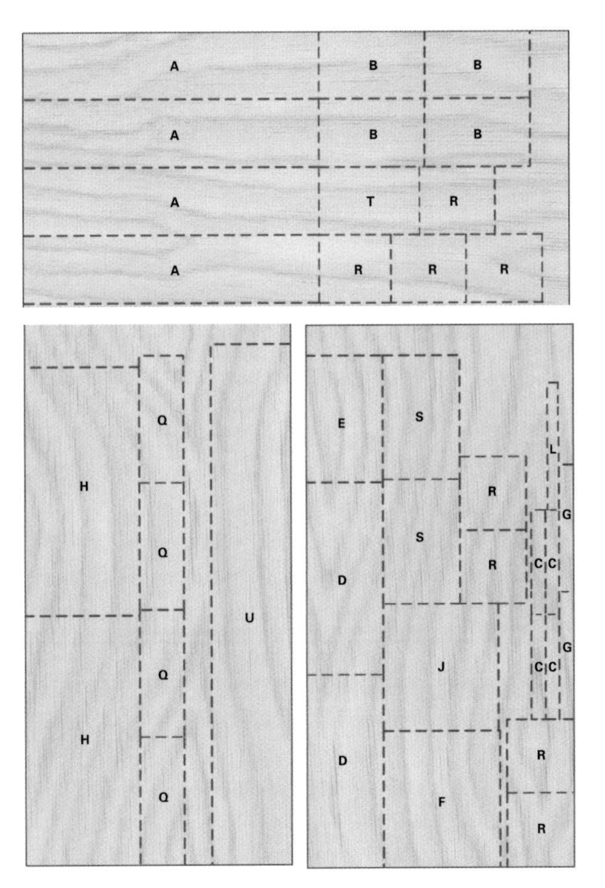

SHOPPING LIST

ITEM	QTY.
4' x 8' x 3/4" plywood	3
4' x 8' x 1/2" plywood	1
4' x 8' x 1/4" plywood	1
8' closet rod	1
Edge banding (iron-on veneer)	2 pkgs.
20" drawer slides	4 prs.
6' shelf standards	10
Closet rod flanges	10
Wire basket	1
2-1/2" screws	1 box
1-5/8" trim screws	1 box
1-1/4" screws	1 box
1" screws	1 box
Wipe-on poly	1 pint

HandyHints®

"Hot" vinyl tile removal tip

Here's a hot tip for removing a damaged vinyl tile that needs replacement. Put a cloth down on the tile and hold an iron set on medium-high on it for about 10 seconds. The cloth keeps the tile from melting but makes it pliable and softens the adhesive backing. Tease a corner free with the tip of a utility knife and the tile will peel right up. This works with both peel-and-stick and glue-down tiles.

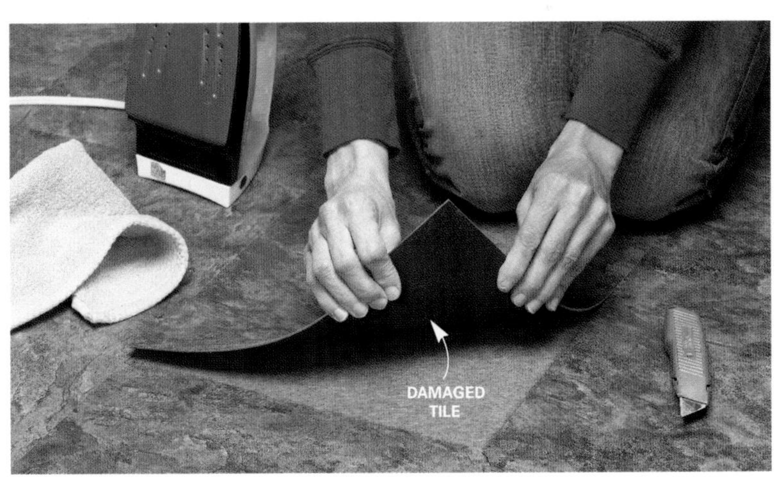

Stay-put insulation

I was insulating the vaulted ceiling in our new bedroom, and I couldn't get the unfaced fiberglass batts to stay put long enough to staple up the plastic moisture barrier. Then I spied a roll of paper drywall tape. Yes! I stapled it across the bottom of the rafters as I pushed the batts into place. It was easy to go back and fluff the batts against the rafters before I stapled up the plastic.

I ♥ KITCHEN ROLLOUTS

They changed my life— and they'll change your yours, too!

by **Elisa Bernick**

It may sound like hype, but adding rollouts to your kitchen cabinets can be life-changing. I speak from personal experience. I recently added rollouts to our entire kitchen, and this is what happened:

- The kids have complete access to everything they need—from cereal to the recycling. Now they can get their own breakfast and take the cans to the curb—no excuses!
- My sore back and my husband's bum knee are less of an issue since we no longer have to constantly stoop to find things in our base cabinets.
- Dinner prep goes a lot faster now that we're not hunting for pot lids and baking pans piled on top of one another on our jumbled, dark shelves.
- We're saving money by not buying things we already have (but that had been lost in the recesses of our cabinets). We can pull our shelves into the light and see everything, including the rancid oil and three boxes of cornstarch we somehow acquired—need some?
- The kitchen feels larger and works better. The rollouts maximize every cubic inch of storage space, so I can store rarely used appliances in my cabinets instead of on my counters.

Are you a convert yet? This article will give you tips for planning, buying and building kitchen rollouts so they can change your life too. You can build a simple rollout drawer like the ones shown in a couple of hours for $20. But don't say I didn't warn you. Once you see that rollout in action, you'll want to retrofit all your kitchen cabinets. What are you waiting for?

Make the most of skinny spaces

Kitchen designer Mary Jane Pappas typically recommends 18- to 30-in.-wide rollout drawers for cabinets: "Any larger and they're too clumsy. Any smaller and too much of the space is used by the rollouts themselves." But there is one type of rollout that makes good use of narrow spaces, even those only 3 to 6 in. wide. Pappas says that pullout pantries—single tall, narrow drawers with long, shelves, drawers, baskets or even pegboard (photo at right)—can be an efficient way to put skinny spaces to work.

REV-A-SHELF

In a small kitchen with little storage space, you can make even narrow filler spaces work harder by installing a vertical pegboard rollout. Shown is the 434 Series 6-in. Base Filler with stainless steel panel, $315, from Rev-A-Shelf.com.

Tip

Make drawer boxes about 1/32 in. smaller than you need. It's easy to shim behind a slide with layers of masking tape to make up for a too-small drawer. It's a lot harder to deal with a drawer that's too wide.

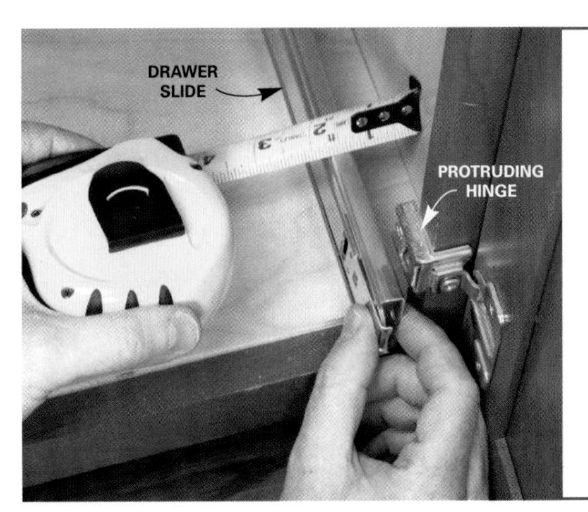

Watch for obstacles

Every cabinetmaker has a story about the rollout that wouldn't roll out but instead collided with something. When you're measuring for the spacer width, watch out for protruding hinges and doors that don't open fully or that protrude into the cabinet opening.

Baltic birch is best

Cabinetmakers love Baltic birch plywood for rollouts because the edges look great. Unlike standard hardwood plywood, Baltic birch never has voids in the inner core. It may not be labeled "Baltic birch" at home centers, but you'll be able to identify it by comparing it with other hardwood plywood in the racks. It'll have more and thinner laminations in the plywood core. The biggest disadvantages of using Baltic birch are that it costs more than standard hardwood plywood and can be harder to find. A 4 x 8-ft. sheet will run you $65 compared with $50 for standard hardwood plywood. If your home center doesn't carry it, try a traditional lumberyard.

Start at the bottom

The most useful rollout shelves and drawers are the ones closest to the floor since these eliminate the most awkward bending and crouching. If you want to limit your time and money investment, you'll get the most bang for your buck by retrofitting these areas first.

Use the right slides

There are a dozen kinds of drawer slides out there, but if you want to keep shopping and installation simple, stick to these two types:

Roller slides glide on plastic wheels. They're inexpensive, a cinch to install (it takes about two minutes) and nearly impossible to screw up. You'll find them at home centers under various names including side mount, under mount and bottom mount. Most are rated to carry 35 to 100 lbs. For heavy-duty rollouts holding items such as canned goods, use slides rated for at least 100 lbs. The big disadvantage: Most roller slides extend only three-quarters of their length—the back of the drawer stays in the cabinet.

Ball-bearing slides glide on tiny bearings. The big advantage of these slides is that they extend fully, giving you complete access to everything in the drawer.

They're about three times the cost of roller slides, and they're usually rated to carry 75 to 100 lbs., but you can get 200-lb. versions for about $40 a pair. Home centers carry ball-bearing slides, but you'll find a wider variety at woodworkershardware.com. The big disadvantage: They're fussy to install. If your drawer is a hair too big or small, these slides won't glide.

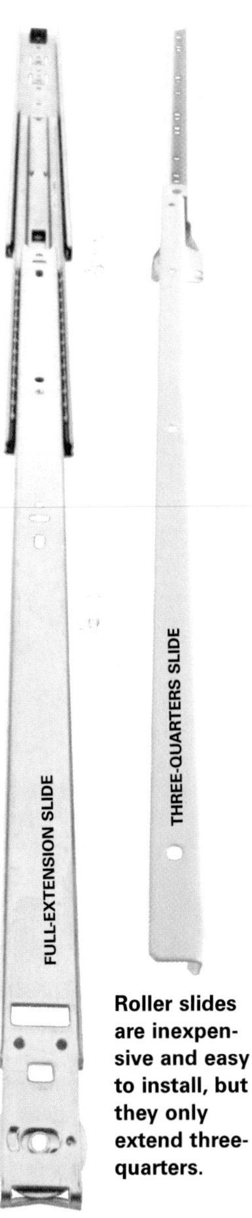

Roller slides are inexpensive and easy to install, but they only extend three-quarters.

Ball-bearing slides cost more and are harder to install, but they can extend fully.

Think inside the box

Building a slew of identical drawer boxes is easier, but having a variety gives you more versatility. Think about what you're going to store and build the boxes to suit your needs.

Rollout drawers with sloping sides keep tall things stable yet still let you see all the way to the back of the shelf. These are good for nesting pots and pans or storing different-size items on the same shelf.

Lower sides (3 in. is typical) work well for smaller items such as canned goods and spices. The low sides make reading labels easier.

Shelves with higher sides all around (6 in. tall rather than the typical 3 in.) are ideal for tippy plastic storage containers or stacks of plates.

Store-bought rollouts—what to look for

You can spend as little as $10 for a simple wire rollout basket or as much as $100. So what's the difference?

- Look for rollouts with quality hardware. Second-rate slides and rollers can sag or seize up under sacks of flour and pots and pans. Examine the slides to check whether they're roller slides (which extend only three-quarters of their length) or ball-bearing (which extend fully). Ball-bearing slides tend to support heavier items and roll more smoothly.
- Choose sturdy, chrome-plated steel rollouts for heavier items. Steel rollouts come in different gauge metals. Before ordering online, shop around at different retailers so you can physically compare the weight and density of the steel used by different manufacturers.
- Epoxy-coated wire rollouts and plastic inserts work fine for light-duty items, but they have a tendency to crack, bend and scratch if packed with heavy loads like canned goods.

IKEA's Rationell Variera pullout basket ($20; ikea.com) works well for medium-weight items.

The Lynk Rollout Undersink Drawer ($65 at home centers) can take heavy use.

Rubbermaid's Slide Out Undersink Basket (No. 80360; $20 at home centers) handles light items.

Avoid mistakes with a story stick

The most obvious way to size rollout parts is to measure the opening of the cabinet and then do the math. But that's a recipe for mistakes because it's easy to forget to subtract one of the components (like the width of the slides or the drawers) from the overall measurement. So try this: Forget the math and mark your measurements on a piece of scrap wood. It's a great visual aid that helps you prevent mistakes and having to walk between your kitchen and your shop constantly to double-check measurements.

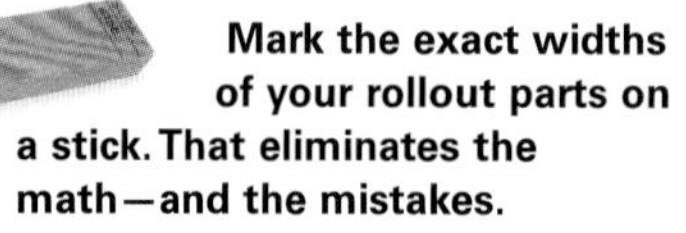

Mark the exact widths of your rollout parts on a stick. That eliminates the math—and the mistakes.

Divide up wide spaces

If the cabinet is more than 30 in. wide, consider installing two narrower rollouts side by side rather than a single wide one. This means some extra building work and buying more slides, but the smaller rollouts will operate more smoothly and easily. Wider shelves and drawers tend to bind or rack as you slide them in and out.

Reader Success Story

"My daughter called her pantry "the black hole" because she could never find what she needed on the deep shelves. I replaced the five full-width shelves with two six-drawer stacks of sturdy full-extension drawers from IKEA, supported by interior center panels. We spaced the drawers carefully for the types of items she planned to store. Finishing touches include soft-close dampers on the drawers and iron-on edge-banding for the birch plywood panels." [The Rationell 18-in.-deep, fully extending drawers cost about $38 each at ikea.com.]

— Jim Wagener

READER PHOTO

Confessions of a rollaholic

I'm addicted to rollouts. Last winter I replaced every single cabinet shelf in our kitchen with rollouts, custom-designed for whatever needed storing. I've built about 15 more for my shop. I've learned that the key to a useful rollout is to decide what you want it to hold and design it around that purpose. These vertical rollouts in my shop are dedicated to jugs, cans and jars of finishes and solvents. Before starting, I carefully laid out exactly what would go on each shelf on the workbench to get the sizes and spacing just right. They work fantastic.

Travis Larson (aka Shop Rat)

Keep drawer boxes simple

All the drawer boxes in my shop are super simple: butt-joint corners and glued-on bottoms. No rabbets, dadoes or dovetails. They don't look very impressive, but they've held up for years. So I built my kitchen rollouts the same way. If simple boxes can carry tools and hardware, I figure they can stand up to kitchen use, too.

—Gary Wentz, Senior Editor

Field editor tip:
Consider having drawer boxes made to your exact specs and then install them yourself. The average cost of a solid maple, dovetailed single drawer that we order is about $35. Compared with buying material and finishing it yourself—not to mention the dovetail joints—you can't beat it. And it looks much nicer.

—Steve Zubik, Nest Woodworking, Northfield, MN

ROLLOUTS GALORE!

Get ideas, inspiration and plans on our new Web site!

BILL ZUEHLKE (4)

Simple pantry rollouts

A great way to get more storage space in even the smallest kitchen is by putting those narrow spaces and filler areas to work with a rollout pantry. We have two great projects to choose from. One is a handle-free version that lets you line up more than one rollout bin in a single cabinet. The other is a more traditional, three-drawer pantry rollout that reuses your existing cabinet door and hardware. Both versions make it possible for you to use every cubic inch of storage space in your kitchen. Visit familyhandyman.com and search "kitchen storage."

Classic rollout shelves plus a trash center

Base cabinets have the least convenient storage in your kitchen. This article will show you how to bring everything in your cabinets within easy reach by retrofitting your base cabinets with classic rollout shelves. It also shows how to construct a special rollout for recycling and trash without using expensive bottom-mount hardware. The article gives you step-by-step instructions for measuring, building the rollout drawer and its carrier, attaching the drawer slides, and mounting the unit in the cabinet. Visit familyhandyman.com and search "kitchen storage."

Rollouts for underused locations

The space under sinks is often overlooked, but it's prime real estate for rollouts. This article gives step-by-step instructions for how to build two types of customizable rollout trays that fit around and below plumbing pipes, garbage disposers and other obstacles beneath your sink. These rollouts transform that "I'm not sure what's under there" storage space into an organized and efficient location for cleaning supplies that lets you see everything you've got in one glance. Visit familyhandyman.com and search "kitchen storage."

Rollouts at ankle level

Turn wasted toe-kick cavities into clever flat storage space for serving trays, cutting boards and baking pans. This article shows you how to construct self-contained rollout shelving units that you assemble in your shop and then just slip into place beneath your existing cabinets. The article steps you through measuring and building the shelf and carrier units, and then installing them in your kitchen. Even if you've never built or installed a drawer before, this article will show you how. Visit familyhandyman.com and search "kitchen storage."

PRO **TILE TIPS**

Specal tricks for special tile

by **Gary Wentz**

LAYOUT LINE

Build a pyramid for diagonal layouts

The usual way to lay tile diagonally is to mark 45-degree diagonal lines on the wall or floor. But when that angle isn't 45 degrees, as with the diamond-shaped tile you see here, getting exact lines is even harder. So we'll show you a better way: Mark a single layout line and center the tiles over it by aligning the corners of the tile with the line. Build a pyramid centered on the line and use the sides of the pyramid to align each diagonal course. Check the sides of the pyramid occasionally with a straightedge.

Nobody knows tile like our guru, Dean Sorem. Over the past 25 years, he's covered thousands of walls and floors with tile of every type. Based in Hudson, WI, Dean is the head honcho of Sorem Tile and Stone (soremtile.com).

Size a niche to suit the tile

If you're planning a wall niche, lay out the tile and take some measurements to determine the size of the niche. If you custom-size the niche to fit between full tiles, you'll get a better-looking installation and avoid some cutting. With a diagonal tile layout like the one shown here, you'll get full tiles and half tiles. If trim will frame the niche, be sure to factor it into the layout.

Eliminate lippage

"Lippage" is the technical term for uneven tile edges (though "@%&#!" is more common). Lippage is hard to avoid with large tile and easy to see with narrow grout lines or tile that has square—rather than rounded—edges. In any of those circumstances, leveling clips and wedges help you lay tile flat. Just slip the clip under the tile and push in the wedge. After the thin-set hardens, break off the exposed clip. LASH brand clips are available at most Home Depot stores ($20 for 96 clips and wedges). To find other retailers, go to qep.com.

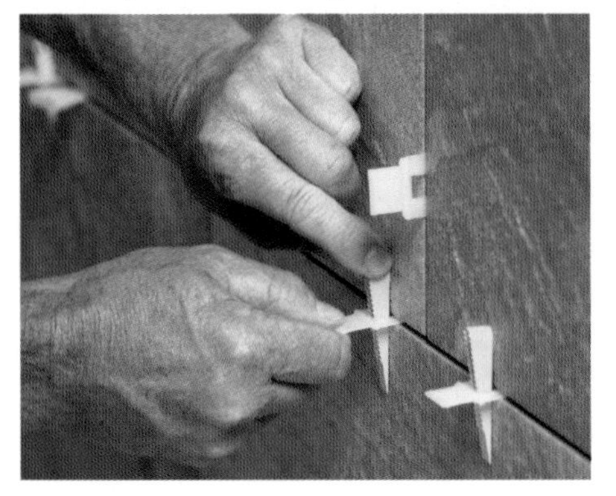

Special mortar for big tiles

Thin-set mortar is the best bedding adhesive for most tile. But if you're setting tiles larger than 12 x 12 in., look for terms like "medium bed," "large tile" or "large format" on the bag label. Bigger tile requires a thicker bed, and unlike standard thin-set, medium-bed mortar doesn't lose its bonding strength when you lay it on thick. It's also firmer and shrinks less, so tiles stay in position better while the mortar hardens. Medium-bed mortar is available at tile stores and some home centers.

Clean cuts in porcelain

Porcelain tile is incredibly hard—and incredibly brittle. So it often chips along cuts or cracks before the cut is complete. Here's a three-step routine that eliminates those problems. The first step only works with saws that allow you to adjust the depth of cut. If yours doesn't, you can still make the second and third cuts to avoid cracks.

1 Score. Make a shallow cut across the tile—about 1/8 in. deep. This minimizes chipping.

2 Slit. Cut a finishing end slit about 2 in. long. This prevents cracking as you approach the end of the main cut.

3 Slice. Make the main cut as usual. Don't rush it; slow, steady pressure creates the cleanest cut.

Don't trust this chart

Your thin-set probably has a chart like this on the label. Don't rely on it. The recommendations are a good starting point, but they don't guarantee a thin-set bed thick enough to provide full contact with the tile. And without full contact, you don't get full support or adhesion.

As the chart shows, larger tiles require larger trowel notches (to provide a thicker bed). But other factors matter too: the flatness of the wall or floor, or the texture of the tile's back. So the only reliable way to know that the bed is thick enough is to set the first few tiles, then immediately pry them up. If the tile hasn't made full contact, you'll see it. The easiest solution is to use the next notch size. With tiles larger than 12 in., it's a good idea to also "back butter" them with thin-set. Also keep an eye on "squeeze-out" during the job. If you don't see thin-set squeezing out between tiles, pull up a tile to check coverage.

AVERAGE COVERAGE / COBERTURA PROMEDIO

TILE SIZE TAMANO DE AZUELOS Y BALDOSAS	TROWEL SIZE TAMANO DE LLANA	PER 25 LB BAG POR BOLSA DE 11 34 KG
Up to 8" Hasta 20 cm	1/4" x 1/4" x 1/4" Square-Notch 6 x 6 x 6 mm Dentada Cuadrada	45 - 50 sq. ft. 4.2 - 4.6 m²
8" to 12" 20 a 30 cm	1/4" x 3/8" x 1/4" Square-Notch 6 x 9 x 6 mm Dentada Cuadrada	32 - 35 sq. ft. 2.9 - 3.3 m²
12" or larger 30 cm o más	1/2" x 1/2" x 1/2" Square-Notch 13 x 13 x 13 mm Dentada Cuadrada	23 - 25 sq. ft. 2.1 - 2.3 m²

Big cuts without a big saw

Huge tiles are popular these days, and the best way to cut them is with a big, expensive tile saw. Here's the next best way: a handheld wet saw guided by a straightedge (we used a plywood scrap). The Ryobi TC400 saw shown ($90), along with the three-step cutting method shown on p. 57, gave us perfectly straight cuts in porcelain tile (but with some chipping). A cement-mixing tub ($10) caught most of the mess.

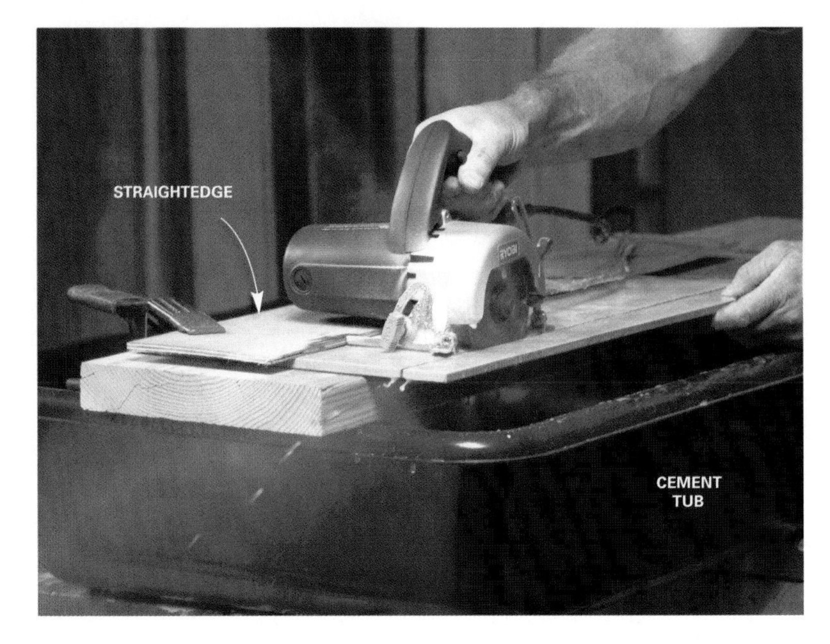

Get a handle on tile

A suction cup ($10) lets you lift a sunken tile or adjust a crooked one. Some home centers and hardware stores carry them; most don't. To shop online, search for "suction cup handle." Keep in mind that they only work on smooth-faced tile.

Gentle smudge remover

When you're shopping for tile supplies, take a detour to the sandpaper aisle and pick up a pack of fine abrasive pads ($2). Along with a little water, they're great for removing stubborn thin-set smudges on the face of tile. And they won't scratch the glossy glaze.

Absolutely essential trowel

Tile setters use a margin trowel for everything: prying up sunken tiles, nudging crooked ones, cleaning out grout lines, mixing up small batches of thin-set or grout, scooping mix out of the bucket and scraping up messes. Makes a great back scratcher, too. If you're setting tile, you've got to have one ($6 at home centers).

NEW-AGE **DRYWALL CORNER BEAD**

Traditional metal corner bead is tedious and time consuming to install, and if you don't cover it with tape, it's likely to develop cracks along the edges. Luckily there's an alternative that's simpler to install and won't crack. If you're an old-school carpenter like me, you've probably dismissed paper-faced corner bead as an inferior DIY product, but trust me, once you try it, you'll never go back.

You'll find paper-faced corner bead alongside standard metal corners in home centers and drywall supply stores. It costs a little more, about $3 for an 8-ft. length vs. $2 for metal bead. But it's worth every penny.

Pros use a special hopper to apply joint compound to the corner bead and an expensive rolling tool to embed the bead, but you can get the same benefits using a 3-in. stiff putty knife, a 5- or 6-in. flexible putty knife and a spray bottle filled with water. Here's how to install paper-faced corner bead, including a few tips to simplify the job and avoid problems.

1 Cut it with tin snips. **If you need to cut pieces to length, simply hold the bead in place, mark the cut, and cut the bead with tin snips. Where pieces run to the floor, cut them about 1/2 in. short. The baseboard will cover the gap.**

2 Mud the corner. **Spread a thick layer of all-purpose joint compound on both sides of the corner and smooth it off with a putty knife. Avoid lightweight joint compound because it doesn't adhere as well to the corner bead. Strive for an even, consistent layer of joint compound about 1/8 in. thick. Don't leave any thin or dry spots.**

3 Mist the bead. **Wetting the paper covering on the corner bead helps create a better bond and better adhesion and cuts down on wrinkles. Do this by spritzing the corner bead before you stick it to the wall. You don't have to soak the corner bead; just dampen it a bit.**

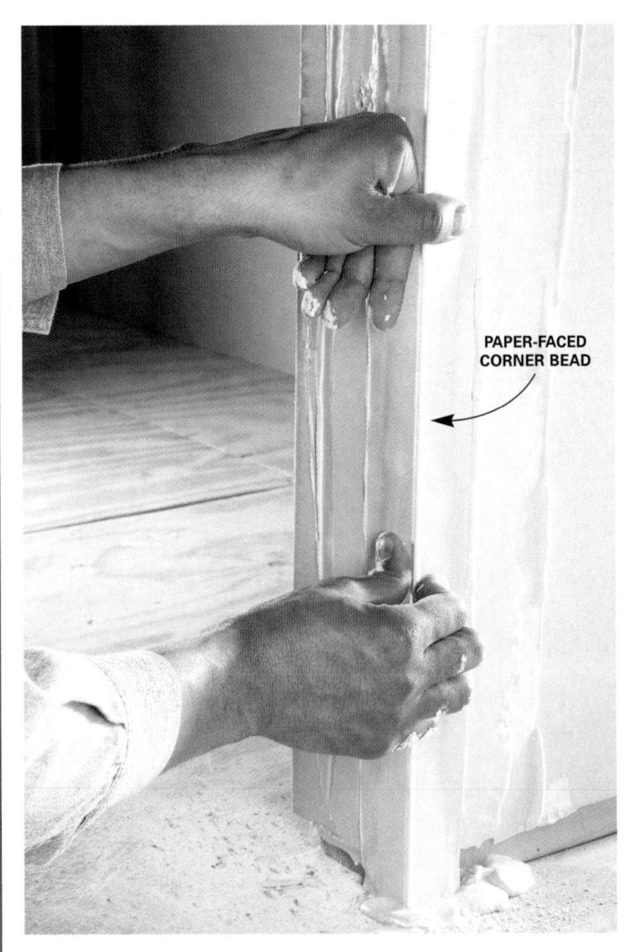

4 Position the bead. **Press the dampened corner bead into the joint compound with your fingers. Run your fingers up and down while pressing evenly on both sides to embed and center the corner bead.**

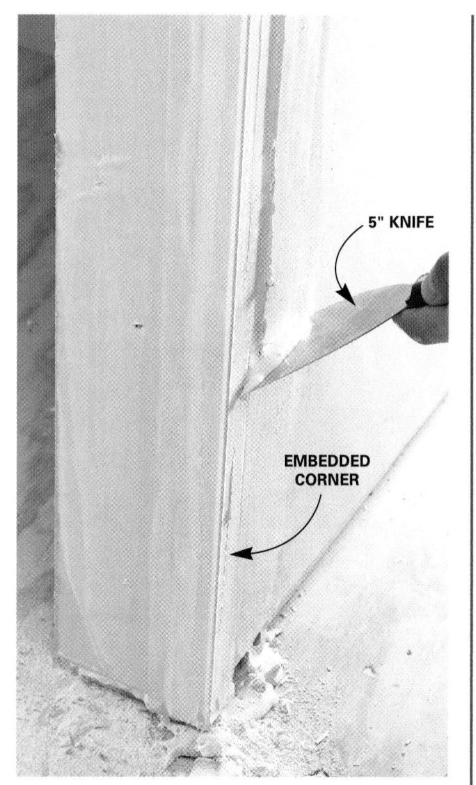

5 Embed the tape. After positioning the bead, wipe and smooth off excess joint compound with a 5- or 6-in. putty knife. Press the edge of the tape with the knife blade to ensure a tight bond with the drywall.

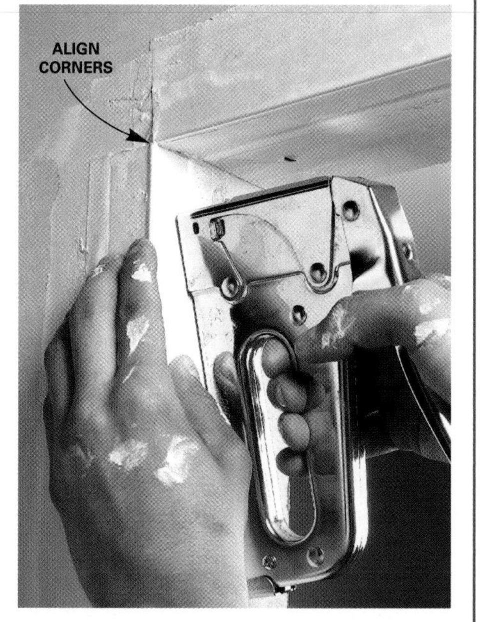

6 Use staples to align corners. Beads that intersect at corners have to align perfectly where they meet. But without nails to hold them in place, the beads can slide out of position. The solution is to slide the corner bead into alignment with the adjoining bead and hold it in place with a few staples.

7 Check the corner with your blade. A perfectly positioned corner bead protrudes slightly at the corner to allow a void for joint compound. After you place the bead, check for a void by setting your 6-in. putty knife against the corner to make sure there's a space under it. Check both sides in several places along the length of the corner. Slide the corner in or out to make adjustments. Use staples to hold the corner in place if it won't stay put.

8 Scrape away excess mud before it hardens. Scraping dried joint compound from the corner can damage the paper tape. Remove excess joint compound before it hardens. Carefully slide a putty knife along the outside edge to knock off excess joint compound.

9 Finish up with two more coats of joint compound. After the embedding coat of mud is dry, apply another coat of joint compound and smooth it. Do a final coat after the second coat dries. Sand the corner with 150-grit drywall sandpaper mounted on a drywall sander. Sand carefully and only enough to blend the joint compound into the drywall and remove high spots. If you sand too much, you'll damage the paper face on the corner bead. If you do sand through the joint compound and create a fuzzy area, cover it with a thin layer of joint compound and resand when it dries.

GreatGoofs®

No way out

I was relocating the shower in a bathroom that was built over a crawl space. To gain access, I cut a hole in the subfloor and slithered down between the joists with all my materials and tools. The floor would be an easy patch since I was retiling anyway. After I spent a few hours down there soldering copper pipes and gluing ABS drain lines, the new plumbing setup was perfect. Then it dawned on me that my beautiful new plumbing job blocked my way out through the opening. Unless I took the whole thing apart, I was trapped! I didn't have the heart to rip it all out, so I used my cell phone to call my son. I cooled my heels down there for an hour until he showed up and cut another hole in the floor to let me out.

Short-circuit shortcut

Mike, a carpenter buddy of mine, shared one of his cool remodeling tricks with me. When he comes across a hump in a wall caused by a badly bowed stud, he cuts right through the drywall and the stud with a long reciprocating saw blade. The cut relieves the stress and the stud straightens itself. Just a little patching to fix the saw kerf and you're done. Brilliant! I had that exact problem in my downstairs bedroom—that hump had always driven me nuts.

I stuck the saw blade into the drywall and started hacking away. All of a sudden, the room went black and the saw stopped. The bad stud happened to be the one with electrical cable stapled to the side to feed the overhead light. I had cut through the cable and blown the circuit breaker. Needless to say, there was a lot more electrical work, drywall patching and painting ahead of me. But at least the wall was flat—mission accomplished!

Mysterious meowing

I volunteered to install a handicap shower for my uncle, who was recovering from knee surgery. To start, I framed in a corner of his bathroom. While I was working, his four cats were constantly underfoot, so I carried them out of the room.

I finished the framing, installed the shower and even built a couple of shelves in the corner. Then I went home, ate and settled down to watch football. Right after kickoff, my uncle called. He'd heard a meowing in the bathroom but couldn't figure out where it was coming from. You guessed it—one of the cats had somehow snuck back into the room and crawled into the space between the studs and the new shower just before I finished hanging the new drywall. I had to cut a hole in the wall to get Midnight out.

I guess I'll find out whether there's any bad luck in store for me for walling off a black cat in a bathroom.

A snag in the shag

A few years ago, I was installing bypass closet doors in a customer's newly finished basement, complete with beautiful, expensive new carpet. Everything was going fine until it was time to screw the door guides to the concrete floor. I got out my hammer drill to drill the pilot holes for the concrete screws.

In a split second, the drill bit grabbed a carpet fiber and ripped a perfectly straight snag right down the middle of the $30 a yard woven carpet. I had to recruit my friend the carpet expert to fix the problem—he said it happens to carpenters all the time. I just wish I had cut a little slit in the carpeting before drilling. Then I wouldn't have lost money on that job.

Sunroof disaster

I finally got around to replacing the flashing on one of our dormers. My extension ladder was too short to let me work comfortably at the peak of the dormer, so I drove my pick-up into the front yard and placed the ladder in the bed, propping the bottom against the tailgate. It worked perfectly, giving me the extra height I needed.

I climbed up the ladder and went to work. No sooner had I gotten down to business than the hammer slipped out of my hand, ricocheted off the ladder rungs and smashed through the sunroof of my truck. A one in a million shot. To look on the bright side, at least it didn't go through my windshield. But from now on, I'll use scaffolding to work on the high points of my house.

Fastest way to unload lumber

I was at the home center, buying yet another load of materials to finish my basement. I strapped the lumber and copper pipe to my truck rack, then hit the highway.

All was well and good until I was almost home and a small dog darted into the street right in front of me, forcing me to slam on my brakes. My truck stopped, but my load didn't. The lumber and piping went flying off the rack, landing on the street. Luckily, there wasn't a car in front of me or it would have had an unexpected delivery through its back window. The dog ran away unscathed, but I swear he was laughing at me.

SPECIAL SECTION

Painting Kitchen Cabinets

A fresh face for your cabinets

by **Brett Martin**

You don't need to spend thousands of dollars on new cabinets to give your kitchen a stunning new look. If your cabinets are in good shape, you can give them a fresh face with paint. Everything you need to give your drab cabinets a silky smooth painted finish costs less than $250—including the sprayer.

Professional painters typically spray-paint doors because it produces an ultra-smooth finish. In this article, we'll show you how to spray-paint your doors and drawers. There's just a short learning curve to use the sprayer effectively. You could also spray the cabinet frames, sides and trim, but masking off the cabinet openings (and the rest of the kitchen) takes a lot of time, so just use a brush for those areas.

Despite our enthusiasm, there are downsides to a painted finish. The paint isn't as tough as a factory finish, and even if you're careful, you can still end up with paint runs and have brush marks on your cabinet sides.

All the materials you need to paint your cabinets are available at home centers and paint stores. Plan to spend four or five days to complete the job—you'll have to let the paint dry overnight between coats, and you can only paint one side of the doors per day.

New-looking cabinets in 3 steps

Is painting right for you?

Not all cabinets are worth painting. They must be structurally sound—paint obviously isn't a cure for doors that are falling apart or don't close properly. If your cabinets are oak or some other species with coarse grain and you want a smooth finish, you'll have to fill the grain on the door panels, cabinet frames and cabinet sides with spackling compound. That nearly doubles the length of this project because sanding the compound takes a long, long time (but if you don't mind a coarse finish, you can skip this step).

If you like the style of your cabinets and they're in good shape, and you're willing to invest the time to paint them, this project is for you.

Wash, rinse, tape, repeat

As with any successful painting project, preparation is the key—and the most time-consuming step. Start by removing the cabinet doors and drawers as well as all the hardware. Label the doors as you remove them so you'll know where to reinstall them. Writing a number in the hinge hole (for Euro hinges) or where the hinge attaches works great—it's the only part that's not painted.

Take the doors and drawers to the garage or another work area and spread them out on a work surface. It's surprising how much space doors and drawers eat up—even if you have a small kitchen. An extension ladder placed over sawhorses gives you a surface to set the doors on. Wash the front and the back of the doors and the drawer fronts to remove grease (**Photo 1**). Then stick tape in the hinge holes or where the hinges attach to keep out the paint.

Wash the grease off the cabinet frames in the kitchen, too. Then tape off everything that abuts the cabinet frames (**Photo 2**). Use plastic sheeting ($13 for six 9 x 12-ft. sheets of 1-mil plastic) or brown masking paper ($3 for 12 in. x 60 yds.) to cover appliances. Use rosin paper ($12 for 3 ft. x 167 ft.) for countertops—it's thick enough to resist tears and won't let small paint spills seep through.

Give cabinets a fresh start with primer

Some cabinets, like ours, have a catalyzed lacquer finish that's very hard. Primer won't form a good bond to this surface unless you scuff it up first. First sand any damaged areas on the doors or cabinet frames with 320-grit sandpaper to remove burrs or ridges, then fill the areas with spackling compound (**Photo 3**).

Lightly sand the doors and cabinet frames, trim and sides with 320-grit sandpaper. Sand just enough to take off the shine—you don't need to sand off the finish. Vacuum the dust off the wood using a bristle attachment. Right before you're ready to apply the primer, wipe down the doors and frames with a tack cloth ($2 for a two-pack).

1 Wash off years of kitchen grease with warm water and dish detergent. Clean away all the grease or the primer and paint won't adhere. Rinse clean with water.

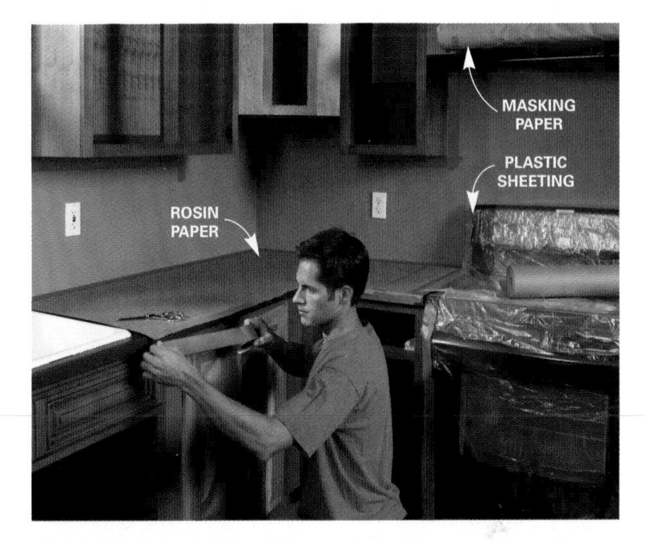

2 Tape off the walls, ceiling and flooring, and cover the countertops with rosin paper. Wrap appliances and the vent hood with plastic sheeting or masking paper.

Running the cloth over the surface is enough—you don't need to scrub to remove the fine dust particles.

Apply a stain-killing primer ($20 per gal.; Bulls Eye 1-2-3 and BIN are two brands) with a paintbrush (**Photo 4**). You can use a cheap brush—even a disposable one—for this. Don't worry about brushstrokes in the primer (you'll remove them later with sandpaper) or getting a uniform finish. The doors and frames don't have to look pretty at this stage. But don't use a roller. It leaves a texture that will affect the finish. Besides, brushing is almost as fast as rolling, and you can use the bristles to work the primer into crevices.

Once the primer is dry (just one or two hours), lightly sand the doors and cabinets with 320-grit sandpaper to remove any brushstrokes (**Photo 5**). Sandpaper works better than a sanding sponge—you can feel the rough spots through the paper, and paper doesn't round over corners like sponges do.

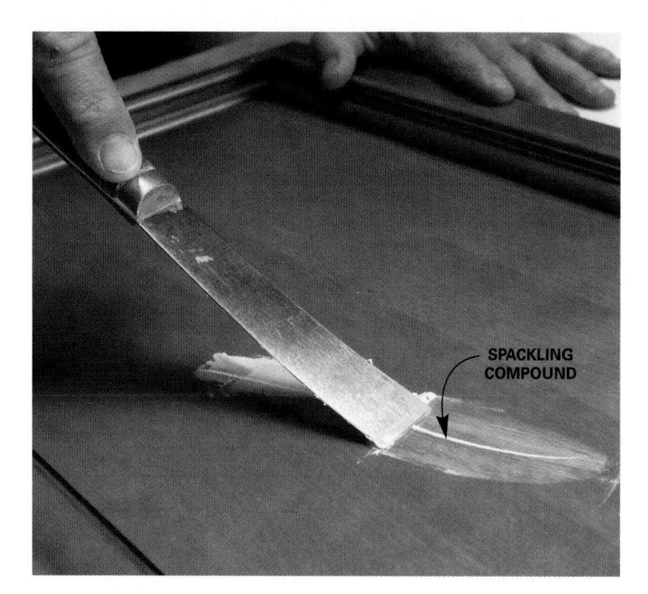

3 **Fix scratches, holes and dings with spackling compound. Work the compound into the damaged area with a putty knife. Fill in holes from handles and hardware if you're replacing the hardware and need holes in different places.**

4 **Prime the doors and cabinet frames with stain-blocking primer. The primer covers any stains and seals in cooking odors. Prime one side of all the doors, let them dry while you prime the cabinet face frames and sides, then come back and prime the other side of the doors.**

5 **Sand the doors and cabinets with fine-grit sandpaper. Sand with the grain. Be careful not to round over corners. Wipe the surface clean with a tack cloth.**

6 **Start in a corner to paint the cabinet frames. Use a high-quality paintbrush to paint an entire rail or stile, including the inside edge, before moving to an adjacent rail or stile.**

Immaculate finish in 90 minutes

For this project, we used a Wagner Control Spray Double Duty spray gun (model No. 0518050; $90 at home centers and amazon.com). The high-volume, low-pressure (HVLP) sprayer gives the doors a thin, even coat of paint and makes quick work of painting. We sprayed our 18 doors and four drawers in less than 90 minutes per coat. The sprayer occasionally "spits" paint, but the Floetrol that you mix in levels out the finish. You can clean the sprayer in about 10 minutes.

The paint experts we talked to say you can get a nice-looking finish with non-HVLP sprayers too. But the advantages of an HVLP sprayer are that the low pressure produces little overspray, so most of your paint ends up where you want it—on the doors—and the spray is easy to control.

Figure A
Painting doors
Spray the door edges first. Then spray any detail work. Then spray the entire door, starting at the top and sweeping your arm back and forth until you reach the bottom. Keep the angle of the spray gun consistent as you spray.

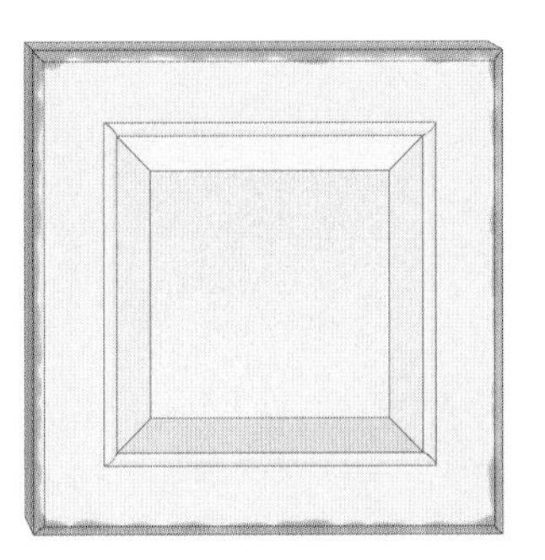

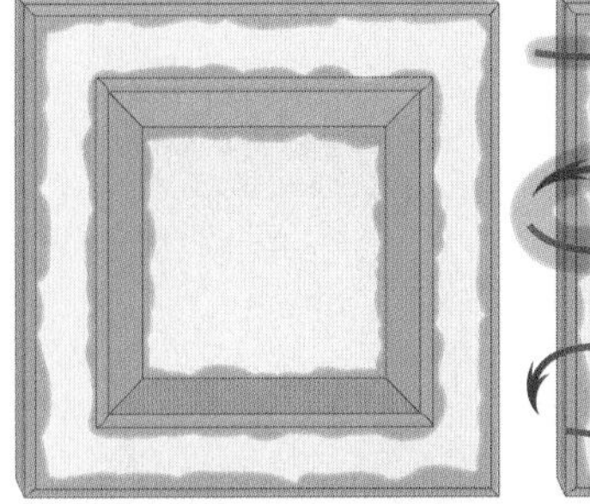

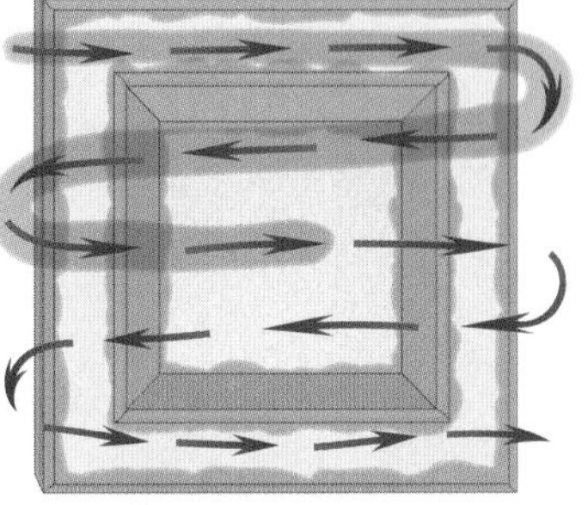

If you have doors with coarse wood grain (like oak) and want a smooth finish, fill in the grain with spackling compound (MH Ready Patch is one brand; $6 at home centers). Use a putty knife to skim-coat the door with compound, working it into the wood grain. Wait for it to dry, sand it with medium-grit sandpaper, then prime it again.

Complete the transformation with paint

Use a gloss or semigloss latex enamel paint for your cabinets. Its hard, shiny finish resists stains and fingerprints.

To get started, pour a gallon of the paint into a bucket and thin it with half a cup of water and half a quart of Floetrol paint additive ($9 per qt.). The water and the Floetrol level out the paint when it's applied and slow the drying process, which helps eliminate brush and lap marks. The thinner paint also provides a more even coat when you're spraying.

Paint the cabinets with a brush (Photo 6). Paint an entire rail, stile or trim piece before the paint dries, then move on to the next part of the cabinet. Paint any exposed sides of cabinets with a brush. Most light brush marks will disappear as the paint dries (thanks to the Floetrol).

Before spray painting, construct a makeshift booth to contain the airborne spray. Assemble a work surface (putting boards over sawhorses works great), then hang plastic sheeting around the work area. Make sure to ventilate the room—even if it's just a fan blowing out an open window.

Fill the spray container with the paint mixed with Floetrol and water. Wear a mask respirator ($8) when spray painting. Test the spray pattern on cardboard, keeping the nozzle 10 to 12 in. from the surface (Photo 7). Sweep your entire arm back and forth across the door panel; don't just use your wrist. Practice spraying on the cardboard to get a feel for the sprayer. When you're ready to paint, set a block of wood or a cardboard box on the work surface to elevate the doors. Place a lazy Susan turntable ($8 at discount stores) over the box, then set the door on top of it (Photo 8).

Spray the back of the doors first. This lets you get used to spraying before you paint the front. Start by spraying the edges. Rotate the door on the turntable to paint each

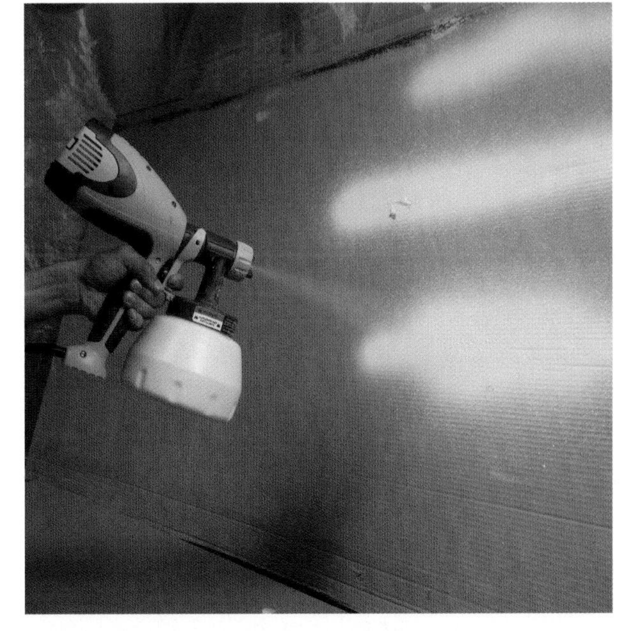

7 Practice spray painting on cardboard. Adjust the nozzle to get a vertical fan pattern. Adjust the flow rate so the paint covers the surface without running.

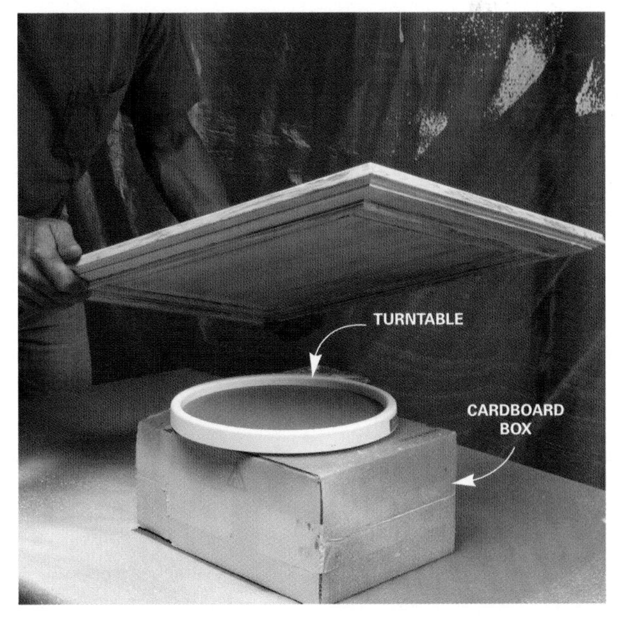

8 Set the doors on a turntable when spray painting. Then you can stand in one spot and rotate the door to paint each side. Keep the nozzle 10 to 12 in. from the door and maintain a consistent angle while spraying.

9 Paint the edge and detail work on one side, then turn the door to paint the adjacent edges and details. Start the spray before the door, and keep spraying past the edge. Don't worry if you missed a spot. You can catch it on the second coat.

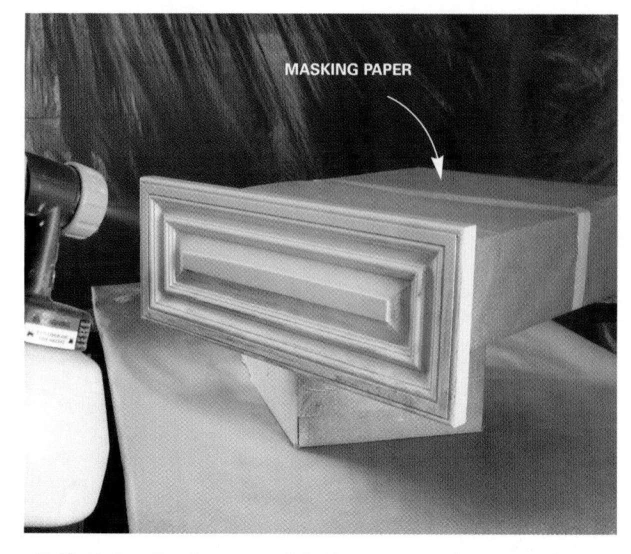

10 Paint the drawers with the sprayer after wrapping the inside with plastic or paper. Paint the backs first, then the edges and then the faces, starting at the top and working down. Start and stop the spray past the sides of the drawer.

11 Fix paint runs with a paintbrush while the paint is still wet. If the paint is dry or tacky, wait until the next day, then sand out the run or imperfection and repaint.

12 Reinstall the doors and drawers in the kitchen. Attach the hinges to the doors first, then screw them to the cabinet frames.

edge so you won't have to change your body position. Move your arm across the entire edge of the door, starting the spray before the paint lands on the door, and keep spraying past the end. Keep the nozzle 10 to 12 in. from the door. After painting all four edges, start at the top of the door and spray in a sweeping motion back and forth, moving down just enough each time to overlap the previous pass by 50 percent until you reach the door bottom.

Let the paint dry overnight. Then give the cabinet frames, sides and trim a second coat. Spray a first coat on the door fronts (**Photo 9**).

Cover the drawers with masking paper or plastic sheeting so only the paintable surface is visible. Set the drawer face down on the turntable and spray the back. Then place the drawer on its bottom and spray the front (**Photo 10**). Be careful not to overspray the drawer. It's easy to get runs in the paint on drawer fronts. Don't worry about areas that are lightly covered. You'll give everything a second coat.

If you catch paint runs while they're still wet, gently brush them out with a paintbrush (**Photo 11**).

Let the doors and drawers dry overnight, then give them a second coat. It's up to you if you want to give the back of the doors two coats. We gave ours just one.

When the doors are dry, install the hardware and hang the doors (**Photo 12**). If any paint seeped into the hinge holes, scrape it out so the hinges will fit snugly.

2 Electrical & High-Tech

IN THIS CHAPTER

Question&Comment

SAVE A CUT EXTENSION CORD

I accidentally cut my good 100-ft. extension cord. A replacement costs almost $50! What's the best way to splice it back together so it's safe and doesn't pull apart?

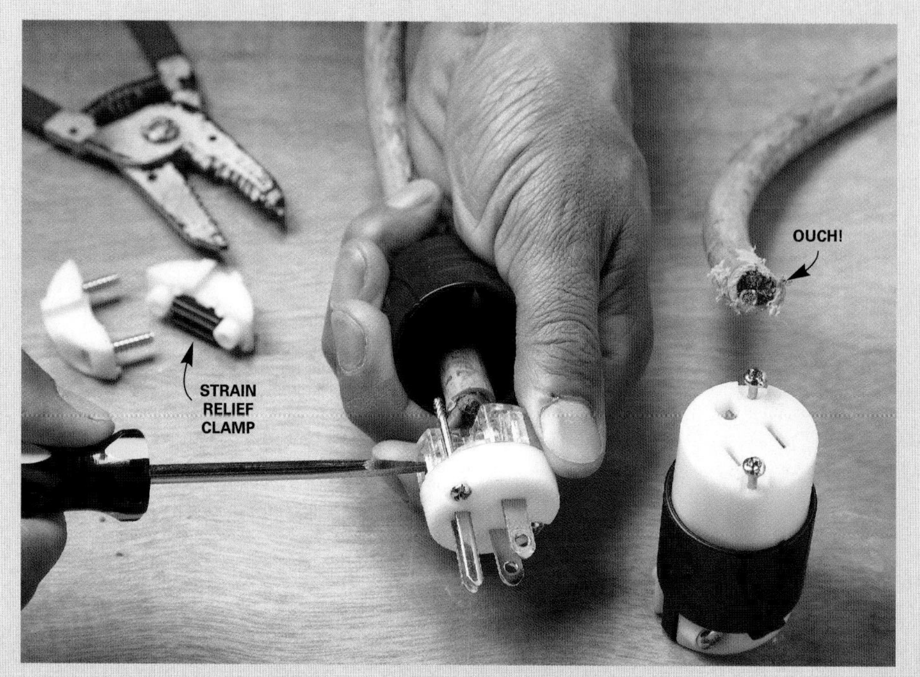

Technically, you're not supposed to splice extension cords. Even if you solder the wires, wrap each wire with electrical tape and encase the whole splice in heat shrinkable tubing, it still won't have the abrasion resistance of a new cord. Plus, it's not permissible under the National Electrical Code.

If both sections are long enough to be worth saving, just buy a high-quality plug and receptacle and make two cords out of one. Be sure the new ends are rated to carry the same load as the old cord and that both have built-in strain relief clamps. Otherwise, just buy one end and accept the fact that your 100-ft. cord is now only 92.56 ft.

USING CFL BULBS IN GARAGE DOOR OPENERS

The lightbulb in my garage door opener burns out frequently. I want to install a CFL bulb for longer life and energy savings. But my neighbor claims that his opener "burned up" after he installed a CFL bulb. If I can't install a CFL, what do you recommend for longer bulb life?

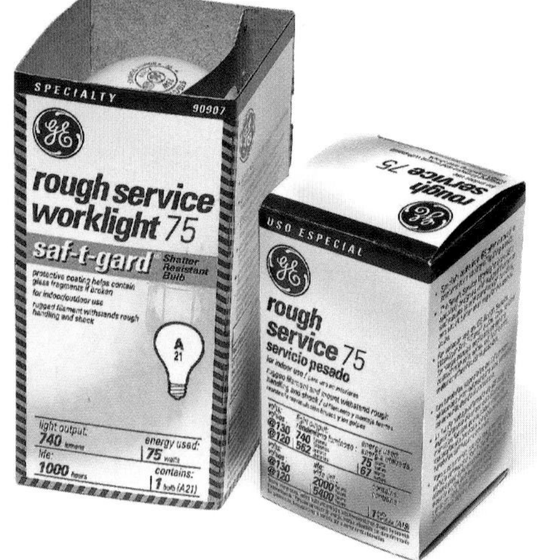

Pick up a standard rough-service bulb ($2.50) or a coated version ($5) at any home center.

We contacted the two largest residential garage door opener companies to ask about CFLs and possible damage to the opener. Both companies state that CFLs will NOT damage your opener. However, since electrical interference from the CFL ballast can reduce the operating range of your transmitter, they recommend always using an incandescent bulb.

Garage door openers produce a lot of vibration, so that's probably what's killing your bulbs. First, tighten all the bolts on your unit and make sure it's solidly mounted to the ceiling. Then, install a "rough service" bulb. These bulbs have heavy-duty filaments with extra support wires to keep them from breaking. Before anyone sends us letters about how "un-green" incandescent bulbs are, wait a minute. The average opener light is on only a few minutes a day.

If your opener doesn't have a plastic lens, the bulb is unprotected, so choose a rough-service bulb with protective coating. The coating prevents the glass from shattering if it's ever struck.

HandyHints®

SLICK CHARGER I.D. TAGS

My electrical drawer was filled with chargers and transformers from our various cameras, phones, portable vacuums and who knows what all. They all looked alike and I could never find the one I needed in the tangled mess. Now I label each one we get, and I can find what I need instantly.

HOW MANY PIECES OF DUCT TAPE...

...does it take to change a lightbulb? One, if you fold it right. If you've ever tried to unscrew a lightbulb from a recessed fixture, you know how tough it is to get your fingers around it. Use duct tape to make a lightbulb "handle." Rip a piece of duct tape off the roll and fold the ends back over themselves, leaving a sticky section in the middle. Put the sticky section on the bulb, grasp the ends and give the tape a twist. This trick works great—and that's no joke!

STICKY SECTION

"HANDLE"

ADD A CIRCUIT

...and live to tell about it

by **Rick Muscoplat**

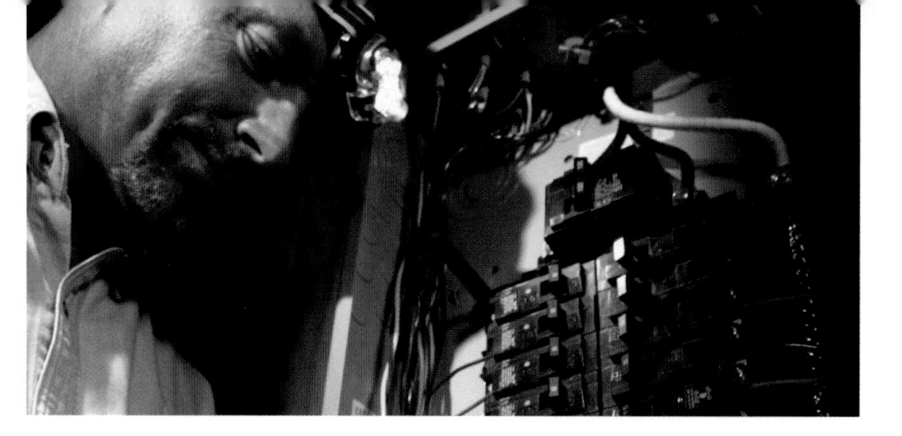

We believe in safe DIY. That's why we've always been reluctant to show readers how to open a breaker box and connect a new circuit. Even with the power shut off, there's a chance you could touch the wrong parts and kill yourself. But then we figured if we didn't show you, you'd just go search the Internet. And that scared us even more. So we're going to walk you through the process, showing you the safest way to open the breaker box, wire a new breaker and test your work.

An inside look at your main panel

Opening the main breaker box and installing a new circuit is actually pretty easy. You only have to connect three wires, and each is color-coded. But there are some safety precautions, and if you ignore them, you could kill yourself. Really. If you follow our safety steps in order and to the letter, you'll be fine. But if at any point you're unsure how to proceed or feel uncomfortable with the project, call an electrician.

Stay away from the large wires and lugs. They're always live, even with the main breaker (service disconnect) shut off. If you touch them, you could die. Cover the live areas with a cardboard shield (Photo 3) to prevent accidental contact while installing the new circuit. If you have any doubts about which areas stay live, contact an electrician.

Your main panel might not be exactly like the one at right. The one shown above, for example, has the large cables and lugs at the right, rather than in the center. With any panel, find the large cables and the lugs they're connected to. They're the parts that are always live, even when the main breakers are switched off.

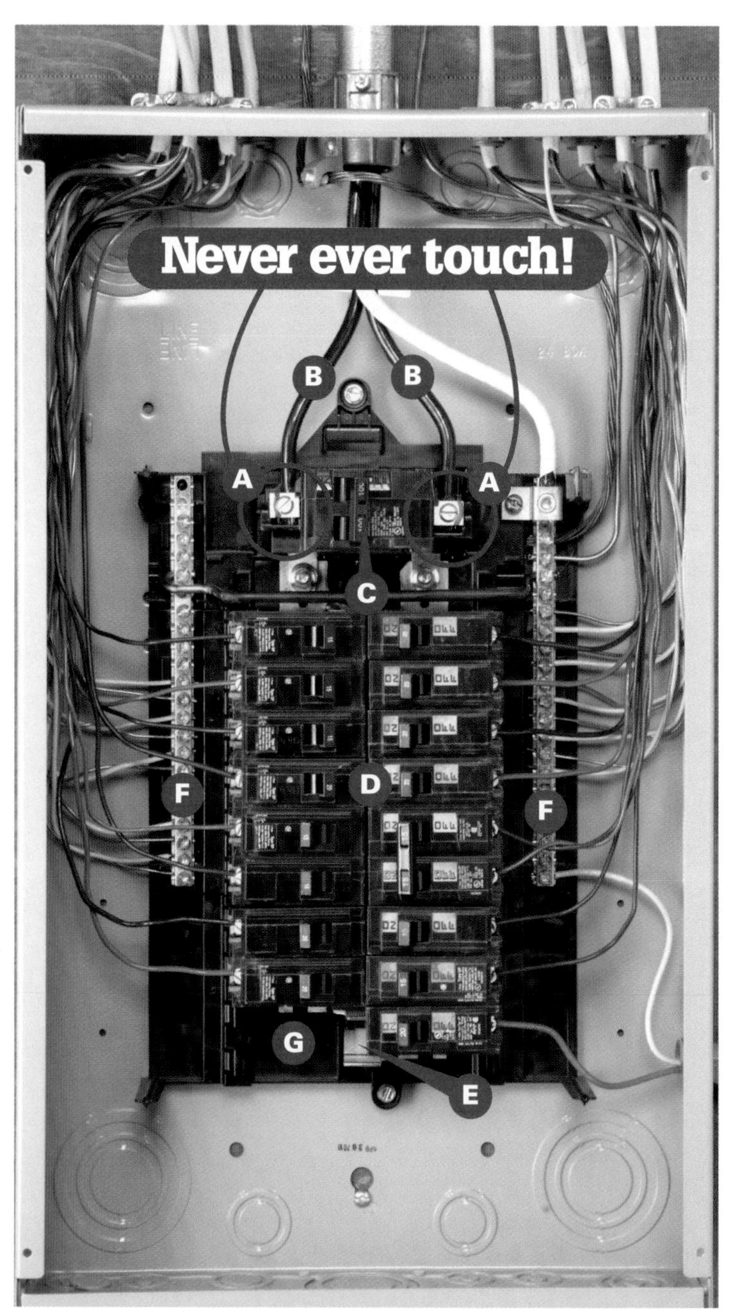

Get the right parts and tools

Before you go shopping, open the door of your breaker box and copy the manufacturer's name, the box model number, and the style numbers of the breakers that are approved for your box. Then buy one of those breakers. If your home center doesn't sell the right model or brand, you'll have to go to an electrical supplier. You cannot install a circuit breaker style that isn't specifically approved for use in your box—even if it fits inside the box. While at the store, pick up a few 1/2-in. plastic snap-in cable clamps to secure the new cable. They're safer than metal clamps because you don't put your hand in the panel to install them.

You have to shut off the power to your whole house, so you'll need a powerful work light. An LED headlamp is also a great idea so you won't have to juggle a flashlight, wire strippers and a screwdriver. Round up a utility knife, wire strippers, electrical tape, a circuit tester (not a voltage sniffer), and a flat-blade screwdriver or No. 2 square-drive tip for your multi-bit driver.

Power down, then remove the cover

Turn off all computers in the house before you switch off the power. Then switch off the main breaker (the service disconnect) and follow the cover removal procedure in Photo 1.

Once the cover is off, cut out a cardboard shield and stick it inside the box to keep you from touching any of the live parts (see Photo 3).

It's dangerous to assume the power is really off just because you've flipped the service disconnect to the off position. There's a slim chance that the service disconnect didn't work properly, keeping power to some breakers. So test each and every breaker to make sure it's really dead (see Photo 2). If the test light lights up, stop and call an electrician.

Remove a knockout and feed in the cable

You can insert the new cable into any knockout on the top, bottom or sides of the box. Find the least congested area and remove one small knockout (Photo 3). Then snap in a plastic cable clamp (the screw-style ones shown aren't as easy to use).

1 Don't break a breaker. Remove three of the panel cover screws. Then hold the cover securely while you remove the fourth screw. If it slips while you're removing screws, it can damage the breaker handles.

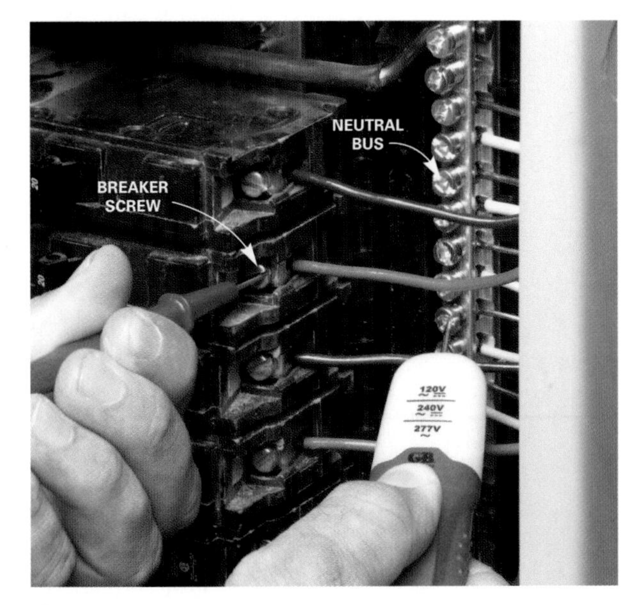

2 No light means no power. Be absolutely certain all the power is off. Touch one lead of a test light to the neutral bus and the other lead to the screw on each breaker.

Know your way

- **A Main lugs. They're always live—even when the main breaker is off. NEVER TOUCH THEM.**
- **B Main cables. The black ones are always live. And although they're insulated, avoid touching them.**
- **C Main breaker. Always switch it off before removing the panel's cover.**
- **D Breaker. The hot wire (usually red or black) from each circuit connects to a breaker. If you're installing an AFCI breaker (as shown on the following pages), you'll also connect the neutral wire to the breaker (Photo 7, p. 75).**
- **E Breaker bus. Distributes power from the main breaker to the individual circuit breakers. Each breaker snaps onto the bus (Photo 6, p. 74).**
- **F Neutral bus. All ground and neutral (white) wires connect here. If you're installing a standard breaker, the neutral (white) wire connects here, too. If you're installing an arc-fault circuit interrupter (AFCI) breaker, you'll connect the neutral to the breaker and run a "pigtail" wire to the neutral bus (Photo 8).**
- **G Breaker space. This panel has room for three more breakers. You can install your new breaker in any open space.**

Hold the cable up to the box to determine how much of the outer jacket you should strip off. Slice off the jacket and remove the paper insulator. Then wrap the ends of the loose wires with electrical tape to prevent them from touching a live portion of the box (see **Photos 4 and 5**).

Route the cable and install the breaker

Neatly route the black and white wires to the empty breaker space. Attach the wires to the breaker and then snap it into the box, or install the breaker first and insert the wires last. Just be aware that wiring an AFCI-style breaker is different from wiring ordinary breakers. The neutral (white) from the new cable attaches to the AFCI (**Photo 7**). On a main panel, you connect the ground wire from the new cable and the neutral (white) pigtail from the AFCI to the neutral bus (**Photo 8**). If you're installing a breaker on a subpanel, place the neutral and ground on separate bus bars.

Test the installation and finish the job

Remove the panel cover plate knockout that corresponds to the slot where you installed the new breaker (bend it back and forth until it breaks off). Then install the cover and turn on the main breaker. Switch the new AFCI to "ON." Wait a few seconds and press the "TEST" button. The breaker should trip. If it doesn't trip, refer to the package instructions for troubleshooting or call an electrician.

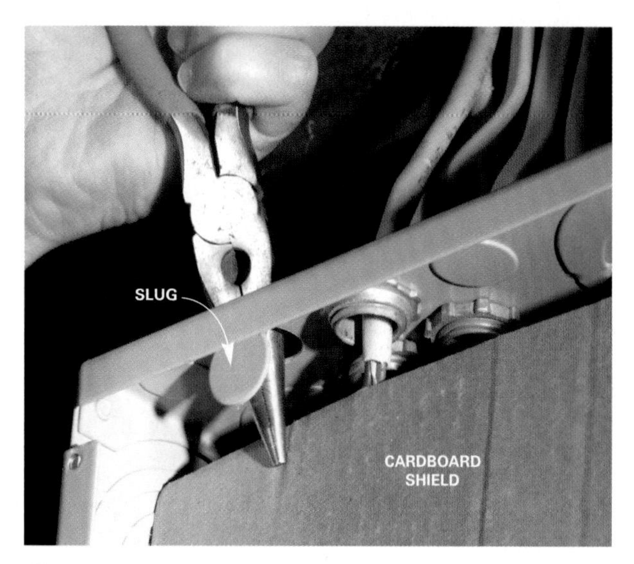

3 Smack it down, twist it out. Jam needle-nose pliers or a short screwdriver into the knockout to bend it down. Then grab the "slug" with your pliers and twist it back and forth until it breaks off.

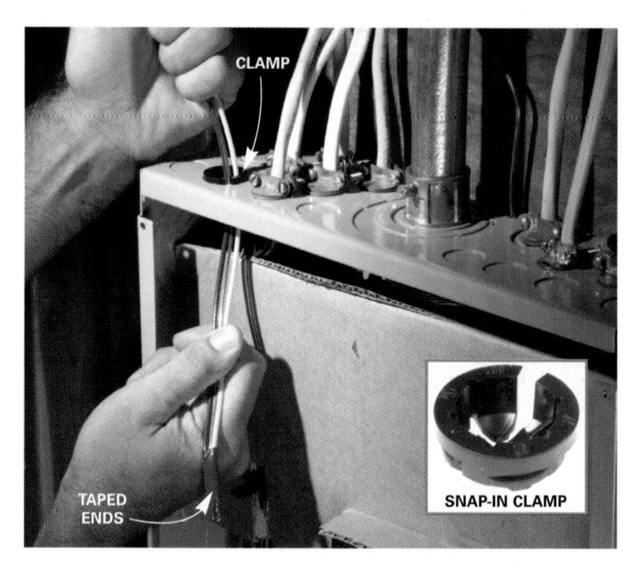

4 Run the cable through the clamp. Snap in a plastic clamp and then feed in the cable. Tape the wires together so one doesn't stray behind the cardboard.

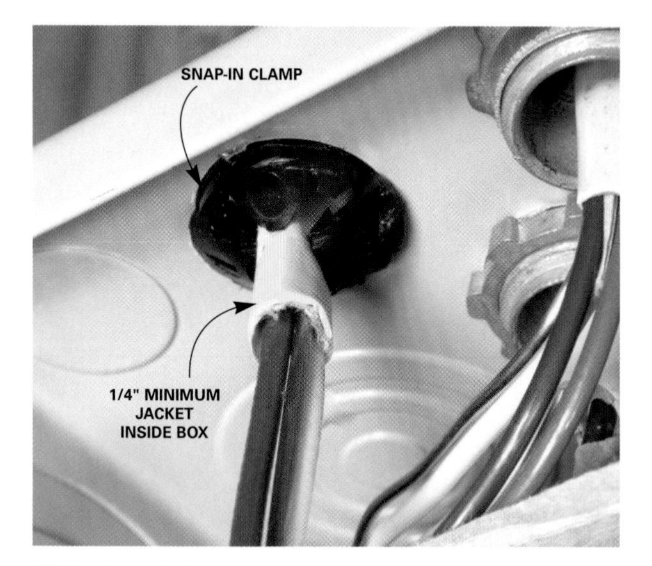

5 Push until the jacket enters the clamp. Keep pushing the cable into the clamp far enough to get at least 1/4 in. of the outer jacket inside the box. Then secure the cable outside the box with an insulated staple within 12 in. of the clamp.

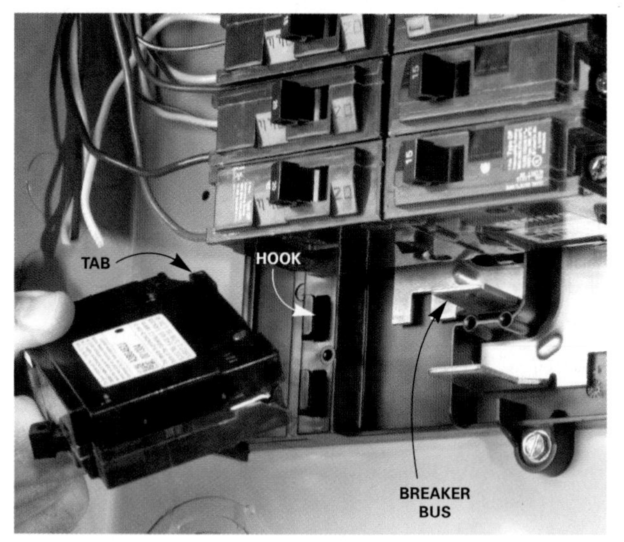

6 Hook and push. Install the breaker by slipping the tab into the hook. Then snap the breaker into place, forcing the slot onto the bus. We're using an AFCI breaker (see above).

7 Strip and clamp. **Strip off 5/8 in. of insulation from the white and black wires and insert them into the AFCI terminals. Tighten until snug.**

8 Ground and pigtail go to the neutral bus. **Route the AFCI neutral pigtail and ground wires to empty screws on the neutral bus and tighten. If you're installing a breaker on a subpanel, place the neutral and ground on separate bus bars.**

How to plan a new branch circuit

DIYers often ask how many receptacles and lights they can install on a branch circuit and what size circuits they should install. We can give you some general guidelines, but electrical codes vary by state and local authority. Since your local codes always trump our advice, contact a local inspector before you start running cable.

1. **You can usually mix lighting and receptacles on the same circuit. But it's not a good idea to place lighting and receptacles in the same room on a single circuit. If the breaker trips, you'll lose all the light fixtures and receptacles at the same time.**
2. **If you're wiring living areas, you can install 10 to 13 lights and receptacles on a single 15-amp circuit. Locate the receptacles so you're never more than 6 ft. away from one on each wall.**
3. **Run a separate 15- or 20-amp circuit for each of these watt-sucking appliances: garbage disposer, dishwasher, microwave, vent hood, trash compactor and space heater.**
4. **Run a separate 20-amp circuit to each bathroom and laundry room. Install a minimum of two 20-amp circuits for the kitchen. Protect the receptacles with a ground-fault circuit interrupter (GFCI) breaker or GFCI-style receptacles.**
5. **Use 12-gauge cable for 20-amp circuits and 14-gauge for 15-amp. Many cable manufacturers color-code the outer jacket of their cable, but the color schemes are not universal. So always double-check the wire itself to be sure (see photo at right).**
6. **New branch circuits to all "living areas" (bedroom, living room, family room, den, dining room, library, sunroom, closet, hallway and similar locations) must be connected to an arc-fault circuit interrupter (AFCI). AFCI breakers are pricey ($40), so you may be tempted to buy an ordinary $5 breaker. Don't. The electrical inspector will just make you change it out.**

Check wire gauge with your loose change

Fourteen-gauge wire is the thickness of a dime; 12-gauge is the thickness of a nickel.

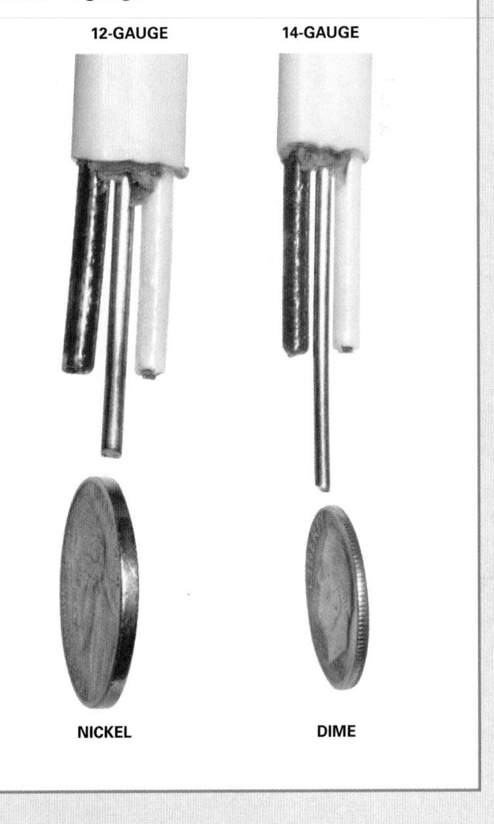

LIGHT UP A DARK ROOM

Is your bathroom dimly lit? Do you have a hallway that could use more light? Here's how to add a wall-mounted light directly above a light switch.

This project requires an understanding of how a switch is wired and a few basic tools. You'll need a noncontact voltage detector ($10), a wire-stripping tool ($6 to $15), a screwdriver and a drywall saw. Then, with our instructions and a few hours' work, you'll be able to add a sconce to any room that has an appropriate switch.

Not all electrical boxes with a light switch in them contain the necessary ground, hot and neutral conductors. To find out, first shut off the power to the switch at the main electrical panel. Then remove the switch cover, and hold the noncontact voltage detector against the wires attached to the switch. This is to ensure the power is off before you remove the screws and pull the switch from the box.

You can add a sconce above nearly any light switch in about three hours.

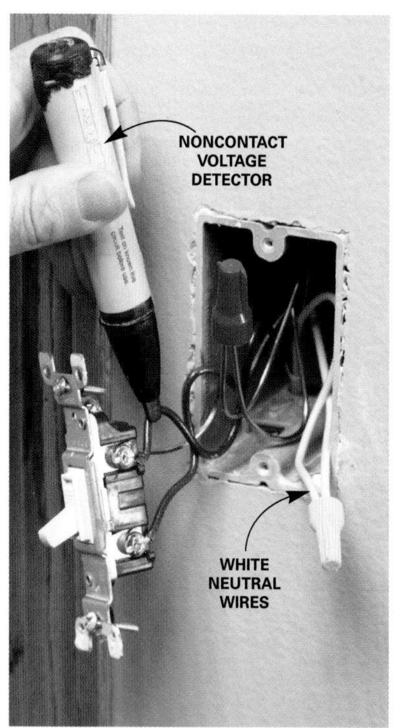

1 Test for power. With the power turned off at the main electrical panel, unscrew the switch and pull it out. Turn the power back on and use a noncontact voltage tester to locate the hot wire.

2 Cut the hole. Trace around the box. Then draw a second line inside the first to indicate the cutout. Cut notches for clamps and other protrusions.

To locate the required neutral, look for two or more white wires joined with a wire connector. If the only white wire entering the box is connected to the switch, then there's no neutral and you can't power a sconce from this box. If your switch wiring looks different from what we show here and you don't understand how it's connected, put everything back together and abandon the project or call a licensed electrician.

There's one more important test you must complete while the power is still turned on. With the light switch turned off, hold the noncontact voltage detector against each of the wires connected to the switch. Take note of which wire causes the tester to light up. This is the hot wire and the one you'll connect to the "hot" side of the new double switch. If you're adding a separate single switch, this is the wire you'll use to power both switches. Now turn off the power to the switch at the main electrical panel. Back at the switch box, *test once again to make sure the power is off* and mark the hot wire with a wrap of black electrical tape.

Finally, complete a simple calculation to see if the existing switch box is large enough to accept more wires. For instructions, go to familyhandyman.com and type "electrical wiring" into the search box.

After you've determined that the existing switch box will work to power the new light, it's time to shop for the sconce and pick up the remodeling box, cable and electrical connectors you'll need. Choose the fixture first. Then pick a rectangular or round remodeling box that is small enough to be covered by the light fixture canopy. You'll need enough cable to reach from the switch to the box plus about 3 ft. Match the cable, either 14-2 or 12-2, to the existing wire gauge. Fourteen-gauge wire is as thick as a dime and 12-gauge wire is as thick as a nickel.

Cut the hole and run the cable

Locate the studs. Then hold the fixture against the wall somewhere between the studs to determine the best location and lightly mark the top and bottom of the canopy with a pencil. Center the remodeling box on the marks and mark the box cutout carefully, taking note of notches needed for the clamps and other protrusions. Cut out the hole (**Photo 2**). Next, punch out one of the knockouts in the top of the switch box and push the cable up to the hole (**Photos 3 and 4**). Prepare the remodeling box for mounting by stripping about 12 in. of sheathing from the cable and pushing it into the box through one of the cable entry points on the back. Make sure at least 1/4 in. of sheathing is visible inside the box. Leave some slack cable inside the wall to allow some leeway when you connect the switch (**Photo 5**). Then fit

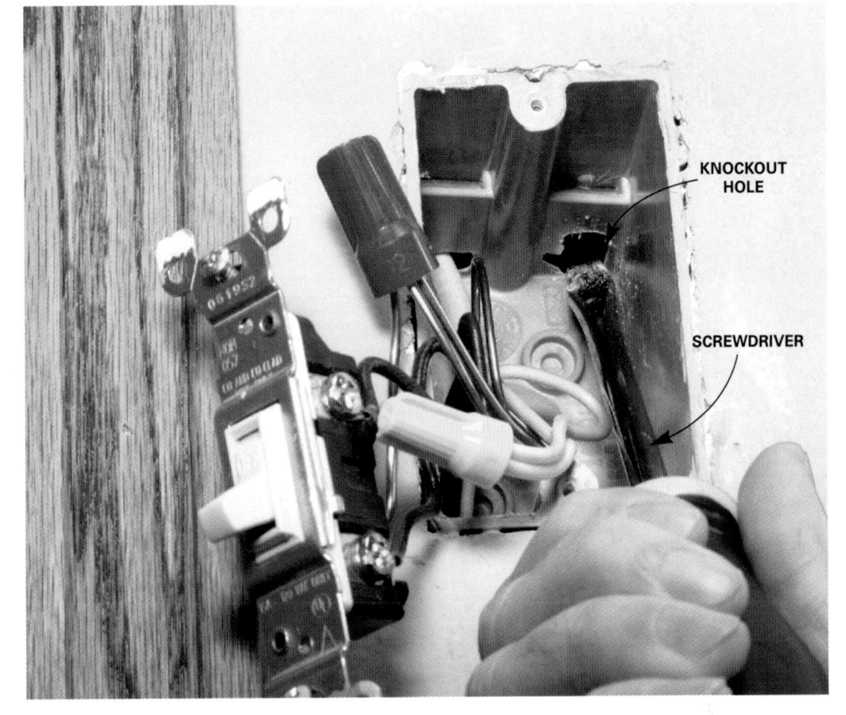

3 Remove the knockout. **Punch out one of the knockouts in the top of the box with a screwdriver. You'll push the cable through this hole.**

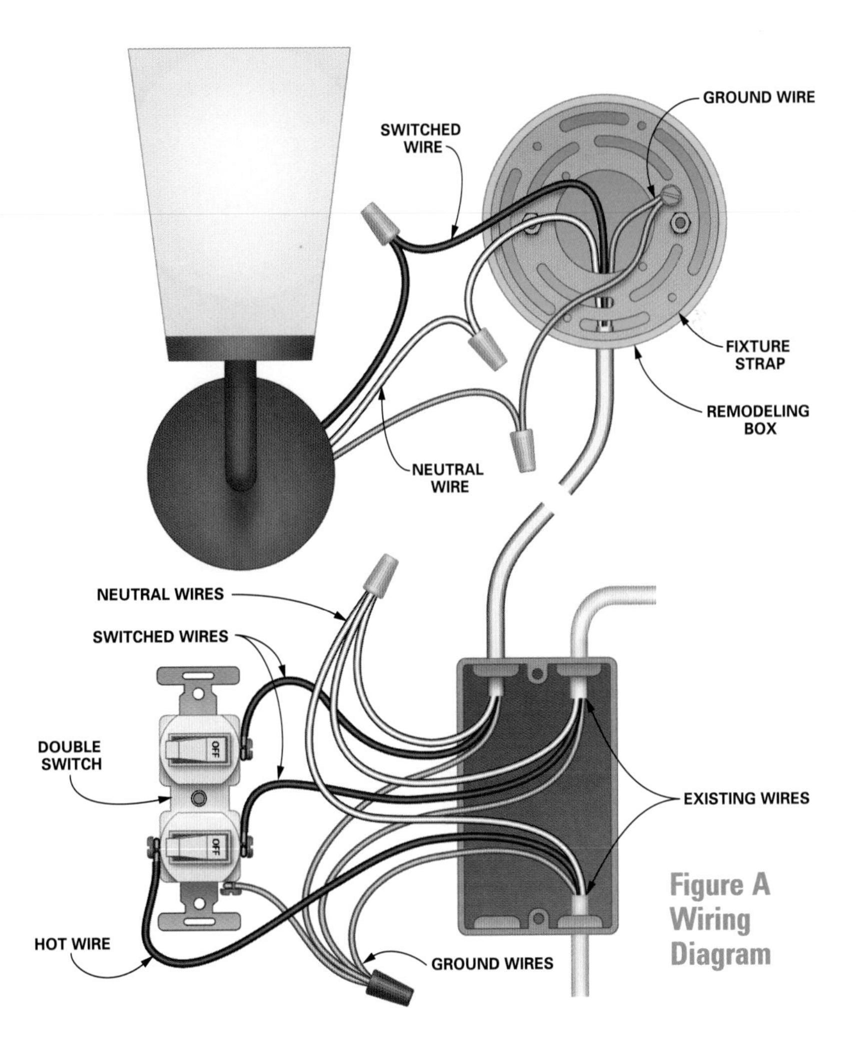

Figure A Wiring Diagram

ELECTRICAL & HIGH-TECH

4 Push in the cable. Push the cable through the knockout and up toward the hole. If you're lucky, it'll come into sight. Otherwise, reach through the hole to grab it.

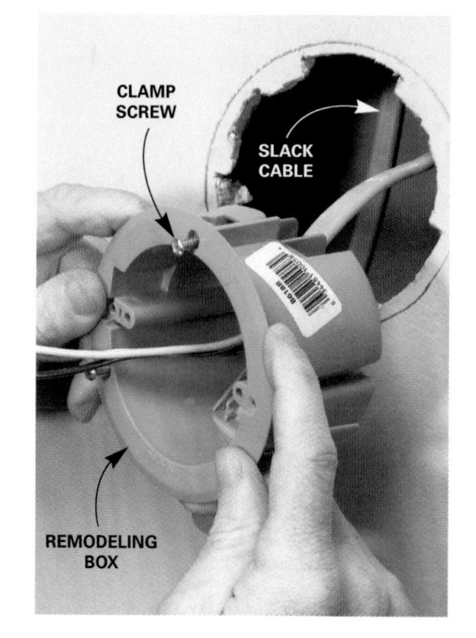

5 Mount the box. Strip the sheathing from about 12 in. of cable. Push the wires through the built-in wire clamp at the back of the box. Make sure at least 1/4 in. of sheathing is visible inside the box. Push the box into the hole and tighten the clamp screws.

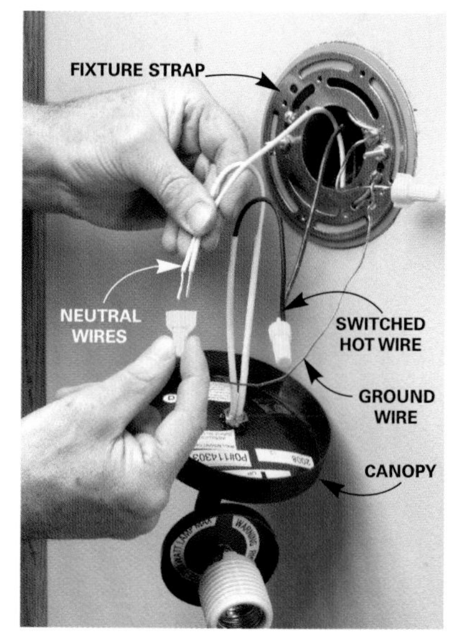

6 Install the fixture. Trim the black and white wires to 8 in., leaving the ground wire long. Strip the ends of the wires. Connect white to white, black to black and bare copper to bare copper. Loop the bare copper wire clockwise around the grounding screw on the fixture strap before connecting it to the fixture ground wire.

What if you have to go fish?

We're showing how to run a cable through the same stud space that contains the switch. Positioning the light in an adjacent stud space is more difficult. For information on how to do this, go to familyhandyman.com and type "fishing electrical wires" into the search box.

the remodeling box into the hole and tighten the clamps.

Connect the fixture and switch

Photo 6 and Figure A show how to connect the light fixture. Start by mounting the fixture strap to the box. Strip the ends of the wires and connect them to the fixture.

At the switch, cut the cable about 12 in. beyond the box. Strip 8 in. of sheathing from the wires and push the cable through the knockout, leaving 1/4 in. or more sheathing visible inside the box. Trim the black and white wires to the same length as the wires they will connect to. Then strip the ends of the wires. Connect the white neutral wires with a wire connector. Connect the wires as shown in Figure A. Connect the hot wire to the side of the double switch that has the "jumper tab" between the terminals (Photo 7). Complete the project by mounting the light fixture, screwing the switch to the box, and installing the cover plate.

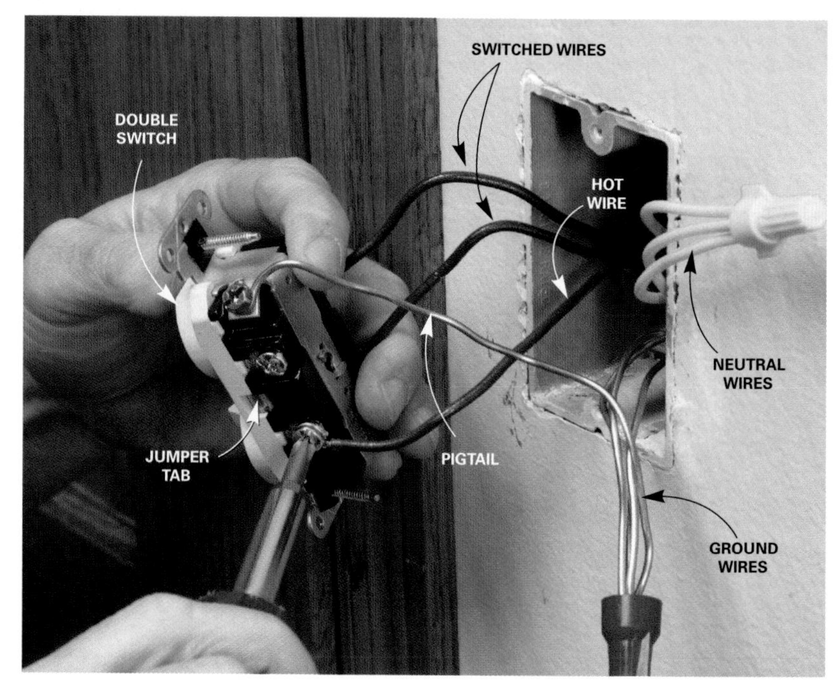

7 Connect the switch. Strip the ends of the wires at the switch box. Connect the neutral white wires with a wire connector. Connect the ground wires with a 6-in.-long pigtail wire leading to the switch. Loop the black wires clockwise around the screws and tighten the screws.

3 Plumbing, Heating & Appliances

IN THIS CHAPTER

REPAIR YOUR LEAKING WATER DISPENSER

If you have a water dispenser in the door of your refrigerator and notice water on the floor when you fill a glass, the vinyl tubing that runs under the refrigerator could be leaking. To find out, pull the refrigerator forward a little. Then tip it back and prop up the front feet on blocks of wood. Look underneath and ask someone to dispense a glass of water. If the tube's leaking, you'll see it.

The fix is simple. **Photos 1 – 3** show the steps. Cut out the section of damaged tubing and take it with you to the home center or hardware store. Buy a new section of vinyl tubing and one or two quick-connect couplings. If you don't have a quick-connect coupling on one end of the damaged tube as shown in **Photo 1**, then cut the tubing in two spots and join it with two new quick-connect couplings.

The tubing for icemakers can also get damaged and leak. So if you ever notice water on the floor under your refrigerator, check for a leaking tube and repair it using the process we show here.

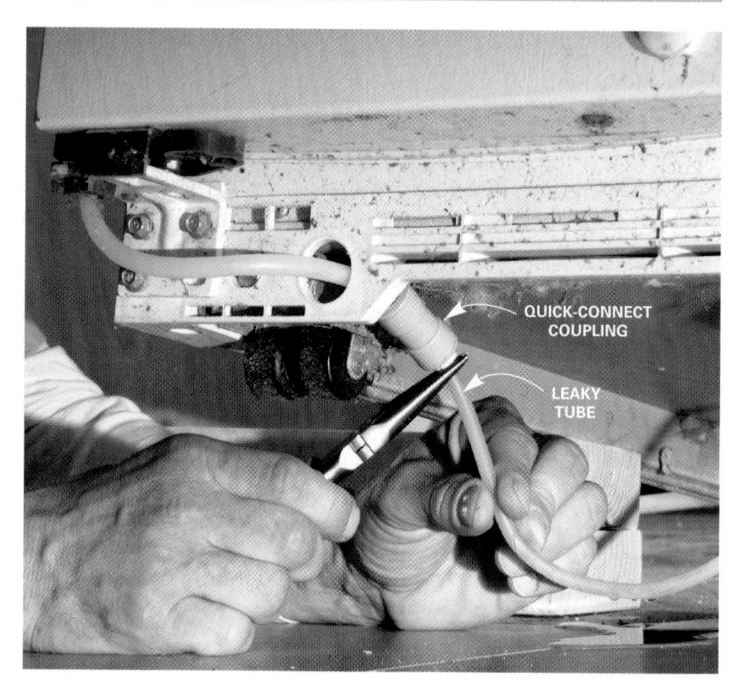

1 Disconnect the leaking tube. **Disconnect one end of the leaking tube by pressing in on the inner ring with needle-nose pliers to release the tube. If there isn't a quick-connect coupling, simply cut the tube with a sharp utility knife.**

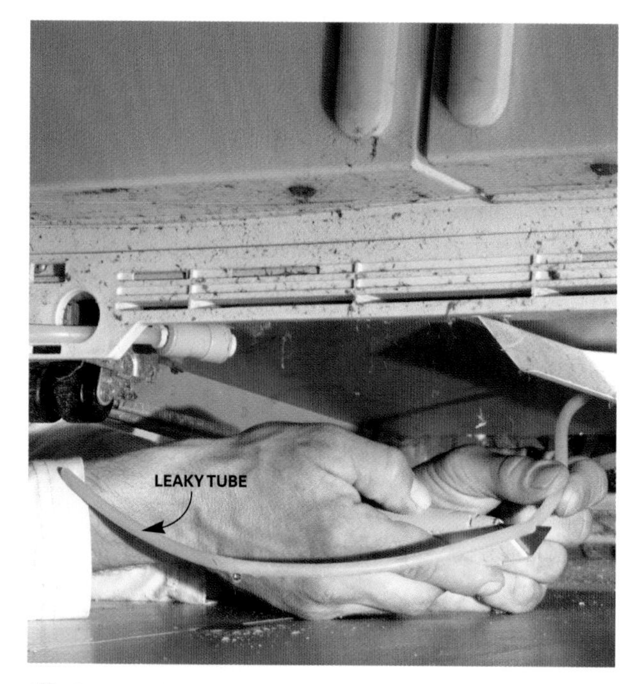

2 Cut out the damaged section of tube. **Cut off the damaged tubing with a sharp utility knife. Don't use a side cutters; it'll distort the tubing and prevent a good seal with the quick-connect coupling.**

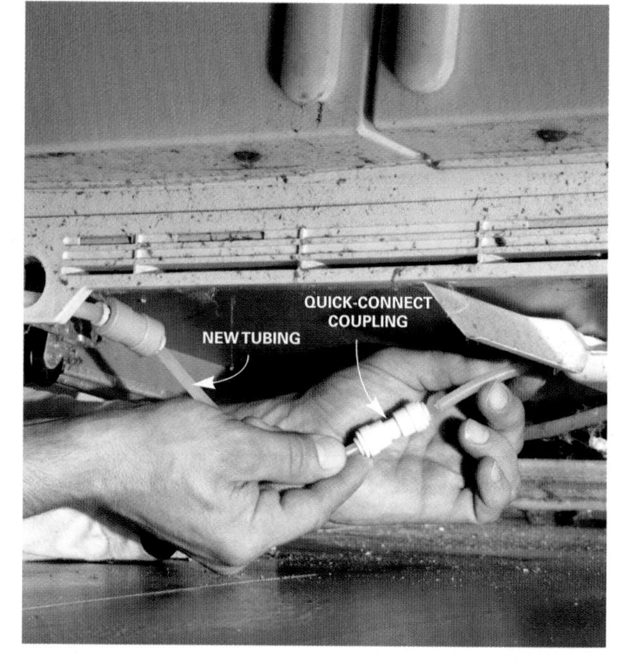

3 Splice in a new section of tubing. **Quick-connect couplings simplify this repair. Just push cut ends of the tubing into the coupling for a leak-free connection.**

SLOW-FLOWING SPRAYER

If your pullout sprayer delivers a weak spray, here's what to do. First, make sure the problem is with the spray head and not farther down the line. Start by removing the sprayer (**Photo 1**). Clip a clothespin or small clamp on the hose to keep it from snaking back down the spout. If water flows from the hose when you turn on the faucet, then you know the problem is in the spray head—unless the flow is still weak. In that case, there's a problem with the faucet or supply lines. Go to familyhandyman.com and type "faucet repair" into the search box for help with this problem.

Most pullout sprayers have an inlet screen (**Photo 2**), a removable aerator (**Photo 4**) or both, which can get clogged with mineral deposits or other debris. But there are dozens of different types of pullout spray faucets, and they all have slightly different parts, so yours may not look exactly like this. The biggest difference is in how you remove the aerator. On some faucets, the aerator has flat spots for a wrench or pliers and you simply unscrew it (**Photo 4**). Other faucets require a special tool (sometimes included with new faucets) for unscrewing the aerator. You can clean out the holes in the inlet screen with a dental pick or other pointed tool (**Photo 2**), but it's not worth trying to clean a clogged aerator since they seldom work quite right when you're done. Take the aerator to a hardware store, home center or plumbing supplier to find a replacement. If it's not available, go to the manufacturer's Web site to find out how to order one.

If these fixes don't work or you don't want to do them, simply replace the entire spray head. First contact the manufacturer of your faucet. It may be guaranteed so that you can get a new spray head free. If not, go to the manufacturer's Web site for information on ordering a new one (it will cost about $30 to $40). Also, many home centers stock a generic replacement that fits most faucets (about $25).

1 Unscrew the sprayer. **Turn off the water at the faucet and use pliers to loosen the nut that holds the sprayer to the flexible hose. Remove the sprayer. Hold the tube facing down into the sink and gradually turn on the water at the faucet to check the water pressure.**

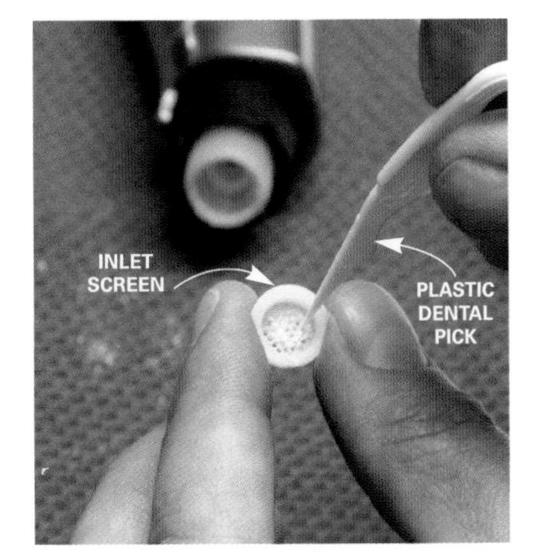

2 Clean the inlet screen. **Look down into the hose end of the sprayer and see if there's a small screen. If there is, remove it by tapping the sprayer or gently prying it out with a small pointed tool. Clean the holes with a toothpick or plastic dental pick.**

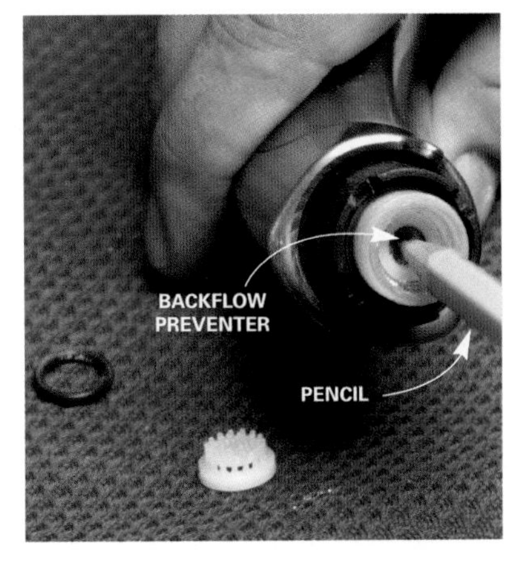

3 Check the backflow preventer. **Inspect the area under the inlet screen to see if there's a backflow preventer. Gently press a pencil against this round disc to make sure it moves freely. Clean off any mineral deposits around the edges.**

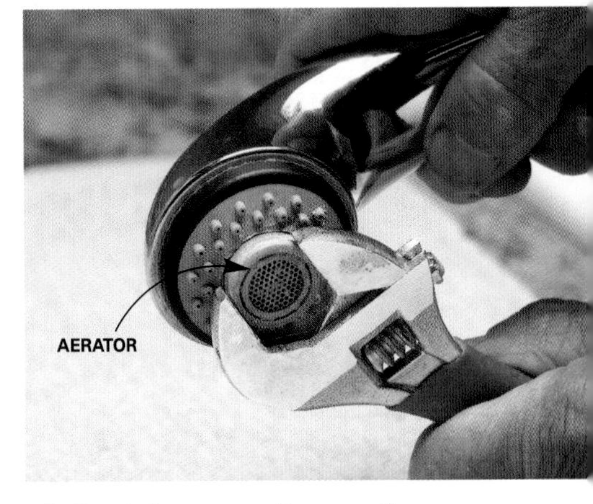

4 Check the aerator. **Unscrew the aerator with pliers or a wrench. Some pullout spray heads don't have removable aerators. Ask the manufacturer if you can't tell.**

WASHING MACHINE WON'T DRAIN?

If the water won't drain out of your washing machine, either something is stuck in the drain hose or pump, or the pump is broken. Both fixes are simple if you're even just a little bit handy with tools. We're showing the repair on a Maytag washing machine.

Start by unplugging the machine and emptying the water. Bail the water out of the tub, or you can drain the tub using gravity by placing the drain hose on the floor near the drain or in a bucket. Clamp the hose to prevent any remaining water from running out (**Photo 3**). Once the washer's empty, support the front of it on paint cans or stacked 2x4s. **Photo 1** shows where to find the screws that hold the front panel in place. Remove the panel and you'll see the pump. The pump has a translucent housing, so you might even see the offending piece of clothing wrapped up in the pump. **Photo 3** shows what to do if the pump is clogged. If you don't see the clog in the pump or in the hose near the pump, then it could be stuck in the outlet where the hose connects to the bottom of the tub.

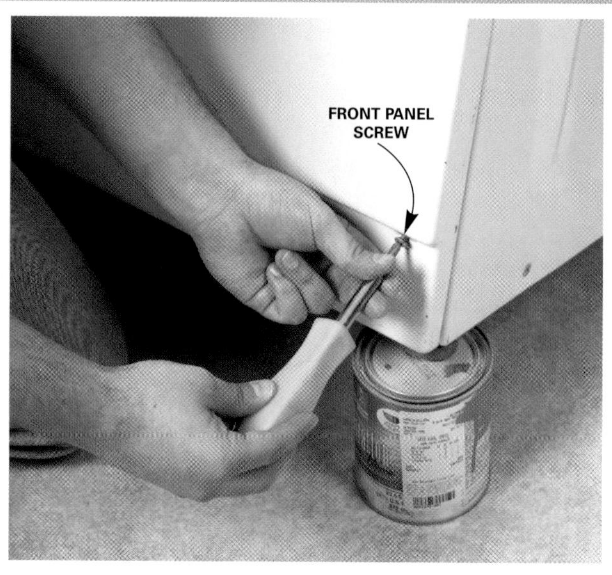

1 Remove panel screws. **Unplug the washer. Then prop up the washer and remove the two screws that secure the front panel.**

2 Remove the front panel. **Pull the lower edge of the panel outward and "unhook" the top. On a Whirlpool washer, you'll have to remove the entire shell to access the pump.**

3 Pull out the clog. **Remove the belt from the pulley on the bottom side of the pump. It's spring-loaded, so it comes off easily. Then remove the hose, and if the clog is visible, pull it out. Twist the pulley to unwind the fabric as you pull it out.**

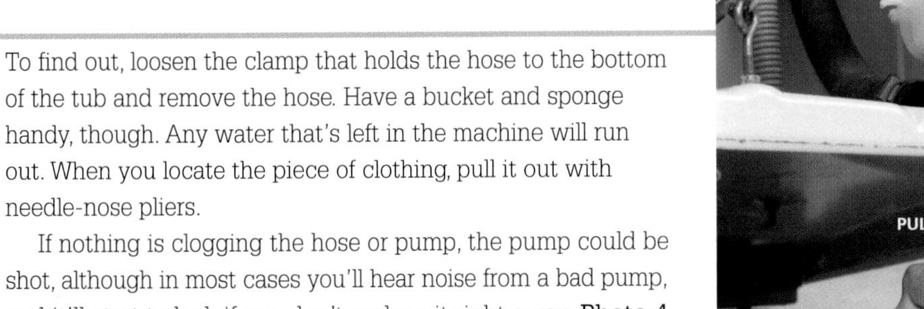

To find out, loosen the clamp that holds the hose to the bottom of the tub and remove the hose. Have a bucket and sponge handy, though. Any water that's left in the machine will run out. When you locate the piece of clothing, pull it out with needle-nose pliers.

If nothing is clogging the hose or pump, the pump could be shot, although in most cases you'll hear noise from a bad pump, and it'll start to leak if you don't replace it right away. **Photo 4** shows how to remove the pump. Buy a new one to match. You can find a new pump online or go to your local appliance parts center. You'll need the brand and model number for proper part identification. Model numbers are usually stamped on a small metal plate located under the tub lid or on the top, side or back of the machine. Copy down all the plate information and use it to access online parts suppliers, or take it along to the parts distributor. Install the new pump by attaching it with screws and connecting the hoses, and then reinstall the belt.

4 Remove the pump. If the impeller inside the pump is damaged (reach your finger inside to feel for broken fins) or if the pump leaks or makes noise, you'll have to replace it. Remove the three screws that hold the pump to the washer. Buy a new pump and install it.

FIX YOUR DRIPPING LAUNDRY FAUCET

Laundry faucets like this are easy and cheap to fix. If it's dripping from the spout, you need a new faucet washer. And if water is leaking around the handle, the rubber O-ring around the valve stem is bad. But since you have to take out the valve stem for either repair, and the fix is simple, we recommend replacing both the hot and cold washers and the O-rings while the faucet is apart. Remember to turn off the water and purge the pressure before you start. If you're lucky, there'll be a separate shutoff for the laundry room. Otherwise, you'll have to shut off the water to the whole house by closing the main valve.

Photos 1 and 2 show how to do the repair. After you've removed the valve stems, take them to the hardware store. You'll find drawers full of faucet washers and O-rings. Just find washers that will fit snugly in the recess, and matching O-rings. If you damaged the screw that holds the washer on when you removed it, buy new brass screws. Now simply reassemble everything in the reverse order. No more drips!

1 Unscrew the valve. Remove the handle. Then turn the valve counterclockwise with a wrench. Pull out the valve.

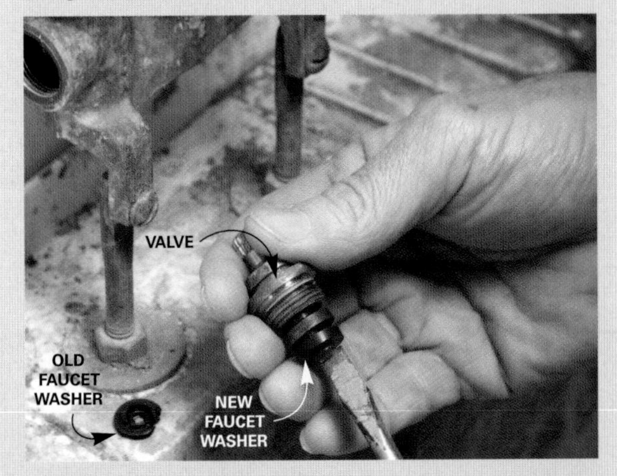

2 Replace the washer. Remove the screw that holds the washer to the valve. Install the new washer and replace the screw.

UNCLOG A BATHROOM SINK—WITHOUT CHEMICALS

Slow-moving or stopped-up drains are common in bathroom sinks, but luckily the fix is usually simple and takes only about 15 minutes. The problem is caused by hair and gummy soap scum that get caught on the stopper or pivot rod and clogs the drain.

To get at the clog, try lifting out the stopper (**Photo 1**). Sometimes it'll come right out. If it doesn't lift out, it's held in by the pivot rod. Release the stopper by removing the pivot rod nut and pulling out the pivot rod (**Photo 3**). If you can't loosen the nut by hand, use pliers. With the pivot rod pulled out, you'll be able to lift out the stopper. Then to get the clog out, bend a wire in a tight hook (a light-duty clothes hanger or short length of electrical wire will do) and fish out the hair (**Photo 2**). If you didn't have to remove the pivot rod to remove the stopper, you can just drop the stopper back down into the drain. If you removed the pivot rod, first drop the stopper into the drain. Then line up the pivot rod with the slot in the stopper and reinsert it. Finally, hand-tighten the pivot rod nut.

Run hot water down the drain to help clear out any remaining soap scum and to check that the clog is gone. Check around the pivot rod nut to make sure it's not leaking. If you see drips, tighten the pivot rod nut slightly with pliers.

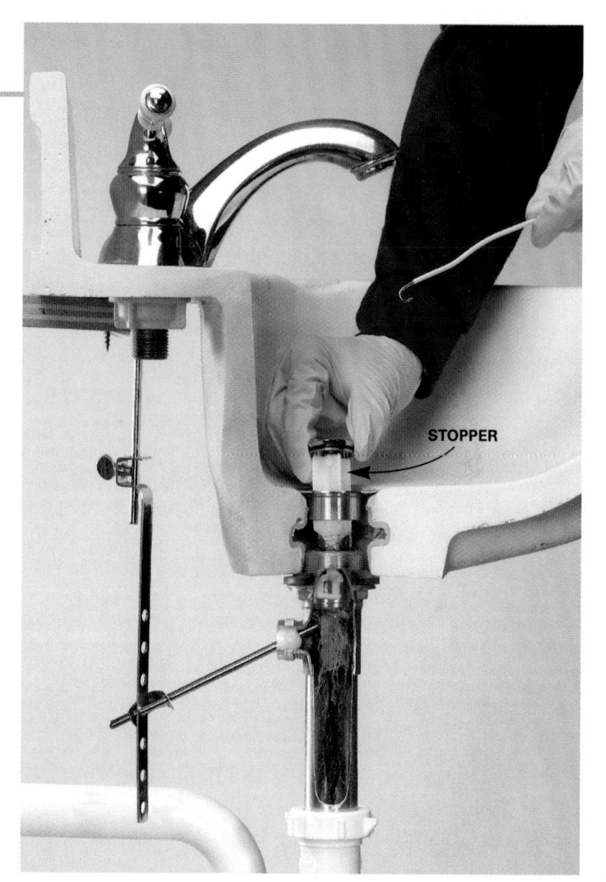

1 If the stopper comes out: **Tug on the stopper to see if it'll come out. If so, remove it.**

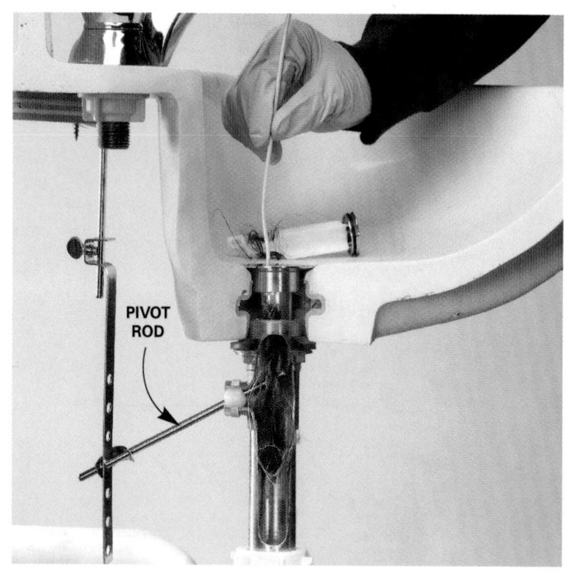

2 Remove the clog. **Fish out the hair clog with a bent wire or other tool. Run water through the drain and replace the stopper.**

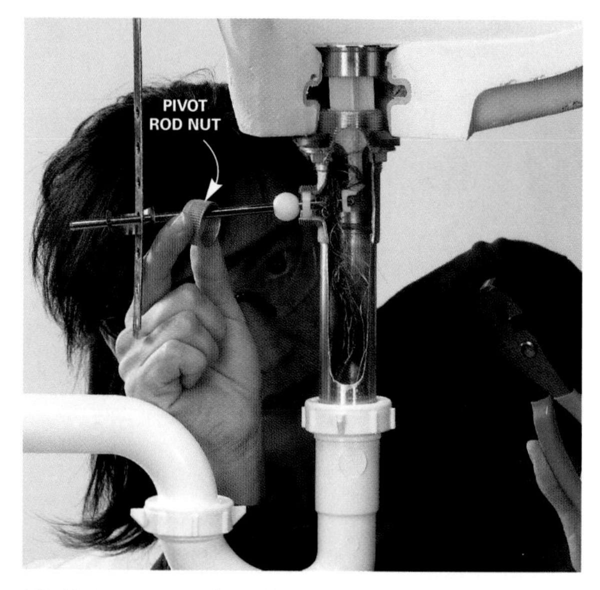

3 If the stopper doesn't come out: **Unscrew the pivot rod nut and pull out the rod. Lift out the stopper. Clean out the hair and reinstall the stopper and pivot rod.**

DRY CLOTHES QUICKER WITH A DRYER DUCT BOOSTER

If it takes forever for your clothes to dry, the problem could be the dryer duct. A dryer vent duct that's too long reduces the airflow and wastes energy. Most dryer manufacturers recommend a maximum duct length of about 25 ft. But the catch is that every bend in the pipe is equivalent to about 5 ft. of straight pipe. It adds up quickly.

A company called Tjernlund Products (search online for "Tjernlund duct booster") has a solution. For about $250, you can buy a dryer duct booster that switches on automatically when it senses airflow through the duct. The booster also has a specially designed fan that won't clog with lint, unlike less expensive boosters.

Mount the booster to the wall or ceiling at least 10 ft. from the dryer and in the path of the existing vent. Connect the vent to the booster and plug it in.

FIX FOR A RUNNING TOILET

If you hear your toilet refilling too often, or if you hear the steady hiss of running water, the flapper may be leaking. The flapper (aka "flush valve seal") is the plug that falls against the drain hole (flush valve drain seat) on the bottom of the tank and holds water in until the next time you flush. When flappers or flush valve seats wear out, water trickles out, causing the water valve to open to refill the tank. Usually the fix is simple. Remove the old flapper and take it with you to the hardware store or home center to find a matching replacement.

Occasionally a new flapper doesn't solve the problem. If you've tried replacing the flapper but the toilet still runs, the flush valve seat is probably rough or pitted. You can replace the entire flush valve, but it's a big job. Here's an easier fix. Look for a flapper kit that contains a flush seat repair. We show a Fluidmaster 555C kit ($7), but others are available. The kit contains a flapper and matching seat that you adhere to the damaged seat with the adhesive provided, as shown.

Start by closing the valve on the water line to the toilet by turning it clockwise. Then flush the toilet and hold the flapper open to allow the water to drain from the tank. Use a sponge to mop out the water that remains. Follow the included instructions to install the new valve seat and flapper. The Fluidmaster flapper we show includes a plastic cup that allows you to adjust the length of time the flapper stays open. It's for toilets that use 3.5 gallons or less for a flush. If your toilet uses more than this, remove the timing cup. Install the new flapper. Then adjust the length of the chain so it's just slightly slack when the flapper is down. Turn on the water and test the flush. You may have to fiddle with the length of the chain to get the flapper working correctly. When you're done, cut off the excess chain to keep it from getting stuck under the flapper.

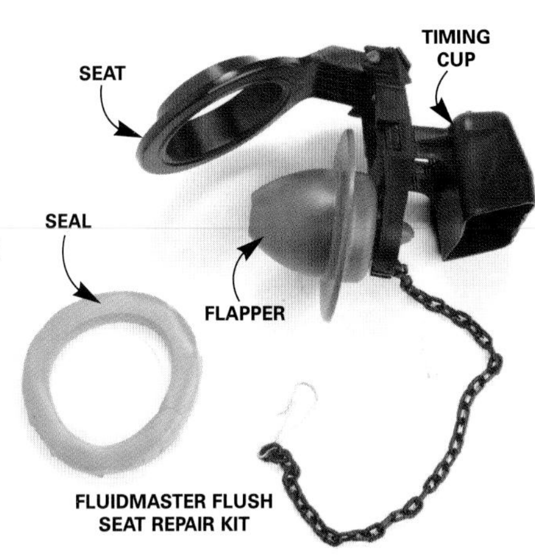

Repair the flush seat. **Follow the directions included with your flush seat repair kit to seal a new repair seat onto the old, damaged seat.**

UNCLOG A KITCHEN SINK

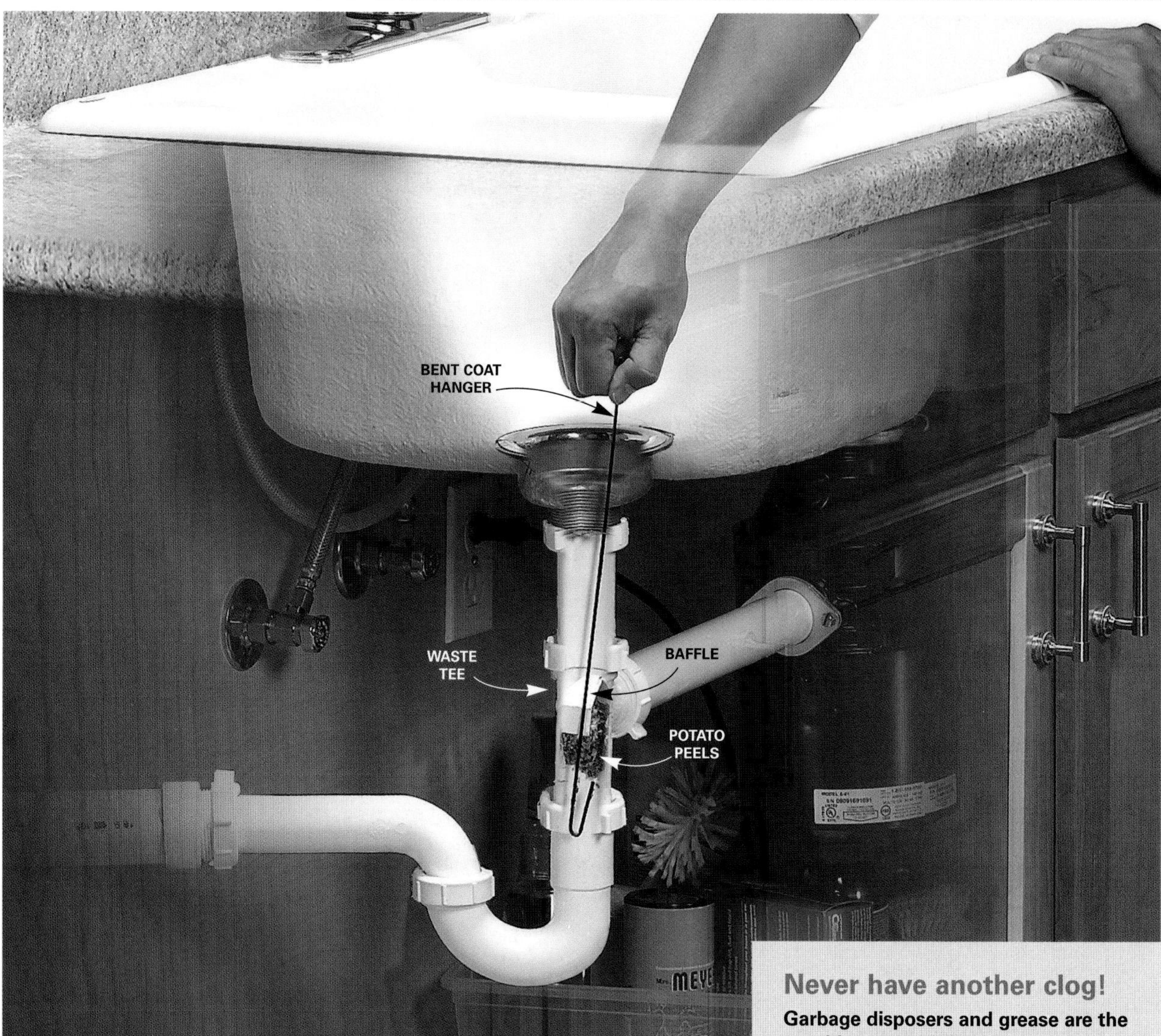

When the water in your kitchen sink won't drain or drains slowly, don't reach for the chemical drain cleaner. Instead, try this three-step method recommended by one of our favorite plumbers. The first two steps we'll show you don't even require you to remove the trap or take anything apart. If you're lucky, all you'll need is a bent coat hanger. But if the clog is in the trap or farther down the drain, you'll need a 1/4-in. drain snake. You can buy an inexpensive snake that's simply a cable running through a bent pipe that allows you to twist the cable, but we recommend spending a little more money for a cable that's enclosed in a drum ($15 to $40). This type is much easier to use.

Before you get started on any of our solutions, suck all the water out of the sink with a wet-dry shop vacuum or sponge it into a bucket. You'll be able to see what you're doing, and if you do have to disassemble plumbing, it'll be less messy.

Never have another clog!

Garbage disposers and grease are the two biggest contributors to clogged sink drains. Here's the first rule for avoiding clogs: Don't use your garbage disposer like a trash can. If your family sends vast amounts of food down the disposer, you'll have a clogged sink someday. Disposing of turkey carcasses, gummy foods like pasta and fibrous items like banana peels in the sink is asking for trouble. The same goes for heaping plates of leftovers. Scrape the big stuff into the garbage can and use the disposer for the small stuff.

The second rule: Never pour grease down the drain. And running hot water along with it won't help. The grease will just congeal farther down the drainpipe where it'll be even harder to clear.

STEP 1: The coat-hanger trick

If you have a two-bowl sink and only one side is clogged, there's a good chance this fix will work. First look under the sink to locate the waste tee. If your drain setup looks something like the one shown here and the water is backing up on the side without the waste tee, you may be able to remove the clog with a bent coat hanger (opening photo). There's a baffle inside the waste tee that is meant to direct water down the drain, but since the baffled area is narrower than the rest of the drain, food often gets stuck there. Garbage disposers are notorious for causing clogs, especially at the baffle. The trick is to bend a hook on the end of a coat hanger wire and use it to dislodge the clog. Use pliers to bend a hook that will fit through the slots in the basket strainer. Peek under the sink to get a rough idea how far down the waste tee is from the basket strainer. Push the bent hanger down the drain. Then twist and pull until you feel it hook onto the baffle. Now wiggle it up and down while twisting it to remove the clog. Run water in the clogged sink to tell if you've removed the obstruction. If the sink still doesn't drain, there's a clog farther down. Move on to Step 2.

STEP 2: Run a snake through the basket strainer

There are several advantages to this approach. You don't have to remove all the stuff from under the sink, struggle to take apart and reassemble drains, or worry about spilling dirty drain water when you remove the trap. Also, pushing the cable down through the basket strainer allows you to clean the slime-covered cable as you withdraw it by running clean water down the drain. (Believe me, this is a nice bonus!) And finally, since the drain is still fully assembled, you'll be able to tell, by running water in the sink, whether you've unclogged the drain.

You have to modify the end of the cable on your drain snake to use this method, however (photo below). Then you snake out the drain by pushing the cable down through one of the slots or holes in the basket strainer. See "The Art of Running a Snake" on p. 88.

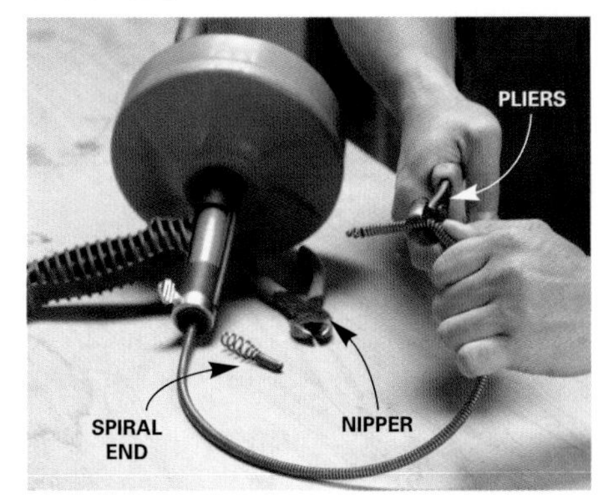

Modify your drain snake to fit through the slot in the basket strainer. First clip off the spiral end. Then bend the last few inches at about a 30-degree angle with pliers. Finally, unwind the tip slightly to form a small hook.

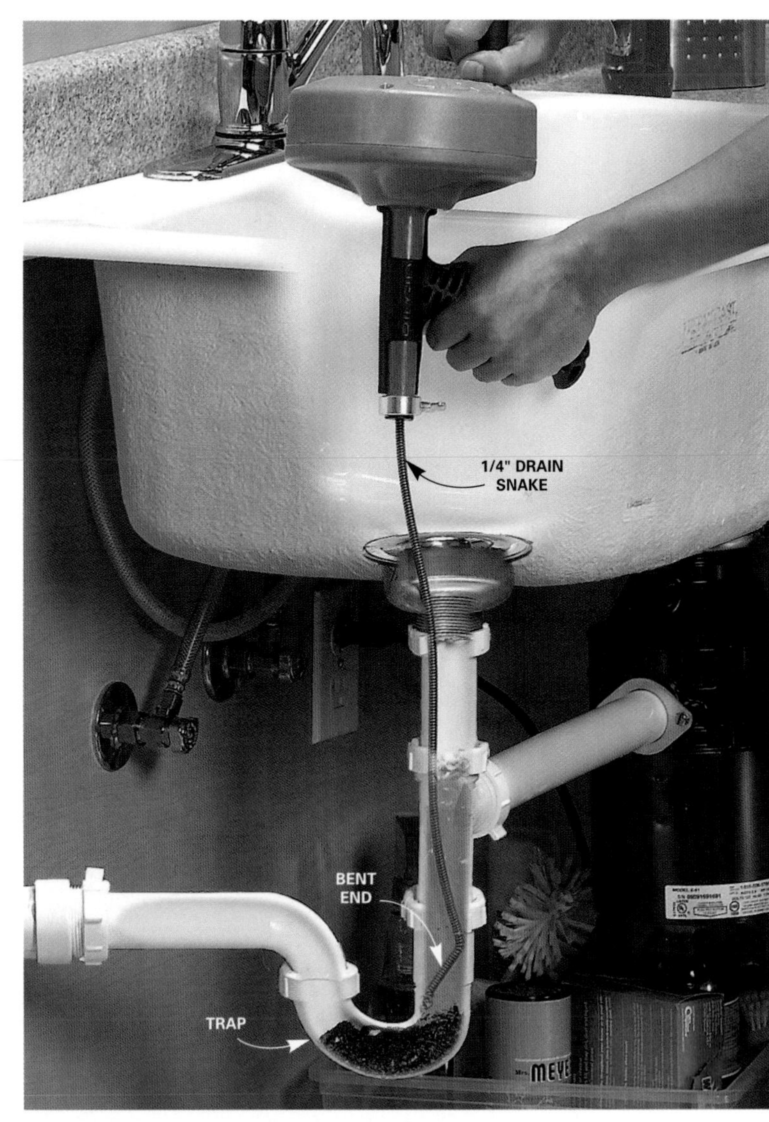

If the bent coat hanger doesn't get the clog, there's a good chance you can clear it without taking your plumbing apart. Run a modified snake (see photo, left) down through the slots in the basket strainer.

STEP 3: Take the trap apart

If you can't unclog the drain using Steps 1 or 2, then it's time to take off the trap and waste arm and feed the drain snake directly into the drainpipe. Remember to remove as much water from the sink as possible before you remove the trap. Then place a bucket under the trap to catch any remaining water. Use large slip-joint pliers to loosen the slip-joint nuts on both ends of the trap. Unscrew the nuts and remove the trap. Do the same with the nut that secures the waste arm to the drain and remove the waste arm.

Before you reach for the drain snake, look up into the baffle tee to make sure the baffle area is clear. Then look into the trap to make sure there's no clog in the bottom. If both spots are clear, then the clog is farther down in the drainpipe and you'll need a drain snake.

With this method, the only way you'll know if you've unclogged the drain is to reassemble the trap and run water down the drain. If you've got a metal trap and drain arm, we recommend replacing them and the other metal drain parts with plastic. Plastic parts are easy to cut and assemble. They're also easier to take apart if you have a problem in the future, and they don't corrode.

If the previous two approaches didn't work, remove the trap and waste arm to get to the clog. You'll have two fewer bends to get around with the snake and have an easier time reaching deep clogs.

The art of running a snake

There's an art to using a drain snake, and the more experience you have, the better you'll be at it. Here's how you do it. Loosen the setscrew or chuck to allow the cable to come out of the drum freely. Now feed the cable into the drain until you can't push it any more. It may be stuck on the clog or simply meeting resistance where the drainpipe bends.

Position the end of the drum so there's about 8 in. of cable showing between the drain and the drum, and tighten the setscrew or chuck onto the cable. Withdraw the cable about an inch so that it's free of the obstruction, and start turning the drum while you push it toward the drain. Continue until you've pushed the exposed cable down the drain. Then repeat the process by loosening the setscrew and withdrawing another 8 in. of cable. If the end of the cable gets stuck and you keep turning the drum, the cable will start to spiral inside the drain. You want to avoid this, so stop turning the drum if you feel that the cable isn't turning freely anymore. Withdraw the cable about 6 in. and try again.

Several things can happen at this point. You might bore through the clog, allowing water to run through and dissolve the remaining clog. You might push the clog to a point where the diameter of the pipes is larger and it can wash down the drain. Or you might hook the clog with the end of the snake and pull it out. This is where your intuition comes into play. When you think you've unclogged the drain, withdraw the snake. If you've pushed the cable down through the basket strainer, you can rinse it off as you retrieve it by running water. Otherwise, put on some gloves and wipe the cable off with a rag as you push it back into the drum.

When you're done cleaning the drain, pull the cable out of the drum, rinse it off, and wipe it down with an oil-soaked rag to keep it from rusting.

PEX EDUCATION

Everything you always wanted to know but were afraid to ask

by **Gary Wentz**

PLUMBING, HEATING & APPLIANCES

I'm not a plumber. But like any remodeler, I occasionally find myself relocating a hose bib or fixing a pipe that managed to get in the way of my Sawzall. For years, my plumbing kit was a torch and a bucket of copper fittings. These days, that bucket mostly holds PEX fittings and tools. And my soldering torch doesn't get used much anymore.

Switching to PEX wasn't difficult; PEX is a whole lot easier to master than copper. The only tricky part was deciding what to carry in my plumbing bucket. Visiting the plumbing aisle at my local home center didn't help matters—all those strange tools, connection systems and unfamiliar thingamajigs made my head spin. But with lots of advice and a little on-the-job training from plumber friends, I figured out what's needed and what isn't. Here's what I learned about getting set up for PEX.

PEX costs less than half the price of copper and installs much faster. And since it's flexible, PEX makes remodeling jobs easier.

LESSON 1: Choose a common connection system

Before you choose a system for connecting PEX to fittings, check what's available at the stores where you like to shop. There are a half-dozen systems out there, but most are available only through specialty plumbing suppliers. If you want to shop at home centers and hardware stores, there are two widely available methods to choose from: copper crimp rings and stainless steel cinch rings. I like the cinch system better because the tool ($45) is smaller and one tool can handle four ring sizes (3/8 to 1 in.). But cinch rings aren't as widely available in my area, so I chose the crimp system instead. Crimp rings require a different tool for each size (and each tool costs at least $50) or a combination tool ($100), and the bigger tools are awkward in tight spots. Still, I'd rather put up with the drawbacks of the crimp system than drive across town to get supplies. If you want to shop online, pexsupply.com is a good place to start. Whatever system you choose, keep an eye on prices: I've found that the costs vary a lot from one supplier to another.

CINCH RINGS
Cinch rings tighten as you pinch the tab with the tool.

CRIMP RINGS
Crimp ring connections are made by compressing a copper ring around the PEX and fitting.

LESSON 2: Buy sticks, not coils

PEX has a strong "memory"; it always wants to spring back to its original shape. So working with a coil of PEX is like wrestling with a giant Slinky. For most jobs, you're better off buying 10-ft. "sticks" instead ($2.50 each for 1/2-in. diameter). You may have to pay a few cents more per foot and install a coupler or two, but you'll avoid frustration and kinks. Even plumbers who run miles of PEX every year often buy sticks rather than coils.

Coils are great when you have lots of long runs, but straight "sticks" are a lot easier to work with. The red and blue colors eliminate hot-and-cold confusion.

LESSON 3: Stock up on push-ins

Don't begin any PEX job without a few push-in elbows, tees and couplings (SharkBite is one brand; sharkbite.com). They're the best solution for cramped quarters where there's no space for a crimping or cinching tool. No tool is needed; just push in the PEX and walk away. Push-in fittings also work with copper and CPVC. Convenience doesn't come cheap, though. You'll spend from $5 to $12 per fitting. Also, check with your local inspector before you use push-in fittings. Some jurisdictions don't allow them in inaccessible locations like inside walls.

Push-in fittings work with copper and CPVC as well as with PEX.

LESSON 4: Bend PEX carefully—or not at all

PEX is easy to kink. With one brand (Uponor Wirsbo), you can restore the tubing by heating it. But with most PEX, you have to cut out the kink and splice in a new section. You can also damage PEX by overbending it. (The minimum bend radius is typically six to eight times the outer diameter, depending on the manufacturer.) One way to avoid kinking and overbending is to use bend sleeves ($2). Keep in mind that—even with a sleeve—a bend requires open working space. In tight situations, save yourself some struggling by using an elbow fitting instead.

A bend sleeve prevents kinking or creating a too-tight bend.

LESSON 5: Get a crimp cutter

PEX fittings cost about three times as much as copper fittings. So you won't want to toss your mistakes in the trash. If you use cinch rings, you can saw or twist off the ring tab, pull off the PEX and reuse the fitting. But sawing through a crimp ring—without damaging the fitting—is a job for a surgeon. For the rest of us, a crimp cutter ($25) is a lifesaver. Just slice off the PEX flush with the fitting and make two cuts in the ring.

A crimp cutter lets you remove crimp rings without damaging the fitting.

LESSON 6: Stub out with copper

You can buy shutoff valves that connect directly to PEX. But don't. PEX can't handle abuse the way copper can—for example, from cramming more and more stuff into a vanity or cranking that crusty valve closed years from now. So use copper rather than PEX for wall stub-outs. For risers coming out of the floor (or extending down from the ceiling to a laundry tub faucet), use lengths of copper pipe.

Copper stub-outs ($5) provide a PEX connection on one end and solid support for shutoff valves on the other.

GreatGoofs®

Two times the water damage

The toilet in the upstairs bathroom had been leaking for some time, which had rotted the floor. I removed the toilet, vanity and sink to replace the plywood. Once the new vinyl floor in and the vanity were reinstalled, I left off the sink to make it easier to solder on new shutoff valves.

With the main water supply to the house turned off, I installed the shutoff valves. Then I went downstairs to turn on the water supply so I could check the joints for leaks. As I walked back upstairs, fancying myself a master plumber, I heard the sound of gushing water. I had forgotten to turn off the shutoff valves! The bathroom was flooded and the ceiling below was ruined. But my soldering job held up perfectly.

Question&Comment

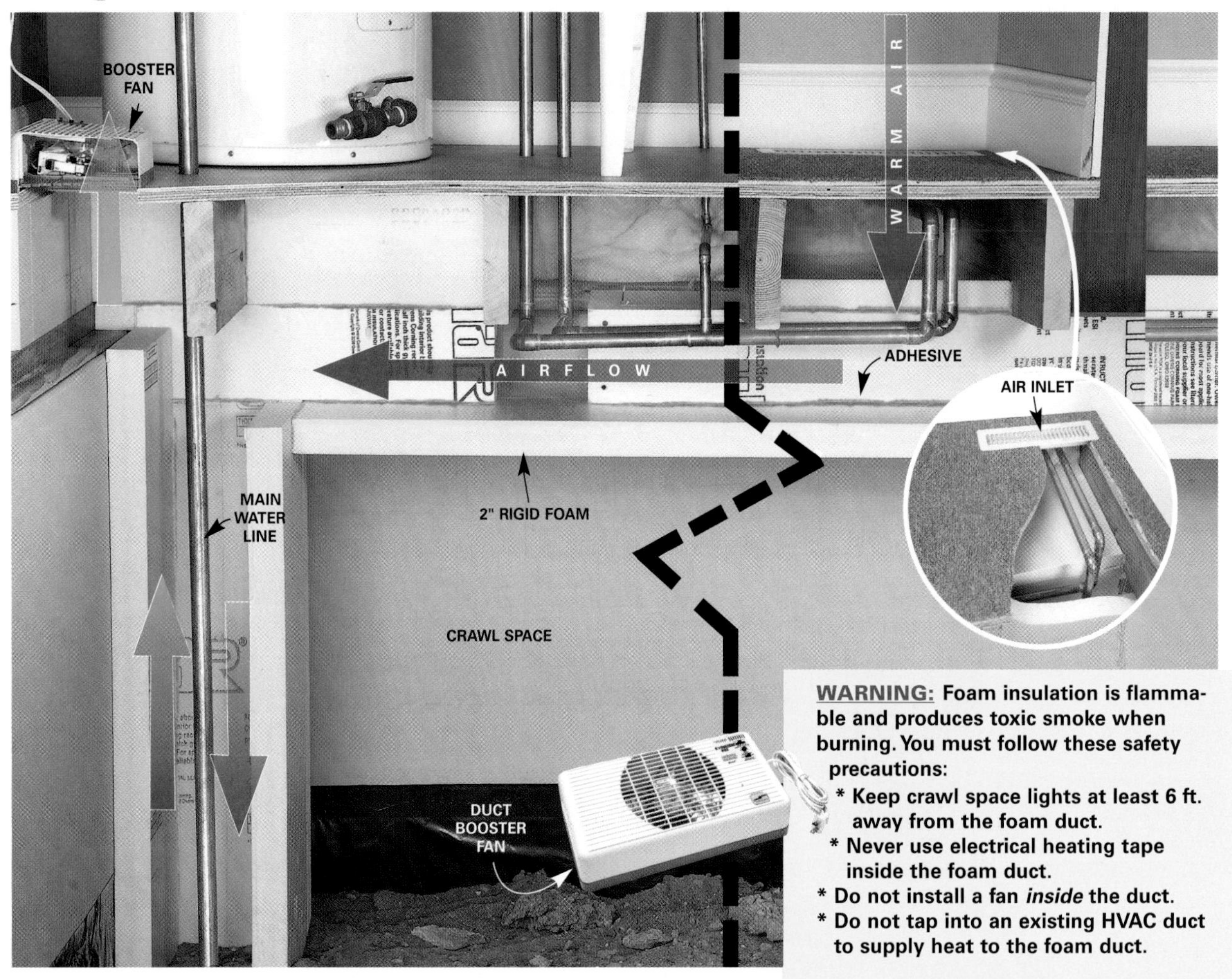

PREVENT PIPES FROM FREEZING

I insulated the heating ducts in my crawl space and my pipes froze. I can't insulate the walls of the crawl space because it's vented to the outside. How can I insulate the pipes to keep them from freezing?

For starters, forget about using fiberglass or the foam pipe insulation sold at home centers. At best, it provides an insulation value of R-3.8. That's not enough to prevent frozen pipes during extended cold periods. Plus, it's difficult to install on existing pipes, especially when the pipes run along the length of a floor joist. So we put our heads together and came up with a solution that we're all but positive will work for you. One of the editors used this fix to successfully insulate freeze-prone pipes on an outside wall.

Here's how it works. Build a duct system around the pipes with 2-in.-thick rigid extruded polystyrene foam (R-10). It works by drawing heated household air through the foam duct and back into the house. Start by locating a spot near the pipes on one end of the crawl space near a wall and cut a 5 x 10-in. hole in the floor above. This exhaust hole should be near an electrical outlet. Cut another hole at the far end of the pipes to fit a conventional floor vent—the size is up to you.

Next, construct the duct by running the foam down a few inches below the pipes to create enough room for airflow. Glue the lengths together with PL-300 blue construction adhesive and pin them with screws or nails until the adhesive sets up. Crosscut individual foam pieces to "cap off" any open joist areas. Cutting is easy with a circular or table saw.

Use the same method to encase vertical riser pipes and pipes that run along the length of a joist. Once all pipes are enclosed, glue on end caps.

Buy a duct booster fan (available in the HVAC department at home centers for $34) and place it over the exhaust vent. Run the fan full time at low speed during freezing weather (that'll cost about $3 per month).

PLUMB A WATER-POWERED SUMP PUMP

REMOTE-CONTROLLED FLOAT SWITCH
WATER-POWERED PUMP
CHECK VALVE
3/4" RESIDENTIAL WATER SUPPLY
OUTSIDE DISCHARGE
TO FLOAT
FROM SUMP

A battery-powered pump is a great backup for your main sump pump, especially if your house is supplied by a well. But if you're on a municipal water system, a water-powered backup pump may be a better option (a well pump won't work if the power's out). The price you'll pay for water consumption during a power outage is a pittance compared with the cost of a flooded basement. And, a water-powered pump never needs new batteries.

The pump shown here (Basepump RB750; $321 from basepump.com) installs on the ceiling above the sump. You'll have to run a 3/4-in. water line to it and connect the remote float and tubing to the switch near the pump. Then run a separate self-draining pipe that drains outside.

REPACK A STEM SEAL ON A STREET VALVE

The street-side valve at my water meter has been dripping for years. I tightened the stem nut, but it still leaks. The utility wants $40 to shut the water off. Can I repack the stem with the water on?

You can repack the stem with the water on, but you'll get some water spray once you loosen the packing nut, so move anything you care about away from the meter area.

Most old valves have rust and mineral deposits in the gate valve's receiving groove. That crud can jam the gate and damage the valve. Gently close the valve (don't force it). Then open the cold faucet at your laundry tub. Next, open the street-side valve slightly. The rush of water will flush out the crud. Shut off the laundry faucet, then the street-side valve (in that order).

Buy Teflon packing rope at any hardware store or home center. With the valve in the off position, loosen the packing nut and slide it toward the handle. Then repack the stem.

Wrap one wind of stem packing rope around the stem. Tighten the packing nut and open the valve. If it still leaks, back off the packing nut and add a few more winds of packing rope.

REPLACE A LEAKING MAIN SHUTOFF VALVE

Every time I do a plumbing job at my house, I crank the main shut-off valve down as tight as I can get it, but water still drips out of the open pipe. Can I replace the main valve myself?

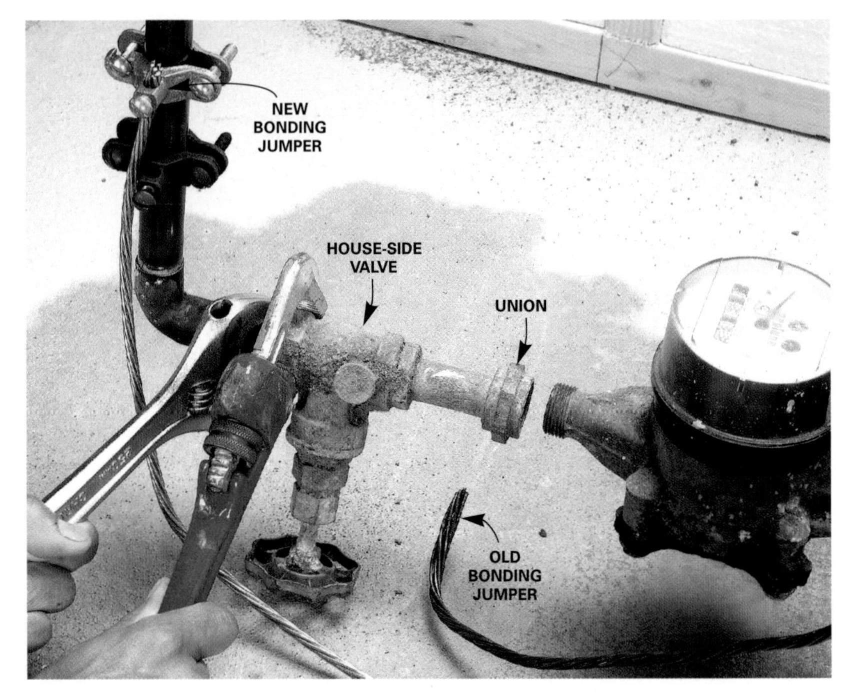

1 Shut off the street-side valve where the water enters the house. Then loosen the coupling nut and remove the nipple from the old valve.

2 Screw on the new ball valve, install the old nipple and the new leather washer (use Teflon tape or pipe dope on the threads). Tighten the coupling nut, turn on the water and check for leaks.

Sure, but you have to get your ducks in a row before you start. To remove the old valve, you'll have to undo the coupling on the "house side" of the water meter. There's usually an oil-impregnated leather sealing washer inside the coupling. Leather washers are tough to find, so look at a plumbing supplier or buy them from Twin Leather Co., twinleather.com; 508-583-3485. (Its "home washer repair kit" contains two 5/8-in. and two 3/4-in. leather washers and costs $5 plus shipping.) Some plumbing suppliers sell neoprene washers, but the "old-timers" swear by leather, because eventually neoprene will dry out and crack. You probably have a 3/4-in. pipe leading to and from the leaky valve. Buy a threaded replacement ball valve; it's a far better choice than the older gate-style valve.

Test the "street-side" valve where the water enters the house. Since that valve is just as old, test it to make sure it closes all the way and reopens again. If that valve needs replacement, contact your water utility to shut off the main valve at the curb.

Then check out the electrical system "bonding jumper" that runs from a clamp on the house side of the meter to a clamp on the street side. If you can unscrew the old valve with the bonding jumper wire in place, fine. If you can't, do not disconnect it. The safe way to work around this problem is to install a longer section of copper wire and two new clamps (6AWG for 100-amp service, 4AWG for 200-amp service). Then remove the short bonding jumper. At that point, you're ready to shut down the water and replace the valve as shown.

FIX ROTTING A/C INSULATION

The black foam on one of my outside A/C lines is rotting and falling off. I suspect it's costing me money because the cold tubing is always covered with condensation. Is this something to worry about?

You're right—that condensation is reducing the efficiency of your A/C and raising your energy costs. You should remove all the old foam insulation and install the correct foam. Unfortunately, you won't find it at any home center. Measure the outside diameter on the larger of the two tubes (the skinny tube doesn't need insulation). Then contact a refrigeration supply house or online supplier for new foam and insulating tape (Insul-Lock tubing insulating foam, $4 for 6-ft. lengths, and Nomaco Poly Tape, $5, both from pexsupply.com).

1 Seal the ends. Wipe off the condensation and wrap a few winds of the sticky poly tape on the tubing where it exits the house. Then dry and wrap the service valve on the condenser end of the tubing. Squeeze it in tight around the tubing.

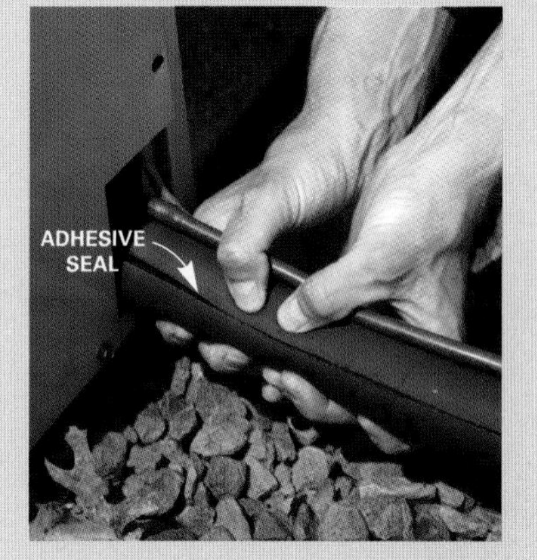

2 Install new foam. Slip the new foam over the tubing and on top of the cork tape. Remove the adhesive liner, align the edges and press the seam together as you go. Be careful. Once the glued ends touch, you can't get them apart again.

KEEPING COLD BREWS IN THE GARAGE

We got a new refrigerator and put the old side-by-side in the garage. The food in the fridge side stays cool, but the freezer doesn't keep the food frozen in cold weather. What gives?

Most refrigerators use a single compressor to cool the freezer and the cold-food compartment. Unfortunately, there's only one thermostat and it's inside the cold-food section. So, if the temperature in the garage stays about 38 degrees F, the thermostat never turns on. The cold air chills the food in the refrigerator, but it's not cold enough to keep frozen food solid (the ideal freezer temperature is 0 degrees).

You may be able to solve your problem by installing a "garage kit," a heating coil to warm the air around the thermostat. The warmer air makes the compressor run longer and keeps frozen food, well, frozen. Check with the manufacturer to see if it makes one for your model.

But before you shell out $20 for the kit, consider how much you'll have to spend to keep your brews chilled and pizzas frozen in the summer. Your old fridge is less efficient than your new one, so it's already costing you more to run. Add 25 percent to run the old clunker in an 80-degree garage. Then double the bill if it's running in a garage at 90 degrees and up. Are you sure you want to pay that much just to save a trip to the kitchen?

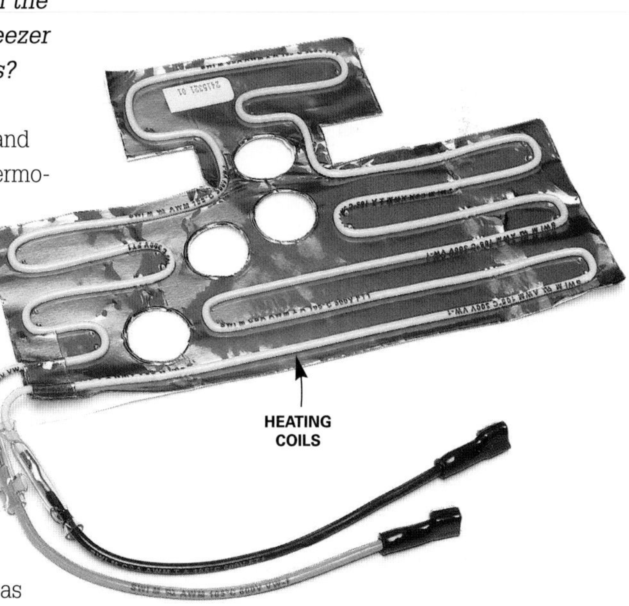

Find the model number of your refrigerator and contact the manufacturer's parts department to see if it offers a garage kit for your unit. This one costs $20.

PLUMBING, HEATING & APPLIANCES

Question&Comment

WATER HEATER PUDDLE? REPLACE THE TPR VALVE

Lately I'm seeing a puddle of water on the floor next to the water heater. The drain valve isn't leaking and I can't find a leak in the pipes. What's going on?

If you've had the heater for a long time and the problem just started, chances are the temperature pressure relief (TPR) valve is bad. The TPR is a safety device that releases water pressure when it becomes dangerously high within the water heater. But before you run out and buy a new TPR valve, check with your local water utility to see if it has made any changes to the system that would boost water pressure. If not, go ahead and replace the valve (less than $10 at a home center). Shut off the gas valve or flip the breaker to your water heater. Wait three hours for it to cool down, or run the hot water until it's lukewarm. Then shut off the water and bleed the pressure by opening a hot water faucet near the heater.

If a new valve doesn't solve the problem, it's time to install an expansion tank (about $40 at home centers). The tank has an internal air bladder that acts like a shock absorber to prevent overpressure in the system. Consult the chart at the home center for proper tank sizing. Install the tank on the cold water line and support the line with metal strapping (photo below).

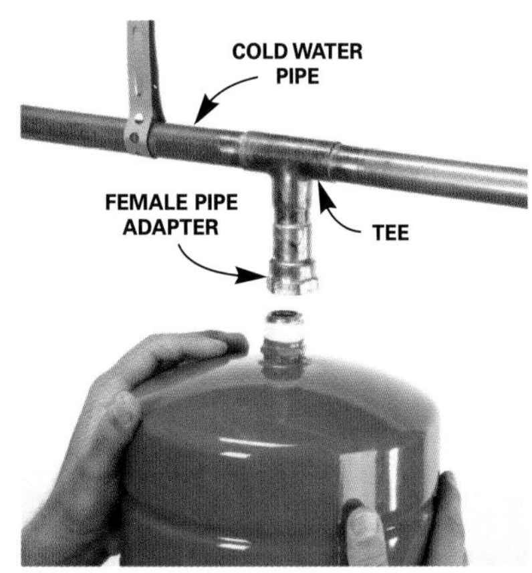

IF THE NEW VALVE LEAKS, ADD AN EXPANSION TANK
If a new TPR valve didn't solve the problem, solder in a "tee" and a female-threaded fitting on a horizontal cold water line near the water heater. Then wrap the tank threads with Teflon tape and screw in the tank. NOTE: Toss the saddle tee that comes with the expansion tank and install a tee and threaded fitting instead. Saddle tees always leak over time.

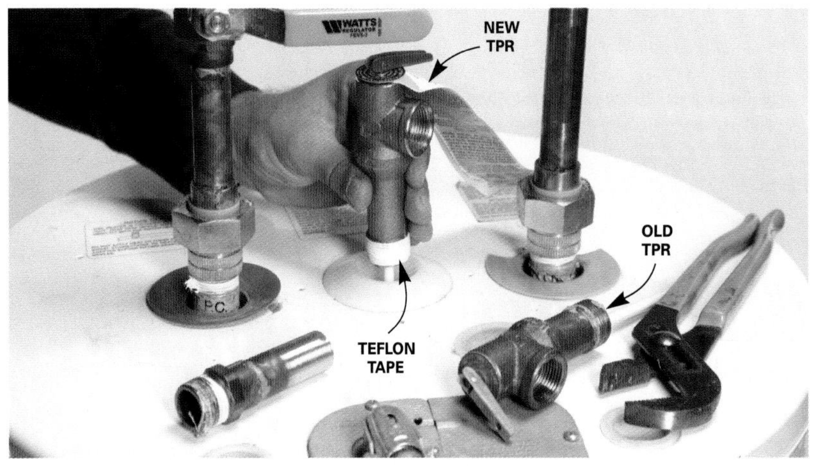

FIRST, REPLACE THE TPR VALVE
Cut the overflow tube on a top-mount TPR with a hacksaw. Then unscrew the threaded fitting from the old TPR valve and install the new valve. Reattach the overflow tube by soldering in a coupler, or use a push-on connector.

GreatGoofs®

Nuts and bolts of washers

When my washing machine suddenly started smoking (the motor, I mean!), I turned it off, pulled the back access panel free and checked the motor. It stank like burned motor windings, but everything else looked fine. Instead of springing for a new washer, I replaced the motor. Everything seemed to be working again, giving me a fine feeling of another DIY conquest. But 10 minutes into the next load, the motor burned out a second time.

At that point, I decided to buy a new machine. After setting aside the old one and wrestling the new unit downstairs and hooking it up, I moved the clothes from the broken washer to the new one. As I pulled out the last pair of blue jeans, I noticed a 3-in. nail that had fallen through a hole in the drum and kept the motor from turning. Now I have two perfectly good washers and one good motor. Oh, well. I'm not the first person to ruin something with an errant nail.

HOW TIGHT IS HAND-TIGHT?

The directions that came with the toilet supply line said to hand-tighten the connectors. Then the connection leaked. So I used pliers to crank it down. It turned almost two full turns. Did I overdo it?

If it were up to us, no manufacturer would be allowed to use cheap plastic compression nuts on supply lines. Your question is one we hear often. In fact, Max Lemberger, one of our field editors, just told us his toilet tale of woe. Hand-tightening caused a leak and pliers-tightening caused the compression nut to crack—days after he installed the supply line. The result was a small flood.

Here's our official advice: Buy a supply line that has a metal nut or a reinforced plastic compression nut. If you can't find one, tighten the regular plastic nut in two stages. First, tighten it enough to stop the water from leaking. Then come back a few hours later (when the rubber gasket has compressed a bit) and snug it up a tad more. Never crank on a plastic nut with pliers.

REINFORCING RIBS

Buy a supply line that has a metal nut or a reinforced plastic nut.

WHOLE LOT OF SHAKIN' GOIN' ON

I've leveled my front-loading washer, but it still vibrates like crazy. I'm thinking about bolting it to the floor.

Whoa! That'll just make more noise. Instead of connecting the washer to the floor, you want to isolate it from the floor. The washer's rubber feet are supposed to do that. Unfortunately, at high spin speeds, they don't do a very good job.

That's where vibration isolation/dampening pads come in. Installers use these heavy-duty rubber pads under furnaces and blowers. One company makes a pad specifically for front-loading washing machines. The puck-shaped pads made by Good Vibrations Inc. (330-606-0978) get good reviews. You can get a set of four for $47 plus shipping from gviinc.net.

Installing the pads is a three-step process, and you'll need a helper for lifting the machine. Start by lifting each corner of the machine and slipping a pad under each foot. Mark each pad location on the floor. Then lift the washer out of the way so you can apply the adhesive discs and mount the pads to the floor as shown.

Clean the floor under the pads. Then stick the adhesive discs to the floor. Apply the primer to the pads and press them onto the discs. Lift the washer back into place, locating the feet in the pad recesses.

Question&Comment

SAVE MONEY ON YOUR WATER BILL

I'm on city water and sewer and my bill keeps climbing. I'm thinking of replacing the water-gulping appliances. Which will pay off the most?

Buying appliances that are more water efficient is one of the last places to start cutting water usage. The No. 1 cause of a rising water/sewer bill is a leak somewhere in the house (10 percent of all homes have a leak of at least 90 gallons per day). And the No. 1 culprit is a running toilet. Toilet parts usually start leaking slowly and get worse over time. So by the time you notice it, months may have passed. When you consider that a leaking toilet can cost you almost $45 per month for water and sewer, it makes sense to fix any leaky toilets in your house before anything else.

Leaking flappers and deteriorated beveled washers are the most common failure points. The parts are cheap (less than $5), so the payback is enormous. Replace them all annually to eliminate a very real water-wasting potential leak.

Even if your toilet isn't leaking, it's probably still wasting water. Consider these water-wasting facts: If your house was built before 1980, the original toilet is wasting $170 every year. If it's newer (1980–1994), it's wasting $99 a year. A new WaterSense–rated toilet costs as little as $100. So that's the fixture to replace first because the payback is huge! Some utilities are even offering rebates to sweeten the deal. Visit epa.gov/watersense/rebate_finder_saving_money_water.html to find rebates in your area.

Next on the fast payback list is a water-saving showerhead. Many older (pre-1992) showerheads had a flow rate of as much as 5.5 gallons per minute. A WaterSense–rated head must use no more than 2.0 gpm. But you can buy super efficient showerheads that provide a vigorous shower using only 1.5 gpm. The Oxygenics 630-XLF15 is one model ($26 from faucetdepot.com). The showerhead sucks in air from around the spray nozzle and uses it to pressurize the shower stream. The water and energy savings make this a one-month payback.

Few know this, but you pay twice for water—once when it enters your house and again when it goes down the sewer. The water meter doesn't know that the water you use for irrigating never goes down the sewer. Ask your water/sewer utility if it has a "deduct" program for

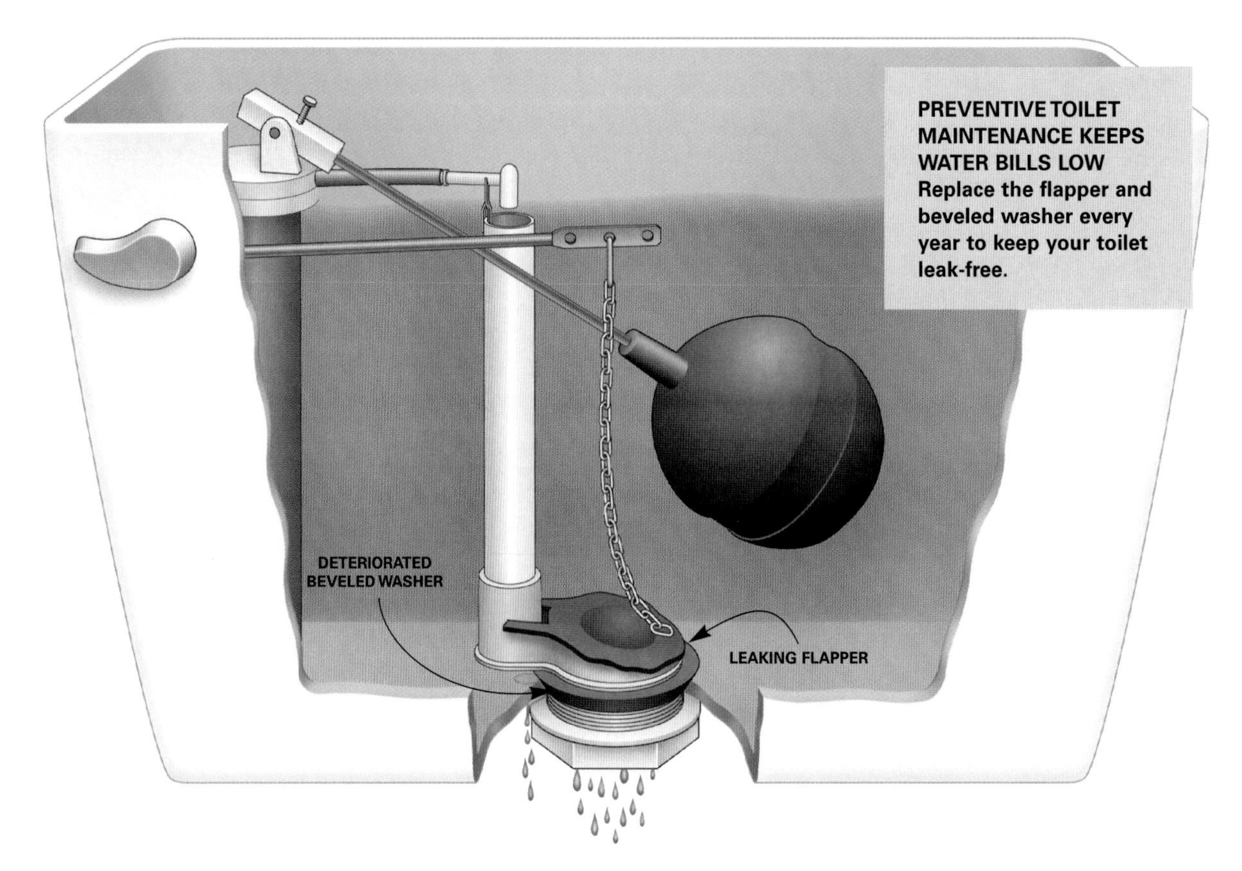

PREVENTIVE TOILET MAINTENANCE KEEPS WATER BILLS LOW
Replace the flapper and beveled washer every year to keep your toilet leak-free.

lawn sprinkling. If so, you can track the amount of water you use for irrigation and deduct that volume from your sewer bill. You'll still have to pay for the water. But since it doesn't go down the drain, it can save you a bundle on the sewer portion of the bill. Of course, you'll have to replumb your hose bibs and water sprinkler system through a separate meter to prove your deduction. But water meters are cheap (the meter shown, far right, the WM75, cost $77 at assuredautomation.com/WM).

I purposely left out new front-loading clothes washers, even though they use half the water of older top-loaders. They're a great choice if you're in the market for a new washer. But don't buy a new efficient washer until you've replaced your toilets and showerheads. The payback on a front-loading washer is a lengthy 5.8 years.

AIR IN

POWERFUL SHOWER STREAM

OXYGENICS

GET A VIGOROUS SHOWER WITH LESS WATER
Twist off your old water-wasting showerhead and spin on a super-efficient 1.5 gpm model. It sucks air into the head to build volume and pressure.

ASSUREDAUTOMATION.COM

SAVE ON THE SEWER BILL
Water meters are a bit of work to install, but they can track the amount of water you use for irrigation to help you save on your sewer bill.

GreatGoofs®

Out-the-window AC

Last fall, we wanted to remove the air conditioner from a second-floor window for the winter. Instead of waiting for my husband to do it, my son and I figured we could handle the job ourselves. We removed the screws and tried to open the window, but it wouldn't budge. So we looked for more screws and pounded on the window sash to make sure it wasn't stuck. No dice.

I told my son to step back as I pried up on the window sash with a big crowbar. The window shot open and the now unfettered AC unit tipped out of the opening, bounced down the entry roof, flew over the gutter, and smashed into several pieces on the ground. I guess I should have waited for my husband's help after all.

HOT ROOM?

Six ways to cool it off!

by **Elisa Bernick**

Do you have a room in your house that swelters all summer long? Most people immediately think of a window air conditioner. That can be a smart solution, but it doesn't work in every case, and it isn't the only option. Check out these six cool alternatives. One of them might be the perfect solution for your hot and sticky problem.

HOT AIR EXITS THROUGH ATTIC VENTS

PAUL PERREAULT (BAKED MEDIA)

A whole-house fan uses one-tenth as much power as AC. It draws cooler outside air in through open doors and windows to create a pleasant breeze that pushes hot air out through attic vents.

1. Cool down with a whole-house fan

Whole-house fans may seem old fashioned, but they're enjoying renewed popularity. The idea behind them is simple. A powerful fan draws cooler early morning and evening air through open doors and windows and forces it up through the attic and out the roof vents. This sends hot air up and out, cooling your house and your attic. These fans are commonly mounted in an upstairs stairwell or hallway ceiling where there's at least 3 ft. of clearance above the fan.

Main advantages

- Energy savings. They use 90 percent less energy than an air conditioner, and in dry climates with cool mornings and evenings, they can actually replace your AC system.
- Easy installation. With a helper and basic tools, you can install a whole-house fan in a weekend.

Main disadvantages

- They can't cool inside temps any lower than outside temps and they can't dehumidify.
- They can make allergies worse. Whole-house fans draw in outdoor pollen and dust.
- Larger fans move air quickly, but they cost more to purchase and install. They also require significant attic ventilation and make more noise than smaller attic fans.

For the best results, match the fan size to your floor plan, cooling needs and available attic ventilation. Call your local utility and check energy-star.gov to see which models qualify for local rebates and any possible federal tax credits. Fans cost $200 to $1,200.

tamtech.com, quietcoolfan.com, airvent.com

R-38–INSULATED SEALED DOORS

REMOTE CONTROL KIT

TAMTECH

Newer attic fans have insulated doors that close in 30 seconds when the fan's not operating.

2. Portable air conditioner lets you chill

Portable air conditioners are similar to window units in operation. They sit on the floor (on casters) and use an adapter kit to vent the hot air through a hose running through a window, a wall or a sliding glass door.

Main advantages

- They are easy to install and use.
- You can move them from room to room.

Main disadvantages

- They're almost twice as expensive and use more energy than a similar-size window unit with the same cooling capacity.
- At this time there are no Energy Star–qualified portable room air conditioners.

Portables range in price from $300 to $1,500 depending on the size, features and efficiency.

friedrich.com, sharpusa.com, sylvane.com

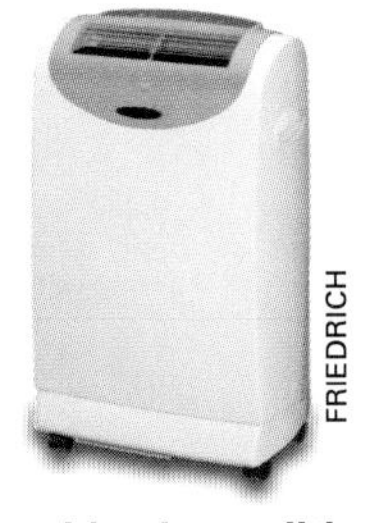

Portable air conditioners are an alternative to a window unit. They're easy to operate and to move from room to room. However, they cost more and use more energy.

3. Mini-split system is cool and quiet

Long popular in Europe and Japan, a mini-split system air conditioner (sometimes called ductless AC), is a hybrid of central air and a window unit. A small condenser sits outside and connects through a conduit to an inside evaporator mounted high on the wall or ceiling.

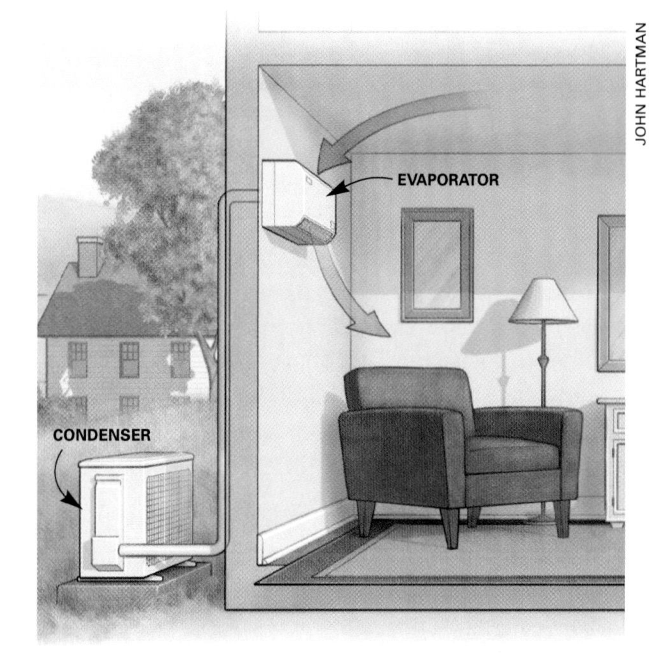

Mini-split AC systems don't require ductwork and can be run to one or more rooms. Their small size, quiet operation and individual zoning let you cool only the room you're using, which can save energy and money.

Main advantages

- Silent operation. The condenser sits outside, it doesn't let in street noise and the indoor fan is whisper quiet.
- The system can be mounted anywhere thanks to the small size of the indoor and outdoor components. The conduit, which houses the power cable, refrigerant tubing, suction tubing and a condensate drain, runs through a 3-in. hole hidden behind the indoor evaporator.
- Zoning flexibility lets you cool rooms individually.

Main disadvantage

- Cost. Professional installation costs $1,500 to $2,500 including parts and labor. You can install it yourself, but it's fairly complicated and you'll most likely void the manufacturer's warranty. Systems with an efficiency rating of 16 or higher may qualify for a federal tax credit.

Sources: mrslim.com, friedrich.com, lge.com

4. In-wall AC unit stays put all year

An in-wall air conditioner is basically the same as a window unit. The primary difference is that it has vents on the back instead of along the sides and it sits flush or extends only slightly farther out from the exterior wall.

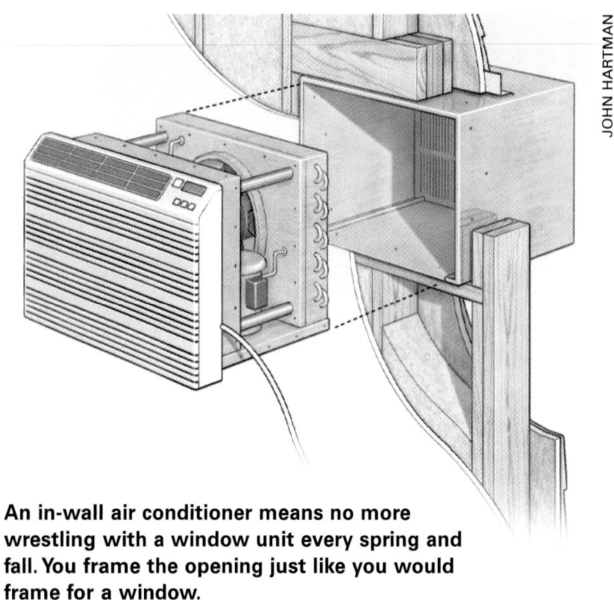

An in-wall air conditioner means no more wrestling with a window unit every spring and fall. You frame the opening just like you would frame for a window.

Main advantages

- Permanent installation means you don't have to lug it in and out twice a year, and it's not an easy entry point for burglars.
- It doesn't block a window.
- The chassis unit sits securely inside a metal sleeve that is installed into the wall. The chassis unit slides out for easy servicing.
- The size of the unit isn't limited to a standard window opening, so it can be bigger and more powerful than a window unit.

Main disadvantages

- Installation is more involved. Cutting a hole in the outside wall of your home may be difficult depending on the exterior sheathing of your home.
- You may need to install a new electrical circuit. Some larger units require 240 volts (although most smaller units can be plugged into a standard 120-volt outlet). Energy Star–qualified models use 25 percent less energy than models made before late 2000. Check with your utility for energy rebates. Some units provide both cooling and heating. Prices range from $400 for cooling a 400- to 700-sq.-ft. room to $700 or so for cooling/heating a 1,000-sq.-ft. space.

friedrich.com, lennox.com, geappliances.com

PLUMBING, HEATING & APPLIANCES

5. Move the cool air with a ventilator fan

If you have a hot room in an otherwise comfortable house, you can pump existing cool air into that hot room using a special fan installed in the wall or floor.

Main advantages

- No extra cooling costs. The Aireshare level-to-level ventilator fan (shown) moves existing cool air from one level (from the basement or a mini-split system, for example) to another level of the house through an adjustable sleeve installed through the floor/ceiling.
- A ventilator fan can blow conditioned air up or down, depending on the position of the blower unit. There are also room-to-room ventilator fans to move the conditioned air.

Main disadvantages

- To install the fan, you'll have to cut a hole through the floor/ceiling and run an electrical line to the unit.
- It's only practical if you have an abundance of existing cool air that's easily accessible to your hot room. Level-to-level ventilator fans (about $190) can also be used to move warm air through the living space during the winter. Search online for "level-to-level fan."

tjernlund.com, aftproducts.com

A ventilator fan can move existing cool air from one level or room to another through the wall or floor.

COOL AIR FROM LOWER LEVEL

JOHN HARTMAN

6. Increase the flow with a duct or a vent booster fan

If you have forced-air cooling but there's still a room that's hotter than all the rest, a duct or vent booster fan can increase the flow of cool air into that room. Two types of booster fans are available.

An in-line duct booster fan fits inside the duct of the room you're trying to cool. You mount the fan near the outlet and it automatically kicks on when your cooling system runs.

TJERNLUND

In-line duct (top) and vent booster fans (below) increase the flow of cool air through ducts and registers.

AIRFLOW TECHNOLOGY

Vent and register booster fans sit directly on top of or replace ceiling, floor or wall registers. Depending on the model, you can set it to operate automatically, control it with a switch or operate it by a remote control.

Main advantages

- Easy to install and use.
- Reasonably priced. In-line duct booster fans are available in both plug-in and hard-wired models and retail for $30 to $150. Vent and register booster units plug into a nearby electrical outlet or can be hard-wired. Register and vent duct booster fans cost $40 to $100.

Main disadvantages

- Less powerful (and cheaper) in-line units have a lighter-gauge housing that is more prone to rattling.
- Duct or vent booster fans may not make a significant cooling difference if your ductwork or overall cooling system is inefficient, sized improperly or faulty.

Search online for "in-line duct booster fan" or "register duct booster fan" to find dealers. (These fans can also be used to increase the flow of warm air through ducts during the winter months.

4 Woodworking & Furniture Projects & Tips

IN THIS CHAPTER

ShopRat

GREATEST SHOP TIP IN HISTORY

Last fall, I was out running the leaf blower and noticed my filthy shop vacuum filter sitting on the slab waiting for a cleaning. That meant hauling the air hose outside and holding the filter at arm's length while I became enveloped in a giant dust cloud. Not this time. It took me about five microseconds to put two and two together. Five more microseconds with the leaf blower and that filter was cleaner than ever. Now the filter—and the dust—are 5 ft. away from my lungs, clothes and hair. Can't call me Pigpen anymore.

LUMBER LIBRARY

OK, you know the drill. You go to the lumber pile and wonder what length the board is, what species of wood it is and then, whether it's worth digging through the pile to get it out. Sometimes it's easier to just go and do the Sunday crossword. Reader Jamie Smith has a simple tip. Label the ends with a permanent marker when you put them in the rack to begin with. Duh, wish I'd thought of it years ago.

HOME CANNING

I had about a quart of leftover stain that I knew would be ruined the next time I wanted to use it. That's because the can rim and lid were so crusty that there was no way it would ever reseal. What to do? My eye rested on all the canning gear my wife uses to can tomatoes and beets in my shop every fall. What could be a more perfect storage vessel than a hermetically sealed glass jar? Plus, it takes up a fraction of the space a gallon can does. I'm going to start using these jars for varnish, paints, everything. Maybe I'll even score a blue ribbon at the county fair.

ELECTROLYSIS—NOT JUST FOR HAIR REMOVAL ANYMORE!

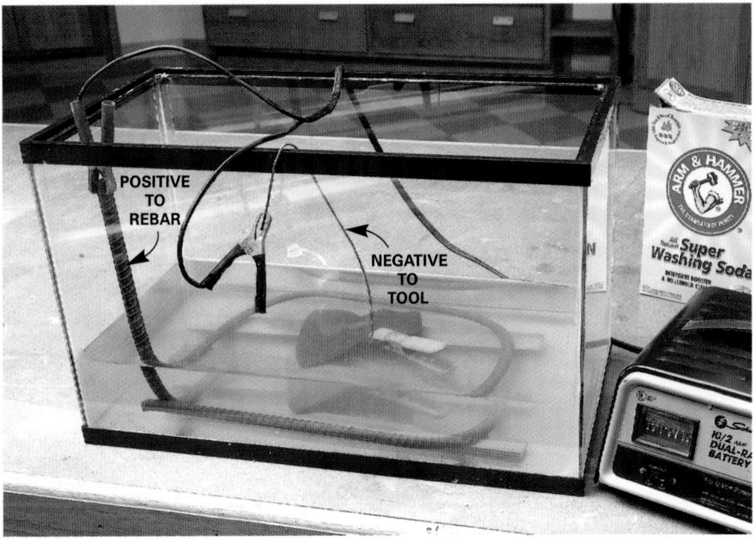

I read about this rust removal technique in *American Woodworker* magazine several years ago and decided to give it a shot. It seems like something you'd see on "MythBusters," but guess what? There's no myth busted here; it really works. I'd like to explain all the neutrinomistic-plasmotical physics involved, but, um...I just don't have the space, so I'll just tell you how to do it.

You'll need a plastic or glass container deep enough to hold enough water to cover your rusty item. And you'll also need a battery charger, a $3 box of washing soda (found with the laundry detergents at just about any big grocery store), a short copper wire and some rebar bent to fit around the object you're restoring. Hook everything up as shown and walk away. Tomorrow morning you'll be amazed to see how rust-free Grandpa's old hatchet is. It gets rid of most of the rust, but you'll still need to polish with sandpaper, steel wool or Scotch pads to get down to bare metal.

When your kid comes home telling you about the science fair project, baby, you are ready! Only you still have to figure out that science-y stuff for the display. And by the way, don't e-mail me for help with that—I'm really busy.

GRANDPA'S HATCHET—BEFORE ELECTROLYSIS

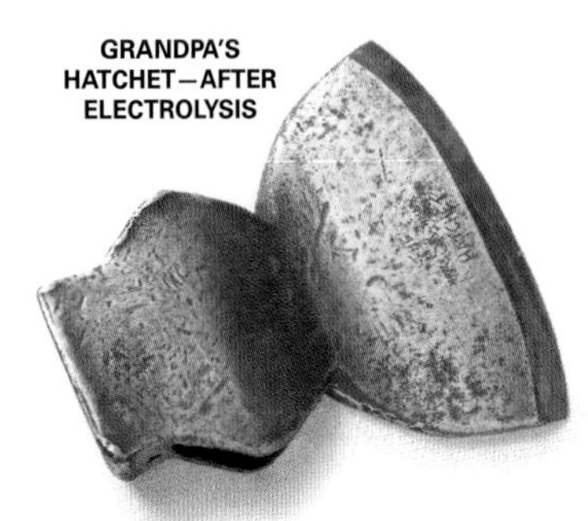

GRANDPA'S HATCHET—AFTER ELECTROLYSIS

READER PHOTO

CLAMP EXTENDERS

My new best buddy, Doug Casper, sent in this gem of a tip. He built some clever plywood clamp extenders to use when his bar clamps are too short to do the job. I think it's brilliant. And it sure beats the old trick of joining two bar clamps in the middle. If you've tried that, you know it never works very well. Plus, this has the advantage of putting more pressure all along the edge of the boards rather than just where the end of the clamp is. Good job, Doug.

*PRE*SAW BEFORE YOU RESAW

The other day, I was "resawing," that is, slicing thicker boards into thinner ones on the band saw. But no matter how careful I tried to be, I couldn't get the blade to stop wandering, rewarding me with two boards of wildly irregular surfaces. Then I remembered this old trick. First send one edge of the board through the table saw, cutting about 1 in. deep. Turn it end for end and cut another kerf on the opposite edge, and then send it through the band saw. The saw kerfs will act as guides to keep the blade in line. Move to the planer for the final smoothing.

SPACE-SAVING DRYING RACK

Have a whole bunch of trim to finish? Lois Mogler sent in this tip, which she and her husband, Rodney, cooked up when they were varnishing miles of trim. The rack is easy to set up and takes up hardly any floor space—and it holds so much that you can finish all your trim at once.

All you do is pound 16d nails about 6 in. apart into 8-ft.-long 2x4s and screw the 2x4s to the wall. No open wall space? Clamp them to your garage door track. Just make sure you unplug the opener! There's your drying rack. Slather on the stain, varnish, paint, whatever—and then rest the pieces on the rack until they're dry.

PETE'S BENCH

Years ago, I worked with a guy named Pete who brought along a cool little bench like this to every trim job. He used it for everything—to stand on, cut on and, of course, to plant his butt on during lunch. After 25 years, I decided to build my own version from 3/4-in. plywood. The bench only takes a couple of hours to cobble together. Give it a whirl; you'll use it more than you think.

Figure A
Pete's bench

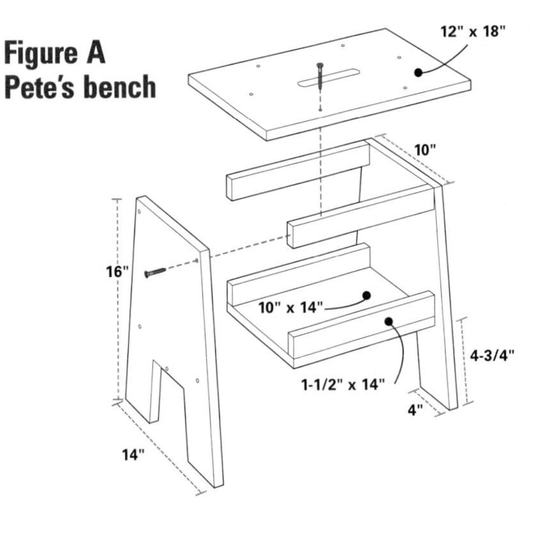

SLED FOR STRIPS

If you've ever ripped thin strips on the table saw, you know it's tough. Leave the guard on, and it blocks the fence from getting close enough to the blade. Leaving off the guard is downright dangerous with that little space between the blade and the fence, where thin strips can get trapped. Then they either get destroyed or are sent right back at you. And push sticks get eaten alive.

The solution is a cutting jig. All you need is a straight, flat 3-ft.-long 2x6. Screw a 10-in.-long 1x3 stop to the end and you're ready to rip. You can make as many identical strips as you need without adjusting the fence. It does gets awkward to use the system for strips longer than 36 in. or so. **CAUTION:** You have to do this without a guard, so be careful!

CHISEL OFF RUNS

Sanding off a drip, run or sag in varnish is a pain. It takes forever and you'll always see evidence of the mistake after the piece is finished. A better fix is to scrape off the drip with a super-sharp wide chisel. Hold the chisel at a low angle and don't try to take it all off at once. Come at it from different angles. With a little practice, you'll be able to remove the drip without damaging the previous coat of finish. When it's gone, lightly sand the area and recoat.

LET'S MEET IN THE MIDDLE

OK, smarty-pants, quick—what's half of 166-13/16 in.? Even if you can do it in your head, I can do it faster with a tape measure. I go to the closest even number, bigger or smaller—in this case, 166 in.—and divide that in half. Even I know the answer is 83 in. Then I measure from both ends 83 in., make two marks and estimate the center of them. The marks will always be less than 1 in. apart. This method is goof-proof as well as fast: If you make a division error, you'll know right away—the marks won't even be close to each other.

IS IT WHITE OAK OR RED?

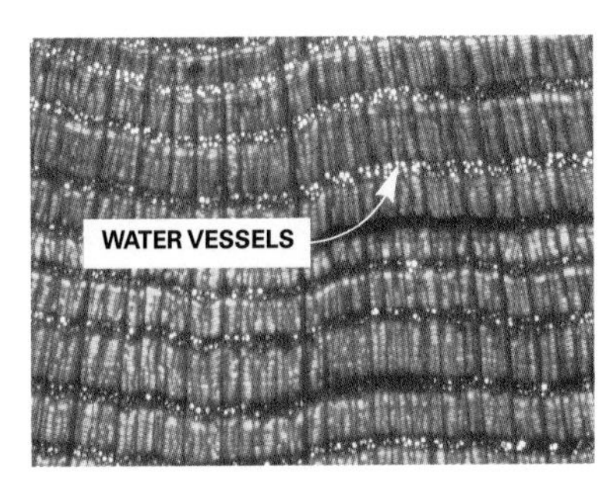

RED OAK

WHITE OAK

White oak and red aren't easy to tell apart, even for serious knot heads. So slice a 1/16-in.-thick piece from the end of the board in question. Hold it up to the light. You'll see dozens of pinholes of light if it's red oak. If it's white oak, no light will shine through. That illustrates why white oak is rot-resistant and well suited for outdoor furniture, while red will rot if you so much as give it a dirty look.

Act like Cliff Clavin at that next party and bore someone with this tidbit: All hardwoods contain long hollow cells called water vessels that conduct water up to the treetop. Red oak's vessels stay hollow like drinking straws, while white oak's vessels get filled with resins during the fall growing season. If you use red oak outside, water will wick its way right up those vessels and start rotting the wood from the inside. But since the channels in white oak are somewhat sealed, it's a fairly rot-resistant wood.

QUICKER HOLE SAWING

If you've ever had to drill holes through joists over your head, you know it's grueling. So I decided to try this tip from Gus Dube. He suggests rubbing wax on hole saws to make them cut faster with less burning. I drilled two holes, one with and one without wax, and timed each method. Then I tried another tip we ran awhile back: drilling 3/4-in. holes just inside the circle to act as ports to let the sawdust escape so it wouldn't clog the teeth and overheat the hole saw. Finally, I drilled holes using both the ports and the wax. Here are the results:

Plain old hole: 55 seconds
With sawdust ports: 23 seconds
With wax: 58 seconds
With sawdust ports and wax: 22 seconds

So, sorry, Gus, the wax just seems to gum things up. The ports are the key. And yeah, I know, it takes time to drill ports. But that's time you won't spend muscling a hole saw through a joist over your head. Score the hole first so you can place the ports right at the perimeter.

DUST-FREE DUST PORTS

My planer has its own blower on it, and even with the dust collector in use, it blows sawdust through the small opening behind the blast gate. That little pile always drove me nuts. So I squeezed a thin bead of caulk over the slit behind the gate. Problem solved. But then I cast an eye on all those blast gate slits, which all bled off valuable suction, and caulked them, too. Sealing the slits won't make a huge difference, but it only takes a few minutes, and the tighter your system is, the better the suction. Just don't fill the slit too deep or you'll glue the gate shut.

ShopRat

CREATE THICK STOCK

Some projects built from MDF—shelving, desktops, sometimes even trim—look more substantial when you use thicker material. Since it's harder to find thick MDF, reader Tim Burnside just glues 1/2- or 3/4-in. layers together. Here are his three keys to building up layers of MDF:

1. Rough-cut the slabs about an inch larger than their final size. That way, you don't have to worry about aligning the edges during glue-up. Trim the perimeter later to create flush edges.
2. Spread on a full-coverage, even coat of wood glue. Spots that remain dry can open up slightly years later and show up as cracks in the edges. Tim's favorite glue spreader is a small disposable paint roller ($2).
3. Apply a lot of pressure to close all the gaps. Inexpensive spring clamps (lots of them!) are a quick way to squeeze the edges. For areas beyond the reach of clamps, apply weight. Buckets of water work well, as long as you don't spill!

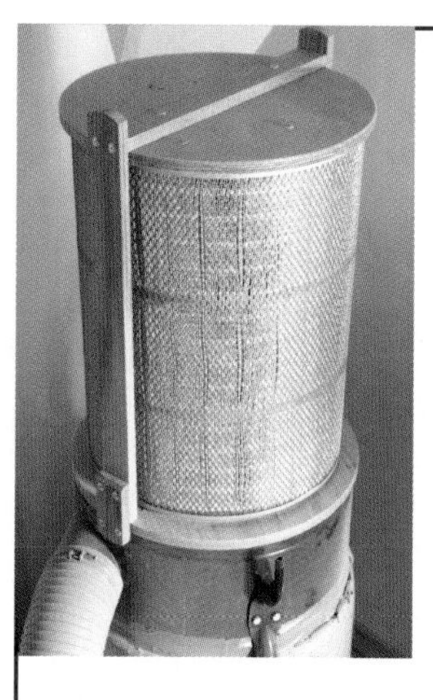

BETTER SHOP DUST FILTRATION

Pleated filters are a much better alternative to the giant dust bags sported by most dust collectors. They filter out the tiny dust particles missed by most bags and take up less room. And they're easier to clean. You can simply hose down the outside of the filter with compressed air—no removal necessary.

You can buy new dust collectors with filters, and some manufacturers offer filter systems to replace bags on older models. Check out oneida-air.com and pennstateind.com.

Dick Wynn of Wynn Environmental sent me this pleated industrial-grade filter to try out. Cheapskate that I am, I made this freebie fit my old collector by cobbling together this adapter to fit the old collar. Chances are, you won't have to rig up a filter like I did—Dick says he has one to fit nearly any collector. He also says the filters only take about 15 minutes to install. Check them out at wynnenv.com. The filters range in price from $106 to $165.

HomeCare & Repair

TIPS, FIXES & GEAR FOR A TROUBLE-FREE HOME

Cures for sticking wooden drawers

Drawers that don't slide smoothly can be a real nuisance. But there's no reason to put up with them since the fix is usually pretty simple. Here are two tips for getting your drawers sliding as smooth as butter.

Rub paraffin on the meeting parts of drawers to keep them working smoothly. You'll find paraffin with the canning supplies in your local grocery store. In a pinch you can also use candles, bar soap or even dry spray lubricant.

For a more permanent fix, apply nylon tape to the parts that come in contact with each other. You'll find self-adhesive nylon tape ($7.60 for a 1/2-in. x 10-ft. piece) at woodworking stores. One source is Rockler Woodworking and Hardware (rockler.com; 800-279-4441). The tape won't stick to wax or dirt, so prep the surface first by lightly sanding it with 100-grit sandpaper and then vacuuming to remove the dust. Then simply cut the tape to length with a scissors, peel off the back and stick it onto the wooden drawer runner.

SUSPENDED **SHELF**

Steel cable and shaft collars add style & strength

by **Jeff Gorton**

This wall-hung bookshelf is one of the easiest we've ever built. If you can stack blocks, you can build it. And installing the cable doesn't require any more skill than drilling a hole. Things will go a lot quicker if you own a table saw, a miter saw and a pneumatic nailer, but you could easily build this project with just basic hand tools and a circular saw. We used a router to bevel the shelf edges, but this is optional.

If you're dead-set on finishing this project in a weekend, here's how. Skip the Friday night movie and cut out the parts and get one coat of finish on. Then get up early on Saturday and apply another coat or two of finish and you'll be ready to assemble and install the shelves on Sunday. We spent a little under $200 for the materials, including the oak boards, cables and other hardware.

It's stronger than it looks

Your first question when you see this bookcase might be "Is it strong enough?" And the answer is a resounding yes. It's extra strong, in fact. The back edges of the shelves are securely supported with screws and blocks, and the front edges are hung from aircraft-strength cable. We even epoxied the top of the cable to the standards just to make sure. Each shelf is held up by shaft collars that are tightened onto the cables with setscrews. So don't worry about the strength. These shelves could hold your dumbbell collection!

SHOPPING LIST

ITEM	QTY.
1x10 x 5' board	2
1x8 x 5' board	2
1x6 x 5' board	1
1x2 x 6' board	4
1-1/4" wood screws	10
3" wood screws	10
No. 10 finish washers	10
3/8" steel washers	2
3/4" wood screws	2
Five-minute epoxy	1
No. 10-32 cap nuts	2
Cable and collars are available from McMaster-Carr (404-629-6500; mcmaster.com). Enter the product numbers into the search box to find the items listed. You may also be able to find cable at home centers or hardware stores. The cable costs 62¢ per ft., and the collars are 89¢ each.	
5/32" bore shaft collars (6432K73)	22
1/8" 6x7 fiber-core cable (3449T16)	14

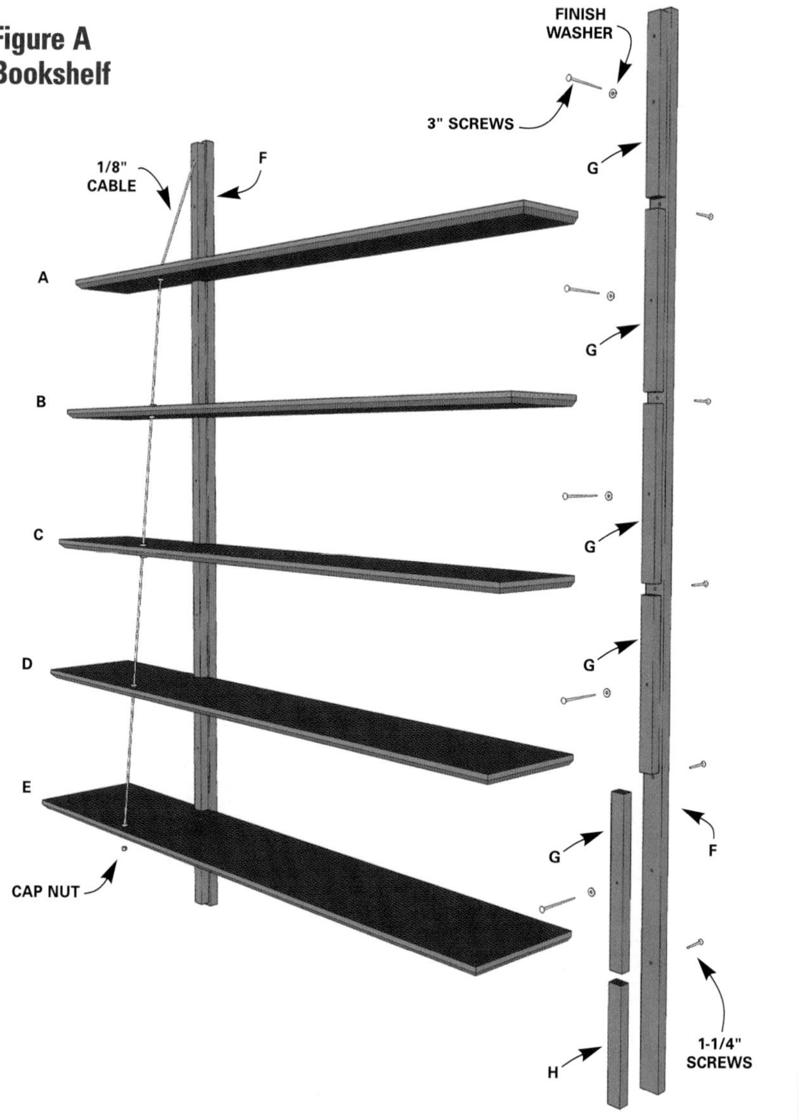

Figure A
Bookshelf

CUTTING LIST

KEY	PCS.	SIZE & DESCRIPTION
A	1	3/4" x 5-1/4" x 59-1/2" shelf
B	1	3/4" x 6-1/4" x 59-1/2" shelf
C	1	3/4" x 7-1/4" x 59-1/2" shelf
D	1	3/4" x 8-1/4" x 59-1/2" shelf
E	1	3/4" x 9-1/4" x 59-1/2" shelf
F	2	3/4" x 1-1/2" x 68-1/4" standards
G	10	3/4" x 1" x 11-1/4" cleats
H	2	3/4" x 1" x 7-3/4" cleats

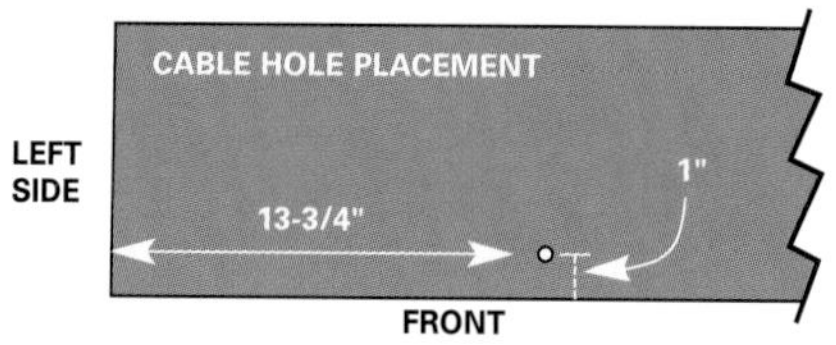

Figure B
Shelf detail

Cut the parts

Start by ripping the shelves to the widths given in the Cutting List (above). We used a full-width 1x10 for the bottom shelf and successively narrower boards as we went up. Making all the shelves the same width would be OK, too. While you're at it, rip two 1-in.-wide strips from the 1x2s for the support cleats. Next, cut the boards to length. We used a 45-degree chamfer bit and router to bevel the ends and front edges of the shelves, but you could leave them square if you'd like. After the parts are cut and prefinished, you're ready to assemble the shelf.

Assemble the shelves

The shelves are too big to build on a normal workbench. If you're young and nimble, you could put them together on the floor. Otherwise, save your back and line up a few old doors on a pair of sawhorses.

Assembly is straightforward; follow **Photos 1 – 6** and the details shown in **Figures A and B**. Here are a few tips to help:

- Mark the back of the shelves 13 in. from the ends so you'll know where to line them up with the standards (**Photo 2**).

1 Drill an angled hole for the cable. Start by drilling straight down about 1/8 in. Then tilt the drill to about a 45-degree angle and use the starter hole to keep the bit in place as you start to drill. The angle of the hole isn't critical.

2 Nail the shelves to the cleats. Drive a brad through the shelf into the support cleat. These brads just hold the shelves in place when you flip the bookshelf over to drive in the shelf screws (Photo 5) and secure the cable (Photo 6).

3 Assemble the shelves. Add a cleat under the shelf and nail it in. Then add another shelf and tack it to the cleat. Continue like this until you get to the bottom. Now do the same thing on the other side.

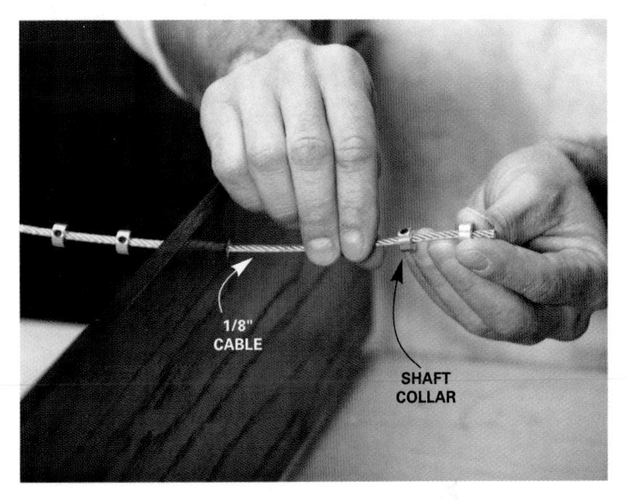

4 Thread the cable. Start at the bottom shelf and run the cable through the collars and shelves. Add two collars between each pair of shelves. At the top, thread the cable through the angled hole.

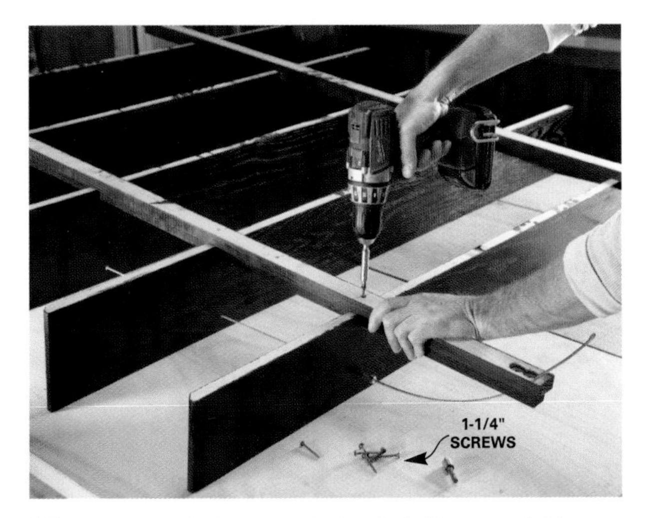

5 Fasten the shelves. Flip the bookshelf over and drive screws into the back of each shelf through the holes in the standards.

- Keep the shelves and standards at a right angle to each other as you attach the cleats. That'll ensure that the cleats fit tight to the shelves.
- Don't drive nails where you'll be drilling holes.
- Drill mounting screw holes after you have all the cleats installed. It's easier to do it before you mount the shelves on the wall.

String the cable

The cable is flexible and easy to cut, so it's a breeze to install. Just remember to put two collars on the cable, between each pair of shelves, as you thread the cable through the holes. Leave about 4 in. of cable sticking out the top and an extra foot or so on the bottom. The extra cable on the bottom lets you use our "cable pedal" method for removing slack (Photo 8). After stringing the cable, flip

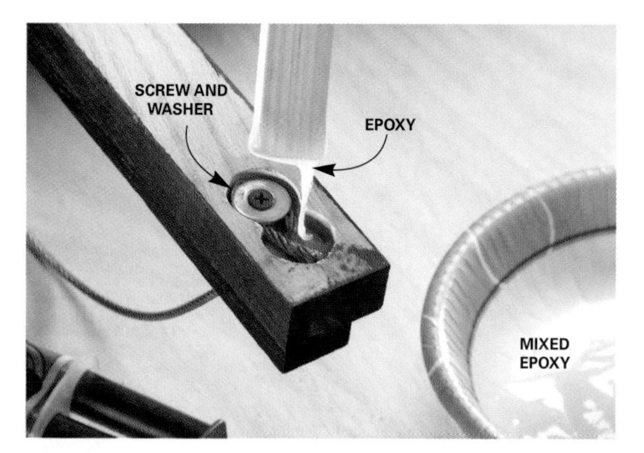

6 **Anchor the cable with epoxy.** Loop the cable in the recess and hold it down with a washer and screw. Then mix five-minute epoxy and fill the recess with it.

7 **Mount the bookshelf.** Locate two studs that are 32 in. apart with a stud finder. Screw the standards to the studs, making sure the shelves are level and the standards are plumb.

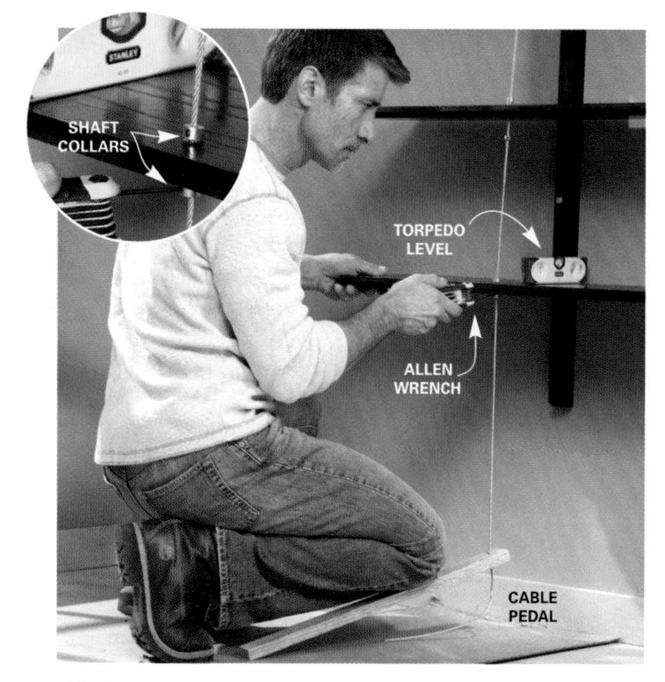

8 **Tension the cables.** Tighten the cable using a scrap of wood with a hole in it to put tension on the cable while you tighten the setscrew on the collar below the lowest shelf. Then snug the remaining collars to the top and bottom of the shelves and tighten the collars.

9 **Trim and cap the cable.** Use side-cutting pliers or lineman's pliers to cut the cable. Leave 1/4 in. protruding. Cover the end of the cable with a cap nut. Use hot-melt glue or silicone caulk to hold the cap nut in place.

the whole works over so you can drive the shelf screws (Photo 5) and anchor the top of the cable (Photo 6). Take a coffee break while the epoxy sets up.

Mount the shelves

The shelf standards are spaced 32 in. on center to align with studs. So all you have to do is locate two studs where you want the shelves to go and mark them with masking tape. Setting the shelves on blocks (Photo 7) is a handy way to hold them up while you drive the first few screws. Start by driving one of the top screws. Before you drive the top screw in the second standard, check to make sure the shelves are level. After the two top screws are in place, make sure the standards are plumb before you drive the remaining screws. We used No. 10 finish washers under the screws for a decorative effect.

Tighten the cable

At this point, the cable is slack and the collars are still loose. Your goal is to take the slack out of the cable and then adjust each shelf so it's level from front to back while you tighten the collars (Photo 8). Use an Allen wrench to tighten the setscrews. Remember, you don't need too much tension on the cable, just enough to remove the slack. Finish up by cutting the cable and covering the end with a cap nut (Photo 9).

SHORTCUTS TO BETTER BUILT-INS

Top-notch doesn't have to mean slow and difficult

by **Gary Wentz**

Sometimes you can speed up, simplify and still build a masterpiece. In the following pages, a veteran cabinetmaker spills some of his best secrets for cutting labor and hassles without sacrificing quality.

Set cabinets on a platform

Most lower cabinets include a base or toe-kick that raises them off the floor. But Ken doesn't build them that way. Instead, he builds a plywood platform that acts as the base for an entire row of cabinets. The platform can be undersized to allow for a toe space or full size for a more traditional look (shown here).

This approach has a couple of major advantages. First, cabinet construction is simpler. The cabinets are just boxes; no extended sides to form a base, no toe-kick cutouts. Second, installation is faster. Leveling one platform is a lot easier than positioning each cabinet individually. Ken sets the box 1/4 in. from walls to allow for wavy or out-of-plumb walls.

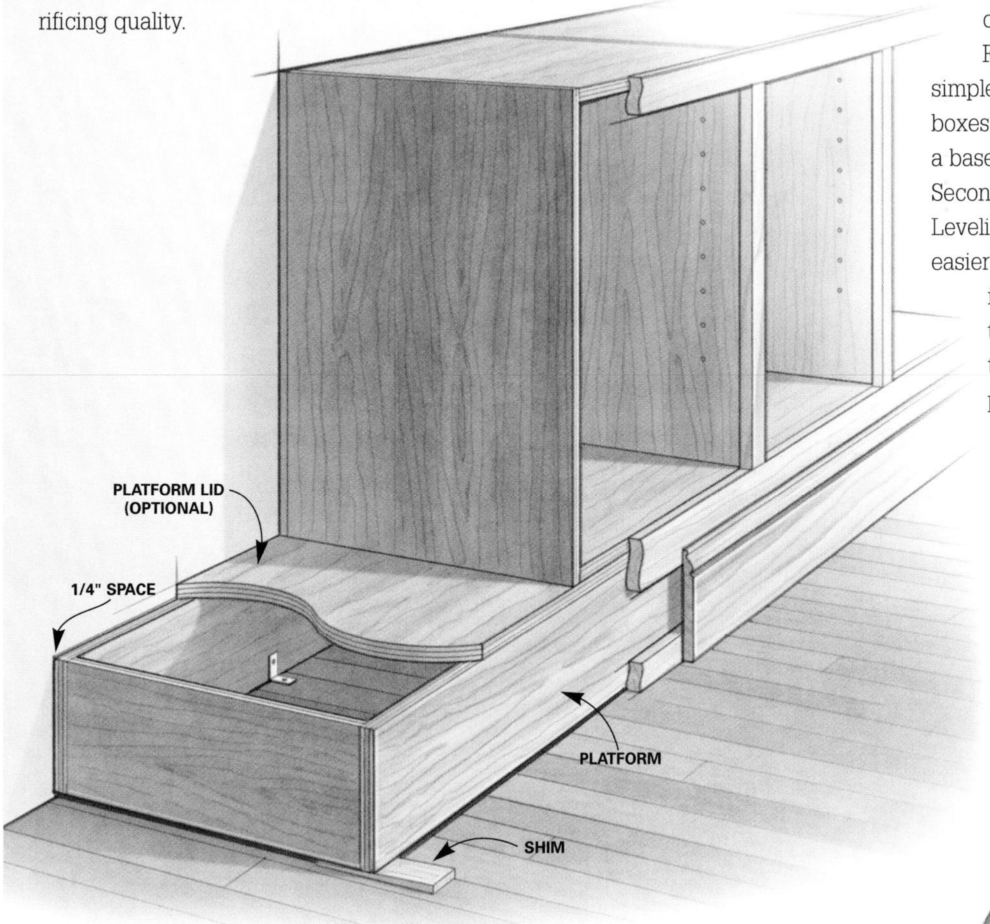

PLATFORM LID (OPTIONAL)

1/4" SPACE

PLATFORM

SHIM

Ken Geisen has been a cabinetmaker in North Branch, MN, for 20 years. And he has a fat brag book full of built-in furniture projects; mostly cabinetry, shelving and entertainment centers. Not just a master woodworker, he often draws on his art background to design his projects. To see some of his work, go to woodwrightworkshop.com.

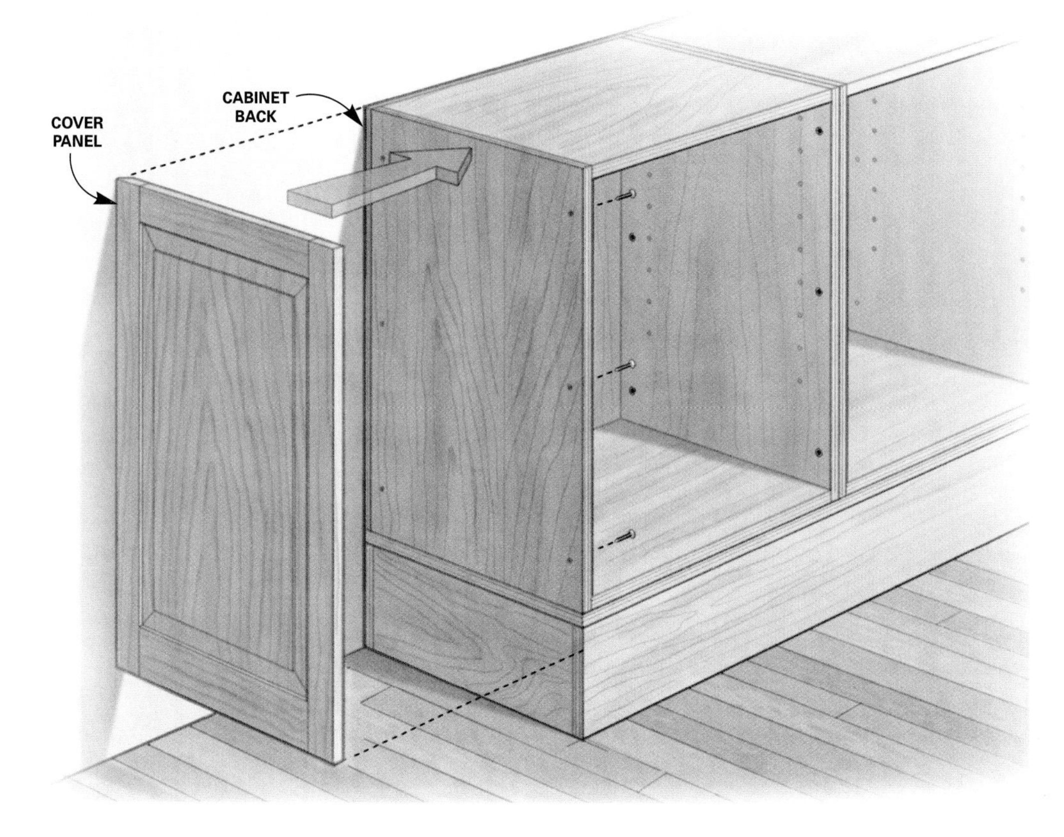

Quick, classic side panels

When the side of a cabinet box will be exposed, you have to hide the cabinet back's edge somehow. The usual method is to rabbet the side and recess the back. But Ken gets a richer look with less hassle. He simply glues and nails the back to the cabinet box and hides the exposed plywood with a frame and panel for a classic look. And since the cover panel is a separate part, it's easy to scribe it to the wall before fastening it to the cabinet.

Back-bevel wall stiles

Before scribing stiles that will meet walls, bevel the back edge on your table saw. That way, you'll have less wood to belt-sand off when you shape the edge to the contour of the wall. Ken cuts a 45-degree bevel about 1/2 in. deep, so he has only 1/4 in. of wood remaining. For more scribing tips, go to familyhandyman.com and search for "scribe."

Thicker backs save time

Most cabinetmakers use 1/4-in. plywood for cabinet backs. But Ken prefers 1/2-in. material. The thicker plywood usually adds less than $5 to the cost of each box and eliminates the need for a hanging strip or "nailer" at the back of the cabinet. That means quicker construction and a cleaner interior look. Best of all, it allows you to drive a screw through the back anywhere, not just at the nailer.

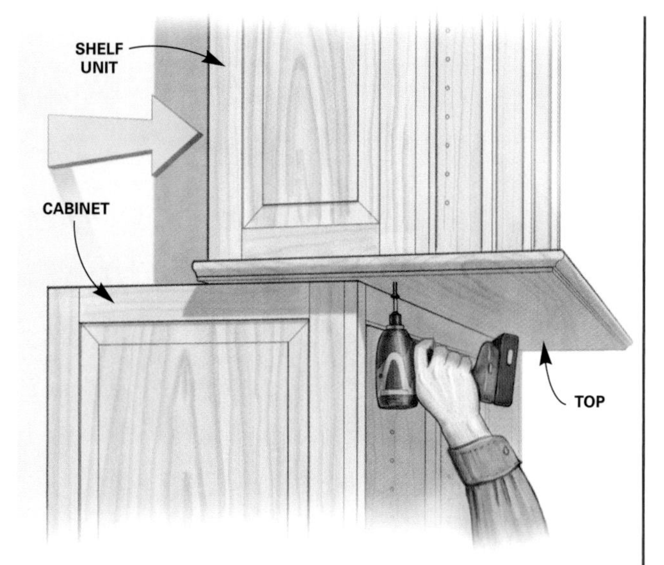

Secret screws for shelves

Lots of designs have upper shelf units that rest on lower cabinets. Here's Ken's trick for fastening the shelf units to the cabinet top so that the screws are hidden: He sets the cabinet top on the lower cabinets and scribes it and sands it to fit the wall. But he doesn't screw it in place yet. Instead, he positions the shelf units on the top and carefully slides the top forward just far enough so that he can drive screws into the shelf sides and dividers. After sliding the top back into place, he screws the top to the cabinets from below and screws the shelf units to the wall.

Use prefinished plywood (sometimes)

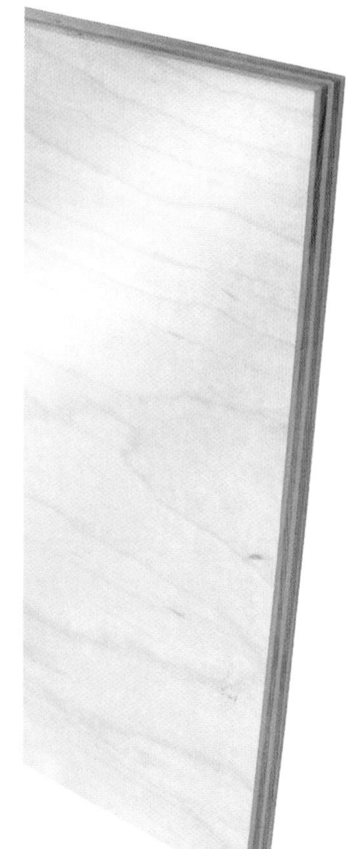

With its tough, flawless clearcoat, prefinished plywood eliminates finishing hassles. But Ken uses it only for "no-show" parts like cabinet boxes and shelves. Finishing other parts to match the color and sheen of the factory-finished plywood is just too difficult.

Finding prefinished plywood can be difficult. Your best bet is a lumberyard that caters to cabinetmakers (search online for "cabinet making supplies" followed by the name of your city). Expect to pay about $40 to $120 per 4 x 8-ft. sheet, depending on the thickness, grade and species.

Break down face frames

Pocket screws are a standard joinery method, but Ken has a nonstandard approach. He assembles face frames with pocket screws, but without glue. He sands the frames, labels the back of each part and then disassembles them for easier finishing. Transport is easier too: Ken can pack a mile of face frame parts into his van and carry them into the house without banging up walls. The cabinet boxes need less TLC too, since they're frameless during transport. Once on-site, Ken reassembles the frames with pocket screws and glue. For pocket joinery, Ken uses a Kreg Jig (kregtool.com).

SATURDAY MORNING **SHELF**

Build it before lunch— spray on the finish after dinner

by **Jeff Gorton**

Sure, you can buy a shelf similar to this one for about $30 at a discount store, but you won't be able to choose the size or finish. We designed ours with a wider top to hold vases and other collectibles, but you can make yours bigger or smaller. Plus, you can finish it to match your room. The shelf is versatile and goes together fast—it would make a great gift. Made from cherry, our shelf cost $64. It would cost about half that in oak or pine.

Tips for building the shelf

- You'll need a miter saw and a table saw for this project. A finish nailer isn't necessary but is very helpful.
- If you don't have a finish nailer, drill pilot holes for the finish nails to avoid splitting the wood.
- You can use scraps of less expensive lumber for the base (E) and cleats since these aren't visible.
- Glue the parts together. Because you can use fewer nails, you'll have fewer nail holes to fill.

We finished this cherry shelf with a coat of Varathane American Walnut stain (test the color on a scrap) and three coats of spray satin lacquer. Photo 5 shows how to mount the cleat that supports the shelf. Then you just drop the shelf over the cleat to hang it on the wall.

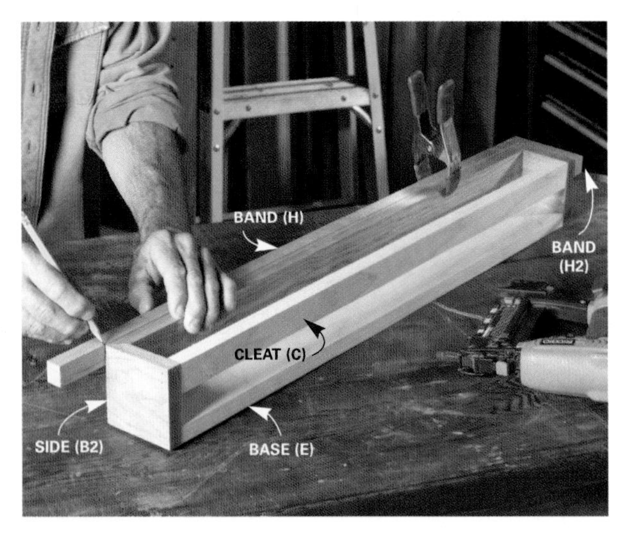

1 Mark trim parts in place. Cut the 1-in. band and the cove moldings extra long. Fit the miter on one end, then mark the opposite end for cutting.

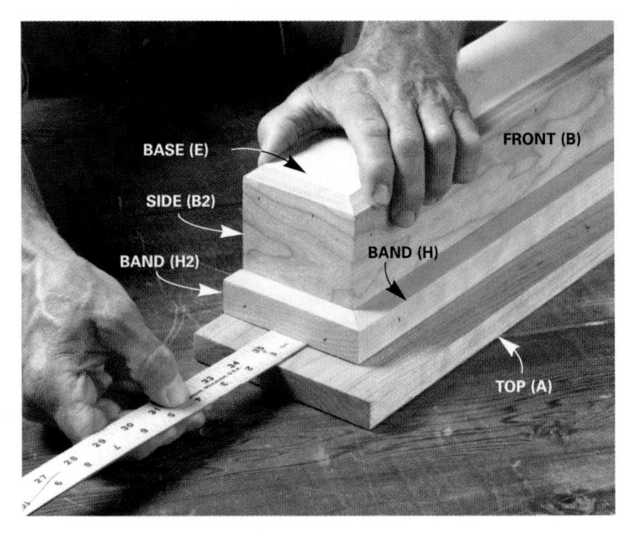

2 Center the top. Measure the overhang on each end and adjust the top until it's centered.

SHOPPING LIST

ITEM	QTY.
3/4" x 5-1/2" x 8' finish-quality board	1
3/4" x 2-1/2" x 3' finish-quality board	1
1/4" x 30" x 2-1/2" plywood	1
3/4" x 5-1/2" x 3' softwood board	1
3/4" x 3/4" x 8' cove molding	1
Finish nails	

CUTTING LIST

The Cutting List gives finished lengths for the top, front, sides, cleats and bottom. You can cut these to the exact width and length listed and nail them together. The lengths listed for the 3/4-in. x 1-in. bands and the 3/4-in. cove moldings are oversized. You'll mark these pieces in place for an exact fit (Photo 1).

KEY	PCS.	SIZE & DESCRIPTION
A	1	3/4" x 5-1/2" x 36" (top)
B	1	3/4" x 3-1/2" x 32" (front); miter both ends at 45°
B2	2	3/4" x 3-1/2" x 3-1/2" (sides); miter one side
C	1	3/4" x 1-1/4" x 30-1/2" (cleat); 30-degree bevel
D	1	3/4" x 1-1/4" x 30" (cleat); 30-degree bevel
E	1	3/4" x 2-3/4" x 30-1/2" (base)
F	1	1/4" x 2-1/2" x 30" (plywood spacer)
G	1	3/4" x 2-1/2" x 30" (bottom)
H	1	3/4" x 1" x 36" (band); miter both ends to fit
H2	2	3/4" x 1" x 6" (bands); miter both ends to fit
J	1	3/4" x 3/4" x 36" (cove); miter both ends to fit
J2	2	3/4" x 3/4" x 6" (coves); miter both ends to fit
K	1	3/4" x 3/4" x 36" (cove); miter both ends to fit
K2	2	3/4" x 3/4" x 6" (coves); miter both ends to fit

Figure A

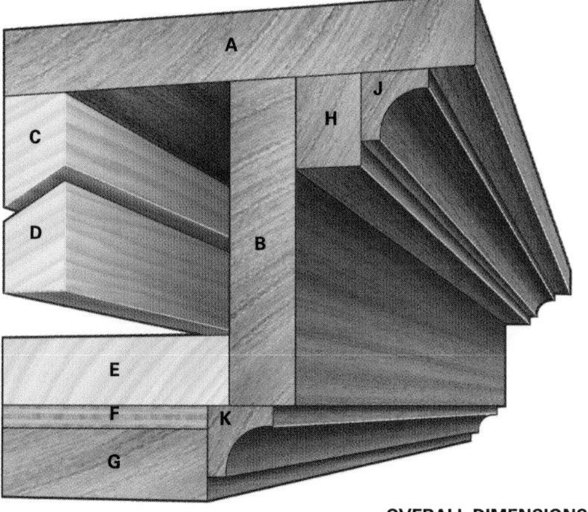

OVERALL DIMENSIONS: 36" x 5-1/2" x 5-1/4"

3 **Nail on the top. Glue the band and nail through it into the top.**

4 **Install the cove moldings. Add the 1/4-in. spacer and bottom board. Then finish up by fitting and nailing the cove molding.**

5 **Mount the cleat. Level the cleat and screw it to the wall. You can locate studs or use drywall anchors.**

WOODWORKING & FURNITURE PROJECTS & TIPS

BIG BOOKCASE... SMALL SHOP

Modular construction makes it easy

by **Gary Wentz**

Before you say to yourself, "I couldn't build that," glance through the following pages. You'll see that this bookcase is an assembly of plywood boxes and square frames dressed up with simple trim. The joinery involves nothing more than screws, glue and biscuits, and there's not a single miter cut in the whole project.

Don't get the wrong idea, though. Fast, easy construction doesn't mean poor quality. This bookcase is sturdy enough to last for generations.

The materials for our cherry bookcase cost about $800. In oak or birch, it would cost about $500. Most home centers carry oak and birch plywood only, so if you want a different species, you have to shop at a lumberyard that caters to pros.

Think of it as 5 small projects—with 5 big advantages

Bookcases like this one are usually built as two big sections: a cabinet unit and a shelf unit. But breaking it into smaller units has huge benefits, during and after construction:

It's perfect for small shops.

Built in small sections, this bookcase doesn't require a big space, a big workbench or big clamps.

Smaller parts mean smaller mistakes.

There are no face frames or other big, complicated assemblies. So you're unlikely to make a mistake that would cost you lots of wasted wood or a whole day of rebuilding.

Quick disassembly makes finishing easier.

By removing some screws, you can separate the five units. By removing more screws, you can break each unit into even smaller, easier-to-finish parts.

Moving it is easy.

When fully dismantled, the bookcase can be easily carried by one person and then reassembled in place.

You can make it half as big—or twice as big.

Our two-section design (two cabinets, two drawers, two shelves) is easy to alter. You'll have to alter the lengths of a few parts, but most will remain the same. Our bookcase is 67-3/4 in. wide x 17-1/2 in. deep x 82-1/4 in. tall.

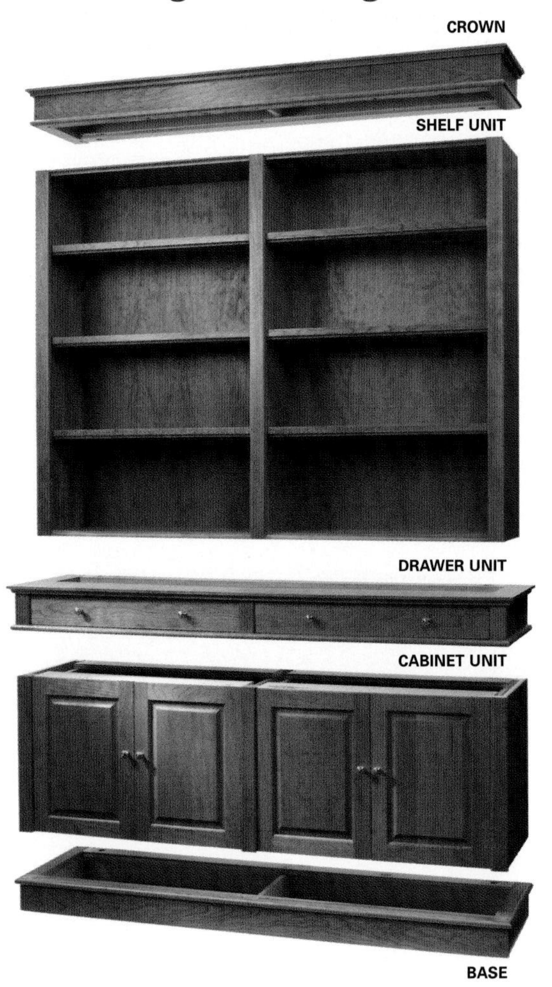

The base

The base is the simplest unit: Just build a plywood box, cover three sides with solid wood boards and then top it off with a round-edged frame. The base frame is identical to the drawer frame (see p. 123), and the crown frame (p. 125) is a smaller version of the two. So you'll save some time by building all three at once.

- Choose a board with an attractive grain pattern for the base face; it's one of the most prominent parts.
- Before you glue the face and sides to the plywood box, position them by driving a few 1-1/4-in. screws from inside the box. Then remove the screws, add glue and screw the parts into place again. Unlike clamps, screws won't allow the parts to slide out of alignment on the slippery glue.
- Center the biscuits 1 in. from the inside of the frame parts (see Photo 1). That keeps the biscuit slots a safe distance from the outer edges (though they'll show slightly inside the frame).
- Round three sides of the frame using a 3/8-in. round-over bit. Rout the left side first, using two blocks to prevent gouging and splintering (Photo 3). Then round the front. Clamp on a block to prevent gouging as you finish up on the right side. Flip the frame over and repeat the process.
- When you screw the frame to the plywood box, drive screws only near the ends and center of the front rail; other screws would be exposed when you open the cabinet doors.

1 **Mark up the frame parts. Position the biscuit center lines fast using a 1-in. block. Avoid "glue-up screwup" later by numbering the joints.**

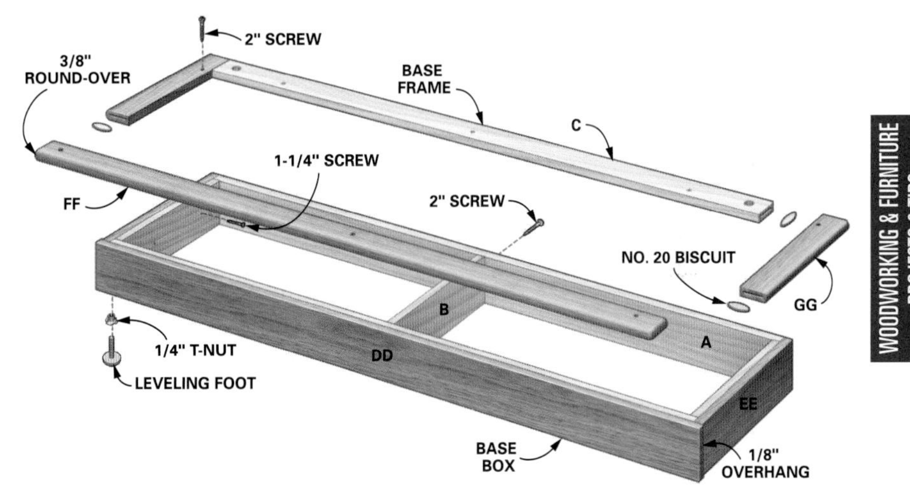

Figure A
Base box and frame

2 **No need for long clamps. A 1-in. hole in the back rail lets you clamp on the side rails without 6-ft.-long clamps. Attach both sides and let the glue set for at least 20 minutes before you add the front rail.**

3 **Don't ruin the frame when routing it. A starting block prevents gouging at the back edge of the side rail. A breakout block prevents end-grain splintering on the front rail.**

The cabinet unit

To build the cabinet unit, start with two plywood boxes. Before you add the side panels and center stile, hang the doors (see p. 126). Then remove the doors and set them aside until the whole project is done.

- Assemble the boxes with screws only. Glue is unnecessary for strength and will leave squeeze-out stains that may show up when you apply your finish.
- Make sure the cabinet boxes are perfectly square by taking diagonal measurements before you attach the backs. Out-of-square boxes will cause headaches when you assemble the cabinet unit and fit the doors.
- The stiles for the cabinet unit are identical to the stiles for the drawer and shelf units. So cut and rout them all at the same time. Three 6-ft. pieces will provide just enough material (but with no room for mistakes!).
- To make spacers, gather 3/4-in. plywood scraps and glue them together. Then cut them to width (1-1/8 in. and 2 in.) on your table saw.
- To build the side panels, glue on the spacers first, then add the stiles (Photo 4). Align the stiles flush with the spacers and let them overhang the panels.
- Before assembly, we covered the plywood edges of the cabinet boxes and shelves with iron-on edge banding.

Mail-order the doors

Building raised-panel doors for this bookcase would take more time and know-how than the rest of the project combined. Plus, you would need a router table and a $150 set of router bits. But for about $200, you can order custom doors.

To find a supplier and browse a variety of styles, search online for "cabinet doors." Our raised-panel cherry doors cost about $50 each (plus delivery). Oak doors would have cost about $43 each. Our doors are from distinctivedoordesigns.com (763-389-1631).

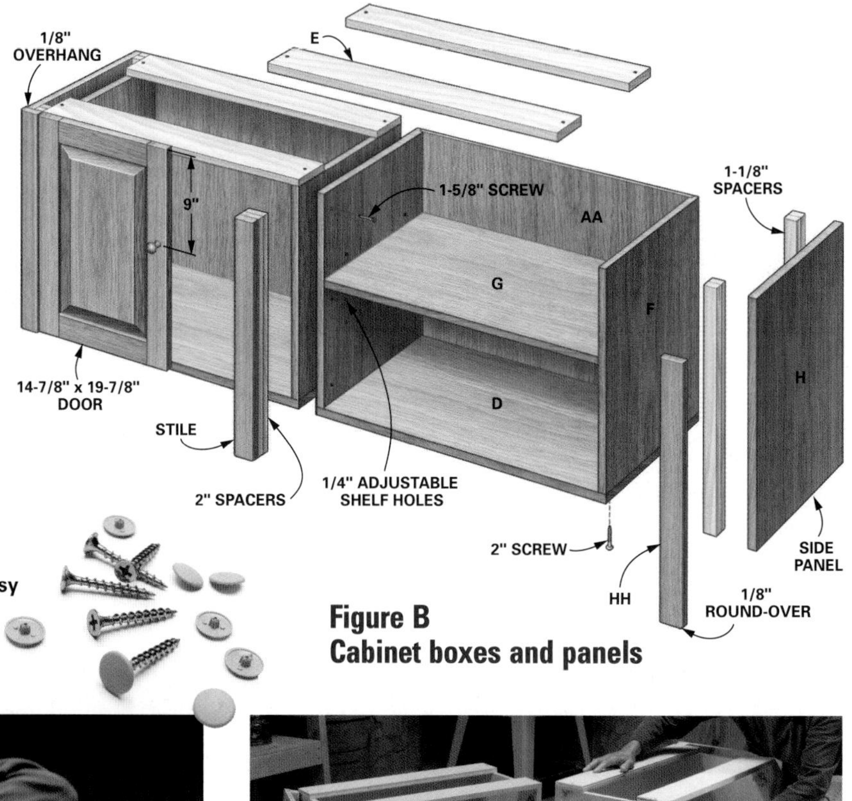

Figure B
Cabinet boxes and panels

Plastic screw caps are a quick, easy cover-up for the screw heads inside the cabinet box. See the Shopping List, p. 126.

4 Stop glue stains with masking tape. **Tape the side panels before you clamp the stiles to the spacers. If you use spring clamps, keep an eye on the stile alignment; spring clamps can let parts slide on the slippery glue.**

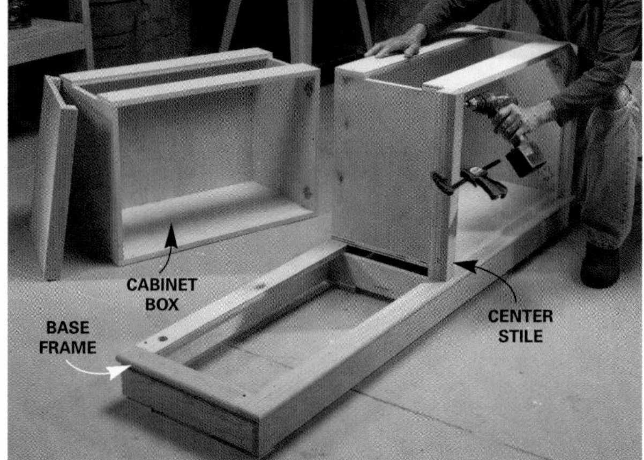

5 Screw it all together. **Fasten the side panels and center stile by driving screws through the cabinet boxes. Then center the whole cabinet unit and screw the boxes to the base frame.**

The drawer unit

To build the drawer unit, start with the drawer boxes and cradles. Add the side panels and center stile just as you did on the cabinet unit. Then sandwich them all between a frame and the drawer top. For a more substantial look, we used 1-in.-thick boards for the drawer top (and for the crown top later). You won't find 1-in.-thick boards at most home centers, so check with a local lumberyard. You can substitute 3/4-in.-thick material without changing the construction of other parts.

- Drawers take a lot of abuse, so assemble the drawer boxes with screws and glue. Trim screws are best. They're skinny enough for the 1/2-in.-thick sides, and their small heads are easy to cover with wood filler.
- Note that the side panel spacers aren't exactly like those on the cabinet unit; they include a top spacer that allows you to drive screws into the drawer top (see Photo 7).
- Instead of using expensive 1-in.-thick cherry for the back rail of the drawer top, we glued together two layers of 1/2-in. plywood scraps.
- The 1/2-in. cove in the drawer top is too deep to rout in a single pass. To avoid splintering, we were extra cautious and made four shallow passes, lowering the router bit after each pass. Better safe than sorry!
- Cut the drawer fronts from a single board so they'll have similar color and grain pattern. Be sure to choose an attractive board for these prominent parts.
- Before you add the drawer fronts (Photo 8), set the drawer unit on the cabinet unit and drive screws through the cabinet boxes into the drawer frame.

6 Mount two drawers in three minutes. Position the slides on the cradle sides using a 3/8-in. spacer. Then screw slides to the drawers and you're done.

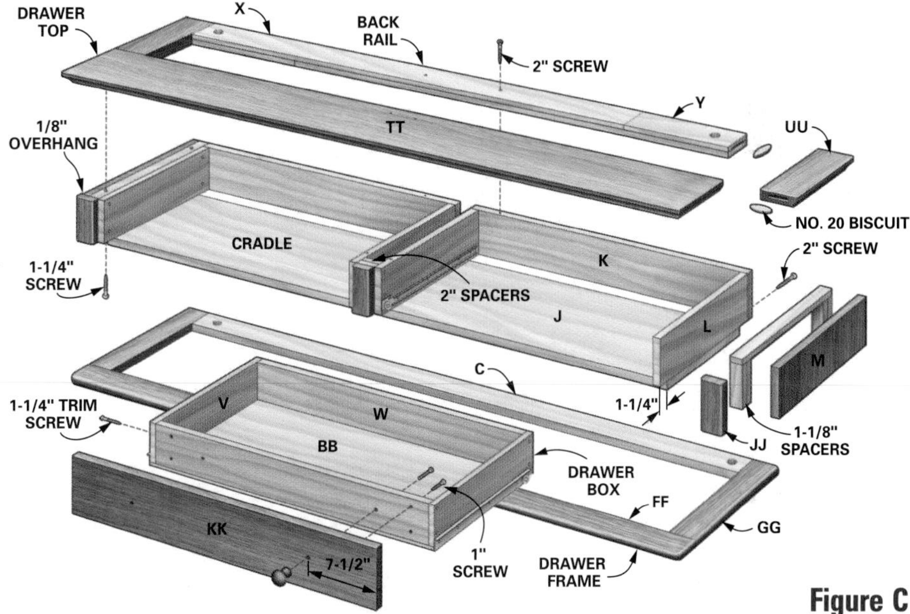

Figure C
Drawer cradles and frames

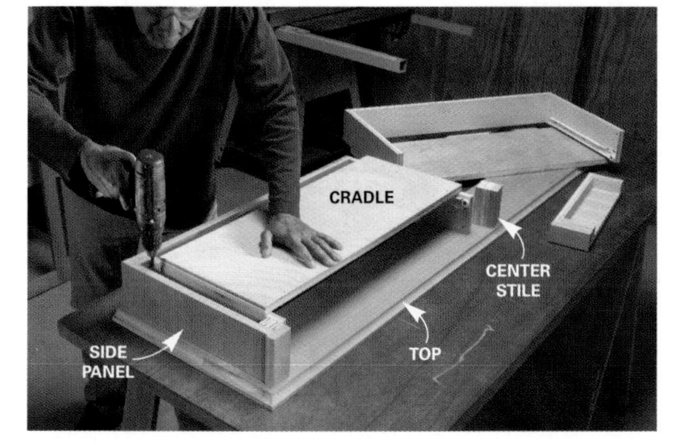

7 Assemble drawer unit upside down. Screw the side panels, center stile and cradles together. Then screw the side panels to the top before you add the frame.

8 Position drawer fronts perfectly. Install the drawers and position the fronts with spacers. Then drive temporary screws through the knob holes. Pull out the drawers and drive screws from inside the drawer boxes.

The shelf unit

The shelf unit is the biggest component—and the simplest. Just build two boxes and glue on stiles and trim.

- Remember that plywood has a good side and a not-so-good side. Be sure the good side faces outward on the shelf box sides, inward on the box top and upward on the shelves.
- Drill holes for the adjustable shelf supports using a 1/4-in. brad-point bit. A scrap of pegboard makes a perfect template for positioning the holes.
- To make sanding easier, sand the insides of the shelf box sides before assembly.
- Fasten the shelf box backs with screws rather than nails. That way, you can remove them later for easier finishing.
- When you glue and clamp the stiles to the sides, remember that the outer stiles protrude 1/8 in. past the box sides.
- Glue the center stile to only one of the shelf box sides. That lets you decouple the two shelf boxes by unscrewing the top and bottom gussets.
- When adding the nosings to the adjustable shelves, use four biscuits. The biscuits aren't needed for strength, but they help align the nosings while clamping.
- The shelf unit simply stands on the drawer unit; there's no need for screws. But you will have to screw the bookcase to the wall (see "Finishing and Installation," p. 125).

CAUTION: The blade guard must be removed for the cuts shown in Photos 9 and 10. Work with extreme caution!

9 Cut rabbets without a dado blade. Set the blade height to 1/2 in. and make two or three passes, moving the fence slightly after each pass. Clamp a wood scrap to the fence so the blade won't damage the fence.

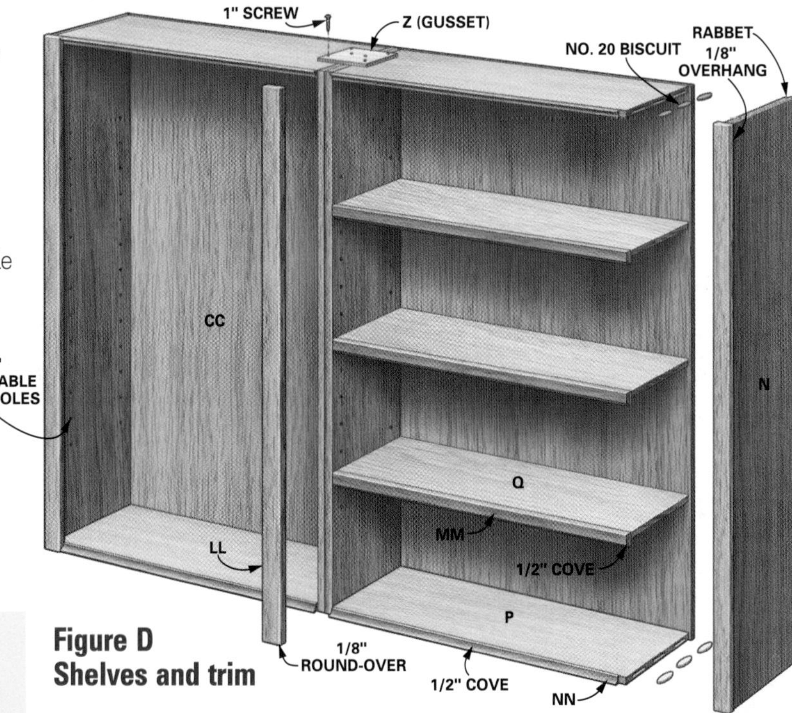

Figure D Shelves and trim

10 Make your own molding. Rout both edges of a board and then cut off the cove moldings. A guide board with a push block screwed to one end lets you cut thin strips safely without moving the fence.

11 Clamp on the molding with tape. Lay the shelf unit on its back and apply tape to protect "show" surfaces from squeezed-out glue. Stretch masking tape over the moldings to hold them while the glue sets. Use the same trick when you glue trim to the shelves.

The crown

The crown parts are similar to parts you built earlier. The box and frame are smaller versions of the box and frame for the base. The crown top is much like the drawer top, with one big difference: Instead of being built as a frame, it's built around a slab of 3/4-in. plywood. That creates a continuous surface for easier dusting and lets you display items on top of the bookshelf.

To assemble the crown, first drive 2-in. screws through the frame into the box. Then set the crown on the shelf unit and screw through the frame into the shelf boxes. (Be sure to use 1-1/4-in. screws so you don't screw through the shelf units!) Then attach the crown top by screwing into the crown box.

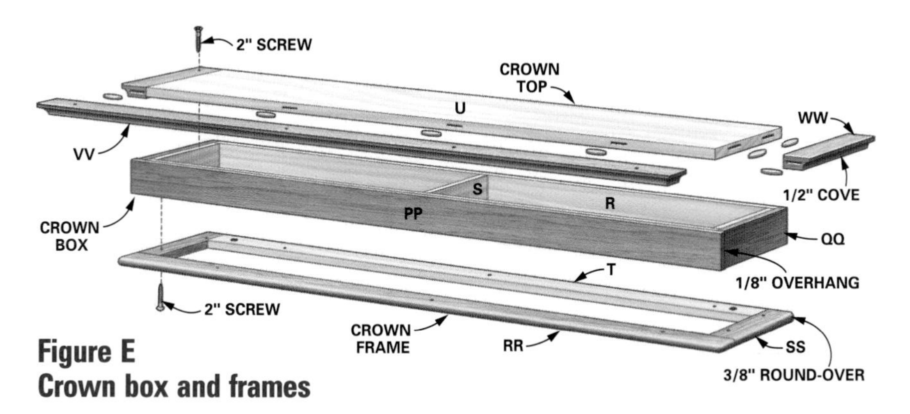

Figure E
Crown box and frames

12 Put it all together. **Test assemble all the parts, including the drawers, doors and shelves. It's better to find a sticking drawer or misfit shelf now than after the finish is on. Take a minute to stand back and admire your work, too.**

Finishing and installation

By removing screws, you can disassemble the bookcase into small parts for easy finishing. Be sure to label the components so they all go back together smoothly. We gave the drawers and cabinet boxes two coats of water-based polyurethane. Cherry often absorbs stain unevenly, creating a blotchy appearance. So we pretreated all exterior surfaces with Minwax Pre-Stain conditioner and then applied two coats of Watco oil finish (Cherry). After allowing the oil to cure for three days, we applied two coats of Minwax wipe-on polyurethane for extra sheen and protection.

Reassembling the bookcase in its new home takes just a few minutes. But before you screw on the crown top for the last time, screw the crown to the wall to prevent the shelf unit from tipping and injuring someone. Drill two 1/2-in. holes through the back of the crown box. Then slip fender washers over 3-in. screws and drive them into wall studs. The oversized holes will allow the bookcase to move slightly as wood shrinks and swells or the carpet below is compressed.

Complex hinges—simple installation

Don't be fooled by the complex look of "Euro" hinges. They're actually fast and easy to install. Once you get used to them, you'll never want to use anything else.

The only tricky step is choosing the right hinge for the job. For this bookcase, you can simply order the hinges and mounting plates we used (see right). For other situations, browse an online retailer such as wwhardware.com or rockler.com.

The best thing about Euro hinges is adjustability. You can adjust the door in three directions with the turn of a screw, so you won't spend hours sanding or planing to get a perfect fit.

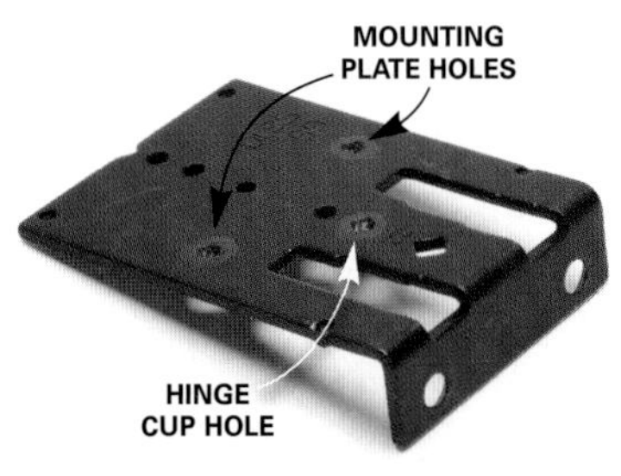

A drilling template isn't absolutely necessary, but well worth the $6 price. Mark the three holes you'll use with dabs of paint to avoid mistakes.

A 1-3/8-in. Forstner bit ($15) and a drill are all you need to bore the cup holes. Don't bother with a drill press unless you're installing lots of doors.

Mark the hinge locations. Lay the cabinet box on its side, center the door against it and mark both using a 2-1/4-in.-wide scrap. The lines mark the center of the hinge.

Position holes precisely. Center the template on the line and drill two 3/32-in. mounting plate holes in the cabinet. On the door, mark the center of the cup hole using the drill bit and template. Then bore the cup hole with a Forstner bit.

Snap on the door. Just slip the hinges over the mounting plates and press. To remove the doors, push the release lever.

SHOPPING LIST

ITEM	QTY.
4' x 8' x 3/4" hardwood plywood	2
4' x 8' x 3/4" utility-grade plywood	1
4' x 8' x 1/4" hardwood plywood	1
3/4" x 5-1/2" x 8' hardwood boards	6
1" x 7-1/4" x 8' hardwood board	1
1" x 2-1/2" x 8' hardwood board	1
We ordered the following items from Woodworker's Hardware, (800) 383-0130, wwhardware.com:	
Leveling feet and T-nuts (HB33 232 and SCT1420)	4
Blum hinges and mounting plates (B075T1550 and B175H710)	8
Hinge drilling template (B065 5310)	1
14" drawer slides (pair) (B230M 14CM)	2
Screw cover caps (bag of 100) (HCI5525 029)	1
Birch iron-on edge band (ET078 PB 25)	25'
Shelf supports (bag of 20) (THB0144)	2
Our drawer and door knobs came from restorationhardware.com (No. 24070461 PN; $8 each).	
Wood glue, masking tape, construction screws (1", 1-1/4", 1-5/8", 2", 3"), 1-1/4" trim screws and No. 20 biscuits	

Tools you'll need

We used a biscuit joiner (starting at about $75), but you could use a pocket screw jig. You'll need clamps with a reach of at least 18 in. and a router and three bits: a 3/8-in. and a 1/8-in. round-over and a 1/2-in. cove (about $40 total). This project requires lots of drilling and countersinking for screws, so pick up a bit that does both at once ($5).

CUTTING LIST

KEY	PCS.	SIZE & DESCRIPTION
¾" plywood (see cutting diagrams)		
A	2	3-1/2" x 64-1/4" base box
B	3	3-1/2" x 14-3/8" base box
C	2	2-1/2" x 62" frame rail
D	2	15-1/4" x 30" cabinet box
E	4	3-1/2" x 30" cabinet box
F	4	15-1/4" x 18-1/2" cabinet box
G	2	15-1/4" x 28-1/4" shelves
H	2	15-7/8" x 20" cabinet panels
J	2	11-1/2" x 30" cradle
K	2	4" x 30" cradle
L	4	4" x 14-3/4" cradle
M	2	4" x 15-7/8" drawer panels
N	4	11-1/2" x 47-1/2" shelf box
P	4	11-1/4" x 30-1/2" shelf box
Q	6	10-3/8" x 30-3/8" shelves
R	2	3" x 62-1/2" crown box
S	3	3" x 10" crown box
T	1	2-1/2" x 60-1/4" crown frame
U	1	10-3/4" x 61" crown top
1/2" plywood (see cutting diagram)		
V	4	2-3/4" x 14-1/2" drawer box
W	4	2-3/4" x 26-1/2" drawer box
X	2	3-1/2" x 48" top frame
Y	2	3-1/2" x 12-3/4" top frame
Z	2	5-1/2" x 5-1/2" gussets
1/4" plywood (see cutting diagram)		
AA	2	19-7/8" x 29-7/8" cabinet box
BB	2	14-1/2" x 27-1/2" drawer box
CC	2	31-3/8" x 47-1/4" shelf box
¾"-thick solid wood		
DD	1	3-1/2" x 66" base face
EE	2	3-1/2" x 15-7/8" base sides
FF	2	2-1/2" x 67" frame front rail
GG	4	2-1/2" x 14-5/8" frame sides
HH	3	2" x 20" cabinet stiles
JJ	3	2" x 4" drawer stiles
KK	2	3-7/8" x 29-7/8" drawer fronts
LL	3	2" x 47-1/2" shelf stiles
MM	6	1-1/4" x 30-3/8" shelf nosings
NN	4	5/8" x 29-1/8" cove moldings
PP	1	3" x 64-1/4" crown box face
QQ	2	3" x 11-1/2" crown box sides
RR	1	2-1/2" x 65-1/4" crown frame
SS	2	2-1/2" x 10-1/4" crown frame
1"-thick solid wood		
TT	1	7-1/4" x 67-3/4" drawer top
UU	2	3-1/2" x 10-1/4" drawer top
VV	1	2-1/2" x 66" crown top
WW	2	2-1/2" x 10-3/4" crown top

Plywood cutting diagrams

We used "utility grade" birch plywood and leftover cherry plywood for the hidden parts.

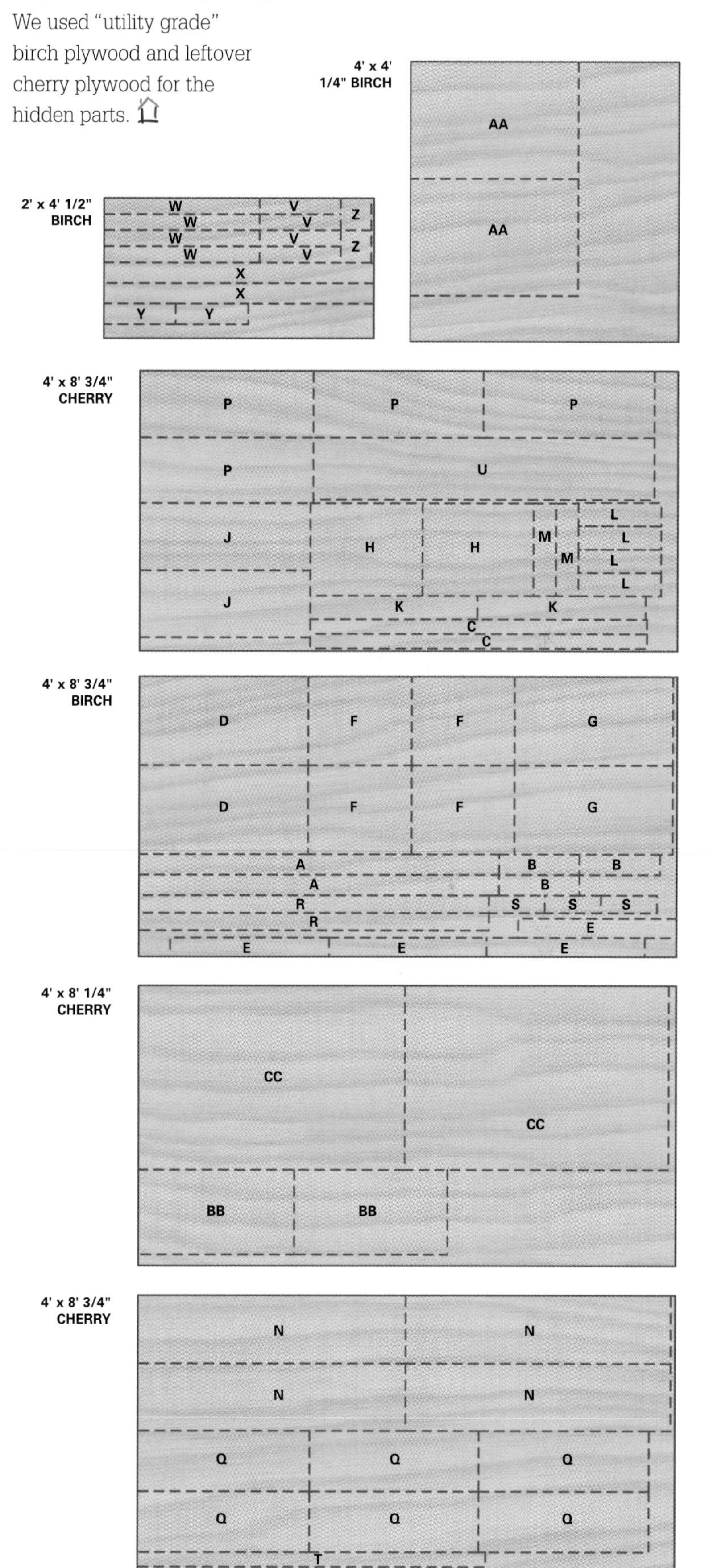

WOODWORKING & FURNITURE PROJECTS & TIPS

SPECIAL SECTION

Tools & Skills

QUICK-DRAW MEASURING TAPE

The clip on my measuring tape used to fray the pockets on my jeans. Here's my solution. I unscrewed the clip from the tape and screwed on a pot magnet in its place. I hook the clip onto my pocket and stick the magnetized tape to it. The clip stays in my pocket all day, and the magnet makes it easy to grab the tape and put it back when I'm done.

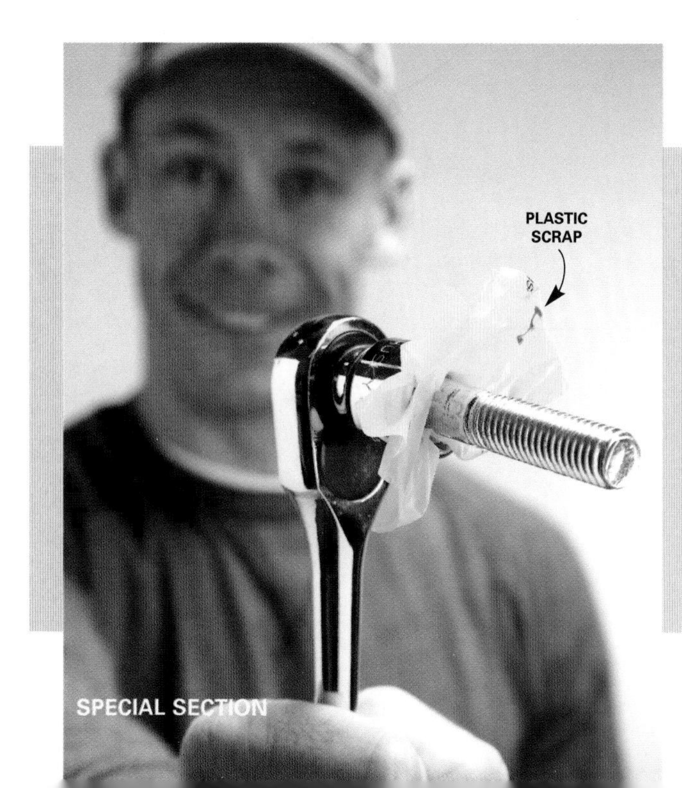

SOCKET WRENCH HINT

When you're using a socket wrench to ratchet on a bolt in a spot where your fingers can't reach, how do you get it started? Simple. Stick a little piece of plastic bag between the bolt head and the socket. The thickness of the plastic will hold the bolt tight until you get it in place, and the plastic will fall right off when you take the socket off the bolt.

READER PHOTO

LOW-COST, LIGHTWEIGHT 8-FT. LEVEL

A good 8-ft. level can cost almost $200, but you can make a good substitute with a steel stud and a 2- or 4-ft. level. Unlike wood, steel studs are always straight and weigh almost nothing. And if your level is magnetic, you can stick it to the stud for vertical work.

EASY-FIND SCREWDRIVERS

Although I have a bunch of screwdrivers, I can never seem to find the one I need. Here's a way to help identify your screwdrivers at a glance. Use a permanent marker to label their size and type on the handle. I use an "X" for a Phillips head and a dash for a flathead.

CLOG-FREE BELT SANDING

Last spring, I was cleaning some new treated deck boards with my belt sander to prep the wood for a semitransparent stain. All the gunk on the boards kept clogging up the belt. To keep the belt clean and make it last longer, I screwed a wire brush to the sawhorse and every so often touched the running belt to the brush. It cleaned the belt up nicely—and my new deck looks great!

Tools & Skills

SIMPLER SKIM-COATING

A new approach that's easy to master

by **Jeff Gorton**

If you're a skilled drywall taper or plasterer, you probably use a hawk and trowel to skim-coat walls. We don't expect to change your mind if you use those tools as second hands. But if you're a remodeler who does only occasional skim-coating to fix wrecked walls, you know it's a tough skill to master.

The method we show isn't faster than traditional skim-coating—you have to do two or three coats and let each one dry in-between. But it's idiot-proof, and the walls will end up flat and smooth. So if you're a contractor who's given up on skim-coating and you always call in a taper for the task, you can save on labor by tackling it yourself next time. It only takes a regular paint roller and a squeegee knife. The 14-in.-wide squeegee knife we used is called a Magic Trowel. It costs $25 and is available at some Sherwin-Williams stores. To find online sources, search for "TexMaster 9927" or "squeegee knife."

Start by prepping the walls

With this method, you don't just spot-prime; you roll the entire wall with a stain-blocking sealer (**Photo 1**). If you've always used solvent-based sealers like traditional BIN and KILZ, it's time to try one of the water-based stain killers. Water-based BIN works well, and you won't have to worry about the smell. But don't rush on to the next step; let the sealer dry thoroughly before applying any joint compound.

These are thin layers that won't fix holes or torn-away paper, or make uneven sections level. Patch these problems with setting-type joint compound. Let the compound harden (it doesn't have to be dry) before you start skim-coating.

Roll on the mud

Mix all-purpose joint compound to about the same consistency as mud you'd use for bedding tape (the consistency of mayonnaise, or just thin enough to roll on the wall). You'll get shrinkage if you mix it too wet. Don't worry if you get cracking on the first coat; just mix the

1 Prime the walls. Roll a fast-drying, stain-sealing primer on the walls. The primer seals loose paper and promotes better adhesion of the joint compound.

2 Roll on the mud. Spread a layer of slightly thinned all-purpose joint compound on the walls with a heavy-nap roller. Work in small sections so you can smooth out the joint compound before it starts to dry.

next coat a little thicker by spooning in some fresh mud from another bucket.

Use a 1/2-in.-nap roller to roll mud on an area about 4 ft. square (**Photo 2**). Try to keep it as even as you can so the squeegee work will go better for you.

Wipe it smooth

Smooth the mud with the squeegee knife. Keep a damp rag and a mud pan handy. Use the rag to wipe the blade after every few strokes and the mud pan to wipe off excess mud that builds up on the blade. Starting at the top corner, set the squeegee knife against the wall and pull it down (**Photo 3**). Overlap each vertical pass until you finish the section. You may have to go over some areas a few times. It won't take you long to get the hang of using the squeegee knife.

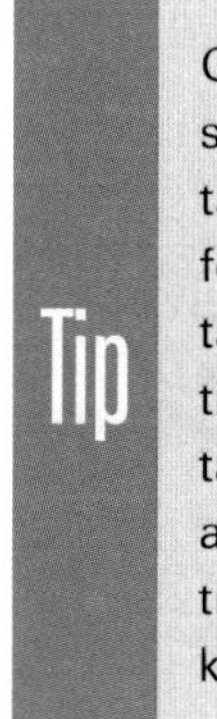

Give this squeegee-like taping knife a shot for smoothing out tape joints next time you tape. It tapers the edges and you'll have no trowel or taping knife marks.

When you're done with the top section, roll joint compound on the lower half. Pull the squeegee knife from the bottom up (**Photo 4**). Touch up along the edges as you go.

Let the first coat of joint compound dry. To speed up drying time, especially if the air is humid, use a space heater and a box fan or two. You don't have to sand between coats; just knock off lumps or proud mud lines with a 5- or 6-in. putty knife to avoid streaks in the next coat (**Photo 5**).

Apply one or two more layers

It sounds like a lot of work to apply two or three coats of joint compound, but the process is quick and the thin layers dry fast. As you know, the smoother you get the wall, the less sanding you'll get stuck with. Trowel off each successive layer at a right angle to the previous one. After the last coat dries, pole-sand the wall with 120-grit paper. If you have too many peaks and valleys, hit the walls with 100-grit first.

3 Trowel the first coat. **Smooth the joint compound with the squeegee knife. Start in the top corner and pull down.**

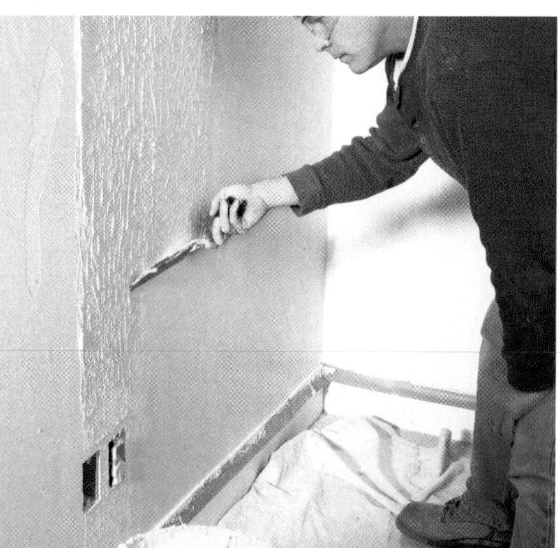

4 Pull up from the bottom. **Roll joint compound onto the lower section and smooth it by pulling the trowel upward.**

5 Scrape off lumps. **Scrape the wall with a 6-in. putty knife to remove lumps and ridges. Brush off the wall and you're ready for the next coat.**

6 Change directions for the second coat. **Trowel the second coat horizontally. If you still see indentations or imperfections after the second coat dries, trowel on a third coat.**

Tools & Skills: Shop Rat

ROUTER LIFTS

If you've seen those slick router lifts in catalogs and wondered whether they're worth the painful price, here's my take: I used to have an under-mounted plunge router on an oversize plastic base, and it was a royal pain in the butt. I'd have to either extract the beast to make fine depth adjustments or crawl under the table like a reptile. Neither option was fun, and both required several tries to get the depth set just right. And there was the hassle of changing bits.

Then I got a router lift and I love it. It makes extremely fine height adjustments simple and fast just by turning a crank. My Jessem model cost about $300, and the dedicated Porter Cable router cost another $300. There are $200 ones on the market, but I haven't given them a try. If you do lots of routing on router tables, a router lift is well worth the big bucks.

WORKBENCH POWER STRIP

This oldie-but-goodie tip comes from David Gersic. Screw a power strip to the side of your workbench and you won't have to monkey with extension cords any-more when using power tools for bench work.

DOUBLE YOUR BATTERY LIFE

Here's a tip for making lithium tool batteries last twice as long. Most kits come with two batteries. Take one of them and stick it in the refrigerator—with the milk, not the ice cream. Lithium-ion batteries have a shelf life of only a few years even if you use them sparingly. And new batteries are expensive. But keeping one cold makes it last at least twice as long. Granted, you'll be a little inconvenienced from time to time waiting for a dead battery to recharge, so this tip won't be practical for pros.

When the first battery finally gives up the ghost, you can start all over with a practically brand new one. And by the way, frequent full discharges will wear out your battery quicker. Several partial discharges with short recharges are better than running the battery dead and then giving it a complete refill.

A WHEEL-Y PORTABLE COMPRESSOR!

Some small air compressors are about as portable as an engine block with a suitcase handle. But Sheldon Buda fixed that: He replaced the rubber feet with casters, and now his compressor rolls around like a shop vacuum. You may have to drill out the mounting holes a bit to fit the caster shafts and shorten the shafts with a hacksaw, but it's worth it.

SAVE BIG BUCKS ON TOOLS

My cheapskate coworker, Gary Wentz, loves two things: power tools and saving a buck. If Dumpster diving were an Olympic event, I'd want him on Team U.S.A. Naturally, you won't find a guy like him at the home center paying full freight for tools—no, sir! Gary goes online and buys factory-reconditioned tools and, according to him, he hasn't been stung yet. Some have been returned because of a mechanical problem or just a dent in the case. Whatever their histories, the tools have been inspected, tested and repaired if necessary. Most are covered by the same warranty as a brand-new tool.

Gary has bought at least a dozen tools in the last few years, and all have performed flawlessly. Here are his shopping tips. First, find out the cost of new before you buy. Though savings are 10 to 40 percent, you may only save $10 and wind up spending more than that on shipping. Second, if you find a bargain, grab it. Supplies of any specific model are limited. To find the tool you want, go online and search for "reconditioned tools."

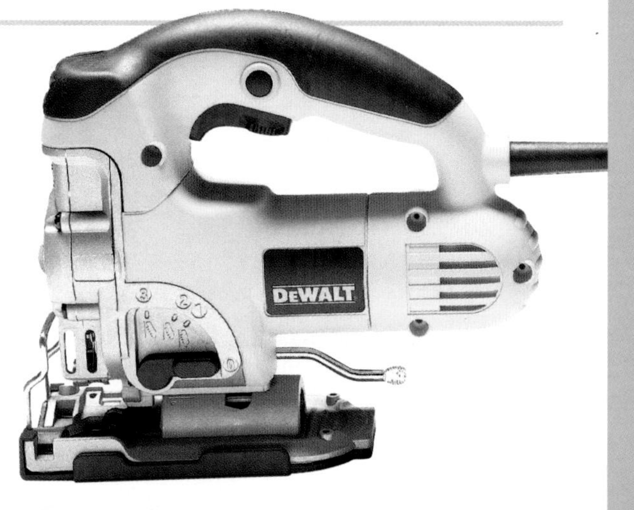

This reconditioned jigsaw was $70 less than a brand-new one.

Tools & Skills: Shop Rat

HOMEMADE BENCH PUCKS

Rockler sells ingenious little things called Bench Cookies for $12 for a set of four (rockler.com; 800-279-4441). Not a bad price, I'd say. They're very useful when you need to space projects above the workbench for clamping, finishing or routing. But if you need lots of them, or you love saving a few bucks, you can buy hockey pucks for about $1.25 each and stick shelf liner on both sides with spray adhesive. Rob Rowe suggested this tip. I'm guessing he's a bored NHL player/woodworker with a mountain of old pucks.

T-BAR ASSEMBLY LIFTS

Ever wonder what makes a woodworker tick? Here's Ken Collier, the editor in chief: "These T-bars are one of my happiest discoveries as a woodworker. They're just 5-in.-wide pieces of 3/4-in. plywood face-glued together, with another 5-in. piece screwed on the bottom for a base. Any larger assembly I do happens on the T-bars because they lift it off the table. It's easy to drive in screws, check the project for squareness and tighten clamps anywhere around the edges. I work alone most of the time, and the T-bars are my extra set of hands."

EASY-OFF SANDING SLEEVES

I couldn't live without my spindle sander for super-smooth sanding of inside curves on projects, but for years I dreaded changing spindle sizes. That's because it was difficult to tighten the bolt enough to expand the rubber drum, so the sanding sleeve often slid up and down the drum while I was sanding. And if I managed to tighten up the bolt enough, it was nearly impossible to loosen it again. Last week, a hand screw miraculously jumped onto the sander table and solved the problem. I tightened it around the drum and easily twisted the bolt. Hallelujah!

MIKE KRIVIT

AUXILIARY FENCE
This fence provides a positive stop at the jig centerline and keeps the jig from tipping during the cut.

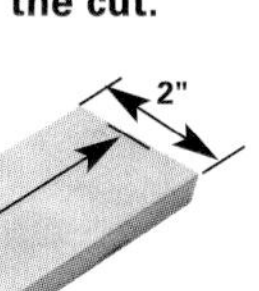

Cutting perfect circles is easy with a band saw—as long as you take a half hour to build yourself a cutting jig. I've cut circles with radiuses ranging from a few inches to a couple of feet. The only limit is the distance from the fence to the saw blade.

Use any 3/4-in. plywood to make the jig, and attach a runner to the underside that fits in the band saw's miter gauge slot. That will hold everything steady while you turn the actual circle stock through the blade. Then make yourself an auxiliary fence from another piece of 3/4-in. plywood as shown. Send the jig through the blade to create the saw kerf, then shut off the saw when the blade reaches the centerline and lock the fence about 1/8 in. away from the jig. Clamp the auxiliary fence to the band saw fence with the stop against the edge of the jig. Hold it slightly above the jig so the jig will slide easily beneath it. The auxiliary fence not only stops the jig at the right spot for turning circles but also keeps the jig from tipping up from the band saw table.

Cutting is simple. You'll need to choose narrow blades for small circles. Push the jig with the mounted cutting blank until you reach the stop and then just twist the blank through the blade. You'll have a small amount of cleanup to do where the cut starts and stops. You're done.

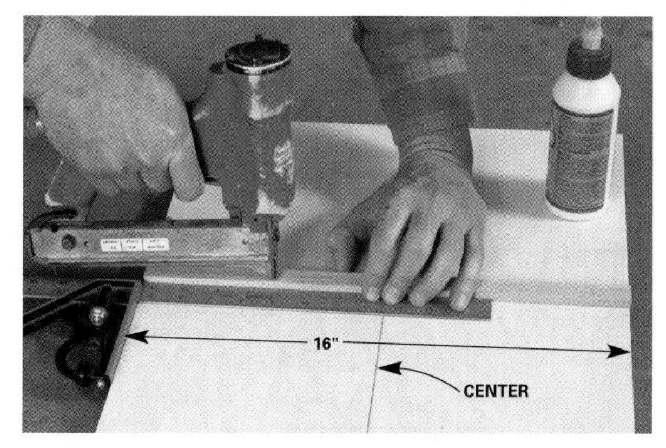

1 Attach the runner. Cut 3/4-in. plywood to 16 x 24 in. Draw centerlines on both sides, then glue and pin the runner to the bottom. Send the jig through the blade until you reach the centerline, then clamp the auxiliary fence to the jigsaw fence.

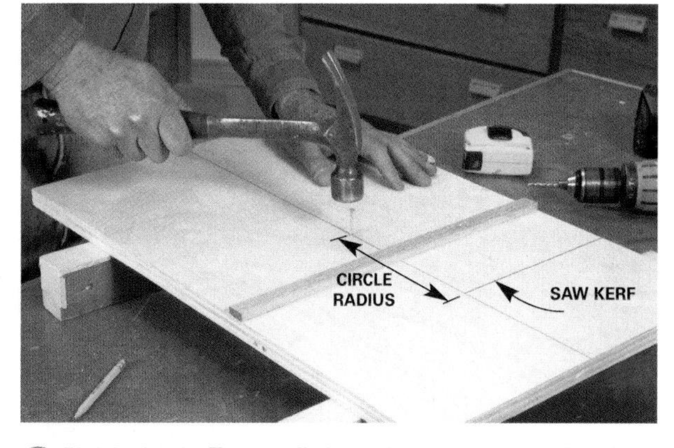

2 Finish the jig. Tap a nail through the hole, then flip the jig over. Drill a hole in the middle of the blank and prop the circle stock over the nail shank.

Tools & Skills: Shop Rat

DRILL PRESS TABLE

Drill presses are designed for working with metal, not wood. That's why, 10 years ago, I screwed an old scrap of 3/4-in. treated plywood to the metal table so I could screw down or clamp stops and fences. Frankly, I was embarrassed by it and finally built this dedicated woodworking drill press table. Mine is a bit over the top, with dadoes, plastic laminate and T-Tracks. Tackle it if you wish. The truth is, you could make a quick and easy top by bolting two glued layers of particleboard to the cast-iron table from the underside. You can screw or clamp temporary stops and fences to that and have a serviceable table. But your table won't be as fetching or as easy to use as mine.

Here's an overview of the construction process. Glue 1-in. oversized particleboard panels together, then cut them to size on the table saw. Edge-band both sides of the table, then belt-sand the top so the hardwood is flush with the surfaces. Cut the laminate squares 1 in. oversize and apply them with contact

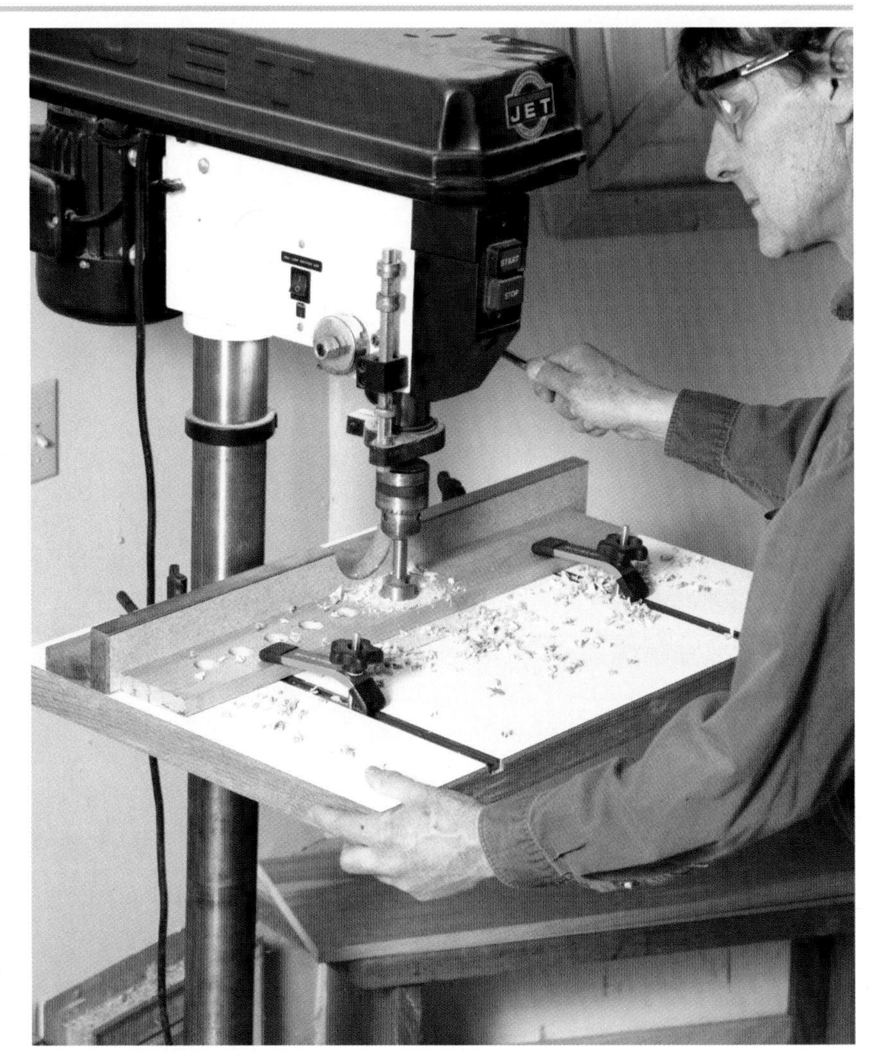

Bells and whistles

FENCE: **A semicircular clearance hole for the chuck allows for drilling holes that are close to the fence.**

THROAT PLATE: **An inset 1/2-in. replaceable throat plate takes the abuse so the top won't have to.**

T-TRACKS: **T-Tracks are universally useful gizmos that allow you to endlessly adjust jigs, fences and hold-downs. On this table, they're used for a sliding fence and hold-downs.**

LAMINATE: **Plastic laminate on both the top and bottom will keep the top from warping with humidity changes.**

EDGING: **A hardwood edge-banding protects the rather delicate core from getting dinged up—plus, it's pretty.**

cement. Then rout the laminate squares flush with a flush-trim bit and chamfer them with a 45-degree bit. Rout out the 1/2-in.-deep recess for the throat plate.

Cut the 3/4-in.-wide dadoes on the table saw. Cut the clearance hole on the fence with a 2-1/2-in. hole saw on the drill press. Screw the fence together before applying the laminate, then rout that as you did with the tabletop.

Lag screws (1-1/2 x 5/16 in.) and washers work great for securing your new top to the existing drill press table. The instructions with the T-Track will tell you the rest.

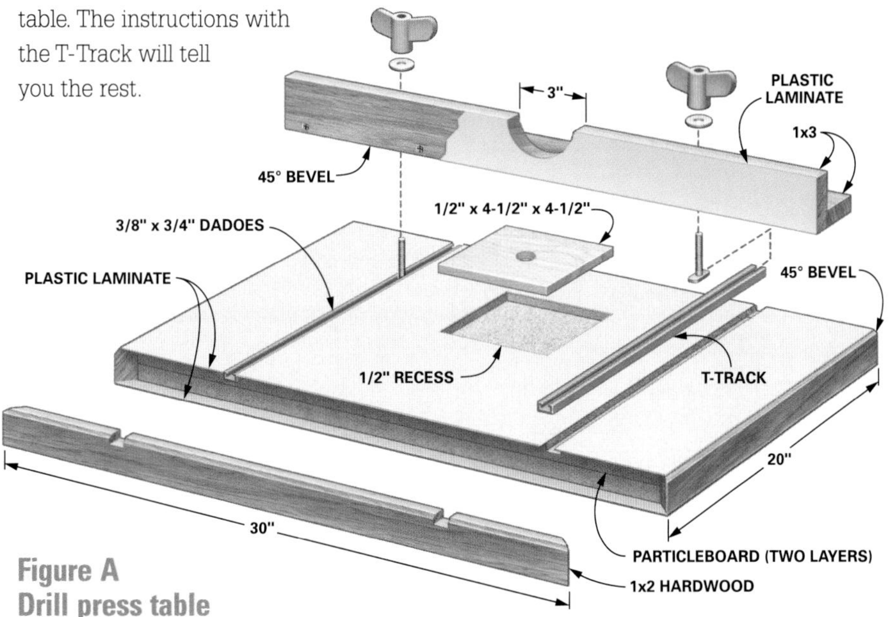

Figure A
Drill press table

SHOPPING LIST

Table: Two 2-ft. squares of particleboard. (You can get 2x2s at most home centers or have them cut them from full sheets.)

Edge band: 8 lin. ft. of 1x2 hardwood.

Fence: 6 lin. ft. of 1x3 hardwood.

Laminate: Buy the smallest size sheet that'll give you two 20 x 30-in. pieces at the home center for anywhere between $20 and $50.

T-Track parts: You'll need two each of these: 24-in. tracks, hold-down clamps, knobs and 2-1/2-in. T-Slot bolts. (These parts cost a total of about $50 available at rockler.com.)

PLANING WARPED BOARDS

A jointer is the best tool for flattening twisted, warped boards. But what if you don't have a jointer or the board is too wide? Set the board on a "sled," a flat piece of 3/4-in. plywood. Then shim the high corner(s) so the board doesn't rock. Also shim high spots in the middle of the board. Mark the shim locations, remove the board and hot-glue the shims into place. Then glue the board to the shims and the plywood with a dab of hot glue. Send that rascal through until it's flat, then pull it free and plane down the other side.

Tools & Skills: Shop Rat

Yes, you can buy a clamp rack similar to this one for about $150, but why not have this good-looking version for a lot less? Plus, it's another shop project!

ULTIMATE CLAMP RACK

If you have a big shop, a roll-around clamp rack is better than any wall-mounted system. It holds every type of clamp in one compact space, and you can wheel it right up to your work area. That saves miles of walking back and forth to the clamp rack.

This version is built from oak legs and 3/4-in. plywood shelves. Note that the front and back edges of the plywood are all the same length but have 7-degree bevels. The shorter pieces of edge trim also have 7-degree angles. When you cut the edge trim to length, it should be measured and cut to the bottom, longest part of each board.

Assemble the legs first and then preassemble the shelves. Then screw on the top and bottom shelves. Rest the rack upside down and slide in each shelf. Make sure they're evenly spaced and screw each one to the legs. Add the wheels, varnish it and you're done.

Figure A
Clamp rack

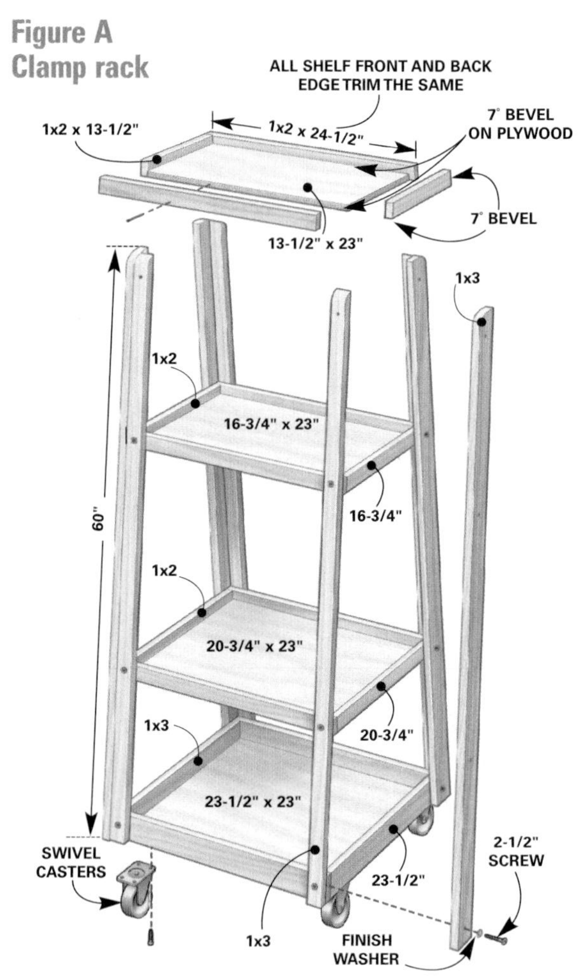

MARKING AND CUTTING CURVES

by **Jeff Gorton**

Whether you're building a frame for an arched opening, making curved brackets or fashioning arch-top casing, marking and cutting curves is part of the process. In this story, we'll show you several techniques and tips for marking, cutting and fine-tuning curves. Some methods are best suited for rough curves. Others are refined enough for furniture making. Choose the technique that works best for the project at hand.

Cut precise curves with a router trammel

This simple router trammel is easy to build and allows you to cut a perfect circle. For circles up to 6 ft. across, use a piece of 1/4-in. plywood, MDF or hardboard that's about 4 ft. long and at least as wide as your router base. Start by removing the base plate from your router and clamping it to one end of the trammel material. If you want your trammel to be stylish, trace around a coffee cup to make a nice-looking rounded end. Then draw tangent lines connecting the circles and cut the sides. If you don't care about looks, simply make a long rectangular trammel.

Trace around the base plate and use the mounting holes as a guide for drilling holes in the trammel (**Photo 1**). Cut out the trammel and drill a 1-1/2-in. hole in the center of the router end to clear the router bit. Countersink the mounting screw holes so the screw heads won't tear up your workpiece. Attach the router to the trammel with the base plate screws.

Screw the trammel to the workpiece, centering it on the circle you want to cut out. Mount a straight plunge-cutting bit in your router and set the router bit to cut about 3/8 in. deep for the first pass. A plunge router works best, but if you don't have one, hold the router above the wood and start it. Carefully plunge it into the wood and begin moving it counterclockwise around the circle. Complete the circle, then readjust the depth and make another pass until you cut all the way through.

1 Lay out the trammel. **Draw the sides and ends of the trammel. Trace around the base plate and drill holes for the mounting screws.**

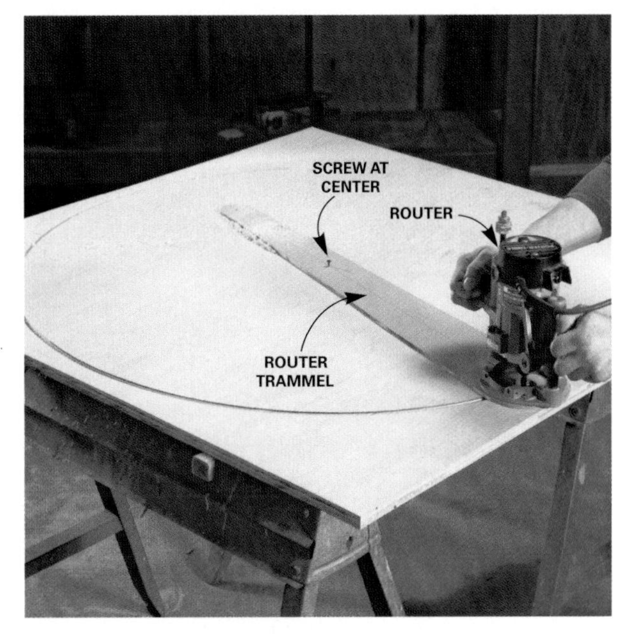

2 Rout a perfect circle. **Screw the trammel to the center of your workpiece and cut out the circle with your router. Make two or three passes in a counterclockwise direction.**

SPECIAL SECTION TOOLS & SKILLS

Tools & Skills

Cut gradual curves with a circular saw

The first tool that comes to mind for cutting curves is a jigsaw, but if the curve is gradual, try a circular saw instead. It's surprisingly quick and easy to cut a smooth curve with a circular saw. This method is for cutting rough curves. Don't try to make furniture with this technique. The trick is to make sure the curve is gradual enough that the blade doesn't bind. If you try this method and the blade binds or starts to heat up and smoke, switch to the jigsaw. The thinner the material you're cutting, the sharper the curve can be. Set the blade depth so it barely projects through the bottom of the wood.

Plastic wood template

Often you can simply "eyeball" the best curve for the job by bending a piece of wood and using it as a template. But variations in wood grain can result in inconsistent curves. Here's a tip to make this technique even better. Use plastic wood or a plastic molding instead. It bends very uniformly and yields near-perfect symmetrical curves. Azek, Fypon, Kleer and Versatex are several brands available at home centers. Choose a thickness that'll bend to the curve you need. For gradual bends or wide curves, use 3/4-in.-thick material. For tighter bends (those with a smaller radius), use a 1/2-in. x 1-1/4-in. plastic stop molding or something similar. Support the ends of the plastic wood with blocks attached to a strip of wood. Adjust the position of the blocks to change the curve.

Draw large curves with a giant compass

Grab any narrow board or strip of plywood and drill a few holes—voilà, instant compass. Drill a pencil-size hole a few inches from the end of the board. Then drill a screw-size hole at the pivot point. The distance between them should be the radius of the curve, if you know what that measurement is. Otherwise, just use the trial-and-error method, drilling a series of pivot holes until you can swing the trammel and draw the right-size arch. It's easy to draw parallel curves too. Just drill two pencil holes spaced the desired distance apart.

There's no limit to the size of the arch you can draw. If your plan calls for a 10-ft. radius, find a long stick and use the floor as your workbench.

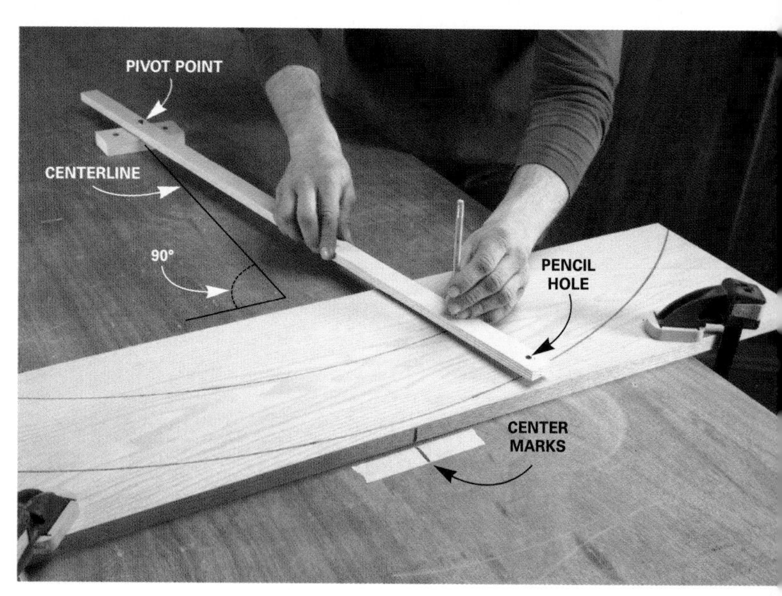

Use a pattern and a router for irregular curves

When your plan calls for cutting curved parts and you need to make two or more, first shape and sand a perfect full-size pattern from a piece of 1/2-in. medium-density fiberboard. Then use a router with a top-bearing pattern bit to cut out the parts.

Here are a few tips for routing with a pattern bit. First, use the pattern to mark the shape. Then remove excess material by cutting about 1/4 to 1/8 in. outside the lines with a jigsaw or a band saw. Elevate the workpiece to avoid cutting into your workbench. We used Bench Cookies (available at rockler.com; $12 for a set of four). But hot-melt glue and scraps of wood are another option. If you're cutting material that's thicker than the pattern bit is deep, cut as deep as you can. Then remove the pattern and use the part as the pattern to complete the cut.

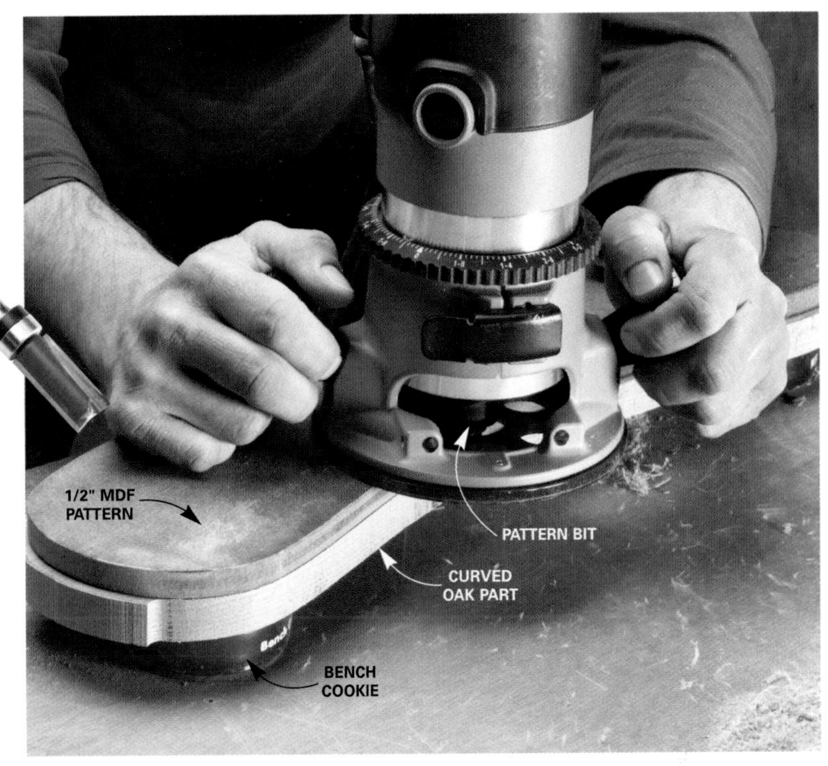

Make matching parts with a pattern
Trace out and rough-cut your part. Attach the pattern with hot-melt glue. Use a top-bearing pattern bit to follow the pattern and shape the part. Move the router counterclockwise around the pattern.

Mark an arch with two sticks

Here's a quick way to draw an accurate curve if you know how wide and tall you want the arch to be. Let's say you want to draw an arch that's 3 ft. wide and 9 in. high. Drive two nails at the ends of the 3-ft. baseline. At the center of the baseline, draw a perpendicular line and make a mark 9 in. above the baseline. Drive a nail at the mark. At one end of the baseline, draw another perpendicular line and make another mark 9 in. above the baseline. Drive another nail at this mark. **Photo 1** shows how to arrange and connect two sticks that you will use to draw the arch (**Photo 2**).

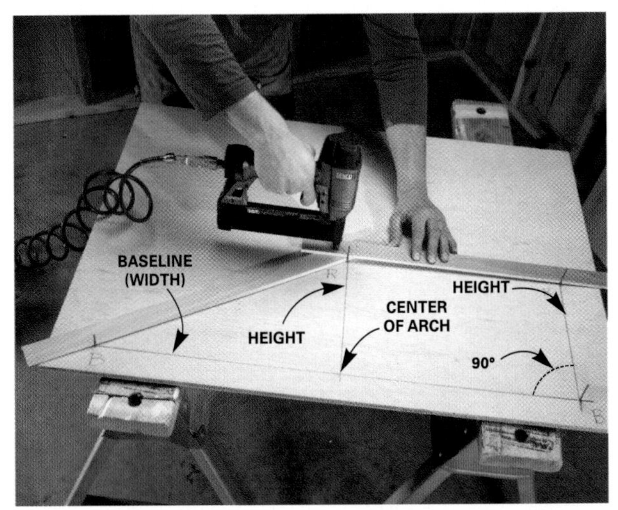

1 Set up for arch drawing with two sticks. **Drive nails at the ends of the baseline and at the height of the arch. Lay one stick across two height nails and lay the other from the center height to the end of the baseline. Connect the sticks with short pins or hot-melt glue.**

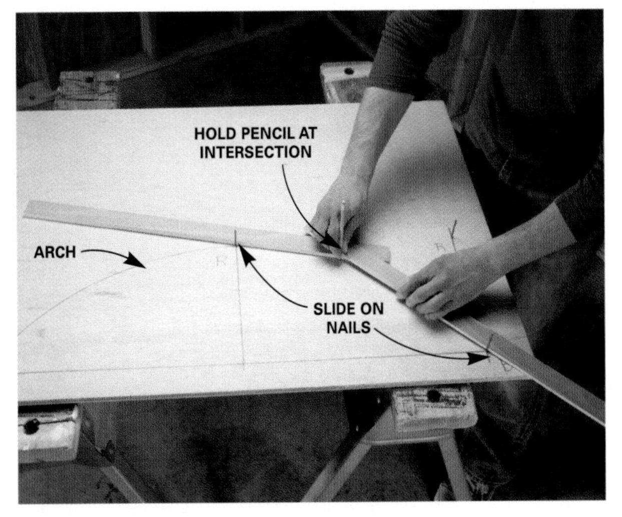

2 Slide the sticks over the nails. **Nestle a pencil into the crook of the sticks. With one end of the sticks resting on the baseline end nail and the other on the center height nail, slide the sticks along the nails to draw the arch. Repeat on the opposite side to complete the arch.**

Tools & Skills

SUCCESS WITH MDF

by **Gary Wentz**

Medium-density fiberboard is the most versatile building material I know of. Because it's inexpensive and fairly durable, it's a good choice for practical projects like shelving and storage cabinets. But MDF is great for decorative projects too. The smooth surface is perfect for painting, and a router leaves crisp profiles with no splintering, burning or tear-out.

Over the past 15 years, I've used MDF to build everything from crude shelving in my shop to fancy trim in upscale homes. I've even used it for furniture and ornate millwork like the trim board shown above. In fact, my own home is entirely trimmed out with MDF moldings made from about 50 sheets of MDF. Yes, I'm a fan of the stuff. This article will cover the most important things I've learned about working with MDF—and help you avoid some of the frustrating mistakes I've made.

MDF is basically sawdust and glue, fused together under pressure and heat. It varies in color from tan to chocolate brown. Common thicknesses range from 1/4 in. to 1 in., but most home centers carry only 1/2-in. and 3/4-in. Full sheets are oversized by 1 in., so a "4 x 8" sheet is actually 49 x 97 in. A full sheet of 3/4-in. MDF costs about $30. Some home centers also carry MDF boards in various lengths and widths. Working with MDF is no different from working with wood or plywood; you use the same tools to cut and shape it.

AVOID FULL SHEETS

I blame my hernia on MDF. A full sheet of 3/4-in. MDF weighs about 100 lbs., and I've lugged lots of them from my pickup to my shop. But there are ways to avoid hernia surgery:

- Buy half (4 x 4-ft.) or quarter (2 x 4-ft.) sheets instead of full sheets.
- Some lumberyards and home centers sell MDF shelving, usually in 1 x 8-ft. sections ($6). I like to slice these long, easy-to-handle shelves into trim stock.
- Some home centers and lumberyards will cut full sheets into manageable sections at no extra charge.

PREPARE FOR A DUST STORM

There's one thing you'll really hate about MDF: the fine, powdery dust that invades your clothes, hangs in the air for hours and clings to every surface like a coat of frost. Cutting MDF is a dusty job, but routing it is even worse.

Whenever possible, I cut and rout MDF outside. When that's not possible, I drape sheets of plastic over shelving and other hard-to-clean areas in my shop and use a fan to blow dust outside. When installing trim in a room, cover doorways, close air vents and expect to vacuum every surface when you're done, even the walls. Clean your vacuum filter often—the fine dust plugs filters quickly. And a tight-fitting dust mask is essential.

MAKE YOUR OWN TRIM—CHEAP!

When a job calls for painted trim, I almost always cut costs with MDF. Even inexpensive wood, like this poplar baseboard, costs four times as much. To make trim, I cut MDF sheets into strips and shape the edges with a router or router table. With the right bit, I can create just about any trim profile, simple or fancy. Eagleamerica.com is one good place to browse for bits. Bits that cut baseboard profiles like the one shown here cost from $40 to $70. Some home centers carry ready-made MDF trim; baseboard similar to the trim shown here costs about $1.70 per foot.

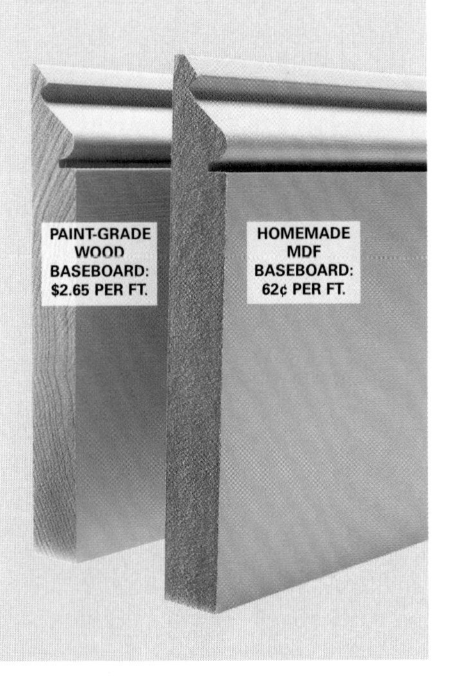

DON'T DROP IT

The face of MDF is harder than most woods, but the inner layers are soft. So edges, and especially corners, are easy to crush. That means you have to handle it with more care than lumber or plywood. Also, avoid scratching the face. Light scratches stand out like a sore thumb on the ultra-smooth surface, so you have to sand them out completely before priming. And wear gloves when handling MDF, especially when carrying heavy sheets. MDF edges can be sharp enough to cut skin—I've got the scars to prove it.

COMBINE MDF WITH WOOD MOLDINGS

Here's one of my favorite tricks for painted trim, cabinets or even furniture: Use MDF for the large, plain parts and dress them up with wood moldings like base cap, coves or base shoe. That gives you the money savings of MDF without the time-consuming work of making MDF trim from scratch. The wainscoting shown here, for example, is simply panels and strips of 1/2-in. MDF trimmed with small-profile pine moldings that cost less than 75¢ per foot. The cap rail is likely to take a beating from chairs, so I make that from wood instead of MDF. Once coated with primer and paint, the wood and MDF parts will look exactly the same.

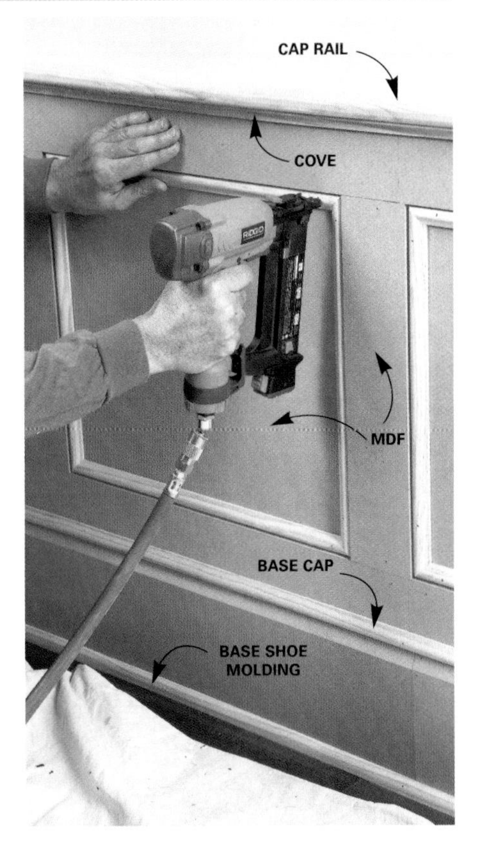

DON'T DRIVE WITHOUT DRILLING

MDF is kind of like an Oreo cookie: two hard faces with a softer core between them. That soft core splits easily when you drive a screw into the edge. The hard face presents different problems for screws. If you don't drill a countersink recess, the screw head may snap off before it sinks into the MDF. Or, if the head does sink, it might push up chips. The cure for both problems is to use a countersinking drill bit ($4), which gives you a pilot hole and a recess for the screw head in one step.

COUNTERSINK BIT

Tools & Skills

SAND, PRIME, SAND...

The face of MDF is smooth, but the edges are fuzzy like the skin of a peach. If you just slap paint on the fuzz, it will look and feel like sandpaper. So you have to get rid of the peach fuzz before you paint. I have two recipes for smooth edges: one for "good-enough" edges and the other for edges that will get a high-gloss finish.

Here's the good-enough process I apply to most projects, including trim: First, lightly sand the edges with 100-grit paper. Foam-backed sanding pads work great on routed profiles. Then prime the MDF. Use a solvent-based primer only. Water-based primer can raise small blisters. My favorite MDF primers are KILZ and Cover Stain because they're easy to sand. When the primer dries, sand off the fuzz with 100-grit pads. A couple of light passes is all it takes. You can sand KILZ or Cover Stain after a couple of hours, but let the primer dry overnight for smoother results. After sanding, wipe away the powdery dust with a damp cloth and you're ready to paint.

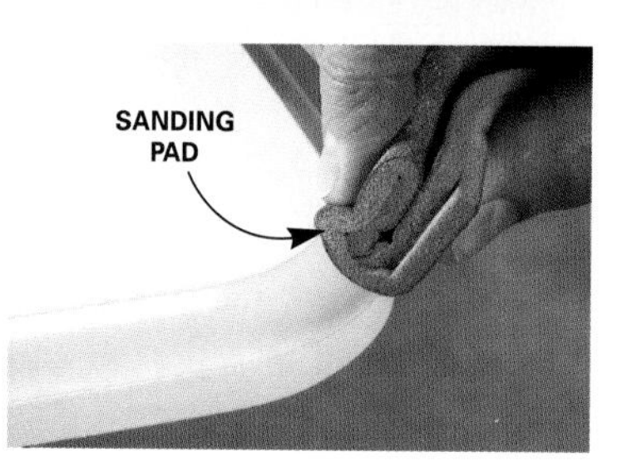

For projects that will get a coat of high-gloss paint, I prime twice: First I prime the edges only. Later I prime the whole project (as described above). When applying the edge-only coat, be sure to feather out any primer on the face of the MDF so brush marks won't show up later. Then sand, prime again and sand again to achieve smooth-as-glass edges.

DON'T LET IT GET WET

MDF stands up to moisture about as well as graham crackers. A few water drops will raise small bumps on the surface. A long soaking will make it swell to twice its original thickness. So MDF is a risky choice for baseboards in entryways and trim near tubs or sinks. My all-time greatest MDF mistake was using it for windowsills in my own home. Condensation from the windows made them swell just like the baseboard shown here. If you use MDF as baseboard, be sure to paint the lower edge before installation. That will provide short-term protection against occasional spills. Also install the baseboard about 1/4 in. above the floor and then cover the gap with wood base shoe molding. There are moisture-resistant versions of MDF, but they're hard to find. To find manufacturers and dealers, search online for "moisture resistant MDF."

DON'T USE A HAMMER

Unless you're willing to drill a hole for every single nail, don't plan on using a hammer. Without a hole, the nail will probably bend in rock-hard MDF. And even if it goes in without bending, the nail will push up a mound of fiber that looks like a mini volcano. A trim nailer, on the other hand, shoots nails through MDF every time. The skinny nails will raise tiny pimples, but you can easily scrape them off with a sharp putty knife before you fill the nail holes.

Question&Comment

WHEN TO USE A ROTARY DRILL

I'm installing a sprinkler system and have to drill a 1-in. hole through my poured concrete foundation for the water line. I own a hammer drill with a 1/2-in. chuck and was able to find a 1-in. masonry bit with a 1/2-in. shank, but it was too short. Can I just mount it in an extension?

Probably not. Those extensions aren't designed to take abuse from a hammer drill. Even if you didn't need an extension, the 1-in. bit likely exceeds the rated capacity of your hammer drill. As a rule, a heavy-duty 1/2-in. hammer drill is limited to a 3/4-in. bit. Even if you could find a stepped-down shank that you could chuck into your drill, you're better off renting a rotary hammer drill with the proper length bit. It'll get the job done in a fraction of the time and with a lot less sweat.

HOLE SAW HASSLES

I dread using hole saws in wood or metal. Wood takes forever, and metal dulls the teeth. I'm also confused by the different varieties—and the huge price range. Which type should I get? Is there a way to speed up the drilling process?

We talked to Matt Savarino, the hole saw expert at Lenox Tools, to get to the bottom of your dilemma. Matt told us that most DIYers don't need expensive hole saws. In fact, for occasional cuts in wood, he says the cheapest carbon steel saws work just fine (see Photo 1). But don't try using them in metal—that'll destroy the saw teeth in seconds.

But if you're cutting a hole in your steel door for a dead bolt, or cut lots of holes, step up to a bimetal hole saw. The teeth are made from a harder steel than the shell, so they last longer. But that doesn't mean they're indestructible. Always provide lubrication when drilling into metal. Cutting oil is best, and even ordinary motor oil is better than nothing (see Photo 2). You can use bimetal saws to cut through all types of materials except ceramic, porcelain, granite and the like. For those, you need a carbide-grit hole saw.

Even if you drill relief holes, hole saws take forever to drill through thick wood. If the holes are less than 1-1/2 in. in diameter, don't bother with hole saws; use spade bits.

1 Holes in wood. **The best way to cut holes faster is to drill relief holes to exhaust wood chips and keep the blade cooler.**

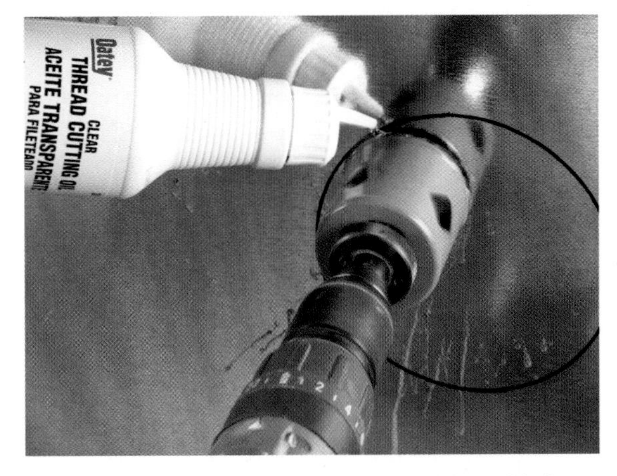

2 Holes in metal. **In metal, always use bimetal hole saws and keep the teeth sharper longer by using lubricating oil.**

SPECIAL SECTION TOOLS & SKILLS

Tools & Skills: Question & Comment

AIR COMPRESSOR QUANDARY

My old air compressor pooped out and I need a new one. I see air compressors advertised for less than $100. Are they even worth having?

It all depends on how much you'll be running it, and what you plan to use it for. Compressors that cost less than $100 are very portable and will do a fine job of running a trim nailer, filling tires or blowing dust off your clothes—but that's about it. You'll have to be patient; they take a long time to get up to pressure and to fill tires. If you do decide on a cheap compressor, consider it a "throw-away" tool and be prepared to replace it when it dies. Virtually any repair will exceed the replacement cost.

If you can afford to spend about $300, you can get a portable compressor that'll power most DIY air tools and last for a couple of decades (see **Photo 2**). Look for a compressor with a cast iron cylinder, oil lubrication and air output of at least 4 cu. ft. per minute (cfm). You'll have to change the oil on schedule to keep it humming. But the longer life outweighs the hassle. Also be aware that oil-lubricated compressors inject a fine oil mist into the air line. So you'll need to invest in a separate hose and a filter if you're going to use a paint sprayer.

You can find less expensive, oilless compressors ($129 to $199) that will put out 4 cfm, but don't expect them to last as long. And you'll need to wear hearing protection—they're LOUD!

If you're a serious motorhead, you'll have to take a larger leap. If you want to run "air-motor" powered tools like impact wrenches and ratchets, you'll have to get serious with a unit that's capable of at least 5.5 cfm with a sizable air tank. Just forget about running air-powered sanders and sandblasters—those guys require almost 9 cfm (see **Photo 3**). Expect to spend $540 plus for a good one. But the only thing that makes them portable is the wheels. They're heavy and bulky.

$89 • .7 CFM • OILLESS

1 Run your brad nailers all day with a low-cost air compressor. It'll run a framing nailer, too, but you'll have to wait for the pressure to rebuild after every few nails.

$300 • 4.2 CFM • OIL SPLASH LUBRICATION

MAKITA

2 Pony up more money to get a quality portable oil-lube compressor that's powerful enough to run all these air tools, including a framing nailer.

$540 • 5.8 CFM • OIL LUBRICATION

CAMPBELL HAUSFELD

3 Blast big bolts with a powerful impact wrench and a heavy-duty compressor. This model has a 20-gallon tank, twin pistons and a fully cast iron pump.

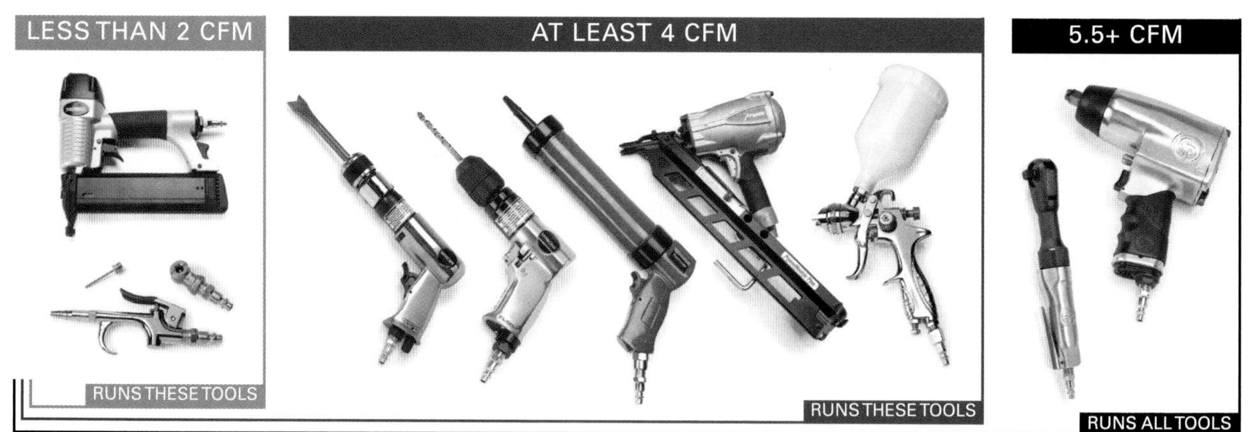

GRAB 'N GO TOOL STORAGE

by **David Radtke**

Do you spend too much time looking for tools on shelves scattered around your garage? If so, this grab-and-go tool cabinet is the answer. You corral all your power tools and accessories in one place and roll them around your garage or shop. The pullout table is great for doing quick repairs, prepping tools and sorting parts. The drawers are removable totes that you can carry to your work area.

You'll also like how easy it is to build. All the parts are glued and screwed together with simple butt joints and overlays. Just build the top section of tool bins first, then build the lower shelving unit to slide under.

Time, money & materials

You can easily build the cabinet in one weekend and then apply the finish and install the hardware the next. Figure on spending about $375 for the entire project including hardware and finish. We chose 3/4-in. birch plywood for the main structure and 1/2-in. plywood for the backs and drawer sides. You'll also need hardwood for the drawer fronts and the edges of the pullout work surface. You can dress up the look with simple moldings to cover the exposed plywood faces.

Build the upper bins first

Cut the plywood parts according to the Cutting List on p. 48. Assemble each of the three bins as shown in **Photo 1**. To make assembly faster, we used self-drilling screws, which means you won't need a pilot hole or a countersink. However, drill a shallow starter hole with a 3/32-in. bit to keep the tip of the screw from wandering off the mark as you start to drive the screw.

When you join the three bins (**Photo 2**), you'll need a work surface that's absolutely flat; an old flush panel door

Meet a pro: David Radtke
David is a custom cabinetmaker, home design consultant, freelance editor and home restoration specialist in Minneapolis. He enjoys archery, bowmaking, woodturning and cycling—whenever he's not standing behind a table saw or sitting in front of the drawing board.

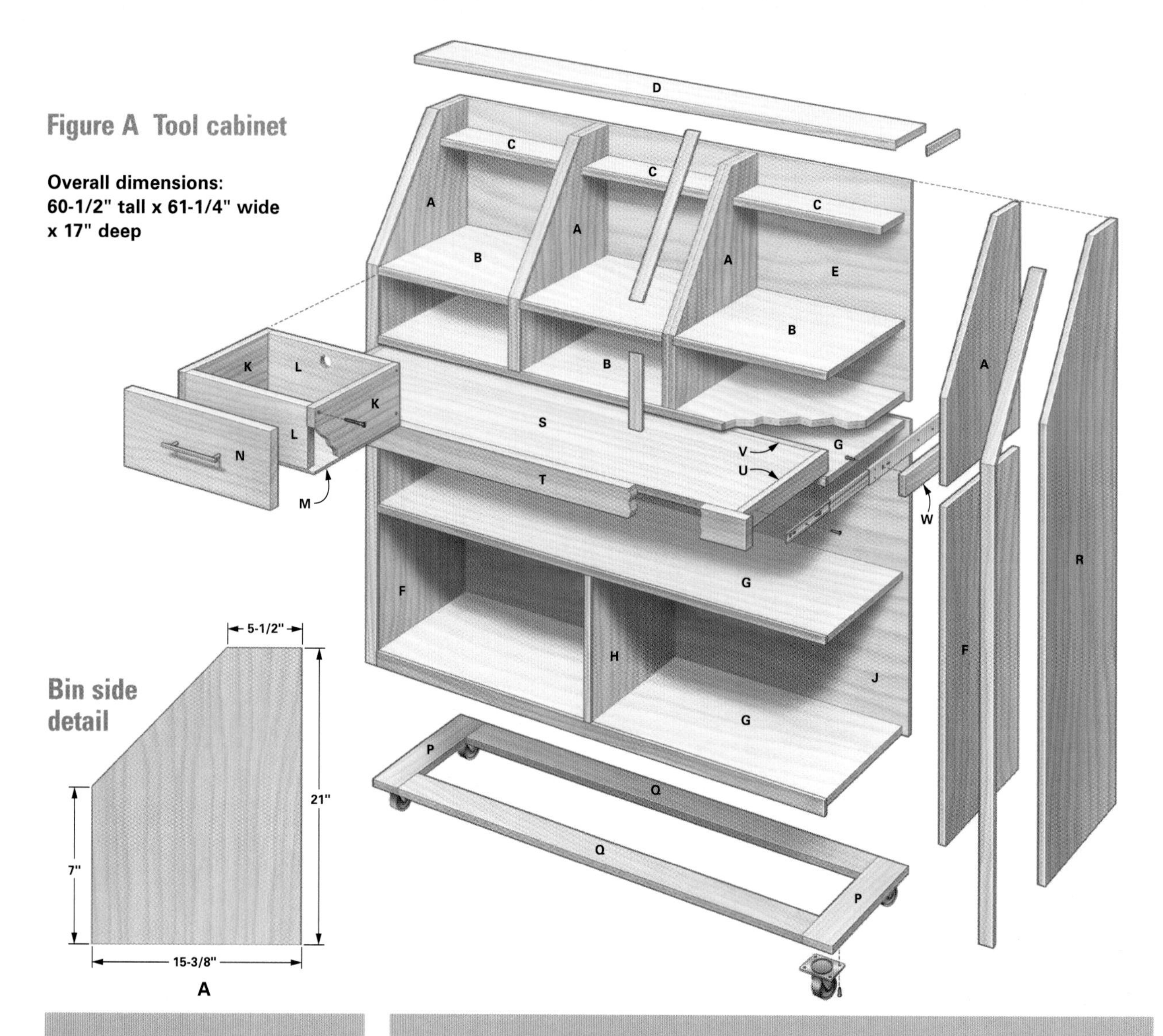

MATERIALS LIST

ITEM	QTY.
3/4" hardwood plywood	4
1/2" hardwood plywood	2
1/4" x 3/4" screen molding	40'
1/4" x 1-1/2" lattice	20'
3/4" x 1-1/2" (hardwood table edging)	5'
1x8 hardwood (drawer facing)	5'
1x4 hardwood (table front)	5'
14" ball-bearing drawer slides	2
3" swivel casters	4
5" drawer pulls	3
8"-wide drawer pulls	2
Wood glue	1 pint
No. 8 x 1-1/4" screws	1 box
No. 8 x 1-1/2" screws	1 box
5/16" x 1-1/2" lag screws	16
1-1/4" 18-gauge nails	1 box
7/8" pneumatic staples	1 box

CUTTING LIST

KEY	QTY.	SIZE & DESCRIPTION
A	6	3/4" x 15-3/8" x 21" bin sides
B	6	3/4" x 15-3/8" x 18" bin shelves
C	3	3/4" x 5" x 18" upper bin shelves
D	1	3/4" x 7" x 60-3/4" top
E*	1	1/2" x 21" x 58-1/4" upper assembly back
F	2	3/4" x 15-3/8" x 32" lower unit sides
G*	3	3/4" x 15-3/8" x 56-7/8" lower unit shelves
H	1	3/4" x 15-3/8" x 14-13/16" lower unit vertical partition
J*	1	1/2" x 32" x 58-1/4" lower unit back
K	6	1/2" x 15-3/8" x 5-1/4" drawer sides
L*	6	3/4" x 17" x 5-1/4" drawer fronts and backs
M*	3	1/4" x 15-3/8" x 17-7/8" plywood drawer bottoms
N	3	3/4" x 6-5/8" x 19-1/4" hardwood drawer face
P	2	3/4" x 3-1/2" x 15-3/4" plywood side base supports
Q*	2	3/4" x 3-1/2" x 51-3/16" plywood front and back base supports
R	2	3/4" x 15-7/8" x 55-7/8" plywood finished sides
S*	1	3/4" x 14-5/8" x 54-3/8" plywood pullout table
T*	1	3/4" x 3-1/4" x 58-1/4" hardwood table face
U*	2	3/4" x 1-1/2" x 15-3/8" hardwood table side edging
V*	1	3/4" x 1-1/2" x 54-3/8" hardwood table back edging
W	2	3/4" x 2" x 15-3/8" plywood spacers

** Measure and cut to fit*

on sawhorses works perfectly for this. Finish the bin unit by gluing and nailing the top into place (Photo 3).

Making the drawers fit

Measure the openings in the bottom of the bins and then downsize the drawer about 1/8 in. in total height and width. Since the drawers don't have slides, this will give you just the right clearance. Take into account the thickness of the plywood drawer bottom. Sometimes "1/4-in. plywood" is actually 3/16 in. thick.

Build the lower shelving section

Measure the width of the top assembly and then cut the parts for the lower shelving unit so it'll be exactly the same width. "Three-quarter-inch" plywood isn't exactly 3/4 in. thick; it's actually 23/32 in. That's why it's critical to measure. Use the Cutting List as a guide, but measure carefully to be sure.

Screw the sides to the shelves using Figure A as your guide. Install the lower partition (H) halfway between the bottom and middle shelf. Cut the 1/2-in. plywood back and check the assembly for square, then glue and nail it to the back of the sides and shelf.

To reinforce the bottom shelf, rip 3-1/2-in. strips of 3/4-in. plywood (parts P and Q) and glue and nail them to the bottom of the assembly. Screw the casters to the strips.

Combine the two sections

Mount the drawer slide that will support the pullout table (Photo 5). Then lay the upper unit onto its back and glue and screw the outer sides (R) to the bin sides (A). You may need to shim underneath to bring the sides perfectly flush.

Next, slide the lower unit into the upper until it contacts the spacers (W). Align the faces of the lower assembly with the outer sides (R) and drive the screws from the inside. You'll need nine screws per side.

At this stage, the project has acquired considerable heft, so get someone to help you tip it upright.

1 Build the bins. Position the shelves with spacers and tack them in place with a brad nailer. Then add screws for strength.

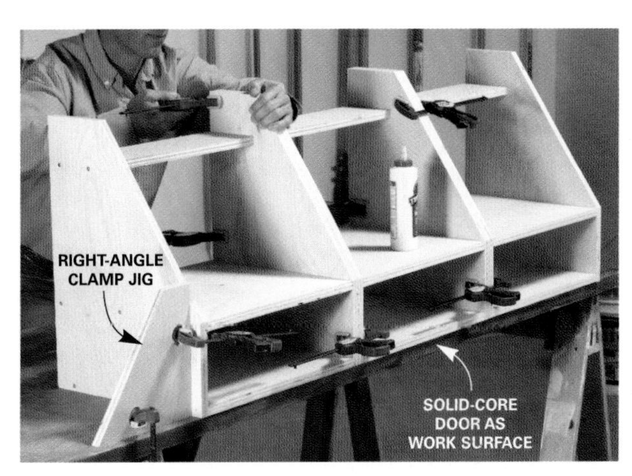

2 Join the bins. Line them up on a flat surface, then glue and clamp them together. A homemade squaring jig holds the bins square until the back is on.

3 Add the back and top. First, glue and nail on the back. Then sand the front edges of the bins so they're flush. Finally, glue and nail on the top.

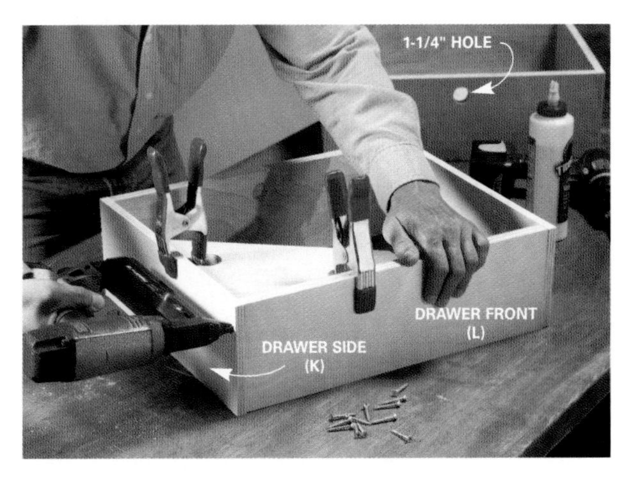

4 Build the drawers. Tack them together with nails and glue, then add screws. A squaring jig makes square assembly easy. Drill holes through the back of each drawer to act as a handle.

> **Tip**
>
> To make sure your drawers don't get trapped inside their openings before you install the fronts, press a strip of masking tape onto the inside front of the drawer and let it hang past the drawer. You can pull on the tape if you accidentally close the drawer.

Nail on the edging

Now you can cut and glue the edge banding to the exposed plywood edges. We used screen molding for the 3/4-in. faces and 1/4-in.-thick lattice for the double-thick faces. You may need to rip the lattice to fit. Keep in mind that you don't want the trim to hang over and obstruct the drawer openings, so be sure to flush the edging with the plywood.

Finishing touches

With the unit nearly finished, you can now make the pullout table. Carefully measure the distance between the side spacers. Subtract 1 in. from this measurement (1/2-in. clearance for each drawer slide) and build the table to this precise width. Now you can cut and screw the drawer faces to the front of the drawers. Be sure you have 1/4-in. clearance between the bottom of the drawer faces and the pullout table. Align the edges of the outer drawer faces so they're even with the table front.

For a fast, easy finish, use a wipe-on polyurethane or Watco oil. Use a brush to get into tight areas and then a lint-free rag to wipe the finish. Let dry and give it a second coat.

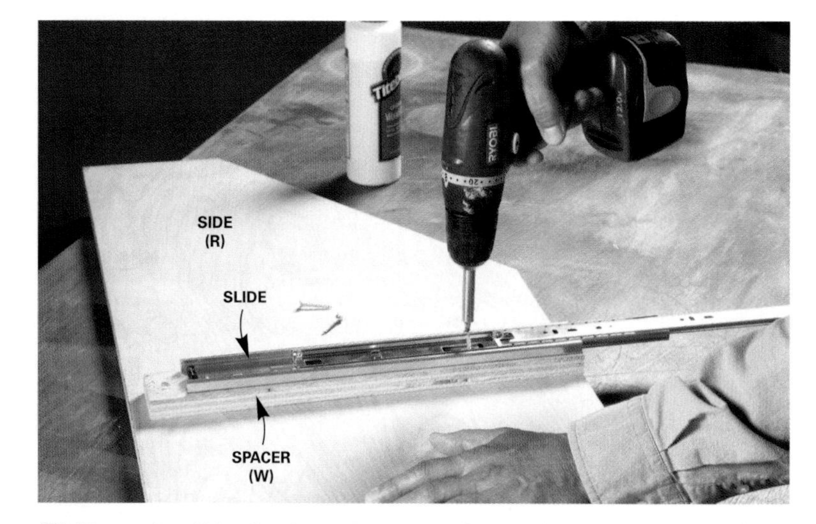

5 Mount the slides for the pullout table. **Glue and nail spacers to sides, then add the slides. This is a lot easier to do before you attach the sides to the bins.**

6 Combine the upper and lower units. **Slide the lower unit into the upper unit until it makes contact with the spacers. Screw the lower unit to the sides.**

7 Cover exposed plywood edges. **If the trim is a bit too wide, you can shave it slightly with your table saw. Glue and nail the edging into place.**

5 Exterior Maintenance & Repairs

IN THIS CHAPTER

HOW TO REPAIR **MORTAR JOINTS**

Crumbling masonry joints start out ugly, and then things get uglier fast—bricks come loose, water seeps behind the wall and bees make their homes in the mortar holes. Let it go and the problem won't go away. In fact, the deterioration will accelerate and you'll have a much bigger fix on your hands. But you can mend the joints yourself with a process called tuckpointing.

Tuckpointing isn't difficult or expensive—the only real investment is your time. But you can pick away at it in your free time, area by area.

The steps we show here will work on any brick walls, chimneys and retaining walls. Tuckpointing won't fix cracking or crumbling bricks, or cracks in walls caused by a shifting foundation. Those problems call for more drastic fixes that we won't cover here.

Pick up tools and materials

First and foremost, you'll need an angle grinder with a 4- or 4-1/4-in. diamond blade. Don't bother renting one unless you only have several feet of bad joints. You can buy one for as little as $40—even a fairly cheap one will do the trick (unless you're a serious tool junkie or you have an entire house that needs extensive tuckpointing).

You'll also need a few simple, inexpensive specialty tools that are available at masonry suppliers and some home centers. You'll need a brick trowel ($10) and a tuck pointer ($11). If you have concave mortar joints, you'll need a masonry jointer ($4) that's the width of your joints. For flat joints, you'll need a joint raker ($9). If you have just a few areas that need work, use a hammer and cold chisel to knock out the old mortar, but for more extensive work, plan on getting a rotary hammer drill fitted with a flat chisel to make the job go a heck of a lot quicker. You can rent one for $40 per day. If you have days' worth of work, rental costs can break the bank. In that case, spend the $120 (or more) to own one.

You'll also need mortar mix. A 60-lb. bag costs $4 at home centers. If you need colored mortar, take a small piece of the old mortar to a masonry supplier and ask for help finding a mortar dye to match. But be aware of this—fresh tuckpointing always stands out against older mortar. However, it will eventually weather to match.

Start small

If you only have a few joints to tuckpoint, dive right in. But if you have a large wall to tackle, start in a small area to get a feel for the operation before you start hogging out entire walls. You'll hone your skills and get a good idea of how much you can tuckpoint at one time. You'll have 30 to 60 minutes of working time once you mix the mortar.

Get ready for the dust

Tuckpointing is a dirty business. Grinding the joints creates a dust storm, with chunks of mortar covering the

1 Grind the horizontal joints first. Grind along the top and bottom of the horizontal joints. Get as close to the bricks as you can. If you accidentally grind against the bricks, the dust will turn the color of the brick.

2 Plunge-cut the vertical joints. Grind both sides of the vertical joints. Plunge the grinder into the joint and work it up and down to make the cuts. But be careful not to grind the bricks above and below the joints.

ground. Spread a drop cloth on the ground to catch the mortar so cleanup will take minutes instead of hours.

Close your house windows to keep out the dust, and tell your neighbors who might be affected to do the same.

Grind out the joints

Before you can put new mortar in the joints, you have to cut out the damaged material. Start by grinding the top and bottom of the horizontal (bed) joints with an angle grinder (**Photo 1**). Hold the grinder with both hands to keep it steady and avoid grinding into the bricks. You only need to grind 3/4 in. into the mortar.

Start at outside corners and work inward. That keeps you from putting extra pressure on the corner bricks, which could knock them out of the wall. After you've finished the horizontal joints, do the vertical (head) joints (**Photo 2**).

Knock out the mortar

Use the rotary hammer drill to pound the mortar out of the joints. Set the drill on the rotating mode (it puts less pressure on the bricks). Again, work from the outside corners inward (**Photo 3**). Keep the chisel point in the mortar joint and keep moving the hammer. The drill makes quick work of removing mortar, but be careful. The powerful tool can also knock out bricks. If that happens, take them all the way out, chisel off all the mortar, then reset them when you fill the joints.

There's really no secret to knocking out the mortar. Just hold the drill at about a 45-degree angle to the wall, squeeze the trigger and watch the mortar fall out. **Caution**: Wear eye protection—mortar pieces can go flying!

Clean out the joints

Once you've chipped out the damaged mortar, use a hand broom to sweep the joints. Sweep away mortar clumps and the dust (**Photo 4**). Use the rotary hammer drill to bust out stubborn chunks.

Then wash out the joints with water. But don't hose down the wall or you'll soak everything, including the ground where you'll be standing or kneeling. Instead, fill a bucket with water and brush the water into the joints (**Photo 5**). Don't worry about slopping water onto the bricks—you want them damp before you fill the joints anyway.

Mix the new mortar

If you're tinting the mortar, stir the dye and the mortar mix in a bucket before adding the water. Dye is typically sold in 1-1/2-lb. bags. Mix one-quarter of the dye with one-quarter of a 60-lb. bag of mortar mix. Stir in water until the mix is the consistency of peanut butter (**Photo 6**).

3 Hammer out the mortar. Keep moving the rotary hammer drill along the joints as you chisel out the mortar. Be sure to keep the chisel off the bricks so you don't knock them out of place.

4 Sweep out the joints. Use a small broom to sweep debris and dust out of the joints. Inspect the joints for any remaining stubborn mortar and knock it out with the drill.

5 Give the joints a bath. Stick a brush into a bucket of water and rinse out the joints. Your goal here isn't to make surfaces pristine, just to get rid of chunks and dust.

6 Whip up the mortar batch. Mix the mortar to the consistency of peanut butter with no dry spots or clumps. You'll know the mix is right when it sticks to your trowel when you hold it at a 45-degree angle. Let the mortar sit for 10 minutes before using it.

7 Fill the joints. Load your brick trowel and hold it next to the joint. Work the mortar into the joint with your tuck pointer. Pack the joint full before moving on to the next one.

8 Strike the mortar joints. Drag the jointer along the vertical joints and the horizontal joints. Apply gentle pressure to tool out the ridges where the joints intersect. Finish one joint before moving on to the next.

9 Wipe down the bricks. Scrub the mortar off the bricks with a stiff brush. This also knocks down and smooths out any high spots along the joint edges.

The mortar will last 30 to 60 minutes, but you may need to add water to keep it workable. After one hour, throw out what's left and mix a new batch.

Work the mortar into the joints

Use a brick trowel and a tuck pointer to pack the mortar into the joints. Most pros prefer this method to using a grout/mortar bag. Mortar that is hand packed is more durable.

Scoop mortar onto the trowel. Hold the trowel next to the joint, then press the mortar into the joint with the tuck pointer (**Photo 7**). Pack the joint until it's flush with the front of the bricks.

Tool the joints

Let the mortar in the filled joints set for about 30 minutes. If you're tuckpointing a large area, continually check the first joints you filled to see if they're ready to tool (finish). Check by pressing the filled joint with your thumb. If your thumb leaves only a slight impression, it's ready to tool. If it goes in deeper, wait five minutes and try again. But don't let the mortar get too stiff—it can start to harden after just 30 minutes, making it difficult to tool the joints.

If you want rounded joints, press a masonry jointer into the top of vertical joints and pull the tool downward. The jointer will push out some of the mortar and leave a concave shape. For horizontal joints, start at a corner (**Photo 8**). Run the tool about halfway across the joint, then stop and finish tooling from the other side.

For flat joints, place a joint raker over an old joint to set the depth. Then run the raker along the new joints to make them flat.

Clean the bricks

Once the joints have set up (about 30 minutes after tooling), use a stiff-bristle brush to clean dried mortar off the bricks (**Photo 9**).

If the mortar refuses to come off, wait three days, then use muriatic acid ($7 for 1 gallon at home centers). Use 10 parts water to 1 part acid (add the acid to the water, not the other way around). **Caution:** Be sure to wear eye protection and rubber gloves when working with acid. Brush the acid onto the bricks with a stiff-bristle brush, scrub the bricks and let the acid fizz. Then rinse the acid off with water. If there's still a little mortar residue left, treat it again.

The acid can slightly alter the bricks' appearance, so test it on a small area first. If it does alter the appearance, increase the ratio of water to acid.

PATCH **ROTTED WOOD**

Do you have rotted wood? It's usually better to simply tear out the old board or molding and replace it than to repair it. But for windowsills and door jambs that are hard to remove and molding that would be tough to duplicate, patching with wood filler makes sense.

Fillers for repair of rotted wood generally fall into three categories. For small holes and cracks, there are fillers like DAP Latex Wood Filler or MH Ready Patch that harden as the water or solvent evaporates. Other fillers, such as Durham's Rock Hard Water Putty, harden by a chemical reaction when water is mixed in. Finally, two-part fillers like Minwax High Performance Wood Filler (polyester) and Abatron's WoodEpox (epoxy) harden after you mix the two parts.

Two-part fillers are the most durable, and the best choice for long-lasting repairs. Although polyester and epoxy are both two-part fillers, they have unique characteristics that make them quite different to work with. We'll show you the differences and give you some tips for working with these two excellent wood repair fillers.

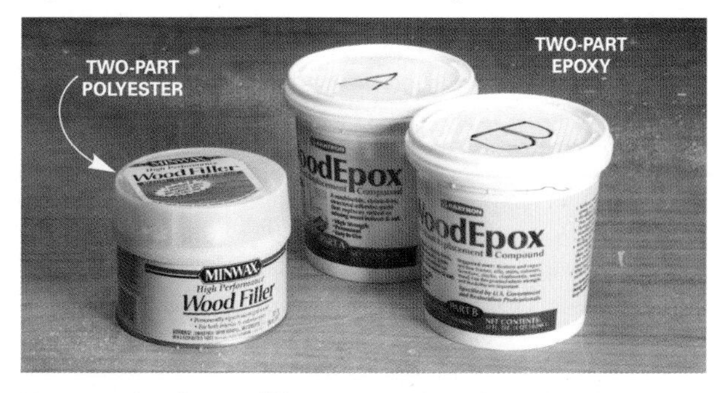

Epoxy and polyester fillers are two-part formulas that harden after you mix the parts. They're both excellent fillers, though with slightly different characteristics.

1 **Gouge out rotted wood with a chisel, screwdriver or other pointy tool.**

Use epoxy for a premium repair

One common brand of epoxy wood filler is Abatron WoodEpox (abatron.com; 800-445-1754). A kit containing pints of LiquidEpoxy consolidant parts A and B and WoodEpox parts A and B costs $76. Unlike polyester filler, epoxy wood filler has a dough-like consistency, so it will stay put even on vertical repairs.

Prepare for an epoxy repair by removing as much rotted wood as possible. Use an old screwdriver, chisel or 5-in-1 painter's tool to gouge out the damaged wood (Photo 1). If the wood is wet, cover it loosely with a poly tent and let it dry completely before starting the repair. Drill a series of 1/4-in. holes around the rotted area if you suspect rotted wood below the surface, but don't drill all the way through. You'll fill these with consolidant to solidify the wood around the repair.

Start the repair by soaking the damaged area with epoxy consolidant (Photo 2). Mix the consolidant according to the directions. Wear rubber gloves and safety glasses when you're working with epoxy. You can mix the consolidant in a squirt bottle or a small plastic container. Use a disposable brush to work the epoxy consolidant into the wood fibers. Epoxy is difficult to remove after it hardens, so clean up drips and runs right away with paper towels. You don't have to wait for

Tips for working with epoxy:

- **Label the caps "A" and "B" and don't mix them up.**
- **Start with a clean container or mixing board each time you mix a new batch.**
- **Save epoxy by filling most of the cavity with a scrap of wood. Glue it in with epoxy filler.**
- **Carve the epoxy before it becomes rock hard.**

2 **Mix two-part epoxy consolidant in a squeeze bottle. Squirt it into the holes and repair area. Use a disposable brush to spread the consolidant and work it into the wood fibers.**

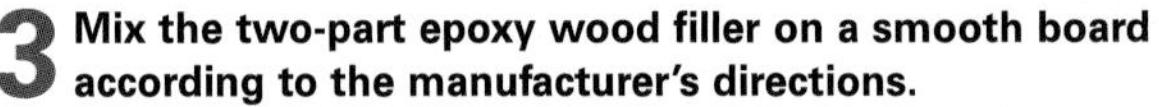
3 **Mix the two-part epoxy wood filler on a smooth board according to the manufacturer's directions.**

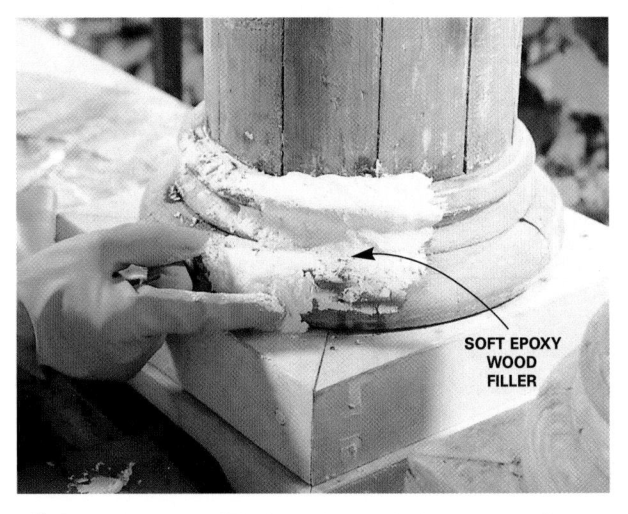

4 **Press the epoxy filler into the repair. Leave enough protruding so you can shape the repair after it starts to harden.**

5 Rough out the shape with a rasp. Mix another batch of epoxy filler and add another layer if necessary. Fine-tune the repair with sandpaper, then prime and paint.

the consolidant to harden before applying the epoxy filler.

Next, mix the two-part epoxy filler on a mixing board (**Photo 3**). Then apply it with a putty knife or simply press it into place with your fingers (**Photo 4**). Roughly shape the epoxy, making sure it protrudes beyond the final profile. When the temperature is 70 degrees F, you'll have about 30 minutes before the epoxy starts to harden. Increase the working time by spreading the epoxy in a thin layer on your mixing board and keeping it cool. On a warm day, the epoxy will harden enough in three or four hours to start shaping it with a Surform plane, rasp and sandpaper (**Photo 5**). After rough-shaping with a plane or rasp, sand the filler with 80-grit and then 120-grit sandpaper. If you sand off too much (or didn't add enough epoxy to begin with), dust off the repair and add another layer. You can make a more spreadable filler by mixing a small batch of consolidant and a small batch of filler and then adding some of the consolidant to the filler to reach the desired consistency.

Polyester is readily available and less expensive

If you've done any auto body repair, you've probably worked with two-part polyester filler. Minwax High Performance Wood Filler is one brand formulated for wood repair, but a gallon container of Bondo or some other brand of two-part auto body polyester will also work and may be less expensive for larger fixes.

The process for repairing wood is much the same whether you're using polyester filler or epoxy. Instead of epoxy consolidant, you'll use High Performance Wood Hardener to solidify and strengthen the wood fibers (**Photo 1**). Polyester begins hardening faster than Abatron WoodEpox. Depending on the temperature, you'll have about 10 to 15 minutes to work before the filler starts to harden.

Also, unlike WoodEpox, polyester tends to sag when you're doing vertical repairs. One trick is to build a form and line it with plastic sheeting. Press the form against the filler and attach it with screws. Then pull it off after the filler hardens. Or you can wait until the sagging filler reaches the hardness of soap and carve it off with a putty knife or chisel or shape it with a Surform plane or rasp (**Photo 2**). Most medium to large repairs will require at least two layers of filler. Complete the repair by sanding and priming the filled area and then painting.

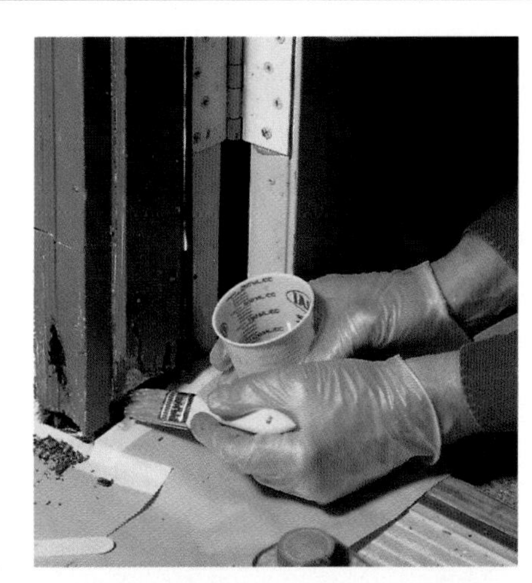

1 Remove rotted wood with a 5-in-1 or other sharp tool. Then coat the area with wood hardener as shown. Mix polyester wood filler and press it into the recess with a putty knife.

2 Carve the partially hardened sagging wood filler with a putty knife or chisel. Add another layer of filler if necessary.

INSTALL A
NEW ENTRY DOOR

A new door in 1 day? Let our old pro teach you a few new tricks!

by **Jeff Gorton**

Robin and Danny's front door was dented and drafty. They needed a new door, and we needed a place to photograph a door installation story. It was a perfect match. Robin and Danny agreed to install the door themselves with my help. I've installed dozens of doors throughout my carpentry career, so I knew how to guide them through the pitfalls. I have to confess, though, there were a few times when I couldn't resist jumping in to lend a hand. Still, the new homeowners did a great job of tearing out the old door and installing a new one. The new door looked terrific—we were all happy with the results. Here's how we went about the project.

One of the biggest mistakes homeowners make is to grab a door off the home center shelf and expect it to fit right. So my first coaching task was to help Robin and Danny measure for and order the door. First we measured the width and height of the door. Then Robin carefully pried off the interior trim (Photo 1) so we could measure the rough opening, which is the width between the studs and the height from the floor to the header. Next we measured from the back of the outside trim, or brick molding, to the face of the interior wall to find the jamb width. Ordering the new door with the right jamb width ensures that the interior trim fits without the need for added jamb extensions. Finally we went back outside and measured the width from the outside of the brick molding and the height from the bottom of the sill to the top of the exterior trim. To avoid having to patch siding, it's best to order a door assembly that will fill the space. This may mean asking for special exterior trim that's wider than standard 2-in.-wide "brick molding." If you're ordering a door and sidelight(s), you can adjust the width by substituting a different size sidelight or by adjusting the space between the door and the sidelight. The door and sidelight were assembled at the plant and arrived as a single unit. Installation of a door without a sidelight is the same.

"Protecting the wall with a putty knife saved the wall paint. Neat trick!" — Robin

With the door size, jamb width and dimensions of the rough and exterior opening in hand, Robin and Danny went door shopping. They discovered that the standard configuration of a 3-ft. door and sidelight was a few inches too narrow and 1/2 in. shorter than their existing door and sidelight. The salesperson recommended spending a little extra

1 Pry off the interior trim. **Robin thought this was a pretty neat trick. Protecting the wall with a putty knife under the pry bar meant she wouldn't have to repaint the entry.**

2 Tear off the brick molding. **Danny cut the caulk along the edges of the brick molding with a utility knife so it would be easier to remove. But the molding was still stubborn and came off in pieces.**

> **"I was shocked at all the door options available. The choices were limitless."**
> **— Danny**

money to add a spacer between the door and the sidelight. This corrected the width problem. Robin and Danny could have ordered a custom height door and frame for several hundred dollars more, but they decided to live with the height difference and cover the gap with trim later. We decided to add a strip of plywood under the sill to raise the door slightly, so in the end the shorter height worked out perfectly.

Robin and Danny wanted a door that looked like wood, minus the maintenance hassles. They chose a Therma-Tru fiberglass door with a surprisingly realistic-looking oak wood grain. The cost of the door and sidelight unit was $1,300. Fortunately (for us, anyway!), the door assembly plant wasn't too busy and the door was delivered about 10 days later.

Remove the old door

Robin was surprised at how easy the door and frame were to remove, especially after the interior and exterior trim were off (Photos 1 and 2). And she got to learn a new skill—operating a reciprocating saw (Photo 3). If you don't have a recip saw, you can use a hacksaw blade. Working in older houses or where the door is exposed to the weather, I often have to repair a water-damaged subfloor or otherwise rebuild the sill area before installing the new door. In this case, the subfloor was in good condition, but we noticed that the new door sill was thinner than the old one. After taking a few measurements, we decided to add a strip of plywood over the subfloor to raise the door so it would clear the entry rug (Photo 5). Robin checked to be sure the sill area was level. We could have shimmed under the plywood with strips of building paper or scrap vinyl flooring to level the floor if necessary.

Since our door was covered by an overhanging roof, we didn't need additional

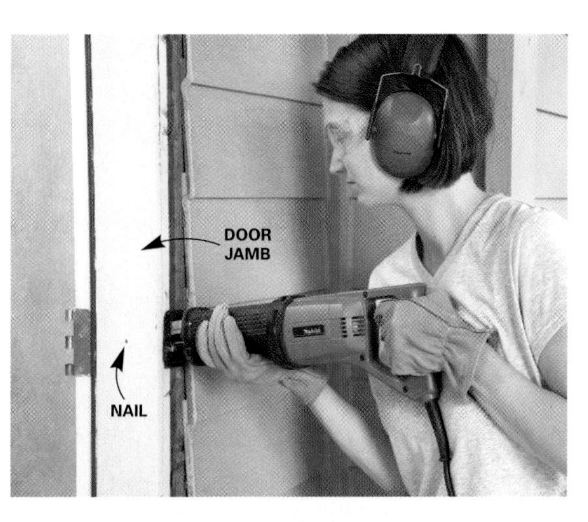

3 Free the door frame. **Here's Robin with her brand new recip saw cutting through the nails so the door frame will come out easily. She's looking forward to the next demolition project so she can hone her sawing skills.**

4 Remove the frame from the opening. **Danny didn't have any trouble getting the frame out after removing the trim and cutting the nails and screws. The sill was stuck down with caulk, but broke free as Danny tilted the frame.**

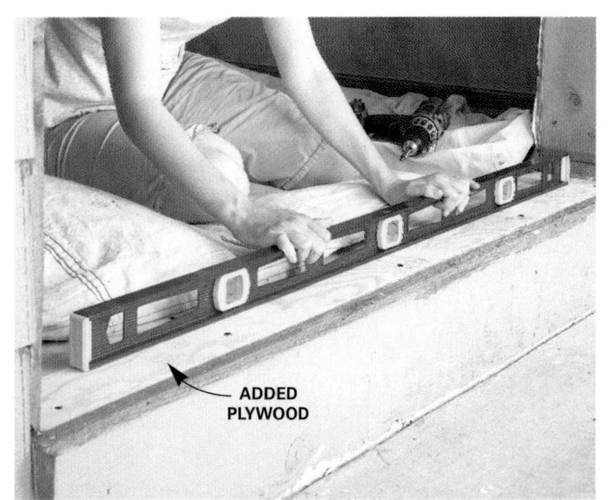

5 Check the sill. **Robin was a lot more flexible than Danny, so he let her do most of the low work. Here she's checking the sill area to make sure it's level. They've already added a layer of plywood to raise the door a little.**

EXTERIOR MAINTENANCE & REPAIRS

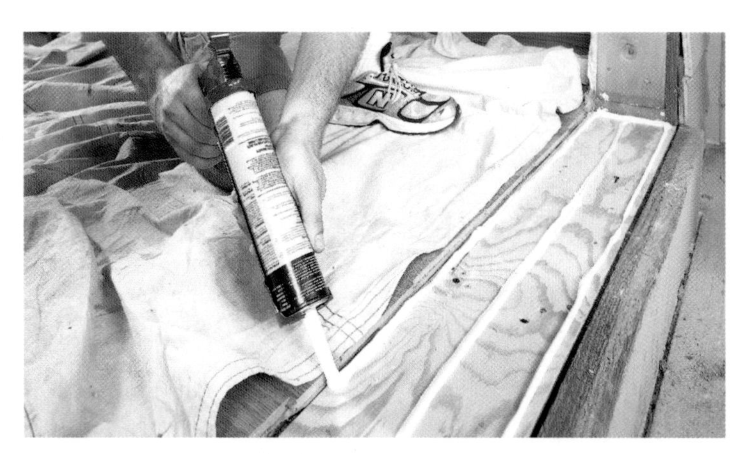

6 Caulk the opening. **Danny's done a lot of caulking, so this part was easy. He inspected the bottom of the door frame and did some measuring to be sure the beads of caulk aligned with flat spots on the sill. When Danny finished caulking the sill, he caulked around the perimeter of the opening too.**

7 Set the door frame. **Robin and Danny could rest easy now. The door frame slid into the opening as planned and the heavy-lifting part of the job was done.**

8 Tack the top corners. **Here Robin is trying out her nailing skills. The 16-penny nails proved a bit much, though, so Danny took over the nailing duty.**

9 Plumb the hinge side. **Robin was a natural with the level, so she's checking to make sure the jamb is plumb while Danny makes adjustments from the inside.**

protection from water, but if you install a door that's exposed to the weather, be sure to add a sill pan to protect the subfloor (one brand is Jamsill Guard, jamsill.com; call 800-526-7455 for ordering information) and a metal drip cap over the exterior trim.

Install the new door

With the old door out and the opening prepared, we were ready to install the new door and sidelight. Before we started, I explained to Robin and Danny that our goal was to set the new door frame in the opening and then adjust it with shims until the door fit perfectly. First we removed all the packing material from the new door and hoisted it into the opening to check the fit. The width was a little tight. We didn't have much wiggle room between the siding and the brick molding, but it was obvious we could make it work. So we removed the door unit and Danny applied heavy beads of polyurethane caulk to the sill and exterior sheathing (Photos 6 and 7). Danny and Robin moved the door to the opening and tilted it into place (Photo 7). Now we were ready to tack it in and add shims.

Shimming a door is the most critical part of the installation since it's when you tweak the frame to make the door fit perfectly and operate smoothly. I helped Robin and Danny center the top of the door frame with an equal caulk space between the siding and the trim on each side, and then tack the two top corners with 16d galvanized casing nails, letting the heads stick out so we could make adjustments later if necessary (Photo 8).

Next, Robin held a level to the hinge-side trim while Danny pried on the frame until the jamb was plumb (Photo 9). We drove another nail at the bottom of the hinge-side jamb to hold the frame plumb. With the door temporarily tacked in place, Danny and I headed around through the back door with a couple of bundles of wood shims. I gave him pointers as he wedged pairs of shims behind the hinges and along the top and far side of the frame. The goal was to create an even gap between the door and the frame (**Photo 10**). The key to shimming is to look at the gap between the door and the frame, and then decide how you can wedge the frame to correct any problems. We spent about 45 minutes adjusting shims before we were satisfied with the way the door fit.

Nails through the exterior trim hold the door frame temporarily, but they don't offer enough support to keep the door square over time. For that we still needed to drive 3-in. screws through the jamb and into the wall framing (**Photo 11**). We drove the screws at the shim locations to hold the shims in place and avoid bending the jamb. Then Danny set the nails that we had left sticking out and added nails about 16 in. apart along the exterior trim. After Danny completed this step, he made one final check of the door's fit in case adjustments were needed before we added insulation and reinstalled the interior trim.

"I didn't know that shimming a door was such a fussy, time-consuming job."

— Danny

Add the finishing touches

It was a relief to have the door securely installed. Robin and Danny relaxed, knowing they could lock the door for the night. I didn't have to warn Danny about the dangers of squirting too much expanding foam into the space around the door (**Photo 12**). He'd already learned that the hard way. With the space between the door and the frame well sealed and insulated, we moved to the outside, where we fitted a piece of trim over the door and caulked around the brick molding to seal the exterior. Now all that was left to do was install new interior trim, finish the door and install the new handle and lock.

10 Shim the door frame. **Danny slid pairs of shims behind the hinges and along the sidelight on the opposite side. He positioned the shims to create an even gap around the door.**

11 Secure the frame with screws. **After checking to make sure the door was contacting the weather stripping evenly and operating smoothly, Danny drilled countersink holes and drove 3-in. screws through the jamb at each hinge location. To secure the hinge side, he removed one short screw from each hinge and replaced it with a long screw.**

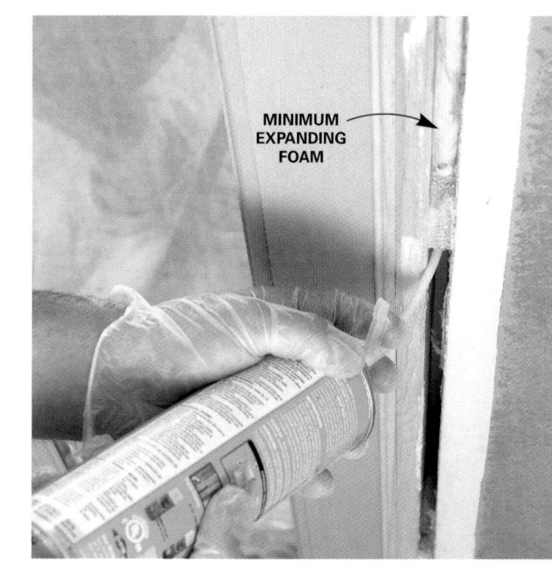

12 Seal the shim space. **Danny was experienced with spray foam, so he handled this task admirably. He managed to fill the space between the jamb and the framing with foam without getting it all over the place.**

Question & Comment

FORGET SELF-CLOSING HINGES

I bought a new spring hinge for the service door to my attached garage, but it's not an exact duplicate. I dread the thought of replacing and remortising all three hinges. What are my other options?

Replacement spring hinges are expensive (about $32 per set). But for just a little more money ($48), you can buy a high-quality hydraulic door closer (shown here is Global No. TC2204; $48 from amazon.com). You can find less expensive door closers ($35), but they don't last as long and are less adjustable.

If you have a steel door, don't use the wood screws that come with the unit (they'll pull out after a week). Instead, drill the mounting holes (make sure the drill is level) all the way through the door and mount the unit with hex bolts, nuts and lock washers. Then fine-tune the door's operation as shown.

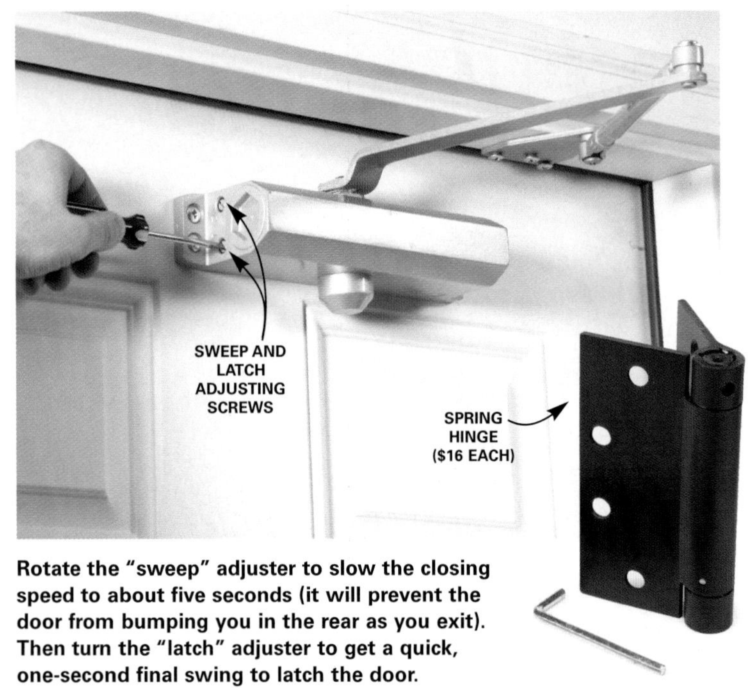

Rotate the "sweep" adjuster to slow the closing speed to about five seconds (it will prevent the door from bumping you in the rear as you exit). Then turn the "latch" adjuster to get a quick, one-second final swing to latch the door.

DO-IT-YOURSELF WINDOW SCREENS

I have some aluminum-framed screens that are beyond repair. The hardware store wants a fortune to make new ones. Is there some way I can make new ones myself?

Most home centers sell screen frame kits and rolls of screen. Just cut the rails to the proper size with a hacksaw and slide in the plastic corners. The kits come with the spline to trap the screen in the channel, but you'll have to buy a spline embedding tool (less than $5 at home centers). For simple screens, just follow the directions. However, if your old screens have latches, spring clips or pull tabs, bring one inside and fire up the computer to order the parts you'll need. Have the old screen handy for measurements and to match the hardware to the catalog images at alcosupply.com or blainewindow.com.

FILL BIG GAPS BEFORE CAULKING

I keep filling the control joints in my concrete patio, but the caulk keeps peeling away from both sides of the crack. What's going on and how can I fix it?

The solution is to use a combination of backer rod ($2.50 to $4 for 20 ft. at home centers) and caulk. First remove the caulk that's in the gap. For latex caulk, pour caulk remover (such as Lift Off; about $6 at home centers and hardware stores) over the caulk, let it sit for two hours, then dig out the caulk with a stiff putty knife. For silicone or polyurethane caulk, use mineral spirits. If you're not sure what type of caulk you have, start with the caulk remover. For stubborn sections, give the remover more time to work, then continue scraping. You don't have to remove every last piece of caulk, especially if it's at the bottom of the gap, but the top 1 in. of the crack needs to be cleaned off pretty well.

Use a backer rod with a diameter that's 1/8 to 1/4 in. larger than the crack. Push the rod into the gap so the top is about 1/4 in. below the concrete surface. Fill the gap with caulk, them smooth the caulk with a plastic spoon. Be sure to use a caulk that's formulated for use with concrete (it'll say so on the label).

BACKER ROD IS THE KEY
Insert backer rod into the gap, then run a bead of caulk over the top. For a smooth, even bead, tool the caulk with a plastic spoon.

REPACK A STEM SEAL ON A STREET VALVE

The street-side valve at my water meter has been dripping for years. I tightened the stem nut, but it still leaks. The utility wants $40 to shut the water off. Can I repack the stem with the water on?

Yes, you can. But you have to close the valve first. The gate valve will keep water from gushing out of the stem when you repack the nut.

Buy Teflon packing cord at any hardware store or home center. You'll get some water spray once you loosen the packing nut, so move anything you care about away from the meter area.

Most old valves have rust and mineral deposits in the gate valve's receiving groove. That crud can jam the gate and damage the valve. So flush the valve before you crank down on the handle.

REPACK THE STEM
With the valve in the off position, loosen the packing nut and slide it toward the handle. Then repack the stem with the Teflon packing cord.

GreatGoofs®

Snow job gone wrong

My wife isn't exactly a farm girl. You know, not well acquainted with running machinery. So I was surprised when she called me at work to say she was going to clear the snow out of our driveway with the garden tractor snowblower. I was quite happy to skip snow-blowing in the dark after work.

But when I got home, the driveway was an absolute mess. Weirdly shaped piles of snow were everywhere, along with ruts across the driveway into the lawn—not exactly the bang-up job I'd been hoping for. We plodded through the drifts to rescue the tractor, which was stuck in a snowbank. I climbed aboard and fired it up. My wife got the most incredulous look on her face—she had no idea there was a switch that existed solely to turn on the snowblower.

Most expensive step ever

We hired a contractor to replace our front step. Once it was removed, he attached an auger to his skid loader and told one of his workers where to drill holes for the footings, then he left. After lunch, he returned to pour the concrete.

All seemed well and good until after supper, when we noticed that our laundry room floor drain had backed up. I thought that tree roots had grown into the sewer line again—it happens every year. But when city workers inspected it, they discovered something else—the contractor and his guys had drilled through the sewer line and filled it with concrete. Replacing the line involved digging up 40 ft. of yard and 12 ft. under the house (taking out my basement floor) and cutting down a 50-year-old tree. What I learned is this: Anytime you're planning to dig big holes, have everything marked, including the sewer line.

Last laugh

My son asked me to help him install a new high-definition roof antenna. I followed him up the extension ladder, carrying everything I needed for the job. Halfway up, I realized that my son had disturbed a hornets' nest behind the gutter, and they were coming out in force to see what the rumble was. Since it was too late to stop climbing, I plowed right past, with only a couple of stings. But now we were stuck on the roof.

I could see the hornets swarming all around the ladder. We sat on the roof for about an hour, waiting for them to settle down, then I braved the swarm once again (two more stings) on the world's fastest ladder descent. I moved the ladder so my son could get down without getting stung. But later that night, I had the last laugh—me and that spray can of hornet killer.

SPECIAL SECTION

Hints & Tips for Pets and their People

PAINT TRAY BIRDBATH

Molly, our cockatiel, loves to take baths—and her favorite bathtub is a plastic paint tray. The ribs on

the bottom of the tray give her traction, and the tray's slope lets her wade in the shallow water until she's ready to move into the deep end. Paint trays are cheap and easy to clean, and they also make great turtle pools (but don't tell Molly).

—Roxie Polnau

ANT-PROOF PET FOOD DISHES

Every summer, ants invade our kitchen, and one of their favorite destinations is our dog's food bowl. We came up with this simple way to keep them out of her bowl—we set her dish in a pan of water. Not only does it keep the ants out of the dog food, but Sage can take a gulp of water from the pan whenever she needs a drink.

—Joanne Jensen

BUNNY RABBIT A/C

Hot summer days are tough on bunnies. Here's a great way to recycle plastic water bottles and keep your bunnies cool at the same time. Fill the bottles with water, freeze them solid and then set them out in the rabbit hutches. The bunnies love to laze

against the bottles as the ice thaws. This works great with puppies, too.

—Maureen McLearen

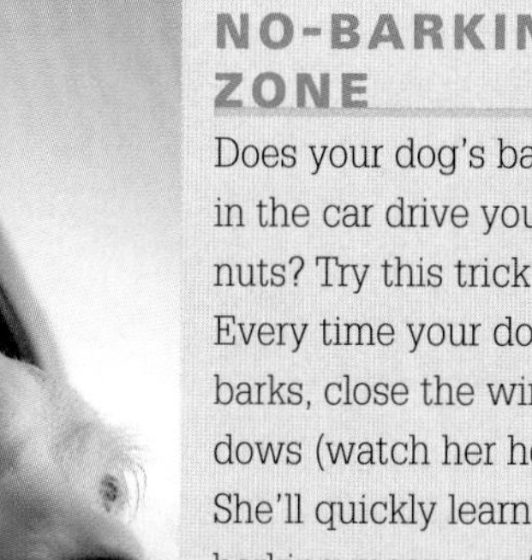

KATHY WYNN / DREAMSTIME.COM

NO-BARKING ZONE

Does your dog's barking in the car drive you nuts? Try this trick: Every time your dog barks, close the windows (watch her head). She'll quickly learn that barking means no fresh air and no slobbery tongue flapping in the breeze. After a few car rides, you'll both be driving around in blissful silence.

—Troy Koonce

Hints & Tips for Pets and their People

BELL TRAINING FOR DOGS

Here's an easy way your dog can let you know she needs to go outside without any barking or scratching at the door. Hang some bells from the doorknob and your dog will quickly learn to associate the sound of the bells with the door opening. Soon she'll nudge them herself. You can speed things along by jiggling the bells and saying "Outside? Wanna go outside?" for a few days every time your dog goes out. Your dog will be able to "talk" to you about going outside even when you're somewhere else in the house.

—Mitch Gustafson

EASIER BATH TIME

For a calmer and easier bath time, make a dog washing station in your shower. Cover the drain with a hair catcher ($3.50 at hardware stores) to prevent fur from clogging it. Cut a hole in a bath mat so it fits over the drain and lay it in the shower to prevent your dog from slipping around. Temporarily replacing your showerhead with a handheld sprayer ($10 at home centers) gives you more control and lets you avoid spraying water into your pet's ears. Dogs like the extra space in the shower, you don't have to reach awkwardly over the tub and everyone involved will find bath day a whole lot more pleasant.

—Jillayne Houlton

DOG-SPOT SOLUTIONS

Growing a neat lawn in an area frequented by dogs is difficult but not impossible. Acidic dog urine discolors and kills the grass, leaving a patchwork of brown spots. Here are a few tricks for keeping the grass green.

1. Apply lime or gypsum regularly to neutralize the acid in the soil and restore the balance that grass prefers.
2. Water the area heavily each week to dilute the urine.
3. Don't fight it! Replace the grass with small round gravel (pea rock) bordered with stone cobbles or brick. Place landscape fabric beneath the rock to prevent weeds from popping up and your problem is solved, permanently. And another plus—less grass to mow!

CHEW-FREE ELECTRICAL CORDS

Our dogs love to gnaw on electrical cords around the house. This is not only dangerous but also really irritating when they destroy my computer cables. I solved the problem by wrapping the cords with split flexible plastic conduit that you get at home centers and automotive stores ($3.50 for 10 ft.). Just cut the length you need and push the cords into the presplit slot. Our dogs have completely lost interest in the cords. Now if we could just get them to stop chewing up our slippers!

—Ann Bursch

SPLIT FLEXIBLE PLASTIC CONDUIT

RAINY-DAY DOGHOUSE

I was eyeing a nice little doghouse that would hold up in the rain, but the $90 price tag was a little rich for my blood. I decided to make my own for a fraction of the price using a plastic storage bin. I cut a small hole in it, flipped it over on its lid and stuck a dog bed inside it. Linus loves watching the rain from inside his snug little house, and I saved $85! The only problem is that our cat likes it so much I can't keep her out of it. Guess I'm going to have to make her one too.

—Corey Ash

PET TIPS FROM OUR FIELD EDITORS

High-tech pet doors

After the neighborhood raccoon discovered my doggy door, I installed a locking door that unlocks when it detects the transmitter on my dog's collar ($100 to $170). Unlocking sometimes takes a few seconds and the door has jammed a few times, but it keeps out the wildlife and stops winter drafts much better than the old low-tech door. There are also motorized models that open the door automatically (starting at about $250). To browse a wide variety of doors, check out petdoors.com (800-826-2871).

PETSAFE

—Thomas Czerwinski, Austin, TX

Paws off countertops

Here's a great way to teach cats that countertops are off limits: Lay contact paper along the edge of the top, sticky side up. Cats hate the stuff and will avoid your countertops after a few sticky experiences.

—Bess Knudsen, Deltona, FL

[Bess isn't just a field editor; she's also a professional animal behaviorist.]

Childproof = pet-proof

Like kids, pets get into places they shouldn't. To stop them, I turn to inexpensive childproofing products: latches for cabinets, locks for doors, and gates for doorways. Discount stores carry some of these products. For a wider selection, shop online. Kidsafeinc.com is a good place to start.

—Jim Duffy, Mays Landing, NJ

Hints & Tips for Pets and their People

WIND-PROOF DOG DISHES

How many times have you gone outside to fill your dog's food or water dish only to find that it's blown halfway across the yard? The really heavy pet dishes are expensive, but here's a cheap dog dish that won't blow away. Fill a plastic ice cream bucket with a couple of inches of sand, and then put a second container the same size inside it. Use the inside bucket as your dog's dish and it'll stay right where you put it.

—Rick Castillo

LOW-FAT DOG TREATS

My vet suggested we replace our overweight dog's high-calorie treats with plain rice cakes. Personally, I think they're tasteless, but our dog goes nuts over them! They're super low fat and they're a lot cheaper than his regular treats too.

—Charlotte Dix

PORTABLE WATER DISH

My dog and I take long walks together, and on hot days we both get pretty thirsty. Before leaving the house, I always stuff a plastic shower cap in my pocket. That way, I can give my dog a drink from any handy tap, drinking fountain or my water bottle whenever she needs a slurp. —Karen Hamilton

PRIVATE DINING

To stop my dog from eating the cat's food, I moved the cat's dish into the laundry room. Then I attached adhesive-backed hook-and-loop fasteners to the back of the laundry room door and to the front of the trim. After filling the dish, I hook up the fasteners so the door only opens 5 in. Now my cat can come and go and eat his meal in peace.

RAMON MORENO

6 Outdoor Structures, Landscaping & Gardening

IN THIS CHAPTER

1 Sand the handles smooth. A random orbital sander makes short work of the sanding job. Keep it moving so you don't create a flat spot.

RENEW YOUR GARDEN TOOL HANDLES

Here's a tip sent in by Ken Werner, one of our field editors: "Each spring I sand our gardening tool handles with 120-grit sandpaper and then rub a coat of boiled linseed oil on them. The handles stay smooth throughout the gardening season. Then I do it again before putting the tools away in the fall." The tools look terrific, and the smooth oiled surface resists cracking and is much easier on the hands.

If you're more like Oscar than Felix and your tool handles have never been sanded, they're probably as rough and worn as ours were. In that case, use a random orbital sander (Photo 1). You'll still have to hand-sand the spots you can't reach with the sander, but it'll save you a lot of effort.

READER PHOTO

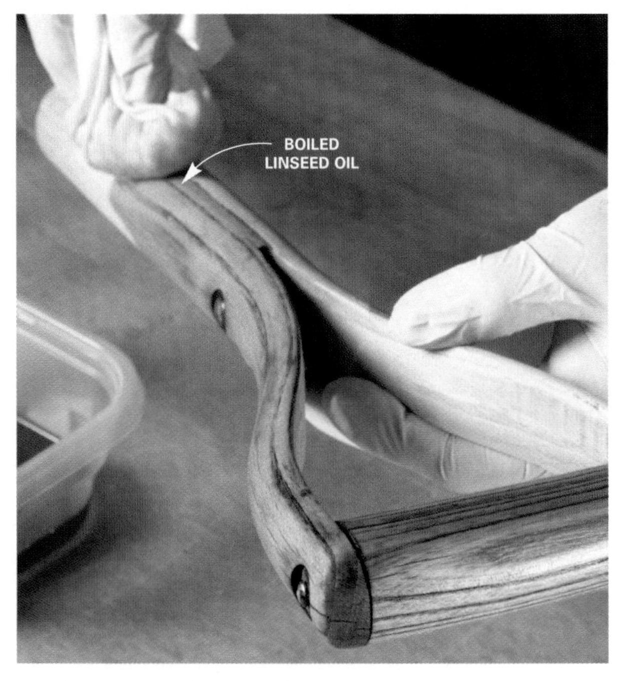

2 Rub on boiled linseed oil. Dip a rag into a container of boiled linseed oil and wipe it onto the sanded tool handle. Let the oil soak in for a few minutes. Then wipe off the excess with a dry rag.

WOODEN WALKWAY

Low cost, low-sweat, low-impact

by **Travis Larson**

■ Faster, easier and cheaper than brick, stone or concrete paths
■ The perfect solution for wet or sloped sites

Paths built with concrete, stone or pavers are expensive and labor intensive. They require a lot of digging, hauling of tons of materials and the disposal of tons of soil. If you're looking for an easier path, consider a wooden walkway, especially for wet or sloped sites. Building with wood is far less back-breaking. You'll have just a few holes to dig, and you'll be hauling wood instead of stone. It's much cheaper, too. The walkway shown, topped with cedar decking, cost only $400. (With treated wood decking, it would have cost $60 less.) A wooden walkway also goes together much faster; this 40-ft. path took two of us two days to build. But enough chitchat—here's how to build a walkway of your own!

Plan your walkway

This walkway design works best for a gradually curving or straight path—whatever length you need it to be. Generally, if it's possible for you (or some kid) to pump your way up the proposed walkway route on a bicycle, you can build this project there. If the path has a steep slope in the middle and you're skilled enough to build deck stairs, end your walkway at the top and bottom of the hill and bridge the hill with steps. If you just want a straight path, your job is simple. Just follow our instructions and skip all the business about curves. Place stakes at both ends and sides of the path, spaced 30 in. apart. Next, string a line and mark your postholes every 8 ft. Then frame up each section using the same steps we show for a curved path.

This is true plan-as-you-go construction. Layout and construction start at one end of the boardwalk and proceed to the other. You determine the length and the number of level changes needed as you go. There's no hard-and-fast materials list or cutting list; you'll do a fair amount of shooting from the hip. Start by picking up a 16-ft. length of hardboard siding and laying out the path. If you can't find hardboard, screw together strips of any 1/2-in. sheet good. Then you'll be able to make up a preliminary materials list and get started.

Rip the 12-in. siding into two 6-in.-wide pieces and get some help to bend it to form the shape of your path (Photo 1). If you need longer lengths, overlap the siding a few feet and screw the pieces together to ensure a smooth curve. Only lay out one side of the walkway for this step. Start at the downhill end at the highest sloped

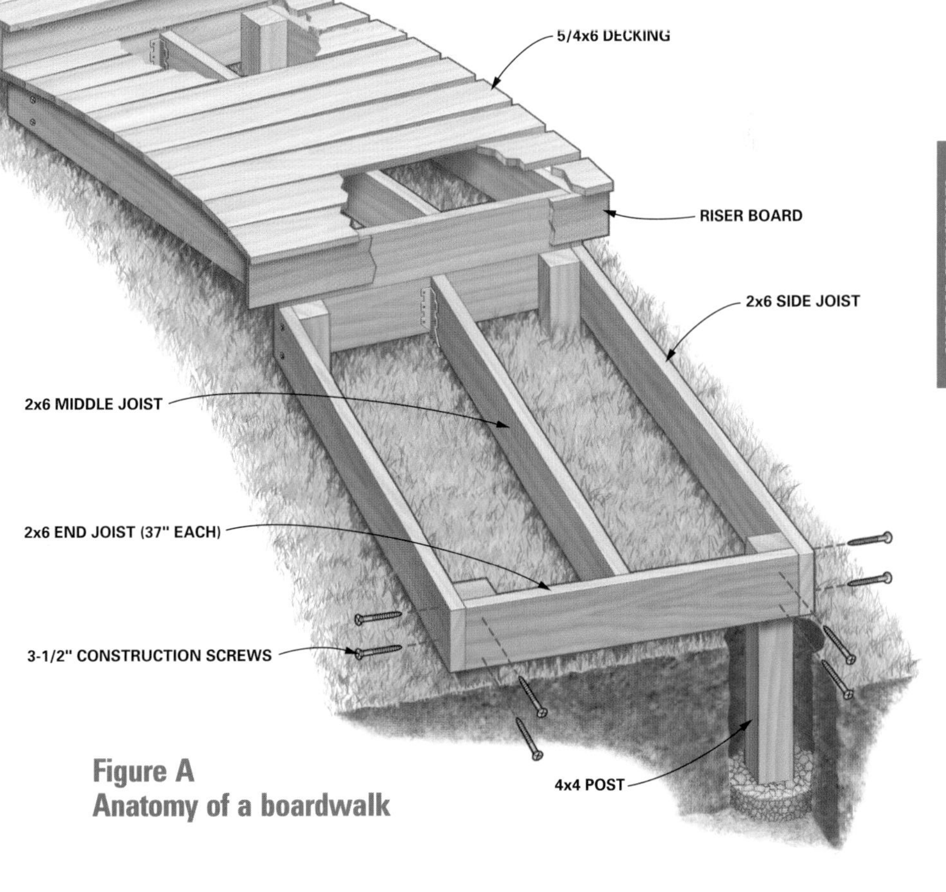

Figure A
Anatomy of a boardwalk

1 **Mark one side of the walkway with hardboard siding, then screw it to stakes to hold the shape. Mark the path with marking paint.**

2 **Establish the length of the first section by keeping the joist level and within 3 in. of the paint line. Mark the post positions and cut the side joist to length.**

side of your pathway, screwing the siding to stakes to hold the shape. Avoid tight curves if possible; gradual ones will simplify construction. When you're satisfied, mark the inside of the form with marking paint and then pull it free. Store the siding indoors or moisture may ruin it. You'll need it later.

This is a foot-traffic-only design—no Harleys or golf carts, please! For that reason, the footings are only 2 ft. deep, and the posts rest solely on gravel.

Buy the materials

This walkway is made completely from treated 2x6 framing and 4x4 posts capped with 5/4x6 cedar decking, but you can use treated or composite decking if you choose. After you establish the length and shape of the walkway, it's time to put together a rudimentary materials list. Because every site is different, we can't provide a precise materials list. We can only give you a rough idea of what to get on your first trip to the lumberyard. We recommend spanning 8 ft. or less with every section even if you have longer runs that don't require steps. The truth is that you'll be constantly adjusting the length of each section, and you'll just have to try to use odd lengths of framing material as wisely as you can. But to get started, for every 8 lin. ft. of walkway, pick up:

- one 4x4 x 10-ft. (treated) post
- three 2x6 x 10-ft. (treated) boards
- eight 5/4x6 x 8-ft. deck boards
- two 2x6 joist hangers
- one 60-lb. bag of pea gravel

3 **Mark the posthole using the joist as your guide. Set aside the joist and dig 2-ft.-deep postholes, add 6 in. of gravel, then rest the uncut posts in the holes.**

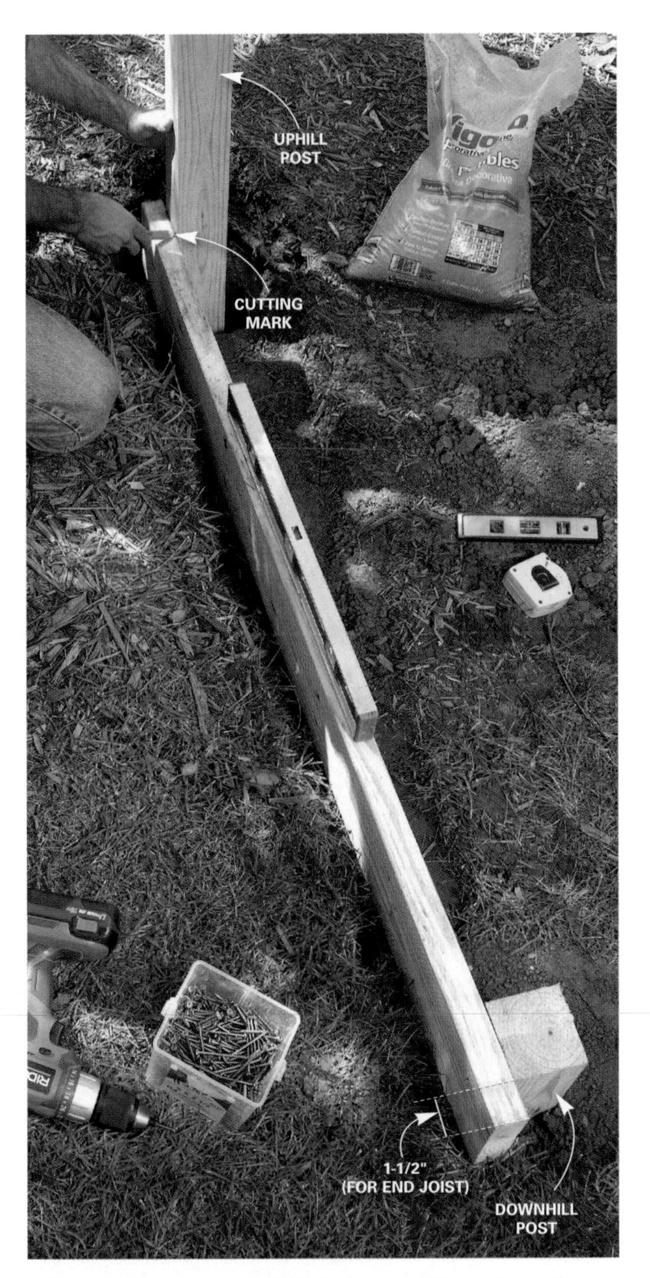

4 **Level the joist to mark each post height and cut the posts to length. Level and screw the side joist to the posts with two 3-1/2-in. construction screws.**

5 **Rest the next stepped side joist on the 4x4 spacer over the first section's side joist. Then adjust the position and cut it to length, allowing for a 1-3/4-in. overlap. Mark and cut the joist and assemble as before.**

6 **Install the end joists, estimating their placement to achieve equal angles with the side rims. Mark and dig the footings. Then set each post and end joist.**

You'll also need a box of screws or nails for joist hangers and special 3-1/2-in. construction screws to anchor the framing to the posts. We used the GRK brand, but you can use whatever construction screw is available at your home center or lumberyard. If you can't find any, it's OK to tack things together with 3-in. deck screws and then go back later and install two 3/8 x 3-1/2-in. lag screws wherever side and end joists rest at each post. And pick up decking fasteners. If you're using synthetic decking, use whatever type is recommended. If you use wood, we recommend 2-1/2-in. stainless-steel finishing screws. They're easy to drive and last forever, and the small heads will be almost invisible when you're through.

Start at the bottom

Use a 4x4 block to support one end of the first 10-ft. 2x6 side joist. Shift the joist up and down the hill until it's level and spaced no more than 3 or 4 in. away from the paint line—anywhere (**Photo 2**). It's OK to dig the uphill end of the board into the hill a few inches to make the section as long as possible. But don't go above the top or your decking will be in the dirt. The uphill end of the board will define one end of the section; the 4x4 defines the other end. Cut the side joist to length and then replace it to mark the post locations. Stake posthole centers about 2 in. in from the board sides and 3 in. away from ends. Then move the joist aside and dig 2-ft.-deep postholes (**Photo 3**).

7 **Cut and attach each side joist for each section before continuing to the next level.**

8 **Support the middle joists with joist hangers after centering and tacking them into place.**

9 **Space the decking, tapering the gap as needed, then screw the boards to the joists.**

Dump about 6 in. of gravel into each hole and place the first post in the hole to mark the cutting height. (Rough-cut long posts shorter to make them easier to work with.) Remove the post, cut it to length and then fill around the post and screw on the side joist. Then level the side joist and use it as a guide for marking and then cutting the uphill post (Photo 4). Screw the side joist to the posts and then start the next section.

Work your way up the hill using the same 4x4 block and leveling and spacing techniques. But when you cut the downhill end of each side joist, leave a 1-3/4-in. overlap and toe-screw this end into place (Photo 5). Finish framing this entire side of the walkway before beginning the other.

10 **Mark the curves on decking using the hardboard siding. Hold the siding in place with stakes or blocks or by hand.**

Finish the framing

Start on the other side of the walkway by cutting a 27-in.-long end joist for each step. Then use the joists to set each post location (**Photo 6**). At both ends of the walkway, set the posts so they're square with the opposite side joist (**Photo 6**). On the others, position the posts so the angle between the end joist and the two side joists is roughly the same. You can just "eyeball it" to compare the angles. They don't have to match perfectly, just close. Then dig each hole and cut and set the posts and end joists as you did on the other side. Then cut and screw the side joists to the posts and end joists (**Photo 7**). Finish up each section by adding the center joists and anchoring them with 2x6 joist hangers (**Photo 8**).

Install the decking

Cut the 8-ft. decking into 4-ft. lengths. Screw one board to each riser at level changes (**Photo 9**). The first board should overhang the riser by 1 in. and overhang equally at both ends. Then dry-fit the other boards, spacing them as needed to handle the curve. You'll have to play with this for a bit on each section. Most of the time you'll be able to simply open up the decking gaps at one side a bit more than at the other (see "Decking Tight Curves," below). Once you're satisfied, screw the boards down. You may have to taper-cut the last filler piece at the step to even everything out. Don't beat yourself up striving for perfection. You'll be the only one who'll notice small variations in the size of the gaps.

Cut the curves

Shape the curves by bending the siding and scribing against it. Do one section and one side at a time. Try to keep the curve 1 to 3 in. away from the joist below. Use blocks or grab a helper to hand-hold the curve while you

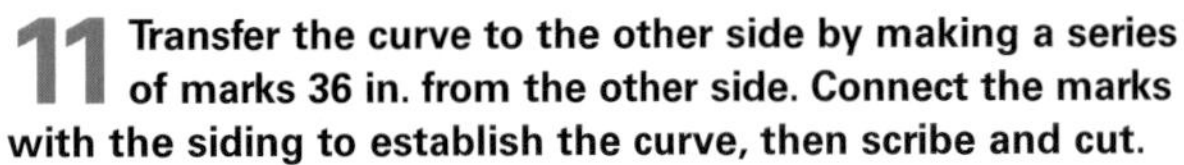

11 **Transfer the curve to the other side by making a series of marks 36 in. from the other side. Connect the marks with the siding to establish the curve, then scribe and cut.**

scribe the first section. Cut off the ends with a circular saw for gradual curves or a jigsaw for tighter ones. At each step, you'll need to remove the riser and the last deck board or two so you can cut them individually (**Photo 11**). Drive stakes against the cutoff ends of the first section. Screw the siding against them to form an even, flowing curve, then anchor the siding onto the next section with blocks while you trace the curve (**Photo 10**). Cut those ends off and repeat the process along the entire side.

When one side is complete, make a series of 36-in. marks on the other side. (Marking every other deck board is enough.) Then use the siding to "connect the dots" to scribe the cutting line on the other side. The last step is to cut the curves. Now your walkway is ready for finishing.

Decking tight curves

If it takes huge tapered gaps to follow a curve, the best-looking solution is to custom-rip each board. But this will require a lot of extra time. Start by laying out the decking in a "fanlike" fashion. Overlap all the decking equally at one end with the edges flush at the other. You'll have to tinker with the overlapped ends until all the overlaps are nearly equal, then scribe the tapers and cut each board. It'll look best if you belt-sand the cut edges to eliminate saw marks and then rout the edges with a round-over bit (we used a 3/8-in. bit) to match the profile on the other side.

InstantProject

GUTTER DECK PLANTER

This lightweight, durable and attractive deck planter is made from a vinyl gutter ($5 per 10-ft. length), two fascia support brackets ($2.50 each) and two end caps ($6.50 a pair). It's a snap to make. Glue one of the end caps in place and drill holes in the bottom of the gutter so the water can drain (**Photo 1**). Slide two fascia support brackets onto the gutter (**Photo 2**) and glue the other end cap into place. If you want a longer planter, be sure to add extra brackets spaced about every 2 ft.—dirt is heavy.

To prevent the soil from slipping through the drainage holes, line the gutter with newspaper or put shards of old broken clay pots along the bottom.

Shallow planters like these have a tendency to dry out. To cut your watering chore in half, mix water-absorbing polymer gel crystals (available at garden centers) with your potting mix. Or buy bags of soilless potting mix with the polymer crystals already added.

If you want a color other than white, use a spray paint formulated for plastic. Screw the planter to your deck rail (**Photo 3**), fill it with potting mix and add your plants. Enjoy!

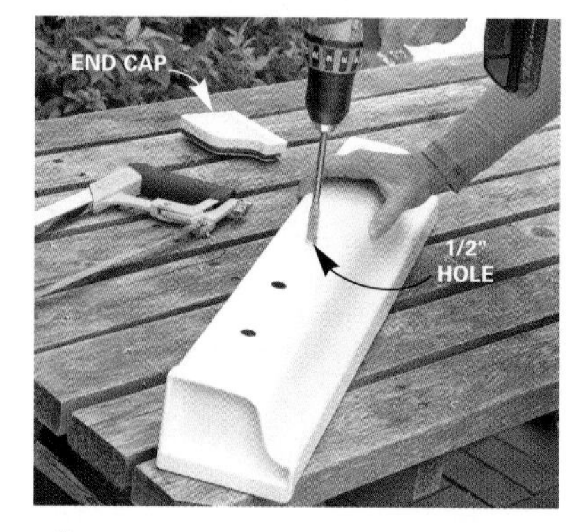

1 Cut a 2-ft. length of vinyl gutter and glue one of the end caps into place with kitchen and bath adhesive caulk. Drill 1/2-in. drainage holes every 4 in. along the bottom of the gutter.

2 Slide both fascia support brackets onto the gutter and glue the other end cap into place.

3 Screw the planter to the deck rail through the fascia support brackets using galvanized screws.

NOTE
Experts recommend you space your wren houses 20 ft. apart.

FENCE POST WREN HOUSE

Attract wrens and other songbirds to your yard with this durable birdhouse made from a plastic fence post. Wrens will nest in almost anything, but other birds have specific requirements for the entrance diameter and house cavity. If you're trying to attract a particular type of bird to your yard, do a little research before you start building this rather small hangout. (Check out wild-bird-watching.com.)

Buy a 4 x 4-in. fence post and cap kit ($25 at home centers). One 6-ft. post is enough for six birdhouses. But the post comes with just one cap, so you'll have to buy caps ($6 each) for all but the first birdhouse.

Cut the house cavity to length and drill the ventilation and entrance holes (**Photo 1**). Then cut the wood bottom and attach it (**Photo 2**). Fit the bottom loosely to allow for ventilation. To clean out the house each year, just remove the screws and release the bottom. Our birdhouse doesn't include a perch. Perches are cute, but they allow predators easier access to eggs and babies.

Attach the eye hook to the top (**Photo 3**), then glue the top to the body with a few dabs of polyurethane glue (Gorilla Glue is one brand). If you want to paint the birdhouse, use spray paint formulated for plastic, but don't paint the inside of the house.

Hang the houses in partially shaded spots with the entrances facing away from prevailing winds and out of jumping range of cats and squirrels.

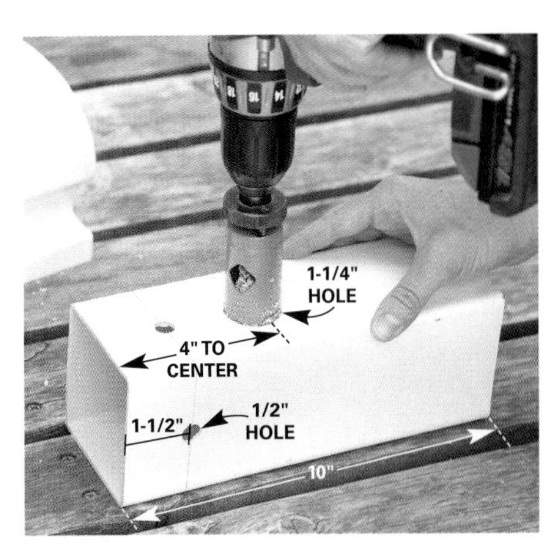

1 Cut 10-in. lengths with a hacksaw or miter saw. Then drill the ventilation and entrance holes. Sand off the sharp edges on the entrance hole with 60-grit sandpaper.

2 Cut a 3/4-in.-thick, 3-1/8-in. square bottom from wood. Predrill and then screw it into place with two No. 8 stainless 3/4-in. pan head screws on opposite sides.

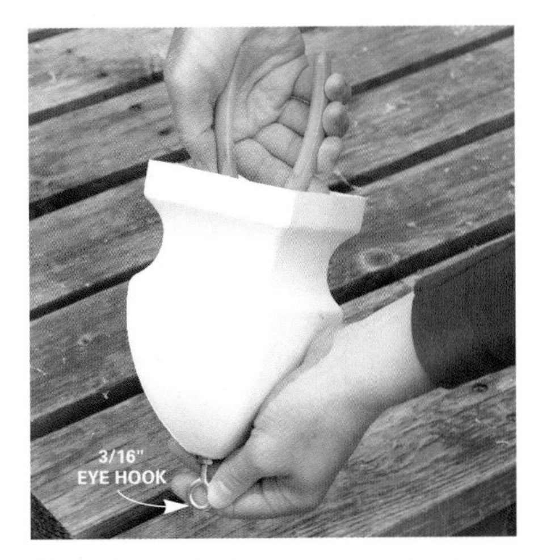

3 Drill a 1/4-in. hole for the eye hook and thread on the nut and washer for the top. Stick it through the top and use needle-nose pliers to hold the bottom nut while you twist the hook tight. Glue on the cap.

CARVE A ROCK— CREATE A FOUNTAIN

Carving stone requires years of training, extraordinary skill and endless patience—or you can cheat and use power tools.

by **Gary Wentz**

If you have a circular saw and an angle grinder, you can spend about an hour in a cloud of dust and emerge with a carved fountain stone like this one. You won't need any special talent, just a few tricks and a couple of diamond saw blades (see "Tools and Gear," p. 180).

A weekend is plenty of time to carve the stone and create a small pond. Your masterpiece could look entirely different from the one I made, depending on the shape of the stone you choose. I purchased all the stone and spent about $200 on the whole project, but if you have access to free stone, you can cut that cost in half.

Selecting a stone

The 6-in.-thick sandstone block I used was about 9 x 20 in. and cost about $15 at a landscape supplier. The stone you use can be any size and shape as long as it has a flat spot that's at least 8-1/2 in. across. The bowl itself will measure just over 6-3/4 in. across and 2 in. deep.

Soft stone is best for this project. Although you can cut and grind very hard stone, it could turn this one-hour task into an all-day chore. Also avoid stone with strong "grain"—layers of harder and softer stone—because it tends to crack along the layers. That makes chisel work risky; one wrong blow can ruin your project.

Hardness and grain aren't always obvious from look and touch. So if you pick up stone alongside the road, you won't know if it's workable until you try it. If you buy stone, be sure to ask for recommendations. In most areas, sandstone and some types of limestone are your best bet.

Getting started

Cutting stone whips up a dust storm—don't even think about doing it in your garage. Work as far away as possible from anything

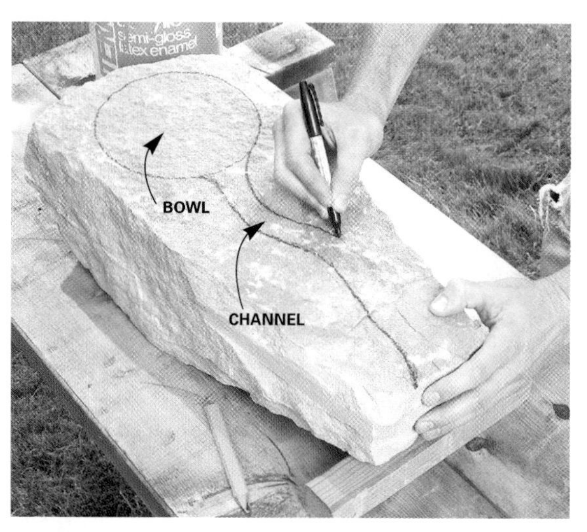

1 Mark the bowl and channel. **Trace around a paint can using a black marker so the circle will show up through a storm of dust. Sketch the channel with a pencil and then darken the lines with a marker.**

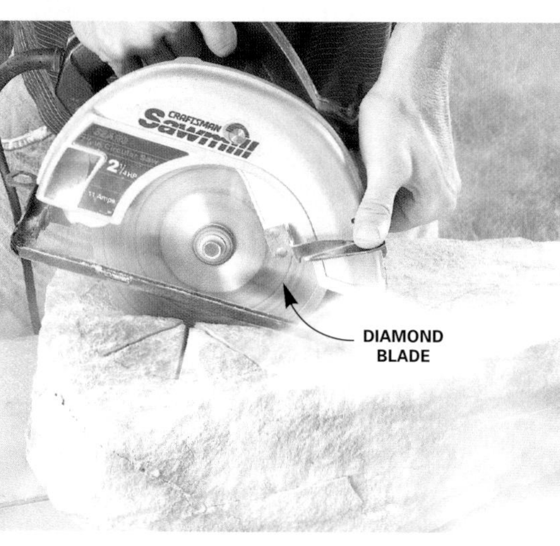

2 Cut the bowl like a pie. **Make plunge cuts across the bowl outline. Hold the saw so that the front of the shoe is resting firmly against the stone. Then slowly lower the blade into the stone. Wear eye protection.**

Building the fountain

This pond is small—a 30 x 36-in. oval, about 14 in. deep. I spent about $100 on the basic pond materials, plus about $90 for the stone. Building a pond couldn't be much simpler. Just dig a hole, line it with pond underlayment followed by an EPDM rubber liner and surround it with stone. Then build a simple stepped-up wall to support the fountain stone. Here are some tips for a smooth project:

- Select larger flagstones for the first layer surrounding the pond. They stay put better and can overhang the edge of the hole by 2 to 3 in. to hide the liner.
- Leave a small gap between two of the flagstones so you can feed the pump tubing through later.
- The flagstone I used for the wall had flat faces that fit together fairly tightly when stacked. That allowed me to glue them together with polyurethane construction adhesive (see **Photo 8**). If you use irregular stone, you'll have bigger gaps and mortar would be a better choice. If you use large stones, you may not need adhesive or mortar. Heavy stones stay put by themselves.
- The pump ($40) I used is rated for 210 gallons per hour. A smaller pump may have worked, but I've learned that it's better to spend an extra $10 than to discover later that a pump was too small.
- Even if your pump has a built-in flow adjustment knob, consider adding a valve (see **Figure B** below) for quicker, more accurate adjustments. The valve and fittings cost less than $10.
- Choose your tubing before you drill the hole in the bowl (**Photo 7**). Depending on the outer diameter of the tube, you need either a 5/8-in. or 3/4-in. drill bit.
- The tubing I used fit snugly into a 3/4-in. hole. So I slathered the tube with silicone caulk, slid it about 1-1/2 in. into the stone and let it set overnight. Don't insert the tube all the way to the top of the drilled hole. The larger diameter of the drilled hole helps to dampen water pulsation caused by the pump.

Figure A Fountain

CHANNEL
BOWL
CORRUGATED TUBING
PUMP
LINER
UNDERLAYMENT
BRICK
POWER CORD

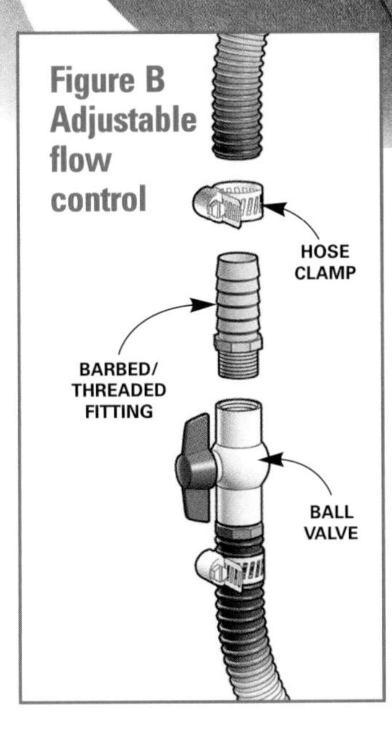

Figure B Adjustable flow control

you don't want coated with dust, especially open windows or your neighbor's convertible. Take five minutes to set up a sturdy work surface (I used a couple of sawhorses and 2x8 planks.) You'll get better results if you're working comfortably, and you'll save your back. If the stone wobbles on your work surface, steady it with shims.

Next, mark out the bowl and channel (Photo 1). If you want a curving channel like ours, avoid tight curves; anything tighter than the curve of a 1-gallon paint can will be tough to cut with your grinder. Make the channel about 1-1/2 in. wide and flare it to a width of 2-1/2 in. at the bowl. The flare helps create strong water flow. The flare at the front of the channel is purely for looks.

Cut, chisel and grind the bowl

Fire up your saw and make the bowl cuts (Photo 2). When making plunge cuts, you have to keep an eye on both the front and the back ends of the blade to make sure

3 Break out the "pie slices." Chip away the first few slices. After that, you'll have space to aim your chisel at the base of each slice, and most will pop out with one blow.

4 Grind the bowl smooth. Drag the edge of the wheel quickly and lightly across the bowl. If you press too hard or hesitate, you'll create gouges that require more grinding to smooth over.

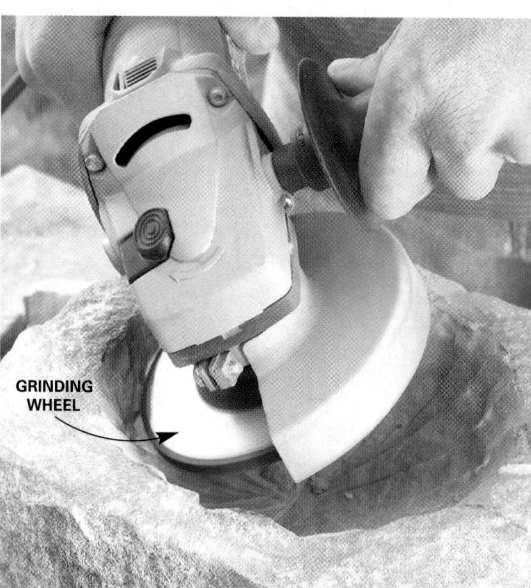

5 Cut the channel. Make cuts along the edges and several in between. Cut in shallow passes, going gradually deeper with each pass. If you make deep passes, the spinning blade will pull itself off course.

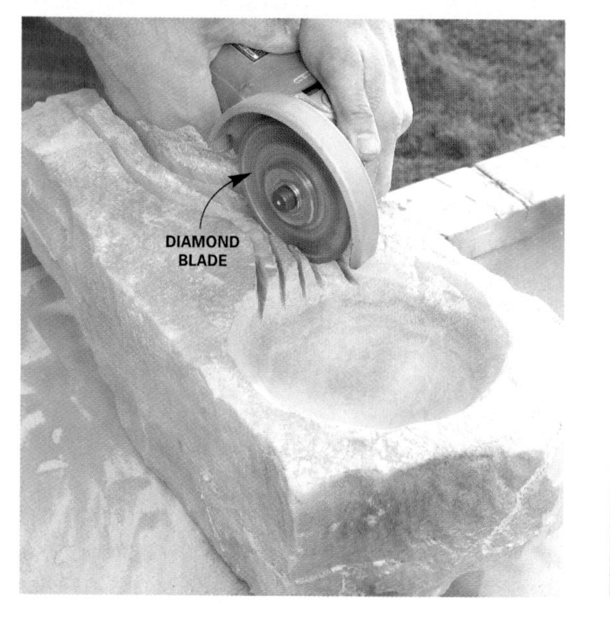

you don't cut beyond the circle. And remember that the spinning blade will try to drag the saw backward. If your circle disappears under a layer of dust, stop and blow off the dust. If you guesstimate where the line is and guess wrong, you'll end up with a lopsided bowl. Make at least eight cuts; the more cuts you make, the easier the next step will be.

Next, chisel out the bowl (**Photo 3**). If any of the slices don't break out easily, rev up your saw again. Better to make more cuts than to whack out a big slice and leave a crater in the bowl. Grinding (**Photo 4**) is tedious, but patience pays off in the form of a smooth, rounded bowl. With very soft stone, like the sandstone I used, you can polish the bowl even smoother by hand-sanding with 80-grit sandpaper.

Cut the channel

Cut the channel as deep as the diamond blade on your grinder will reach (about 7/8 in., depending on your grinder). But the key to controlling that spinning blade

Tools and gear

- To cut the bowl, you'll need a standard circular saw and a 7-in. diamond blade. Diamond blades can cost $75 or more. But for this small job, cheaper is better. I spent about $30.
- To smooth the bowl, you'll need a small angle grinder ($60) and a grinding wheel ($3). Don't balk at buying a grinder just for this project; you'll find other uses for it. If you want to cut a curved channel, you'll need a 4- or 4-1/2-in. diamond blade ($20). Or you can cut a straight channel with your circular saw.
- I used a hammer drill to drill the hole in the bowl. But a standard drill, along with a little extra patience, will do the job if you're using soft stone. Use a masonry drill bit ($6) diameter that matches the outer diameter of the pump tubing.
- This project whips up a tornado of dust and grit, making a dust mask and eye protection mandatory. Safety glasses will do, but I prefer a face shield ($15). Those flying slivers of stone sting!

DIY Success Story: Ode to my angle grinder

Words can't express the passion
I feel
When you cut mortar or stone,
tile or steel
When you sharpen an ax or
grind away rust
I cherish the noise, the sparks
and the dust
With you by my side, there's no
job I fear
If you could drink, I would buy
you a beer

— **Gary Wentz**

is to make all cuts in shallow passes (1/8 to 1/4 in.). Start by cutting the outer edges of the channel. Don't worry about forming perfectly smooth curves yet; if you have to form a rough curve with a series of short, straight cuts, that's OK. Next, cut grooves in the middle of the channel (Photo 5). Then chisel out the channel (Photo 6). That will open up space to smooth out the curved edges with the diamond blade, a grinding disc or a combination of both. When the channel is done, drill a hole in the bowl (Photo 7) sized to accept the tube from the pump.

Set the fountain stone

Positioning the stone takes some care. You have to adjust the flow from the pump, level and shim the stone from side to side so water doesn't spill out of the bowl, and tilt the stone slightly for a strong, spilling stream. When you have it right, remove the stone, apply a bed of mortar or generous beads of construction adhesive, and reset the stone. Keep the 2x4 bridge in place overnight. If water clings to the underside of the stone and runs back toward the stone wall, apply a bead of clear silicone caulk under the front of the stone. The silicone "drip edge" will force the water to drop off.

6 Chip out the channel. Break out the slivers of stone to open up the channel. Then rev up your grinder again to perfect the edge cuts and smooth the bottom of the channel.

7 Drill a hole in the bowl. To avoid chipping around the edges of the hole, start with the drill's hammer action turned off. When the hole is about 1/2 in. deep, switch the hammer action on for faster drilling.

8 Set the stone. Run the pump and adjust the stone until you get a strong stream. Shims and a 2x4 "bridge" hold the fountain stone in position until the adhesive or mortar hardens.

Question&Comment

BUILD A RAIN BARREL

I see rain barrels for sale, but they're expensive—$150 to $200 each. There has to be a way to make one for less than that. Where can I get a barrel and how do I plumb it?

You're right—it's pretty easy to build your own rain barrels from plastic drums or trash cans. Look online or in the yellow pages under "bottles" or "containers" to find an "open head" plastic 55-gallon drum with a cover (about $60). Or find a used barrel by talking to car wash managers (they buy soap and wax by the barrel). If you can't find a container you like, buy a large, heavy-duty garbage can (about $35) at a home center. All the other plumbing parts will add up to about $40.

Place the drum near a downspout, drill a hole in the side near the bottom and screw in a drain valve. That's an OK installation if you plan to run a soaker hose to your garden. But if you want to use a wand or a spray nozzle, you'll need to elevate the barrel on a stand for more water pressure. Water is heavy (55 gallons weighs 440 lbs.), so use 4x4 treated lumber for the legs and secure everything with construction screws or stainless steel lags. But don't place the stand on soft ground. You could kill somebody if the rig toppled over. If you have large gardens and want to store more water, double-size the stand and add a second barrel.

Cut holes in the bottoms of the barrels with a 2-1/4-in. hole saw. Then screw in a 2-in. male threaded electrical (gray PVC) conduit adapter (electrical adapters aren't tapered like plumbing adapters, so you can tighten them down all the way). Squirt a thin bead of silicone caulk around the opening and screw on a threaded electrical PVC coupler to cinch the barrel between the two fittings (see Figure A). Next, glue together sections of 2-in. PVC pipe, unions (to make winter

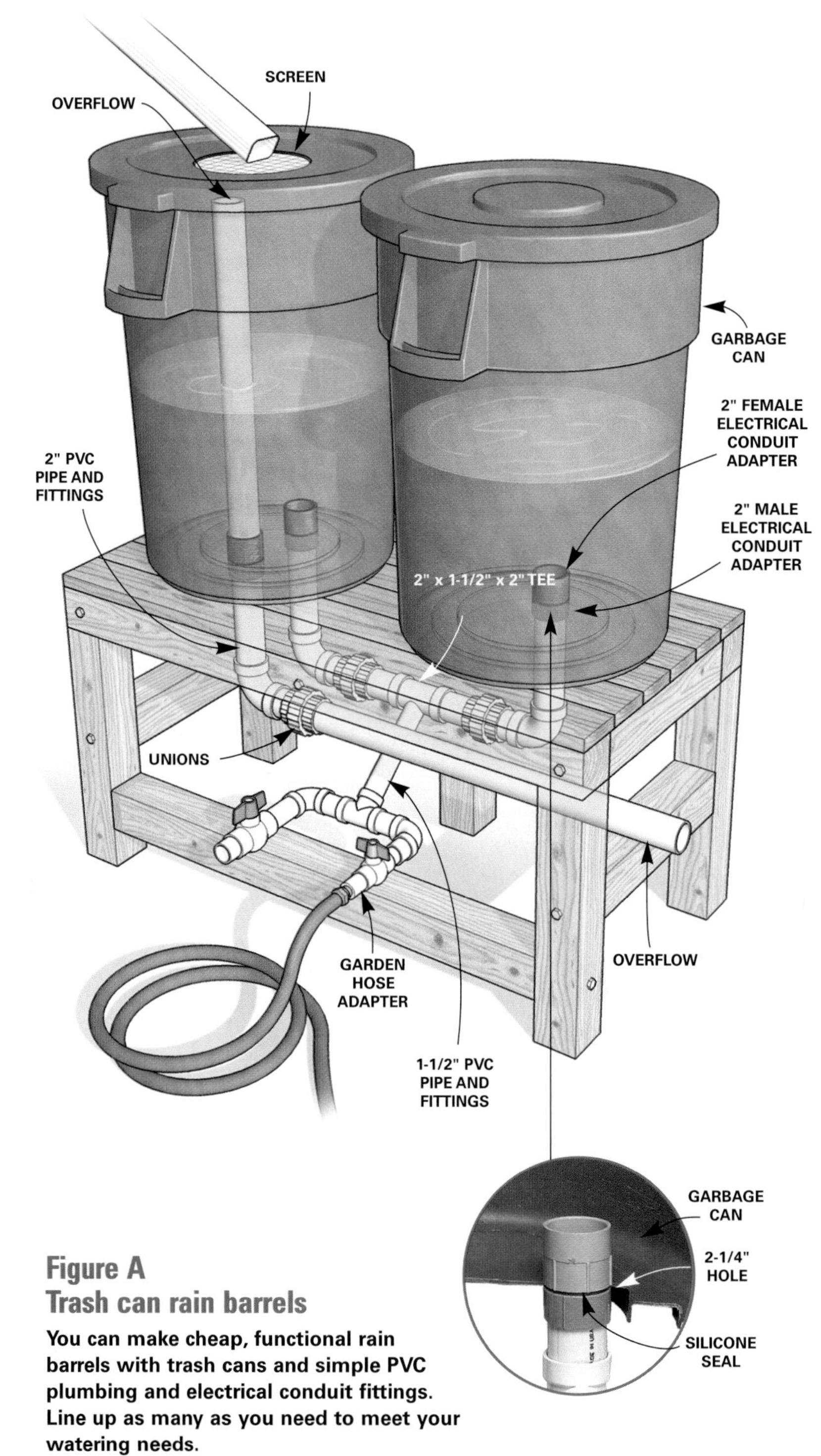

Figure A
Trash can rain barrels

You can make cheap, functional rain barrels with trash cans and simple PVC plumbing and electrical conduit fittings. Line up as many as you need to meet your watering needs.

disassembly easier), reducers and valves. As long as you're at it, install an overflow pipe so you can direct the excess where you want it.

Finally, cut a hole in one of the covers and mount a screen to filter out leaves and debris. Then just wait for the next big rain.

Install a large valve to quickly fill watering cans and a smaller valve for a garden hose. Secure the valves to the cross brace with J-brackets.

PESTICIDE SAFETY

Reader Eric McCumber is an inspector for the Michigan Department of Agriculture. Eric wrote to us with his comments about the pesticide application methods we've shown in previous stories. While pleased that our photos showed people wearing protective gloves and eyewear, he advises us that we left out some important precautions. Here are Eric's additional tips for safe use of pesticides:

1. Wear long-sleeve shirts and pants (never shorts) to protect your skin from contact with the pesticide. Also, tuck your pant legs inside your boots to keep them from dragging through the treated area. Then wash your shirt and pants separately from your regular laundry. Wash all exposed skin with soap and water before you go back into the house.
2. Wear high-top rubber boots and wash them off before taking them inside (or leave them in the garage). Leather boots absorb pesticide and re-expose you to it every time you put them on. That can cause chronic long-term exposure reactions long after you've applied the pesticide. Leather boots also track the pesticide into the house and deposit it on your carpets. Then you'll spread it around the whole house every time you walk on those areas.
3. Wear protective gloves. Cloth or leather gloves are not protective wear. Buy inexpensive nitrile gloves and toss them when you finish the job.
4. Follow the label directions—and then some. Most over-the-counter consumer-oriented pesticides are not strong enough to require a respirator. But there's no downside to wearing one.

Wear rubber boots, chemical-resistant gloves, eye protection and long sleeves when applying pesticides.

Question&Comment

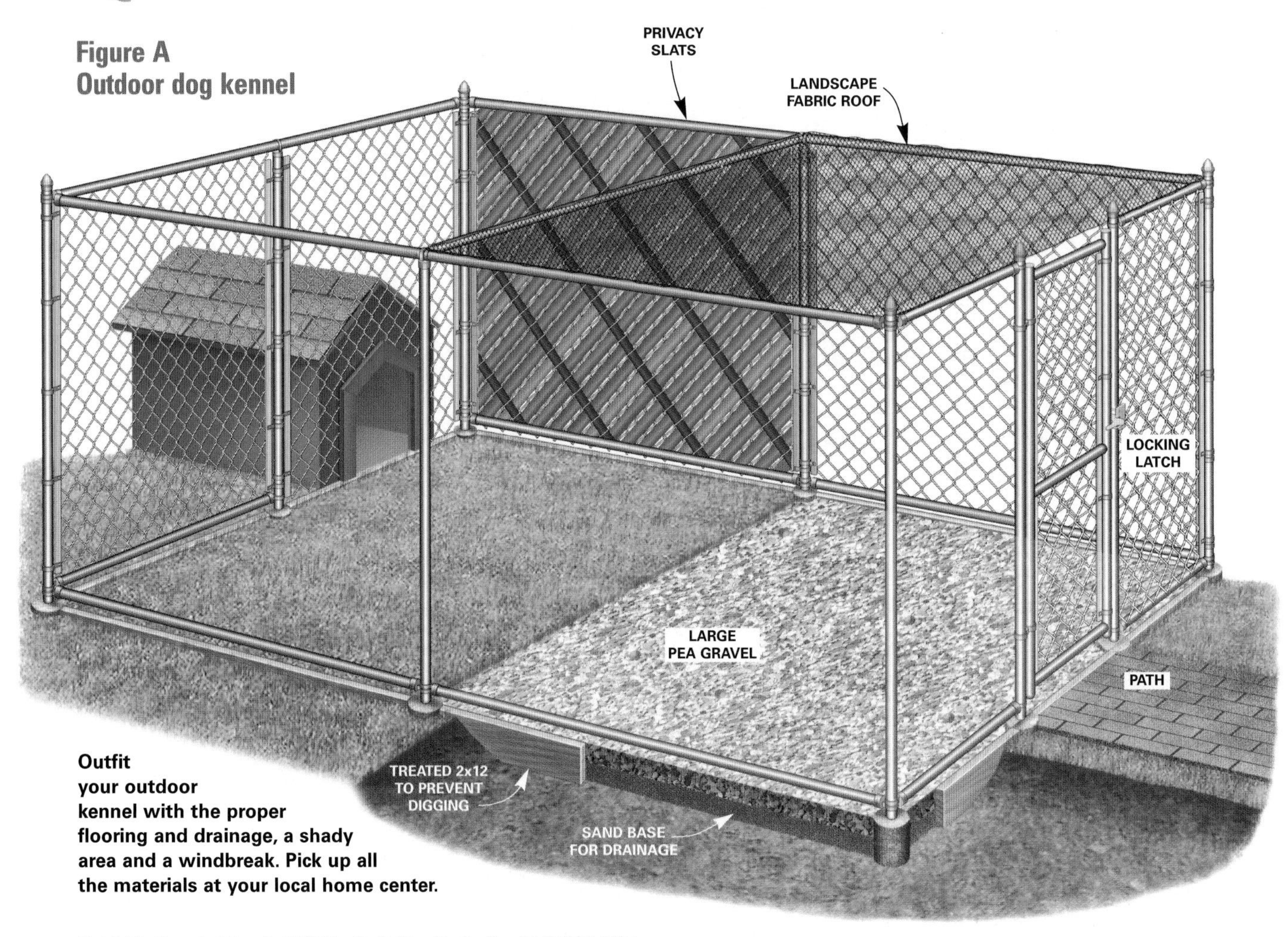

BUILD AN OUTDOOR DOG KENNEL

I want to build an outdoor dog kennel. Can you give me some guidelines for sizing the kennel and choosing materials?

We contacted Lisa Peterson, director of communications for the American Kennel Club, for design advice and to find out some of the most common mistakes.

We were hoping to get a sizing formula. But it turns out there's no such thing. Kennel sizing is based on how much time your dog will be spending in the kennel and how much room you have to spare. If your dog is going to be outside all day, he needs a larger kennel so he can run and exercise. If you make it too small, he'll take every opportunity to "get even" with you and your neighbors with non-stop barking and other bad behaviors. So larger is better.

For walls and doors, chain link fencing is your best bet (4 ft. tall minimum, and taller if you have a larger dog). It's affordable and easy to assemble, and you can buy premade wall and door sections at any home center. Buy a spring-loaded "snap clip" to secure the swing-down latch (some dogs can figure out how to open those latches and escape).

If your dog is a digger, you'll have to embed a "direct burial" treated 2x12 below the fence. Or bury the fence itself about 1 ft. into the soil (see Figure A). Those methods aren't foolproof, but they'll usually prevent a "great escape." Screen off any sides that face streets or sidewalks by sliding privacy slats through the fencing. That'll cut down on barking and overall stress.

When it comes to flooring material, concrete may seem like the best choice because you can slope it for drainage and it's easy to clean. But it's actually a mistake. The hard floor will, over time, cause calluses, worn pads, splayed toes and painful joints. Instead, Lisa recommends either large pea gravel (some dogs eat smaller gravel) or large flat stones (flagstone). The irregular shapes actually help your dog develop stronger paws. But before you throw down gravel or set the stones, take the time to install a sand base for drainage at least 6 in. deep if you're building on

WHICH DECK HARDWARE TO USE?

I'm shopping for hardware for my new deck. I see galvanized, triple galvanized, something called Gold Coat and stainless steel. There's a huge difference in price. Is the pricey stuff worth it?

If you live in a coastal area (near salt water), you don't have a choice—the building codes require stainless steel hangers, plates and fasteners. But if you live inland, you have more options. Most codes allow you to use hot-dipped galvanized (sometimes called triple-zinc) hardware (see Photo 1).

However, if you want to take a step up in corrosion protection, you can buy Gold Coat galvanized hardware that's been treated with an inert barrier coating (see Photo 2). It costs three times more than traditional hot-dipped hardware, but lasts longer (for more info, visit uspconnectors.com). Or you can increase the life of triple zinc hardware by installing corrosion-resistant flashing between the wood and the hot-dipped galvanized hardware (Photo 3). Grace Vycor Deck Protector (graceathome.com) and Protecto Deck Flashing are two brands; they're available from your lumber supplier. It's ugly, so you might not like it on a raised deck where you can view the deck from beneath.

Before you decide on hardware, consider this. The newer arsenic-free treated lumber hasn't been in the field long enough for anyone to know how long hot-dipped hardware will last. Since the hardware is the least costly part of your deck, you might want to hedge your bets by upgrading to stainless steel even though it's seven times more expensive. That way, you'll never have to replace hardware. This advice is especially germane for decks sporting super-long-lasting composite materials. There's a real chance the decking materials will outlive all the hardware.

Note: Never mix fasteners. Use stainless nails with stainless hardware, and galvanized fasteners with galvanized hardware.

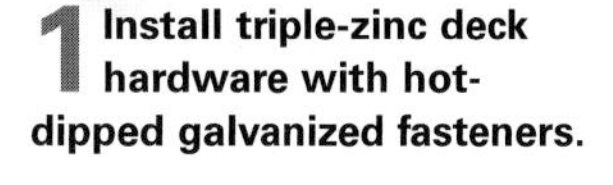

1 **Install triple-zinc deck hardware with hot-dipped galvanized fasteners.**

2 **Secure the coated hangers with the manufacturer's matching nails. They're colored to blend with wood tones.**

3 **Increase the life of zinc-plated hardware by applying corrosion-resistant flashing to the top and sides of the joists.**

clay. Then lay down landscaping fabric to prevent weed growth. You'll probably scoop out gravel along with the poop, so it'll need replenishing every year. If you have enough space, the ultimate dog oasis is a grassy area within the kennel.

Several companies offer composite flooring materials for dog kennels. It definitely looks better than gravel and is easy to clean. But if your dog likes to chew things, it's not a good choice—unless, of course, your vet does free surgery. Plan on a surfaced path to the kennel. If you just have grass, you'll soon have a muddy path. All that mud will get tracked into the house.

Finally, dogs need protection from the elements. A doghouse isn't mandatory, but if you don't provide one, you should at least install a small roof and a windbreak. Dogs can withstand cold, but not cold and wind or rain. An elevated cot will get them off a freezing cold or searing hot floor. Even if you include a doghouse, provide other shaded areas in the kennel (landscape fabric stretched across the top works well).

When placing a doghouse, avoid the common DIY mistake of setting it in a corner (the roof is a perfect launching pad for a jump-over). Instead, locate it outside the kennel with an entrance hole cut through the fence. Or place it in the center of the kennel. If you're stuck with a corner location, make the fence higher in that area to prevent jump-outs.

Question&Comment

BUYING A GOOD GARDEN HOSE

I'm sick of buying "kink-free" rated garden hoses that constantly kink. Another problem is that they flatten out on the hose reel, so I have to unreel the whole thing just to get good water flow. How do I select a hose that really works?

First, stop reading (and believing) the marketing hype on the hose packaging. Instead of reading the specifications (which don't correlate to hose quality at all), perform your own tests on the hoses right in the store. Remove a few twist ties from the hose packaging and unroll about 2 ft. of hose. Then coil it back against itself to see if it kinks. A hose that kinks in the store will kink even easier after it's been baking in the sun all day.

Next, compare the wall thicknesses of different hoses by bending them at a 90-degree angle. The hoses with thicker walls will be harder to bend because they're made with more material. Sure, they cost more, but they also last longer. Finally, check the quality of the connection fittings. You want solid "crush-proof" brass fittings (see photos at right), as opposed to flimsy stamped-brass fittings. That way the ends won't get destroyed when Junior drives over them.

Before you leave the store, make sure you reassemble the packaging on the hoses that failed the test.

Don't believe the labels about "kink-worthiness." Perform a kink test in the store by looping a section back onto itself. The black hose had the most plies and an "anti-kink" rib, but was easiest to kink.

BILL ZUEHLKE (3)

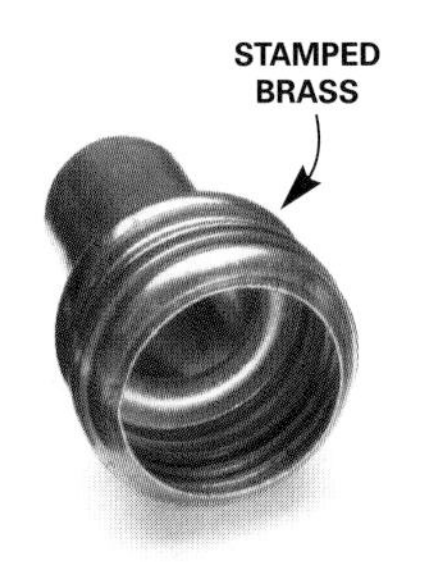

Forget hoses with crummy stamped-brass fittings. You may save a few bucks up front, but you won't be happy with the hose.

Buy a hose with heavy-duty crush-proof cast-brass fittings. They're a good indication of overall hose quality, and they'll last the life of the hose.

GreatGoofs®

How not to kill weeds

This spring, I noticed my neighbor spot-spraying weeds that had invaded his yard. He told me he'd bought a weed killer at our local hardware store to wipe them out. I had weeds in my yard too, so I decided to give his remedy a try. I went to the same hardware store, bought weed killer, then came home and attacked the weeds.

After a few days, my yard looked like a spotted leopard. The weeds were dead, but so was the grass around them. Turns out, the product I had purchased was grass and weed killer. Now I'm the talk of the neighborhood for my goof. I guess no one will be asking me for lawn care advice this summer!

MR. LAWN **CAN WHIP YOUR SORRY GRASS** INTO SHAPE!

Grassroots advice from a guy who knows lawns!

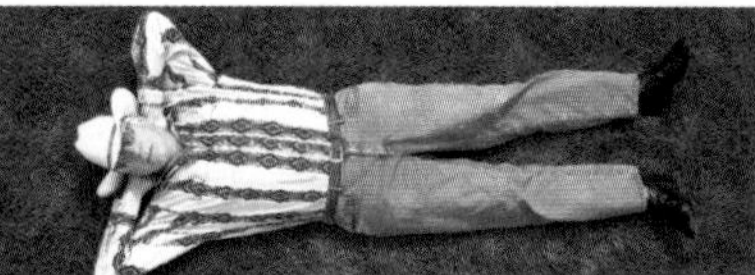

by **Brett Martin**

Achieving a lush lawn doesn't have to be a constant struggle. And you don't have to pay big bucks for a lawn service to douse your yard with chemicals either. Growing healthy, green grass is mainly just a matter of knowing what to give your lawn, and when to give it.

In this story, we'll show you what to do in the spring, summer and fall to get a lawn so nice you could cut it up and sell it as sod. These steps will work for any yard, regardless of climate or soil type. The products shown in this article are available at lawn and garden centers and some home centers.

We worked with lawn care expert George Dege, better known as Mr. Lawn. He has been teaching lawn care classes since the 1970s and has helped thousands of homeowners improve their lawns. As the third-generation owner of a lawn and garden center, he has been in the lawn care business "forever."

SPRING CARE

Once the grass starts turning green, it's time to start your lawn care. That's usually mid to late March for Northerners, early March for Southerners. Don't fret if your lawn is slow to green up. That's good. The thicker the lawn, the less sunlight that reaches the individual blades and the longer it takes for the grass to turn green.

Get rid of the stones and sand that the snowplow or snow blower threw into your yard over the winter. Raking isn't effective—you'll only get about 15 percent of the stones and pebbles. Instead, use a shop vacuum (**Photo 1**).

The snow piles that sat on your lawn all winter compacted the soil. You can loosen the soil and improve water penetration by applying gypsum ($3.50 for a 40-lb. bag that covers 200 sq. ft.). Test your broadcast spreader's dispersal pattern on your driveway. Fill the hopper, set the spread rate so the holes are wide open for gypsum and walk at your normal speed. Then measure how far the gypsum is dispersed on each side of the spreader (**Photo 2**). This tells you the distance to move over with each row when you're spreading—you want the spread patterns to overlap by 6 to 8 in. Broadcast spreaders always "throw" farther on the right side than they do the left. You don't need to spread gypsum over the entire lawn; just 10 ft. back from the street and the driveway.

For your spring and summer mowings, cut just the top third of the grass. So if your grass is 3 in. high, take 1 in. off the top. Mowing more than one-third stresses the grass. You can mow the grass shorter in the fall.

Between your second and third mowings, apply a lawn fertilizer with slow-release (time release) nitrogen ($15 for a 20-lb. bag that covers 5,000 sq. ft.). Always fill your spreader over a tarp or driveway (**Photo 3**). Follow the spread rate listed on the fertilizer bag and spread it on the entire lawn.

Fifteen days after applying the fertilizer, spread soil activator on the lawn (**Photo 4**; $28 for a 40-lb. bag that covers 4,000 sq. ft.).

1 Vacuum the pebbles. **Gravel and sand hinder grass growth, so vacuum them up. Start along the street and vacuum into the yard until you no longer hear stones getting sucked up. Then do the same thing along the driveway.**

2 Check the spreader's "throw". **To apply the right amount of fertilizer, measure from the wheel to the edge of the dispersal pattern. Then space your passes across the lawn so the coverage overlaps by 6 to 8 in. Do this test every time you spread a new product.**

3 Don't spill on the grass. **Park your spreader over a tarp or your driveway when filling the hopper. Spills and leaks can saturate one spot of your lawn and kill your grass.**

Proper watering is crucial to a healthy lawn. The best time to water is early morning, when the sun starts to rise. You lose some water to evaporation in the middle of the day. And watering at night leaves the grass wet too long, which can cause fungus and other diseases in the summer.

Give your lawn 3/8 in. of water three times a week. Calculate the amount of time it takes your sprinkler to dispense that much water (**Photo 5**). Set a timer ($15 at home centers and lawn and garden centers) on your hose spigot so you won't have to watch the clock (**Photo 6**). Increase from 3/8 in. to 1/2 in. when the daytime temperatures are above 80 degrees F.

If you have bare spots in your lawn caused by your dog, sprinkle gypsum on the spot and saturate it with water (**Photo 7**). Plant new grass seed in the bare spots and keep it watered.

Crabgrass will grow when the soil warms up to 55 degrees F. Apply a crabgrass preventer to keep that nasty weed from coming back.

Timing is everything. If you apply the preventer too early, it will be ineffective. And once the seeds germinate, it's too late. In northern states, late April is the best time. Mid-March is recommended for southern states. Check with a local garden center to find the best time for your area.

Apply the preventer wherever you had crabgrass the previous year, which is typically along the street, driveway and sidewalk (**Photo 8**).

In mid-May, give your lawn its second application of lawn fertilizer.

4 Improve your soil. Soil activator helps retain water in sandy soils and loosens clay soils. It also helps aerate the soil, decompose grass clippings and reduce erosion.

5 Measure the right amount of water. Set a cake pan halfway between your sprinkler and the edge of the spray pattern. Watch your clock to see how long it takes the sprinkler to fill the pan with 3/8 in. of water. Water for that amount of time three times a week, unless it rains.

> **"Soil activator contains humate, a natural product that's older than dinosaurs. This is one of the best things you can put on your lawn."**
>
> **— Mr. Lawn**

6 Water with a timer. If you don't have an automatic sprinkler, a $15 timer frees you from watching the clock every time you water. The timer controls the sprinkler, so you'll be sure the lawn gets the proper amount of water.

7 Neutralize dog spots. Gypsum and water are the antidote for dog spots in your yard. Gypsum neutralizes the dog urine, and the water soaks the area for new grass seed. If you treat the brown spots early, your grass won't die.

8 Stop crabgrass before it starts. Apply crabgrass preventer to any areas where crabgrass previously grew. A hand spreader is perfect for small areas, like along the pavement where crabgrass tends to grow.

MID TO LATE SUMMER

By midsummer, you should notice a thicker, greener lawn. You'll probably also notice weeds. Spot-kill patches of weeds with herbicide in a hand-held pressure sprayer ($9; Photo 9).

If weeds are popping up all over the lawn, spray them with a dial sprayer ($20 at home centers and lawn and garden centers). Pour concentrated herbicide into the sprayer and hook it up to your garden hose. Turn the dial on the top of the sprayer to the setting recommended on the herbicide container (such as 2 tablespoons per gallon of water). Then spray the weeds (Photo 10).

In mid-August, you could give your lawn a third application of fertilizer, but chicken manure works even better because it contains more nitrogen, which gives the grass a healthy, green look (there's hardly any odor). Mr. Lawn is a fan of Chickity Doo Doo because it also contains 9 percent calcium, which improves root growth. (A 40-lb. bag that covers 4,000 sq. ft. costs $17. Find retailers at chickitydoodoo.com.) Within two or three days of applying the manure, you'll see the lawn really green up.

Your lawn and chicken doo-doo—a marriage made in heaven!

Chicken manure is rich in nitrogen, which is a key nutrient for a healthy lawn. No need to get your own flock—it's a whole lot easier to just buy it by the bag.

9 Spot-spray individual weeds. **Don't treat the entire lawn if you have just a few weeds. A pump sprayer is more economical than buying spray bottles. Be sure there's no rain in the forecast for 24 hours.**

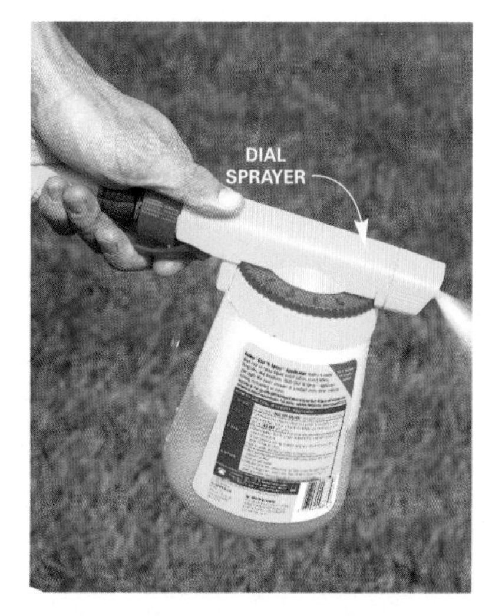

10 Use your hose for large areas. **Use a dial sprayer hooked up to your hose to kill large areas of weeds. Spray the herbicide on a calm day so the weed killer won't drift onto your plants and flowers.**

FALL CARE

Don't neglect your lawn as the growing season comes to an end. It's important to keep treating your soil before the grass goes dormant for the winter. In early to mid September, apply soil activator over your yard, just as you did in the spring.

Two weeks after that, give your lawn its final application of fertilizer for the year. Use a winterizer fertilizer ($38 for a 40-lb. bag that covers 10,000 sq. ft.). This specialized fertilizer has more potassium to help the grass roots grow deeper, which lets the roots absorb and store nutrients until the ground freezes. When the ground warms up in the spring, the grass uses those nutrients to jump-start its growth.

Keep mowing your lawn until the grass stops growing. Even in Minnesota, that sometimes doesn't happen until the first part of December. On your final mowing of the year, cut the grass to 1 to 1-1/2 in. high (Photo 11).

Now you're done caring for your lawn until spring!

11 Face winter with short grass. **Mow the grass short at the end of the year. This reduces the chance that your lawn will get snow mold and vole damage.**

TIPS FOR A LOW-UPKEEP POND

A little more building work means a lot less maintenance and repair

by **Gary Wentz**

A pond can become the best feature in your backyard, your favorite hangout, a project you'll be proud of for years. But if you don't plan for the maintenance up front, many ponds become just another source of chores and frustration. So we asked professional pond builders and longtime pond owners for their best advice on avoiding problems and maintenance. Before you grab your shovel or buy a bucket of goldfish, check out what they had to say.

Choose a tough liner

A leaking liner is one of the most common complaints of pond owners. Patching a leak is no big deal, but finding it can be a hole 'nother story. So a durable liner is a good investment. Most experts recommend 45-mil-thick EPDM rubber pond liners ($1 per sq. ft.).

Buy a one-piece liner; most suppliers can order liners 50 ft. wide or even larger. It's possible to bond smaller sections of EPDM together yourself, but your seam won't be as tough as a seamless or factory-seamed liner.

Protect the liner

Even the toughest liner won't stand up to sharp stones or roots. So when you're done digging the pond hole, take a few minutes to pick out stones and cut back any exposed tree roots. Before you install the liner, cushion the hole with underlayment, a spongy synthetic fabric that helps protect against stones and growing roots.

After you trim the liner, lay the cutoff scraps over areas where you'll place large stones. That shields the liner from direct contact with the heavy, abrasive stones.

Tips & lessons from our Field Editors

Several of our field editors are pond veterans who've built and lived with water features for years. Here's some of their best advice:

Best tip:

JIM BOYLE
HOUSTON, TX

The soil in my area is thick "gumbo" that sticks to the shovel like peanut butter. So when I dug my pond hole, I took a tip from some local excavators: I continuously dipped the shovel in a bucket of water and the sticky soil slipped right off.

Lesson learned the hard way:

I have a 10-year-old pond liner that's in good shape—except for one area that's cracking beyond repair. My mistake was leaving that section of the liner exposed to direct sunlight. Some liner materials—like EPDM—stand up to the sun better than others, but none are completely immune to UV light damage. The underwater part of the liner doesn't have to be shaded, but protect the rest with stones, gravel or plants.

Best tip:

KEN WERNER
HAMILTON, NY

Filling my 6,000-gallon pond would have run my well dry, and the local pool service wanted $400 to fill it. So I bought 100 ft. of plastic corrugated tubing ($50) and connected it to my downspouts. That filled my pond with rainwater in about two weeks.

Lesson learned the hard way:

Water attracts wildlife. That's sometimes good, sometimes bad. Our worst visitor was a heron that poked holes in the liner while trying to catch goldfish with its beak. We found that the best critter deterrent is a sprinkler controlled by a motion sensor (the Contech Scarecrow is one brand; about $50 at amazon.com).

Best tip:

MARK
RIPPLINGER
DELTONA, FL

When I ran the wiring to power my pond pump, I installed a switch by the back porch. We just flip the switch, sit back and enjoy the sound.

Lesson learned the hard way:

The first waterfall I built lost a lot of water because it trickled back between the stones just below the waterfall ledge. Take some extra time to carefully seal the stones behind and below the ledge. You can use mortar or "pond foam," black expanding foam sealant that's less visible than the yellowish stuff.

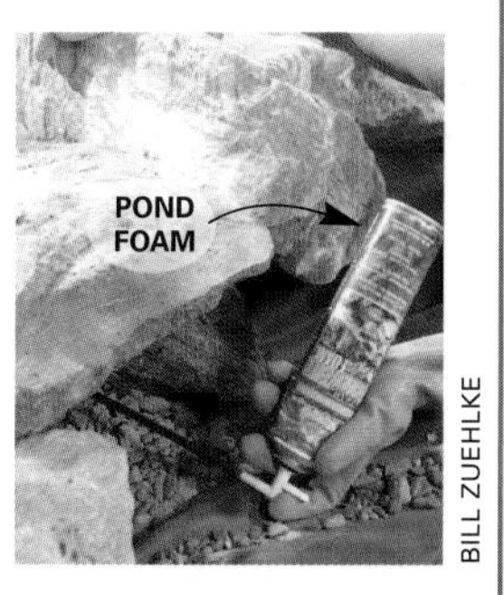

Pump and plumbing tips

If your pond will include a fountain or waterfall, you'll need a pump and tubing to move water.

- Don't set the pump directly on the pond floor where it will suck up damaging sludge. Elevate it on a brick or stone.
- For good water circulation, place the pump as far as possible from the waterfall or other inflow point. "Dead zones" where water stagnates are bad for fish and good for algae.
- Even if your pump has a built-in flow adjustment dial, install a valve in the tubing for more convenient adjustment (see right).

Leave a gap between stones and make sure the tubing can slide through. Do the same for the pump's power cord so you can remove or replace the pump without moving stones.

Keep runoff water out

Rainwater can carry soil, grass clippings and lawn chemicals into your pond. That means sludge buildup, algae growth, maybe even dead fish or pond plants. Keeping runoff out of pond water requires just a little extra care while you dig the pond hole: Make sure the rim of the hole is about 3 in. above the surrounding soil. If you're building in a low spot that becomes a swamp during heavy rains, make the rim a bit higher.

SHAWN NIELSEN

Build up a ridge—about 3 in. high—around your pond. If there's an uphill slope next to the pond, dig a shallow ditch to channel water away.

Make it easy to empty

To prepare for winter or to clean the pond, most pond owners occasionally empty the pond using the pond pump. A sump hole makes that easier. But don't place the pump in the hole during normal operation—the hole will be a gathering spot for debris that can damage the pump. If your pond will include a waterfall, install a tee in the tubing behind the waterfall. That lets you empty the pond without disconnecting the tubing at the waterfall.

THREADED FITTING

CAP

Install a tee in the tubing. When you want to drain the pond, just unscrew the cap.

SHAWN NIELSEN

When you dig the pond hole, slope the bottom toward a shallow sump hole. That way, you can set the pump in the sump to drain the pond dry.

Use tough tubing

Beefy corrugated tubing won't get kinked or crushed and is well worth the extra few bucks you'll pay for it.

CORRUGATED TUBING

WIMPY VINYL TUBING

MIKE KRIVIT

BUILD YOUR DREAM DECK

Our best tips to make it extraordinary!

by **Jeff Gorton**

Here at *The Family Handyman* magazine, we've been building decks for more than two decades, and in that time, we've learned a lot about what makes a deck a special place. In its most basic form, a deck is just a platform. It's the unique features you add that turn a simple structure into a perfect spot to while away the hours. In this article, we'll show you some of the features we've built into our dream decks over the years and give you some construction tips to help you incorporate them into your next deck. If you already have a deck, most of these projects can be added on with only minor changes to your existing structure.

Green up your deck with planters

Add a planter or two to your deck design and take advantage of your green thumb to provide color and greenery in your deck environment. You could even grow fresh veggies for the grill. Planters can take the place of low rails and double as seating. The photos here show a few construction details to keep in mind when you're building planters.

BUILD THE ULTIMATE MAINTENANCE-FREE PLANTER
Stack stones to build planters along the sides or in front of the deck. Here we covered the spaces under the deck with stone planters. We laid these stones with mortar but kept the mortar away from the face of the stones for a dry-laid look. Fill the lower section of the interior with stones or gravel to allow drainage.

DON'T FORGET THE BRACING
Even a little soil can add a lot of pressure to the sides of a planter. For large planter boxes like these, tie the sides together with crossbraces that are screwed to the upright framing on both sides. We finished off this planter with cedar siding.

Keep cool in the shade

When it's 20 degrees F outside, the prospect of relaxing on your deck in the warm sun sounds wonderful. But on a scorching summer day you may have a different opinion. When you're planning your deck, don't forget about shade. Unless you buy a freestanding shade awning or canopy, you can't just build on top of the deck. Depending on the covering, you may need extra support under the posts to hold the weight or extra bracing to prevent the wind from lifting or racking the structure.

Shade structures can be a simple pergola design or more elaborate fabric-covered frames. Pergolas let in more light and can double as a lattice for vines. Fabric covers provide complete shade and offer some protection from rain. Keep in mind that in snowy climates you'll have to bring the fabric cover in for the winter.

PLAN AHEAD TO ANCHOR THE POSTS

One good way to lock the posts into the deck is to build a "socket" into the deck framing, then sandwich a 2x4 between 2x6 lumber for the post. Extend the center member of the "sandwich" so it will fit into the socket. Drop the post in and secure it with construction screws to keep the shade structure from lifting off during windy storms and help prevent sway. Then add decorative braces between the posts and the beams at the top.

NOTCH POSTS FOR EXTRA SUPPORT

Another method for providing strong support at the top and bottom of posts is to notch them to fit around the joists and the beams. Then drive construction screws through the notched posts to ensure a strong connection for maximum strength.

Deck tips from our Field Editors

KEN HUNTINGTON, BURLESON, TX

Oversize your joists

If your deck plan calls for 2x8 joists, consider using 2x10s instead. That might add $100 or more to your materials cost, but it would also eliminate that bouncy feel you get when you use "just-big-enough" joists.

KEVIN ZOOK, BELLINGHAM, MA

Keep a router handy

A router equipped with a 1/4-in. round-over bit is an essential deck tool for me. That 1/4-in. radius matches the rounded factory edge on most decking, so I can quickly put a matching edge on a ripped deck board. And you'd be surprised how often you can dress up a deck or railing part with a rounded edge.

KEVIN LIND, NORTHPORT, AL

Save time with a palm nailer

I'll never build another deck without a palm nailer. It's noisy but saves tons of time when nailing joist hangers. Great for nailing in tight spots too. (Name brand palm nailers start at about $80.)

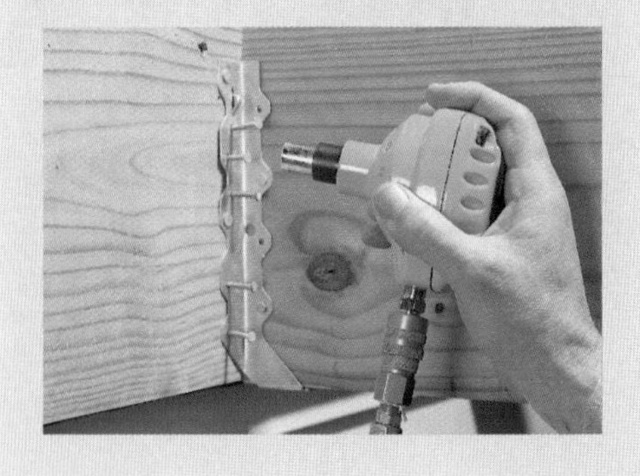

Build elegant cascading steps

If your deck is low to the ground, consider building wraparound steps rather than a conventional 3-ft.-wide stairway. Wraparound steps visually anchor the deck and tie it to the landscape. They also provide access from all directions, freeing up traffic patterns and spreading out wear and tear on the lawn. Finally, these steps serve as bleachers for extra seating at a party or a place to just sit back and watch the grass grow. For information on how to calculate the rise and run of deck steps, go to familyhandyman.com and type "deck stairs" into the search box. If you decide to add wraparound steps to your design, here's a tip to help simplify construction:

STACK BOXES FOR WRAPAROUND STEPS
It's easy to build cascading steps like these if you just build boxes and stack them up. You may have to shim each layer to get the correct rise, but it's still simpler than cutting a bunch of notched stringers.

Create a cozy hideaway with a privacy screen

If you need a little break from your chatty neighbor or just want your deck to feel more intimate, add a privacy screen. The basics are simple. You build a frame and fill it in with something—slatted wood, lattice, fabric stretched over a frame, bamboo curtains or even a vine-covered trellis. Consider whether you want to block wind or allow it to pass through, whether your privacy screen can do double duty as a shade structure in the late afternoon, and whether you want to totally block the view or just create a sense of separation, and then choose the appropriate material. Here are a few construction details to keep in mind when you build the screen.

REINFORCE THE JOISTS
Privacy screens have to withstand natural forces like the wind and people who like to lean on them. Where the joists run parallel to the screen, strengthen them by cutting tight-fitting blocks to fit between the outermost joists every 2 ft. Nail the bridging to the joists. The bridging will prevent the joists from twisting and keep the screen strong, whether the posts are placed inside the framing as shown here or outside as shown above right.

PREBUILD THE PANELS
Notch 4x4s and bolt them to the rim joist. For a design like this, measure the exact distance between 4x4s after you bolt them on and build panels to fit between them. Slip the panels into place and attach them with angled screws.

Curves add class

Looking for that little something to set your deck apart? Work a sweeping curve into the design. Building a curve into the deck framing is straightforward. It's a little trickier to build curved rails and benches. But if you're up to the challenge, here are some tips to make the job easier.

SWING AN ARC FOR CURVED DECK FRAMING

The easiest way to frame a curve is to run joists long. Then hook a marker to the end of a wire, chain or non-stretchy cord and swing an arc from the center of the circle. Cut the joists at the marks and you're on your way to a curved deck.

BEND PLYWOOD FOR A CURVED RIM

You're not going to bend a 2x10 around a curve. But strips of 1/2-in. treated plywood will bend easily. Glue and screw three layers together to form your curved rim joist.

LAMINATE SIDING FOR A CURVED RAIL

Standard 3/4-in.-thick boards are too stiff to bend around a curve. But 1/2-in. x 3-1/2-in. cedar lap siding will work. Rip 1/4 in. from each edge to make square edges. Spread waterproof wood glue over the meeting faces and use lots of clamps to hold it together while the glue sets. In this photo, we ripped the center pieces narrower to create a groove for the rail parts.

DIY Success Story

When our deck was built, the piers were left exposed above the concrete patio. They stuck up about 3 in., and the paper from the forms was exposed as well. Because the deck provided nice shade, my wife suggested that I build flower boxes for impatiens that would surround the piers and post. I built forms out of pressure-treated 2x2s and then used cedar 1x3s to cap the boxes. I also wrapped the posts with landscape fabric to keep the topsoil in the box and prevent the outside of the boxes from getting dirty. Don't do this if your posts aren't treated wood.

— Michael Hanson

OUR **ULTIMATE SHED**

Tons of space, easy-care materials and eye-catching details make this shed our best yet

by **Jeff Gorton**

This year we decided to pull out all the stops and build a really big shed. It's 16 x 20 ft. with 9-ft.-tall sidewalls. We spared no expense in fitting this building with a Craftsman-style fir entry door, a custom 8-ft.-wide by 7-ft.-tall garage door, and matching awning windows. Then we finished the outside with composite trim and fiber cement lap siding and gable end shingles. You might follow our lead and build a shed just like this one, but our real intent is to show you construction techniques that you can use to build any size structure, from a yard shed to an entire house. Big construction jobs go smoothly if you plan ahead and do things in the right order. And we'll show you how.

Go to familyhandyman.com/2010shed to find more building details. At familyhandyman.com, you'll also find more information on concrete pouring; wall framing; roofing, siding, window and door installation; and painting. Just type the appropriate term into the search box. And you can order a photocopy of the article for $3 at (800) 285-4961. Ask for the September 2010 Ultimate Shed.

Not including the $4,000 or so we spent on the windows, entry door and garage door, this shed cost us about $6,000.

Raise the first wall and brace it.

HandyHints®

DECORATE A LAMPPOST

You can train an annual like morning glory or hyacinth bean vine to crawl up a handsome lamppost on the boulevard (or lawn light). Wrap the post with chicken wire and then plant seeds (or seedlings you started indoors) at the base of the lamppost each spring. By midsummer, the vine will have encircled the lamppost. By August, it will have reached the top and be in full flower.

BILL ZUEHLKE (2)

WEED I.D.

Each spring, I battle the pesky weeds in my yard with a spray bottle of herbicide. But I can never tell which weeds I've sprayed and which ones I've missed. This year I mixed a tiny amount of red food coloring into the herbicide. Now when I spray those evil creatures, I can actually see their "bloody" wounds and I know I've hit 'em where it hurts. I save time and money, and it actually gives me hope that I might someday win the war against all that creeping Charlie!

GARDEN TOOL NOOK

Here's a classic handy hint that puts an old mailbox to work and really brightens up the garden. Screw the mailbox to a post and sink the post in the garden. It's a great place to store gardening gloves and small tools. If you're feeling artistic, paint something clever on the mailbox. It's a charming way to add a convenient storage nook outside.

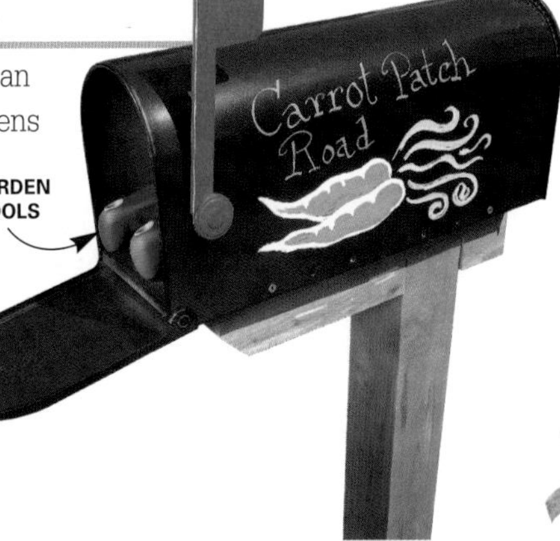

TIPPY BATHS AREN'T FOR THE BIRDS

To keep your birdbath from tipping over and to keep the water in the bowl level, install a level paver stone under your birdbath. Round or square paving stones like the one we're using are readily available at garden centers ($3 to $6 each).

Dig a hole about 2 in. deeper than the thickness of the paver and pack the loose soil to prevent settling. Spread and roughly level a 2-in. layer of sand in the hole. Set the paver on the sand and check it with a level. Lift one edge of the paver and add or remove sand to level it.

KEEP POND PUMPS FROM CLOGGING

Filters on small outdoor pond pumps can clog up quickly with leaves and debris from nearby plants. You can keep your pump flowing freely for longer just by enclosing it in a simple filter made from fiberglass screen mesh. Wrap the pump loosely with a square of mesh, then close the top with a zip tie or piece of wire. When you notice the water flow weakening, just rinse the gunk off the screen.

HandyHints®

BACK-SAVING FERTILIZER FUNNEL

I have a large yard with a lot of shrubs, and fertilizing them each year was a real backbreaker. Granular fertilizer doesn't do any good unless it's spread at the base of the plant near the root zone, and leaning over to fertilize each shrub was killing me. To make this chore easier, I invented the "fert shooter." I duct-taped a funnel to a length of PVC pipe and slit some holes in a plastic coffee container and clamped it to the pipe. Now I just fill the container with fertilizer and move the pipe from shrub to shrub. The fertilizer goes right where I need it and I don't have to fight my way to the base of dense shrubs—or spend the night lying on a heating pad.

SOFT SAPLING PROTECTION

When you plant a new tree, wrap the trunk with a piece of foam pipe insulation before you attach the support wire. The foam is already split, so it's easy to wrap around the trunk. Then twist the wire around it and around the stake. That way, the wire won't cut into the sapling's fragile bark.

OUCHLESS ROSE DEADHEADING

Deadheading my roses was a real pain because all the thorns would prick me through my gloves. Now I use long-handled tongs to hold the rose heads while I snip them off with the other hand. It's also easier on my back and cuts my deadheading time in half.

BILL ZUEHLKE

NO-NONSENSE WEEDER

When tough tree and shrub "volunteer seedlings" (weeds) just won't give, grab the stem with a pair of pliers. Up they'll come in a flash! It's especially effective on woody plants. Plants with a long tap root or spreading roots still require some digging.

A MOVABLE FEAST

Late frosts in the spring and early frosts in the fall can kill your tender veggies and herbs. You can extend the gardening season by planting these annuals in a shallow wheelbarrow. Wheel your small crop around to follow the sun, shade or rain, and when the weather threatens to turn cold overnight, just roll your portable garden into the garage for protection.

DOG-PROOF YOUR SHRUBS

Does your dog love to dig holes beneath your shrubs to lounge in? It's great for Bingo, but not so great for the roots of the plants. Keep him from digging around your shrubs by staking chicken wire around the roots. To hold the wire in place, dig a 3-in. trench under the edges of the wire, bend the edges down into the trench and stake it every 12 in. in all directions. Your dog will hate getting his nails caught in the mesh, and his digging days will be over—in that spot, anyway.

MIKE KRIVIT (3)

UNDERGROUND SPRINKLER PHOTOS

When we installed an underground sprinkler system, I made a map of it before the grass grew back. I turned the water on to each zone and snapped photos of all the sprinkler heads and water lines. I labeled the photos with the zone number and the number of spray heads and rotors and put them in a bag with the controller instructions. We check the photos whenever we need to find a spray head or dig in the yard.

PERMANENT TIKI TORCH HOLDERS

We like to set tiki torches around our patio in the backyard. But the ground is rock hard, so it's not easy to push them in, and I didn't want to remove them every time I had to mow. I came up with this solution: I cut 5-in.-long pieces of PVC pipe to hold the torches and used a maul and a block of wood to pound them into the ground. (I had to pull them out a couple of times during the process to dig out the clay plugs.)

Now I just slip the torches in and out of their sleeves, and I can mow right over the PVC holders without a problem.

NO MORE SPROUTING BIRDSEED

Birdseed that drops to the ground often makes a mess, kills the grass and then grows into an odd jumble of plants. A carpet scrap keeps the seed off, allowing the area to be neat and weed-free.

To get rid of the hulls, sweep the carpet or shake it off in the garbage can. However, the carpet scrap will kill the grass and plants underneath. Be sure you move any plants that you want to save.

BILL ZUEHLKE

HANDY BENCH AND TOOL BUCKET

A 5-gallon bucket comes in handy out in the garden—and not just for collecting weeds. You can load it up with all your gardening tools and carry them easily from place to place. If it starts to rain, protect the tools with the lid. But here's the best part—it doubles as a portable stool when you need to rest or do some pruning. The only problem is that the lid can be hard to pry off. Solve that by cutting off all but two of the plastic tabs. The lid will go on and off in a snap.

My plaid lawn

I bought a drop spreader to fertilize our malnourished lawn. I loaded the hopper, set the drop rate and went to work. After spreading fertilizer down one row, I measured over to the next row and pulled the spreader backward across the lawn. I covered the entire yard this way—pushing the spreader in one direction, then pulling it back the other way. Then I spread fertilizer again, this time going perpendicular to my first pattern.

All seemed well and good until the lawn greened up a few days later. That's when my wife called me upstairs. From the second-story window, we could see an unmistakable plaid pattern over the whole lawn. It turns out that my spreader only drops fertilizer when you're pushing, not pulling. Oops!

Brush-cutter blues

My friend Debby had a ton of brush cutting to do in the woods behind her house. "Debby, you have to borrow my commercial-grade brush cutter. This thing cuts brush like a razor cuts hair!" I bragged. Before she came to pick it up, I installed a new blade to really impress her. The following week, she let me know that she wasn't impressed at all with my macho tool. She worked her tail off for three sweaty hours on a 90-degree F day without getting very much brush cleared. I was puzzled—until I noticed that all the teeth were nearly ground off the brand-new blade. You guessed it. I'd installed the blade upside down and the teeth were facing backward. I couldn't let her buy me a new $30 blade, even though she offered.

BAMBOO PLANTER & TRELLIS

If you're wishing for wisteria or craving clematis, you can plant them just steps away in this planter and trellis for your deck or patio. And if you build a pair of them, you can create a privacy screen or provide shade from the late afternoon sun.

Similar planter/trellis combinations—made of wood or plastic—can cost $200 or more at garden centers. But you can build this one for as little as $100 in one weekend.

Bring flowers and foliage to your deck or patio

by **Gary Wentz**

MASTER A NEW MATERIAL

Bamboo is one of the world's greatest building materials. It's incredibly strong, good-looking and cheap. And if you're a weekend woodworker, you already have the tools to work with it. But bamboo doesn't behave exactly like wood, so you'll also need some new tricks up your sleeve. We'll show you how to build with this hard and brittle, irregular and hollow material.

Figure A
Bamboo planter & trellis

Overall dimensions: 40 in. wide x 18 in. deep x 72 in. tall. All wood parts are 3/4 in. thick. Bamboo parts vary in diameter from 3/8 to 3/4 in. unless otherwise noted.

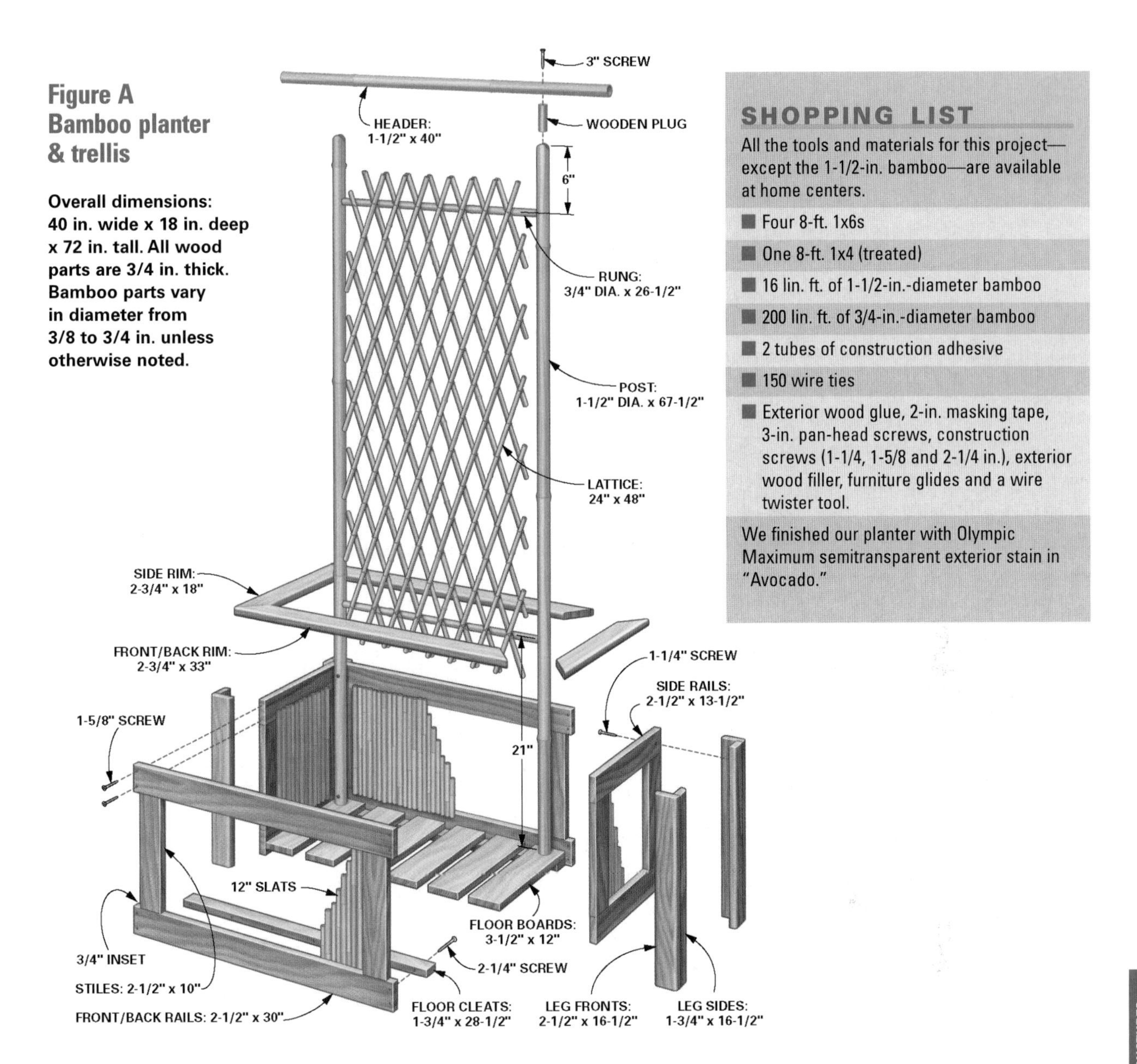

SHOPPING LIST

All the tools and materials for this project—except the 1-1/2-in. bamboo—are available at home centers.

- Four 8-ft. 1x6s
- One 8-ft. 1x4 (treated)
- 16 lin. ft. of 1-1/2-in.-diameter bamboo
- 200 lin. ft. of 3/4-in.-diameter bamboo
- 2 tubes of construction adhesive
- 150 wire ties
- Exterior wood glue, 2-in. masking tape, 3-in. pan-head screws, construction screws (1-1/4, 1-5/8 and 2-1/4 in.), exterior wood filler, furniture glides and a wire twister tool.

We finished our planter with Olympic Maximum semitransparent exterior stain in "Avocado."

To build this planter, you'll need standard woodworking tools like a table saw and a miter saw. If you want to round the edges of the wooden parts as we did, you'll also need a router and two round-over bits (1/4- and 1/2-in. radius). Our total materials bill was about $140. Your cost will depend mostly on the wood you choose for the planter box. We built our planter from "select-grade" pine boards, which cost about $60 altogether. If you don't mind a few knots, use construction-grade pine, which will cost about $20. If you live in a damp climate, consider rot-resistant choices like cedar or teak. Pressure-treated lumber is another good choice because it costs about the same as construction-grade pine and lasts practically forever. The drawback is that you may have to let it dry for a month before you start building.

Small-diameter bamboo for the planter box slats and lattice is in stock at most home centers and garden centers. The bamboo we used was labeled "3/4 inch." To find 1-1/2-in.-diameter bamboo for the trellis posts and header, visit a large garden center or shop online (search for "bamboo poles"). You'll find lower prices online, but those savings may be offset by shipping charges. We bought our bamboo at a garden center and spent about $50. Select straight poles for the trellis posts and header.

Build the planter box

To get started, rip four 8-ft.-long 1x6s into strips on your table saw. You'll need two 2-3/4-in.-wide strips for the top rim, two 1-3/4-in.-wide strips for the cleats and legs, and four 2-1/2-in.-wide strips for the legs, rails and stiles. Glue the rails and stiles together to make frames (**Photo 1**). Sand the frames and round the inside edges with your router and a 1/4-in. round-over bit. Then mask around the frames (**Photo 2**).

1 Build four frames. **Glue together the frames that form the sides of the planter box. Clamp a framing square to your workbench to help align the parts.**

2 Mask the frames. **Line the backs of the frames with wide masking tape. When you finish the wood later, the tape will keep stain off the bamboo.**

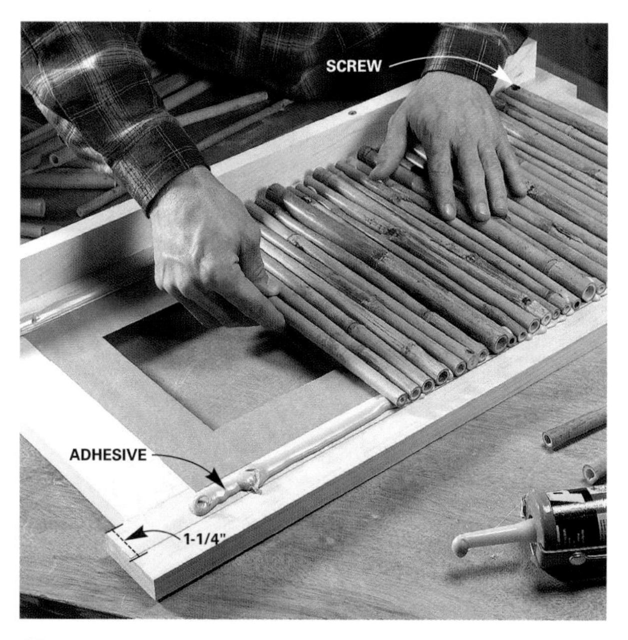

3 Glue on the bamboo. **Fill the frames with bamboo slats. Screw the first slat in place and set the rest in heavy beads of construction adhesive.**

4 Assemble the planter box. **First screw the frames together at the corners. Then screw on the legs from inside the box and add the floor and top rim.**

HANDLE CUT OFF

WIRE TIE

Using wire ties

Wire ties are simple to use: Bend each tie in half and slip it over the bamboo. Then hook the looped ends with the twister tool and spin. For faster twisting, cut the handle off the tool and chuck it into a drill (Photo 6).

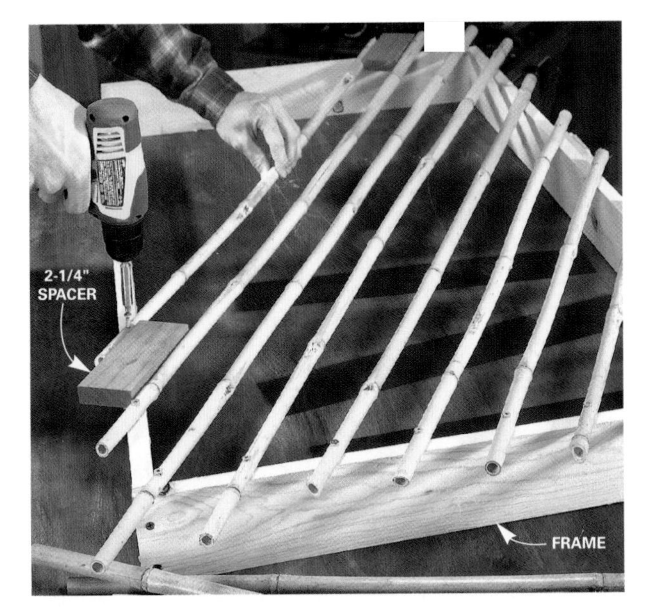

5 Build the lattice on a frame. **Screw the first layer of bamboo poles directly to the frame, using spacer blocks to position them. Drill a pilot hole for every screw; bamboo splits easily.**

6 Wire the lattice together. **Tie the second layer of bamboo to the first with wire ties. Twist until the looped ends snap off. Then bend the remaining wire flat against the bamboo.**

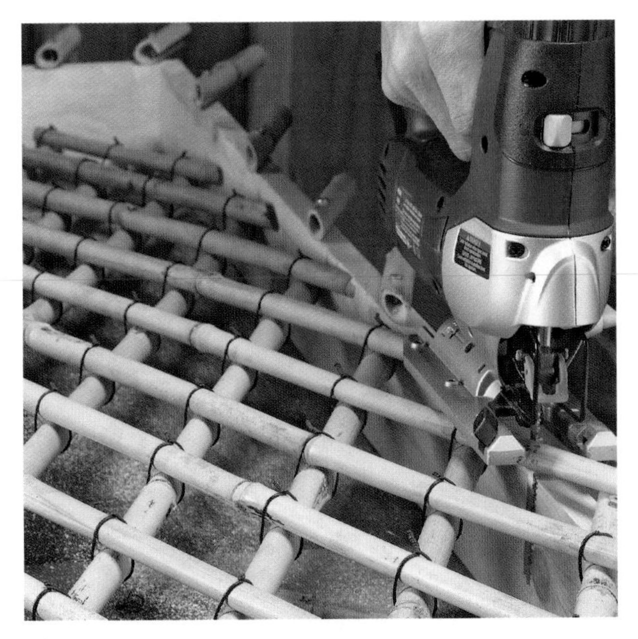

7 Cut out the lattice. **Trim the completed lattice off the frame by guiding a jigsaw or reciprocating saw along the inner edge of the frame.**

8 Prevent cracks with kerfs. **Cut saw kerfs in the posts and header. This prevents random cracks from developing later. To cut safely, screw the bamboo to a 2x4.**

You'll need to cut about 120 slats to fill the frames. To avoid measuring them all, clamp a stop block next to your miter saw. With the slats cut, mark guidelines 1-1/4 in. from the top and bottom of the frames and glue the slats between them (Photo 3). Place the best side of each slat face down. Alternate thin and thick slats, and the direction of the tapers—one narrow end up, the next down.

While you're waiting for the adhesive to harden, glue together the planter legs. Round the edges with a 1/2-in. round-over bit.

Assemble the planter box (Photo 4). Take diagonal corner-to-corner measurements to make sure the box is square before you screw the pressure-treated floor boards to the cleats. Top off the planter box with rim boards, mitered at the corners and screwed to the frames. We rounded the edges of our rim material with a 1/4-in.

round-over bit before cutting it to length. The rim overhangs the inside of the box by 1/2 in.

Build the trellis

To assemble the lattice, first grab any 1x4s or 2x4s you have handy and build a 1x4 frame with inner dimensions of 2 x 4 ft. Take diagonal corner-to-corner measurements to make sure the frame is square. Lay the first pole across the frame from one corner to the other and screw it to the frame. Then add more poles, screwing each to the frame (**Photo 5**). Although it's time-consuming, you must drill a pilot hole for every screw—otherwise, the bamboo will split.

Attach the second layer of bamboo with wire ties and a "twister" tool (**Photo 6**). Wire ties are designed to connect the rebar that reinforces concrete, so you'll find them and a twister in the masonry aisle at home centers. For a neat, tight connection, pull upward on the twister as it spins. When the lattice is done, cut it out of the frame (**Photo 7**).

Next, build the bamboo frame that will hold the lattice. Start by cutting kerfs in the posts and header (**Photo 8**). Bamboo can develop wide cracks as it dries out. Cutting a kerf creates a single, straight opening and prevents random splitting. Then cut the tops of the posts using a 1-1/2-in. hole saw (**Photo 9**). Glue 4-in.-long 3/4 x 3/4-in. wooden plugs into the posts to provide anchors for the screws that fasten the header. The plugs don't have to fit tight; just use lots of construction adhesive.

Drill the posts with a 3/4-in. hole saw to create sockets for the rungs. Don't use a spade bit; the bamboo will split. Insert the rungs and measure the spread of the posts. To fit into the planter box, the spread must be no more than 27-1/2 in. Cut the rungs a bit shorter if needed and then glue them into the posts with construction adhesive. Attach the header (**Photo 10**). Leave the trellis frame on a flat surface until the adhesive hardens, then attach the lattice to the rungs. When you screw the completed trellis to the planter box, insert wooden blocks behind the bottom ends of the posts. Bamboo isn't perfectly straight, so you'll have to experiment with blocks of different thicknesses to make the posts plumb.

We finished our planter box with deck stain. When you're done finishing, slice the masking tape around the box frames with a utility knife and peel off the tape. Add plastic furniture glides to the legs to keep the wood from soaking up moisture. To hold soil, we used a 12-1/2-in. x 27-in. plastic planter. You could use two or three smaller pots instead.

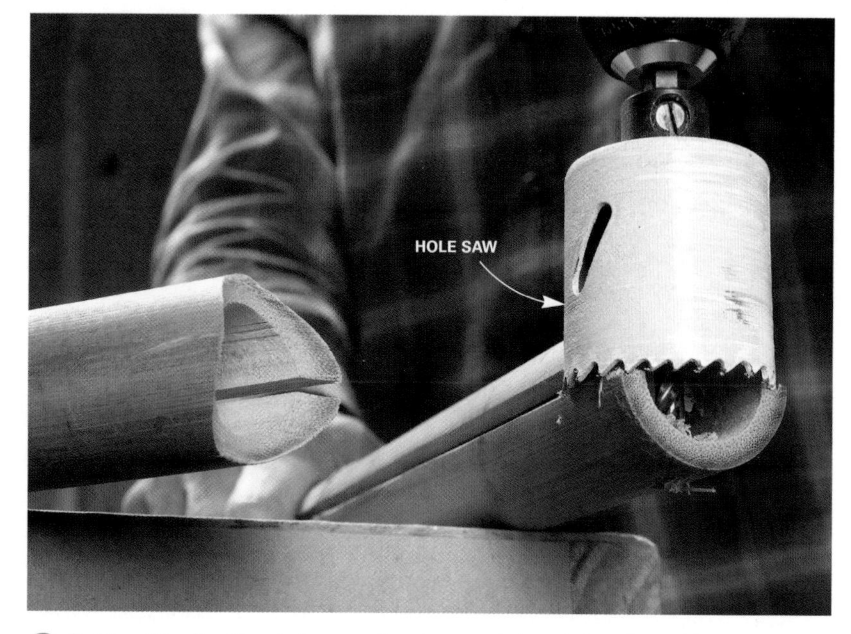

9 Cut "saddles" with a hole saw. **Create rounded ends on the trellis posts to hold the header. For a clean cut, run the drill at high speed and apply light pressure.**

10 Screw on the header. **Screw the header to the posts. Drill pilot holes to avoid splitting the bamboo. Attach the lattice to the rungs using wire ties.**

DECK BUILDING TIPS FROM A PRO

Avoid headaches and save time

by **Travis Larson**

If building about 100 decks over the past 25 years makes someone an expert deck builder, I guess I qualify.

Several of these tips are original and unique. I know—I invented them. Some I figured out by actually constructing the decks; others, by watching them age over the years. Either way, these are some of my favorite deck-building techniques, ones that I'd recommend to anyone planning to build a deck.

RISERS

2x12 SKIRT

Build better stairs

Simple notched stair jacks are fine for interior stairs. They get nailed to wall studs for stability and are hidden once the house is finished. Not so with deck stairs. Naked, notched treated-wood stair jacks are unattractive and wobbly, and because there isn't much meat to attach posts or pickets to, you'll have wobbly handrails, too. But it's easy to strengthen them and spruce them up. Adding sturdy, solid 2x12 skirts to the outside jacks and stair risers does it all.

OUTDOOR STRUCTURES, LANDSCAPING & GARDENING

Get over lag screws

There are few reasons to use lag screws anymore. Construction screws may look wimpy, but they're actually stronger than lags. And you don't have to spend five minutes cranking each one in with a ratchet.

CONSTRUCTION SCREWS

Give construction screws a try on your next deck. You can drive them with any 18-volt screw gun without predrilling—they don't split wood. The price may shock you (they cost four times as much), but you'll never go back to lags.

Avoid miters

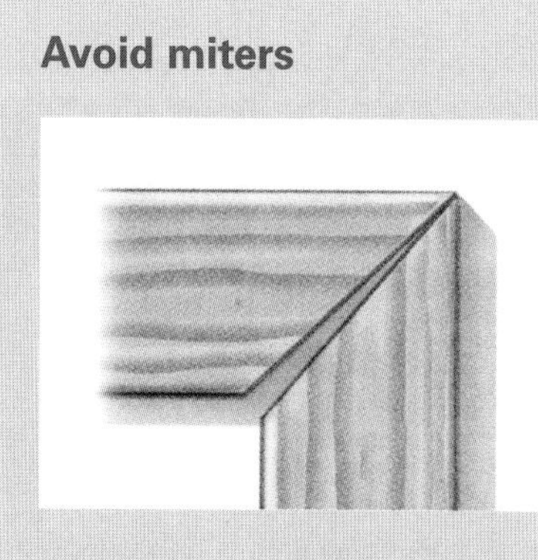

Avoid miters when you can, especially in wide boards. Here's why. Wood installed outdoors immediately starts shrinking—or in some conditions, expanding—mostly in width. Miters will always open up unevenly, and your perfect miter will look like a hack job in no time. Whenever possible, use simple butt joints. They don't look as professional as miters at first, but they look better in the long run.

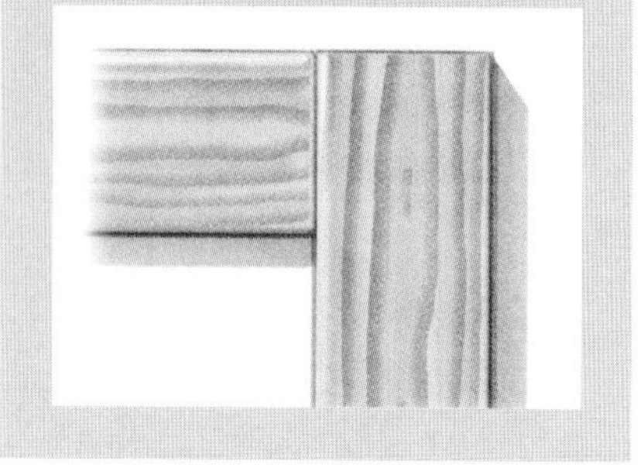

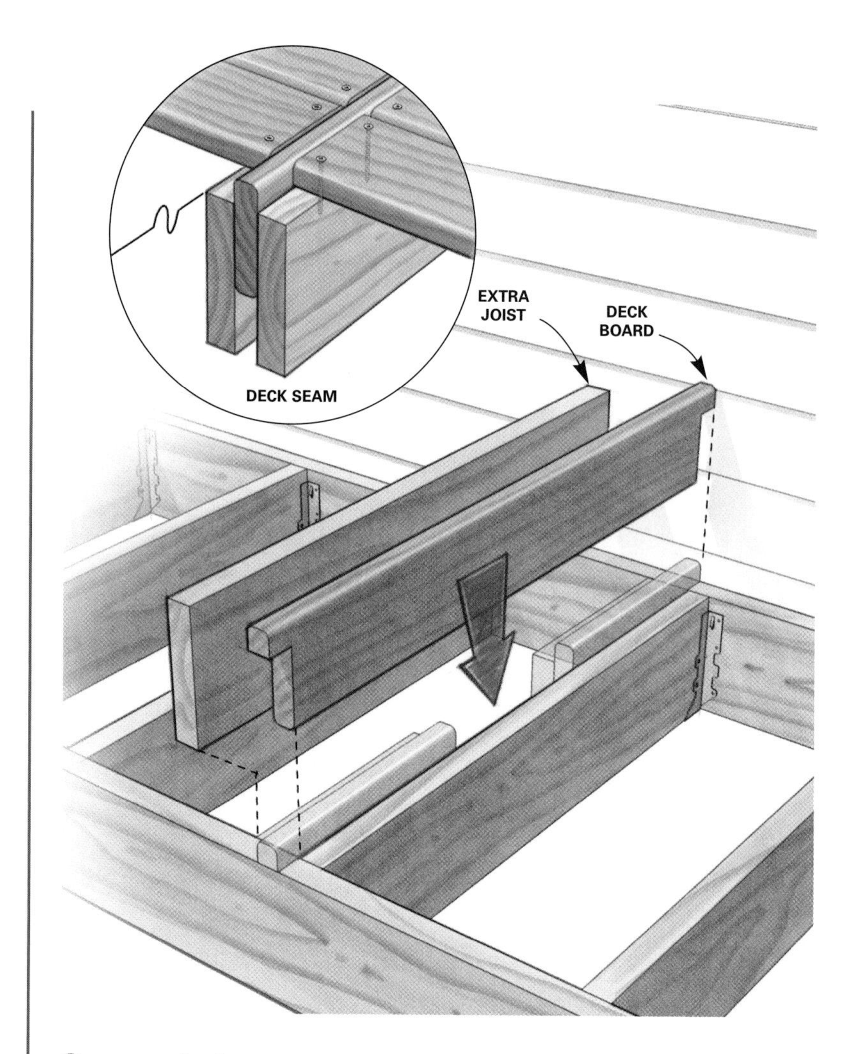

Seam a deck

The traditional way most builders go about decking is to randomly stagger joints. The result is that end-to-end deck boards share the 1-1/2-in. thickness of each joist. That can cause problems, especially with wood decks. With only 3/4 in. of nailing surface, fasteners will cause ends to split, and since the board ends have to be tight, untreated wood will rot.

I use a faster, more material-efficient method I call seaming. It's simply strategically placing a seam (or seams, on bigger decks) and using the same length boards for each section. Each seam is a sandwich made of an elevated vertical decking board with joists on both sides. The advantages are many. It's faster than random seaming; all decking ends have a full 1-1/2 in. of framing, so it cuts down on fastener splits; and you can leave 1/4-in. gaps at the ends so end grain can dry out after it gets wet.

The vertical deck board is for looks only. It makes everything look planned and polished. And there's virtually no waste. If I need to build a 20-ft.-wide deck, I'll make it about 19 ft. 6 in. and use all 10-ft. decking on both halves. That allows for 1-in. overhangs and cutting off some bad ends.

Seaming also works well for solid composite decking, which comes in fewer lengths. If, for example, I'm building a composite deck, 12- and 20-ft. lengths might be the only options. For a 16-ft.-wide deck, I might seam it to have a 4-ft. "sidewalk" down the middle for zero waste. Of course, everything depends on the design. But think about it next time to figure out the best approach.

Leave a little step below doors

There are so many reasons not to snug decks right under door thresholds. The screen and sliding door tracks on patio doors get full of debris. Storm doors have to bulldoze their way through leaves in the fall. And those leaves will get blown or kicked into the house every time the door opens. Splashing water rots out wood casing and jamb trim. And last but not least, water will inevitably work its way under any threshold and rot out the subfloor and then the framing. It's nearly impossible to flash between ledgers and thresholds if the decking is flush to thresholds. Leave a 3-in. step: The house and you will be a lot happier in the long run.

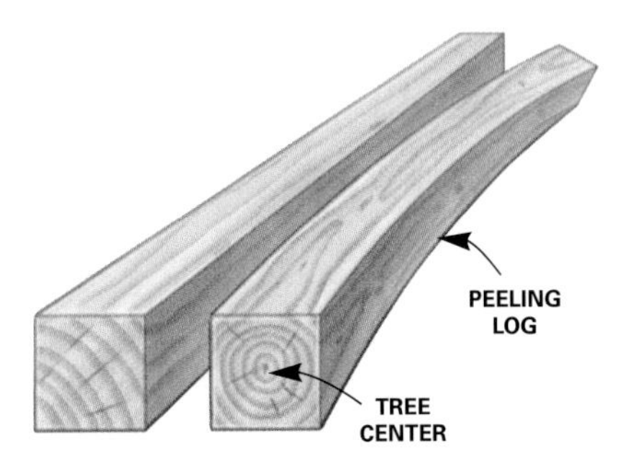

Check the end grain on 4x4s

When buying 4x4s, don't just sight them for straightness; always look at the ends. Try to avoid 4x4s that include the center of the tree, especially anywhere near the center of the 4x4. Those can twist into airplane propellers in no time. This is particularly true of 8-footers because those are often the leftovers from "peeling logs," the outer layers of which have been shaved off to make plywood veneer. When I order 4x4s over the phone and need eights, I always order tens to reduce the chances of getting 4x4 leftovers from peelers.

Cobble together a layout frame

Home improvement books and TV shows always recommend laying out deck footings with batter boards and string. But I gave that up years ago. It's faster and easier to build a layout frame from deck boards or joists. And unlike string, a frame gives you a solid guide to mark footing holes and align post bases. You can mark the location of the frame by driving a few stakes and then remove it to dig holes or pour footings. Then you can quickly replace the frame to align post bases or set posts. You can even screw posts to the frame to hold them in perfect position while you backfill.

5 WAYS TO MAKE YOUR LAWN **ORGANIC**

by **Elisa Bernick**

Going organic isn't difficult, but it does take some effort, especially if you're making the switch from chemical fertilizers. And although an organic lawn eventually looks great, it can take two or three years for it to look as thick and deep green each spring as a lawn on a chemical diet. If that sounds OK, then going organic is really about continuing the basic lawn maintenance you've been doing all along, with a few important differences. This article will tell you the five most important things you need to do to have a healthy and attractive organic lawn.

1 Adjust your expectations

You can have a beautiful lawn without chemicals, but it's not going to be as weed-free. Going organic with your lawn means following good basic lawn care practices and using organic fertilizers and natural weed control methods. It also means accepting the reality of a chemical-free lawn—a slower green-up each spring and a lawn with a few more weeds.

2 Find out what nutrients your soil needs

Testing your soil is crucial, especially if you've been using chemical fertilizers and pesticides, which can destroy soil nutrients and beneficial microbes. Store-bought testing kits aren't very accurate. Instead, contact your local Cooperative Extension Service lab (to find yours, visit csrees.usda.gov). For $10 to $20, most labs will provide detailed soil collection instructions and pre-addressed soil-testing bags that you can use to send in your soil sample. After testing, the lab will send you specific information about your lawn's soil type, nutrient levels and pH. Most important, the lab will make suggestions for improving your soil.

Because extreme moisture levels and low temperatures can skew pH readings, the best time to test your soil is mid to late spring or early fall.

3 Use organic fertilizers

Grass clippings provide about half the nutrients your lawn needs. For the other half, use organic fertilizer, which is made from composted plant waste, manure and other natural materials.

Use your soil test as a guide to selecting the right kind and amount of fertilizer. Organic fertilizers cost about a third more per pound than chemical fertilizers, and you need to use more of them at a time. But since they feed the grass over a longer period of time, you apply them less often and the price difference generally equals out. The main drawback of organic fertilizers is that they release nutrients more slowly, so grass doesn't green up as quickly in the spring.

Feed cool-season grasses before their growth spurt in late May and again in late September to mid-October. Give warm-season grasses frequent light feedings (three to five times) from late spring through early fall.

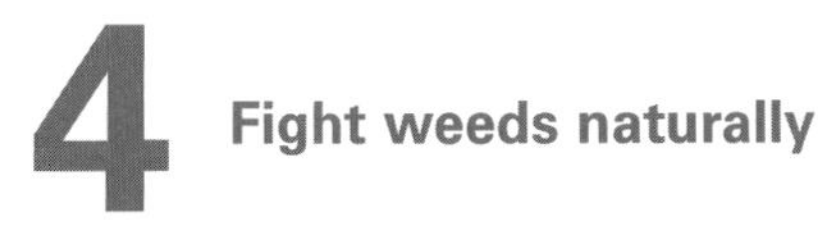

4 Fight weeds naturally

Over time, a healthy chemical-free lawn will discourage most weeds on its own. But if weeds start to take over, try these options:

- Pull them manually.
- Spot-spray with a vinegar or orange oil–based weed killer ($7 for 32-oz. concentrate at garden centers).
- Spread new grass seed over your existing lawn (see sidebar at right).
- Sprinkle corn gluten over your lawn in early spring or in fall ($30 for 25 lbs. at garden centers). Corn gluten will prevent crabgrass and other annual weeds, but it takes a few years to become effective.

Corn gluten can prevent annual weeds, but don't use it when you're overseeding the lawn since it will keep the grass seeds from germinating.

5 Top dress with compost

Add microbes back into your soil by top-dressing your lawn with a 1/2-in. layer of compost once a year. That's about 1 cu. yd. of compost per 1,000 sq. ft. of lawn. Spread it around your yard, and use a push broom to sweep it off the grass blades so you don't smother the lawn. Then water it into the soil. This is most effective if you aerate your lawn first.

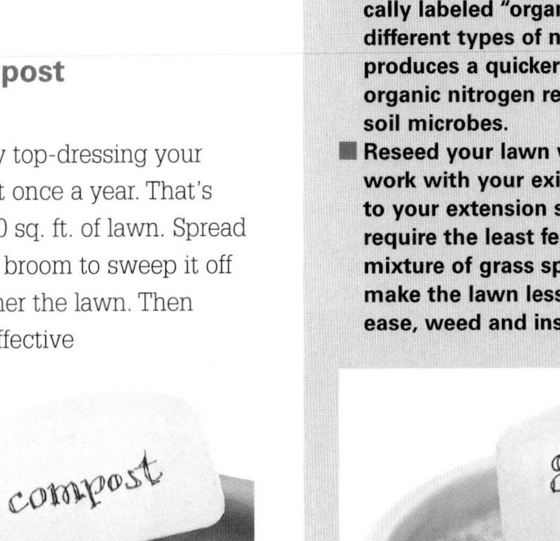

Compost acts like a sponge to retain moisture and nutrients and adds microbes back into the soil.

Wean your lawn from chemicals gradually

If you've had your lawn on a chemical diet and you want to "go green" gradually, here are two things that will help your lawn look better while you make the switch.

- **Use a "bridge" fertilizer that contains both organic and synthetic nitrogen to wean your lawn from chemicals over two to four years. These are typically labeled "organic-based" and the label will list different types of nitrogen. The synthetic nitrogen produces a quicker spring green-up while the organic nitrogen releases slowly and encourages soil microbes.**
- **Reseed your lawn with grass varieties that will work with your existing turf, climate and soil. Talk to your extension service about varieties that require the least fertilizing and watering. Use a mixture of grass species when overseeding to make the lawn less susceptible to drought, disease, weed and insect problems.**

PLANT A TREE THAT WILL THRIVE

If you want your newly planted tree to grow and be healthy, you can't just stick it in a hole in the ground and hope for the best. We'll show you how to plant a tree that will thrive, extend its roots and enhance your landscape. The steps are the same for any variety. Be sure to call "811" to get your utilities marked before you dig.

Pick a tree variety that grows well in your area and soil conditions (a nursery can help you with this). If you're planting a fruit tree, find out if you need to plant a second one within a certain distance for pollination. And ask the nursery (or research online) how big the tree will be when it's full grown. Then plant it far enough away from your house so that once the tree reaches maturity, its branches won't scrape against your siding or roof.

Plant in the spring or fall

Plant a tree in early spring before the buds open or in the fall before the tree goes dormant. A tree planted during the hot summer months can get stressed and is harder to keep watered. If you insist on a summer planting, keep the soil moist but not sodden. During dry, sunny weather, that might mean watering a few times a day. If you have clay soil and the ground stays damp 3 in. below the surface, you can cut back on watering.

When you buy your tree, ask the nursery to wrap it with plastic for the drive home (our local nursery did it for free). The branches are grouped tightly together so they won't be damaged by wind in the back of a pickup or during unloading. The plastic also keeps the soil from spilling out of the container (although a little water may leak).

Place the tree on its side in the truck bed, strap down the container and wedge scraps of wood under both sides of the container to keep it from rolling around during the drive home. If you're hauling the tree in a van or an SUV, put plastic on the floor to catch any water leaks.

Dig a hole the right size and depth

You want to plant the tree so its root collar—the trunk flare right above the root system—is about 1 in. above ground level. Take the tree out of the container (slitting the container sides) or cut away the wire cage and burlap. Then

1 Take off the plastic. Remove the plastic when you get home, even if you won't plant the tree until the next day. The plastic can suffocate the tree if it's left on too long.

2 Grab a shovel and start digging. Make the hole two to three times as wide as the root ball. As you dig, place the soil on a tarp to make backfilling easier and to avoid damaging surrounding grass.

measure the distance from the root collar to the bottom of the root ball and dig the hole to that depth. Dig the hole two to three times as wide as the root ball.

Don't rely on the container size, the wires or the wrapping around the roots as an indication of the depth you want to plant your tree. If the tree is planted too shallow, the roots could be exposed above the ground, especially as the tree grows. But don't plant it too deep either (a common mistake!). The roots need oxygen to get established, and there's more oxygen near the surface.

Before placing the tree in the hole, break up the tightly wound root ball and carefully fan out the roots. Don't pull too hard or the roots will break. It's OK if some of the soil in the root ball crumbles and falls off. It'll help free the roots. Pulling apart the root ball encourages the roots to expand into the surrounding soil.

You'll have to be careful when you handle the tree, or what's left of the root ball will fall apart and you could tear the smaller roots. Never pick up the tree by its trunk. Instead, support the tree from under or from the side of the root ball. Set the tree in the center of the hole.

Keep the root collar about 1 in. above ground level. If it's too high, remove the tree and dig the hole a little deeper. If the trunk flare is too low, add soil under the roots.

Mix the backfill

Don't backfill with only compost manure or peat moss. The roots will be so comfortable in the nutrient-rich backfill that they'll never penetrate the native soil outside the hole.

Mix the backfill material in a wheelbarrow. Use these proportions: two-thirds soil that you dug out of the hole and one-third compost manure. Mix them with a hoe, then use a spade to backfill around the tree. Soak the hole as you backfill. Add backfill until the hole is filled.

Weed trimmers and rodents and other animals can kill a tree by damaging the bark. Install a plastic guard (about $3.50 at nurseries) over the trunk to protect it.

3 Break up the root clump. **Gently unwind and spread out the roots so they don't go into the hole as a big ball. But be careful not to break or pull off the thin roots.**

4 Check the root collar height. **Lay your shovel across the hole to make sure the root collar is at the right height (ours is too low). If needed, adjust the hole depth.**

5 Backfill around the tree. **Shovel in the soil evenly around the roots and make sure to keep the tree straight as you fill in around it. The tree will move easily until the hole is completely filled.**

Tools & Skills

Besides safeguarding against weed trimmer strings and critters, the guard protects young trees against "frost cracking," which happens when the side of the tree that gets more sun grows at a faster rate than the shady side.

Spread a 2- to 3-in.-thick bed of mulch to help the soil hold moisture and to keep weeds from growing. Keep it at least 3 in. from the tree trunk. Mulch, like other organic matter, can have bacteria and fungus, which can spread to the tree and harm or even kill it.

Check your soil before watering

There's no magic formula for how much water to give your tree in its first year. Too little water can kill a tree. But overwatering in clay soil can cause root rot, which can also kill it. The best thing to do is to check your soil conditions. Poke a popsicle stick into the ground near the tree. If the soil is damp down 3 in., you're giving it enough water. If not, water once or twice a day—whatever's needed to keep the soil damp but not saturated.

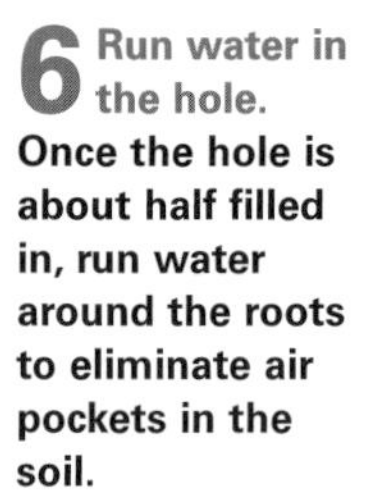

6 Run water in the hole. Once the hole is about half filled in, run water around the roots to eliminate air pockets in the soil.

7 Protect the bark. Slip a corrugated tree guard over the trunk. It'll keep weed trimmers, lawn mowers and pesky animals from damaging the bark.

8 Surround the tree with mulch. Mulch helps maintain moisture in the soil, and it also helps insulate the ground, keeping it cooler in the summer and warmer in the winter.

Great Goofs®

More brawn than brain

We had just purchased a small cottage out in the country, and I wanted to install a wire fence for our dogs. I bought steel fence posts and a roll of white wire fencing. Then I carefully laid out the fence line so it would be nice and straight. Using a sledgehammer, I set the first few posts and was feeling pretty good about my progress. But then the next post met with some resistance. The post seemed bouncy as I hit it. I told my wife to stand back so I could get a good swing. Then I hit the post with my best "carnival strong man" swing and was immediately sprayed with water. I had driven the post through the water line that ran from the well to the house. Several hours later, after I had repaired the water line and finished the fence, my dogs got to run in their new yard, although it was a bit on the muddy side.

SPECIAL SECTION

DIY Hodgepodge

HOME EMERGENCIES

Do you know what to do first? by **Elisa Bernick**

According to disaster experts, 9 out of 10 people either panic or freeze during an emergency; only one is able to jump into effective action. We have no doubt that TFH readers are part of the 10 percent who deliver—you're hands-on kinds of folks. To make sure you're ready for anything, here are 12 big and little home emergencies and the steps you should take first to tackle these disasters head on.

Flooded basement

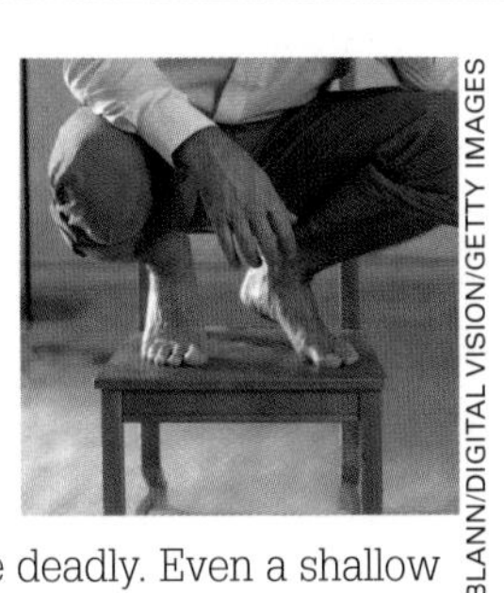

MICHAEL BLANN/DIGITAL VISION/GETTY IMAGES

Your first impulse will be to wade in and rescue your stuff. But that water might be dangerous, so put on your boots and take these precautions.

Don't get fried: Any water in contact with electricity might be deadly. Even a shallow puddle could be electrified by a cord on the floor. Stay out of the water until you've turned off the power to your basement. If you can't reach the circuit breaker box, call an electrician or your utility to cut the power to your home.

Don't get sick: If the flooding is due to flash floods or your belongings are leaching toxins, the floodwaters may contain toxic chemicals and will almost certainly breed dangerous bacteria. Protect cuts and open sores from floodwaters and wear plastic gloves when handling your possessions.

Bat in the house

In most people, bats cause a visceral reaction (like screaming and covering your head). But keep in mind that a bat doesn't want to tangle with you (or your hair) any more than you want to tangle with it.

Plan A: Open a window and get out of the way. There's a good chance the bat will leave on its own.

Plan B: If the bat lands before it can exit, look for it in places it can hang, such as behind drapes or upholstered furniture. When you find the bat, throw a thick towel over it and carry it outside (just to warn you, the bat will complain loudly, but don't drop it!). Shake out the towel so the bat can fly away.

Worst move: Don't approach a bat with bare hands. Bats can carry rabies. Wear thick gloves to avoid bites.

DIGITAL ZOO/DIGITAL VISION/GETTY IMAGES

Power outage

Surprisingly enough, the worst trouble caused by power outages often occurs when the problem is resolved and the power comes back on.

Prepare for surges: Turn off and unplug all electrical equipment, including your tools, appliances and electronics, and turn your heating thermostat down (or cooling thermostat up) to prevent damage from surges when the power returns. (Major appliances can be turned off at the breaker box.) Leave one light on so you'll know when the power is restored.

What not to do: Once the power is restored, don't turn everything back on at once, which can create internal power surges. First restore the thermostat setting on the heating or cooling system and turn on your larger appliances. Give the electrical system a few minutes to stabilize before plugging in your remaining appliances and electronics.

Watch for more trouble: If your lights are noticeably dimmer or brighter after the power is restored, turn off all the power at the breaker or fuse box and call your electric utility.

BILL ZUEHLKE

Electrical storm

Lightning strikes can burn out circuit boards in appliances, computers and telephones, doing thousands of dollars in damage in less than a second. If you hear thunder, power surges are possible, even if you don't see any lightning.

Protect your gadgets: Unplug computers and phone lines, and unplug corded telephones and sensitive electronics to prevent damage from power surges.

Don't wait for flames: If your home gets hit, call the fire department immediately. Lightning strikes can cause small fires inside walls that smolder for hours before you notice anything.

Play it safe: Lightning may strike nearby electrical and phone lines and travel to your home. Avoid contact with electrical appliances and telephones (landlines).

Wacky but true: Lightning strikes can travel through metal plumbing pipes. Avoid sitting on the toilet and don't shower or bathe during electrical storms.

Carbon monoxide alert

Carbon monoxide is the leading cause of accidental poisoning deaths in the United States. Take it seriously and make sure you have working CO detectors in your home.

Check for symptoms: The early symptoms of carbon monoxide poisoning resemble those of the flu. If the alarm sounds and anyone is experiencing headaches, dizziness, fatigue or vomiting, get everyone out of the house and call 911.

Never ignore the alarm: Don't assume all is well if no one feels ill. Open your doors and windows to thoroughly ventilate the house. Turn off all potential sources of CO—your oil or gas furnace, gas water heater, gas range and oven, gas dryer, gas or kerosene space heater, and any vehicle or small engine. Have a qualified technician inspect your fuel-burning appliances and chimneys to make sure they're operating correctly and that there's nothing blocking the vents that let fumes out of the house.

Tip

Backup water supply

If your water supply shuts down, remember that your water heater holds enough drinking and cooking water to last several days. Let the water cool for a few hours before you open the drain valve at the bottom of the tank.

Lightning is the second-leading weather-related killer in the United States. More deadly than hurricanes or tornadoes, lightning strikes kill an average of 70 people and injure 300 others each year.

Kitchen fire

More than any other emergency, fire makes people panic and do dumb things. But armed with a few basic rules, you'll reduce the panic and respond effectively.

React fast: If it's a toaster fire, unplug the cord and use an ABC (dry chemical) fire extinguisher or pour baking soda into the toaster (and then get a new toaster). If it's a stove-top fire, turn off the burner and smother the flames by dousing them with baking soda or putting the lid on the pan.

Or do nothing: If it's an oven fire, the most dangerous thing you can do is open the door. Just leave the oven door closed and turn off the heat to the oven. The fire will eventually smother itself.

Bad move: Don't use water to put out a grease fire. It can splash the burning grease and cause burns.

Worse move: Never carry a burning pan outside. It can cause a full-scale house fire if flaming grease spills and ignites something else.

BILL ZUEHLKE

Each year, one out of every eight homes has a kitchen cooking fire.

Top 5 causes of home fires

- Cooking fires
- Heating equipment
- Smoking
- Electrical (wiring, lamps, outlets, etc.)
- Children playing with lighters and matches

Tornado or high winds

Straight-line winds cause as much damage as tornadoes, but they're more unpredictable. So when a storm with high winds approaches your area, don't wait for the sirens to sound before you take action.

Take cover: Move to a protected interior room on the lowest floor of the house, as far as possible from exterior walls and windows. Use pillows, cushions, blankets or mattresses to protect yourself from flying debris.

Ignore the myths: Don't open windows to "equalize the pressure" no matter what your grandparents told you. This can cause even greater damage. And the southwest corner of the basement may not be the safest spot to hunker down, especially if it's near an outside wall or window.

DON FARRALL/PHOTODISC RED/GETTY IMAGES

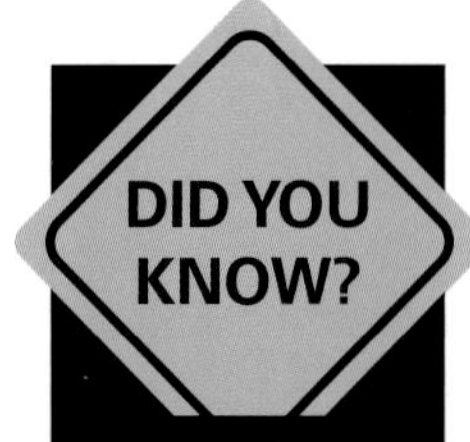

About 1,000 tornadoes are recorded each year in the United States—over 10 times more than in any other country.

Burst pipe

A gushing plumbing leak can dump several gallons per minute into your home. You have to act fast to stop the stream—and that's just the beginning.

Stop the flow: Shutting off the main water valve is an obvious move. But there may still be a few gallons of water held in pipes above the leak. Turn on the lowest faucet in the house, which will let the water harmlessly drain out of the faucet instead of through the leaking pipe.

Don't delay cleanup: The longer things stay wet, the more likely you'll have permanent damage. Delay can even lead to mold problems inside walls, which can cost thousands to eradicate. So before you run off to buy plumbing parts, clean up the mess. Pronto.

Tip

Emergency drain

If your basement is flooding, remove the basement toilet to create an instant, high-capacity floor drain. That will also let in nasty sewer gases, so don't leave the drain unplugged any longer than necessary.

Leaking roof

High winds that tear off shingles or send broken tree branches through your roof are usually accompanied by rain, so you have to act fast to minimize water damage.

Quick fix: For damage larger than a shingle or two, the fastest bandage is a plastic tarp. Secure a tarp over the damaged area with 2x4s or lath nailed to the roof. If possible, secure the tarp over the roof ridge; it's difficult to make the tarp waterproof at the upper end.

Don't kill yourself: Trying to patch a slippery, wet roof during a storm is dangerous. Add in high winds or lightning and the situation is deadly. So think twice before you head up there.

SIEDE PREIS/PHOTODISC/GETTY IMAGES

Wild animal invasion

A squirrel or raccoon in the house may not seem like an emergency, but those critters can do a lot of damage quickly. If all else fails, you may have to call in a wildlife removal service or your town's animal control officer.

What to do first: Isolate the varmint by closing the doors to all the other rooms in the house. Then open a window. Leave the room and shut the door. The animal will eventually find its way out the window.

What not to do: Don't try to chase the invader out. It'll just panic and hide. If it crawls into a hidden spot and poops, has babies or dies...that's a smelly set of different problems.

The worst thing to do: Don't let your dog or cat help with the eviction. That could result in an expensive trip to the vet or a gory mess.

Tip

Bucket flush

You don't have to live without a toilet just because the water supply is off. If you have a pool or other water source, you can flush with a bucket. Pour about 3 gallons into the bowl (not the tank) to get a fine flush.

Dead furnace

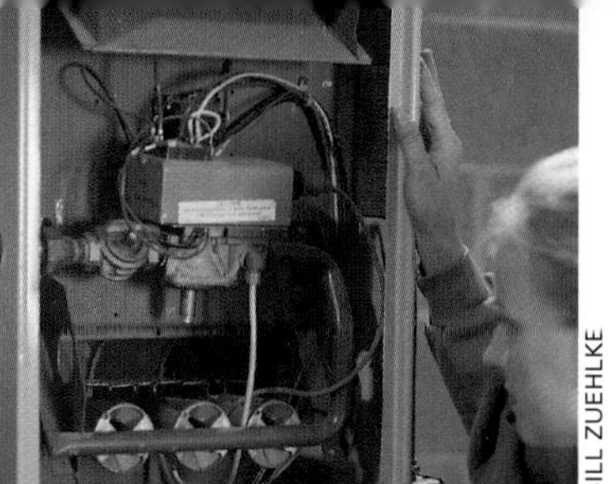
BILL ZUEHLKE

As the temperature drops inside your house, your first worry may be the budget-busting cost of an after-hours service call. But there are things you can troubleshoot before you pick up the phone.

Check the simple stuff first:

- Is the filter filthy? A clogged filter can cause the furnace to shut down.
- Is it getting power? There's a switch (just like a standard light switch) near the furnace. Make sure it's on. Check the circuit breaker or fuse box, too. A natural gas furnace won't work without power either—the thermostat, fan motor and gas valve all need electricity to operate.
- Is the gas valve on? The handle should be parallel to the gas pipe.
- Is the exhaust pipe clear? Sometimes heavy snow can cover up the exhaust vent to the outside.
- Does the thermostat need to be reset? Turn it down, then turn it back up.

Prepare for the worst: If the inside temperature continues to fall, take action to prevent burst pipes. Turn off the main water valve and drain the pipes by turning on the faucets to let out the remaining water. Use a plunger to drive water out of the toilets and drain traps.

DID YOU KNOW?

If the damage to your home isn't covered by your homeowner's insurance, don't report it to your insurance company. The report may still go on your insurance record and look like a claim when you shop for new insurance in the future.

Tip

Don't get locked in

Garage door openers lock up when the power goes off. Make sure everyone in your home knows about the cord that releases the door from the opener. That way, they can lift the door open and get the car out in an emergency.

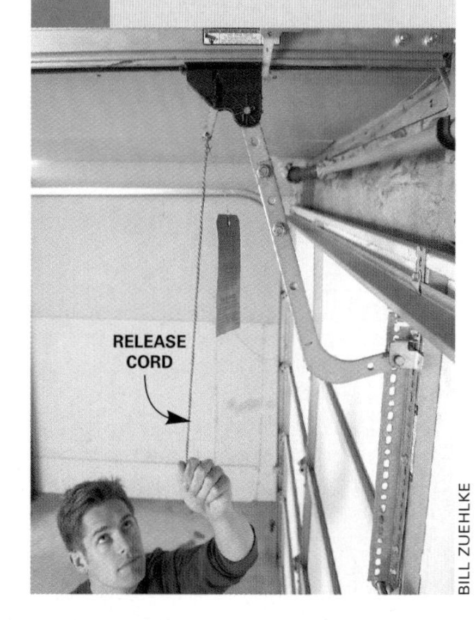

BILL ZUEHLKE

EMMA LEE/LIFE FILE/PHOTOGRAPHER'S CHOICE/GETTY IMAGES

After a hurricane

High winds and storm surges cause a lot of property damage during a hurricane. But more people die in the aftermath of a hurricane than during the storm itself—primarily from carbon monoxide poisoning and electrocution.

Act wisely: Don't use generators, charcoal grills or propane camping stoves indoors. And don't clear debris from your home and yard without surveying the area carefully. Downed or damaged power lines can send electrical currents through tree branches and metal fences.

What not to do: Avoid an "every man for himself" mentality. Once officials have signaled the "all clear," survey the damage to your home and reach out to your neighbors. It will be difficult to drive anywhere for supplies (if stores are even open), and you'll conserve resources by pooling them. Assess your neighbors' stocks of food, water and other resources. Eating meals collectively will reduce the amount of food that spoils (use fresh foods first) and will conserve cooking fuel.

DID YOU KNOW?

Hurricanes, tornadoes and winter storms are the top three causes of catastrophic home insurance losses.

◆

Emergencies are dramatic, but far more people are injured in ordinary household accidents. To find out how to make your home safer, visit homesafetycouncil.org.

Q&C Hodgepodge

OSB VS. PLYWOOD

My neighbor built a shed and used OSB for the sheathing and roof deck. He said it's just as good as plywood. I always thought it was an inferior product. What's the deal with OSB?

OSB panels are edge-sealed at the factory. If you cut the panel, sealing the edge is recommended.

Opinions run pretty strong on both sides of this argument. Some builders swear by OSB. Others swear at it. Just don't confuse OSB (oriented strand board) with wafer board, which was introduced in the early '60s. OSB is wafer board on steroids. It's made from about 50 layers of 3- to 4-in. wood strands piled at right angles and sealed with water-resistant adhesives and wax.

OSB experienced some failures when it was introduced (plywood suffered similar failures when it first came out in 1905). But those early failures have been addressed, and modern OSB is a quality product. The Engineered Wood Association now states that "when used as intended, OSB and plywood are interchangeable." In fact, the shear strength of OSB is twice that of plywood. And, despite opinions to the contrary, lab tests prove that it holds nails just as well as plywood.

Those findings mean you can substitute OSB on your project without any worries. Just follow these simple precautions:

First, keep it (and plywood for that matter) dry on the job site. OSB can resist the normal rainfall you encounter during construction. But keep it off the ground and covered with a tarp until you're ready to use it.

Next, seal all cut edges with a high-quality 100 percent acrylic latex paint. Most carpenters skip this step. But cut edges can swell up to 15 percent if they get wet, and edge sealing helps with water resistance, especially if a new building won't get buttoned up right away. Finally, check your local building codes to make sure that OSB is approved for your application.

WINTERIZED MINI BLINDS

Every winter I put that shrink film on my windows. But since my mini blinds are mounted on the interior of the casing, I can't open or close them until the following spring. Is there a way to keep out the chill and still have light during the day and privacy at night?

Cut holes in the shrink film so you can access the wand and lift cords. Start by removing the rotating wand from the blinds before you apply the shrink film. To unhook the wand, lift the retaining ring (if any) and lift the wand off the hook. Apply the window film, shrink it in place, apply tape and cut holes (see Photos 1 and 2).

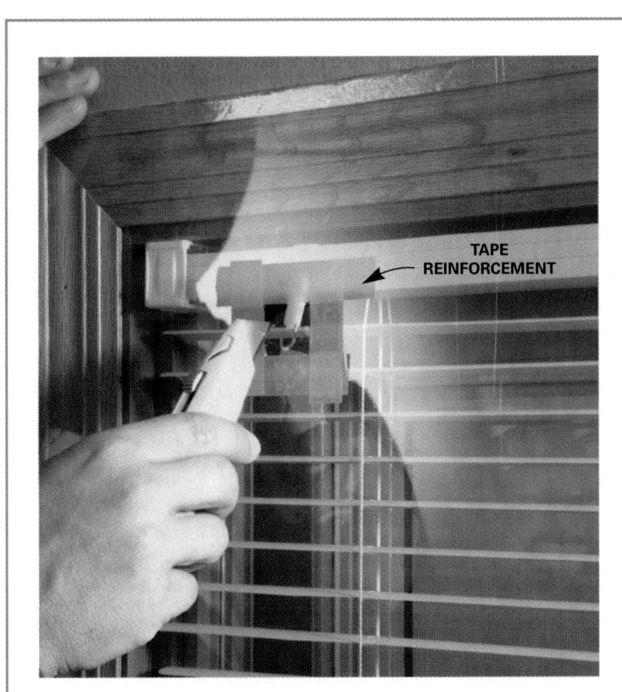

1 Reinforce the film with tape and cut the hole. Apply four strips of cellophane tape to the window film surrounding the wand hook. Overlap each strip at the corners so they reinforce each other. Then cut out the center of the square with a new utility blade (a dull blade will rip the film).

2 Extract the lift cords. Pull the lifting cords out of the hole. Then you can raise and lower the blinds all winter with the shrink film in place.

HandyHints® Hodgepodge

HOLIDAY

LAZY SUSAN TREE STAND FOR WOOD FLOORS

Winding the lights around our Christmas tree was always a pain. Then we found a great way to rotate the tree in its stand—without scratching up our hardwood floor. We put a bath rug underneath the tree stand, fabric side down, rubber side up. Now we can easily turn the tree to string our lights and place our ornaments just where we want them. It makes "undecorating" the tree a breeze too. We fold the rug under the tree skirt to keep it hidden.

EASY BOLT TIGHTENING

Tightening tree-stand nuts by hand is tiring and takes forever. Try this, our favorite Christmas tree hint from our archives: Cut off the little L's at the end of the tree stand bolts with a hacksaw. Chuck the ends of the bolts into a variable-speed drill and tighten them into the trunk. Your tree will be secure, and you can get out from underneath the tree and get decorating.

TIP-PROOF, DRIP-PROOF LAZY SUSAN FOR CARPET

We've tried different tree stands over the years, but we've still had trees fall over—because they either were top heavy with ornaments or got tipped over by the cat. I came up with this easy solution: I cut a 2-ft.-diameter circle out of plywood, screwed my tree stand to it and then stapled plastic sheeting to the plywood. The wooden base gives our tree solid footing and even the cat can't topple it (not that she doesn't keep trying). The plastic helps us slide the tree around on the carpet for easy decorating and protects the carpet from any watering spills.

LABELED TREE LAYERS

Artificial Christmas trees are assembled in color-coded layers. After a few years, the colors rub off (or you lose the instructions), and putting the tree together gets confusing. Try this simple trick. When you disassemble the tree at the end of the season, do it one level at a time. Once all the branches from one level are off, duct-tape them together and number each layer with a marker. Next year, the tree will go together in a snap!

TREE IN A TUBE— TO GO, PLEASE

We like the convenience of our artificial tree but dislike storing it because it takes up so darn much space. I came up with this idea. I use two 8-in.-diameter concrete form tubes, wrap each layer of the tree in twine and store half the tree layers in one tube and half in the other. I mark the layer numbers on each tube and stow the tubes in my garage rafters. A perfect solution!

HOSE REEL FOR HOLIDAY LIGHTS

They call me "Mr. Christmas" because I love decorating my house with tons of lights inside and out. My wife calls this my holiday obsession. I prefer to think of it as my holiday passion. To keep all the lights from getting tangled and make it easy to string them around my yard, I rolled about 30 strings of lights onto a portable hose reel that has wheels and a handle. Now I can pull the lights around my yard and roll off as many as I need without any help from elves (or my wife), and everybody's happy. Ho ho ho.

HANDY CLIPS FOR OUTDOOR LIGHTS

We use plastic picnic tablecloth clips to attach Christmas lights to our deck railing. It makes putting them up and taking them down a cinch!

HandyHints® Hodgepodge

MAGIC LABEL REMOVER

When you buy new plastic food storage containers, the gummed label always turns into a gooey smeared mess when you try to peel it off. You can scrub, scrape and soak it, but there always seems to be a little adhesive left behind. Here's a simple trick. Fill the container with hot tap water, but keep the label dry. Let it sit for a few minutes to soften the adhesive and then slowly peel off the label. Voilà! A perfectly clean plastic container.

STAY-PUT SOFA

The back of our sofa kept rubbing against the wall, scuffing our beautiful paint job. We kept pulling the sofa out from the wall, but it kept slipping backward every time someone plopped down. My husband finally fixed the problem by making wooden "shoes" for the back two sofa legs. He cut a scrap 1x4 into two short sections and then cut holes to fit the legs. The "sofa shoes" keep our sofa in its place. If your sofa doesn't have a skirt to hide the shoes, you could stain them to blend in with your flooring.

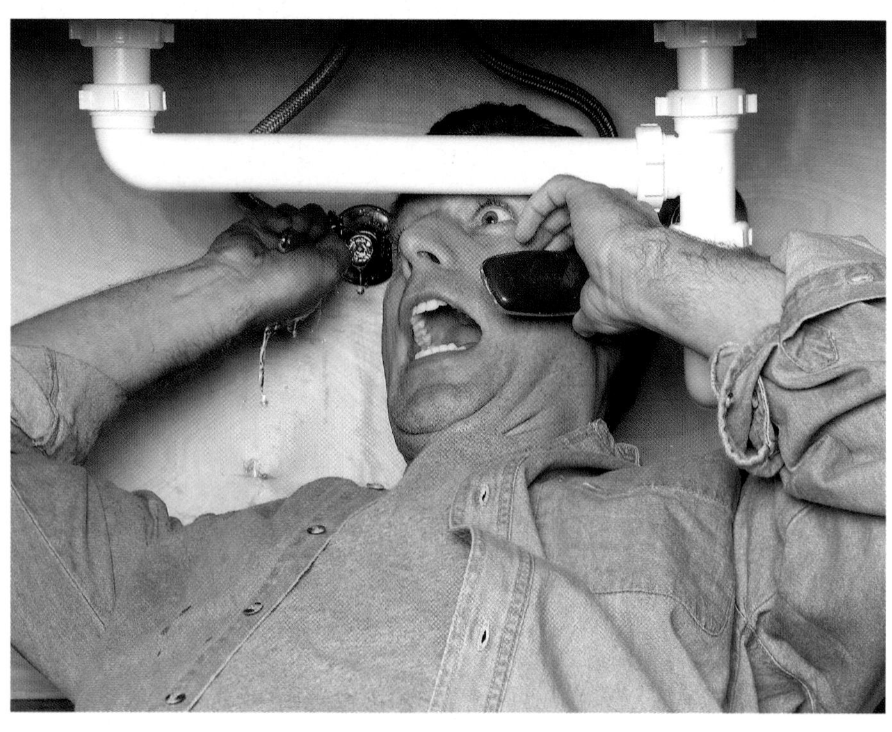

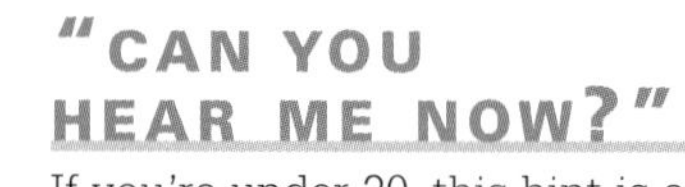

"CAN YOU HEAR ME NOW?"

If you're under 30, this hint is a "duh." But those of us who didn't grow up with cell phones attached to our ears may not realize how useful they are for communicating with a helper when you're doing home repairs. This is a great tip when you're trying to locate an electrical circuit or when you're adding shutoffs or trying to fix a leak and you need someone to turn the water on and off at the main valve. Here's a bonus tip. Use the soft glow of the screen as an ad hoc flashlight. Not a lot of light, but in a pinch...

SIDEWALK SALT SHAKER

Lugging a heavy bag of deicer out to the sidewalk is no fun, and it's tough to spread deicer evenly with a shovel or cup. You get a clump in one spot and none in another, so you're wasting both time and deicer. Here's a great solution. Make a "sidewalk salt shaker" from a big plastic coffee container with a handle. Poke 1/4-in. holes in the lid and fill it with sand, cat litter, deicer, or a mix of whatever you want and shake away!

COFFEE CONTAINER

SIDEWALK SALT

LAWN CHAIR UMBRELLA HOLDER

My wife and I love to watch our grandkids play outdoor sports. To escape the hot sun, we always take along our large golf umbrella. The umbrella shades both our chairs, but holding it the whole game gets tiring. I came up with this simple umbrella holder, which clamps right to the lawn chair. Bolt a piece of 1-1/2-in. PVC to the chair and secure it with a 4-in. hose clamp. It works great, and all you have to remember is to collapse the umbrella when you get up or a sudden breeze will blow it over.

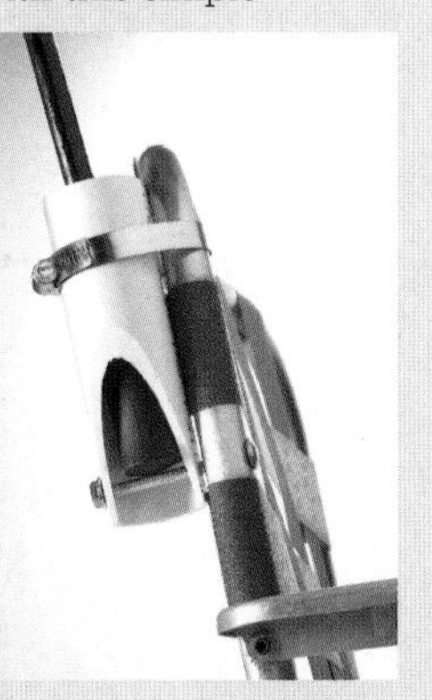

HASSLE-FREE PICTURE HANGING

When you're hanging a picture that has a wire across the back, it's hard to get your hand behind the picture to guide the wire over the hook. Try this: Slide a piece of string between the hook and the wall. Put the wire over the string and lower the picture into place. The string will guide the wire right over the hook. Drop one end of the string and pull it off the hook. Done.

HandyHints® Hodgepodge

WEDDING GIFT FOR A DIYER

Need the perfect wedding present for your favorite newlyweds? Or a house-warming gift for a first-time home buyer? A blender is nice, but a bucket of essential household tools and supplies is even nicer. Put crumpled tissue or newspaper into the bottom of the bucket to keep the gifts near the top, and include things like a hammer, slip pliers, a level, screwdrivers, a gift card to a local home improvement store and, of course, a subscription to *The Family Handyman*. It's sure to be a hit with the groom (and most brides, too!).

DIGITAL PERISCOPE

A digital camera is one of the handiest DIY tools I own. It's perfect for peering into places where your head won't fit. Use it to read inaccessible product labels, like the ones that list the model and serial number of a water heater or furnace. They're often deep inside the front panel. You can even mount your camera on a pole and peer into gutters or your chimney, or check out the roof without a ladder.

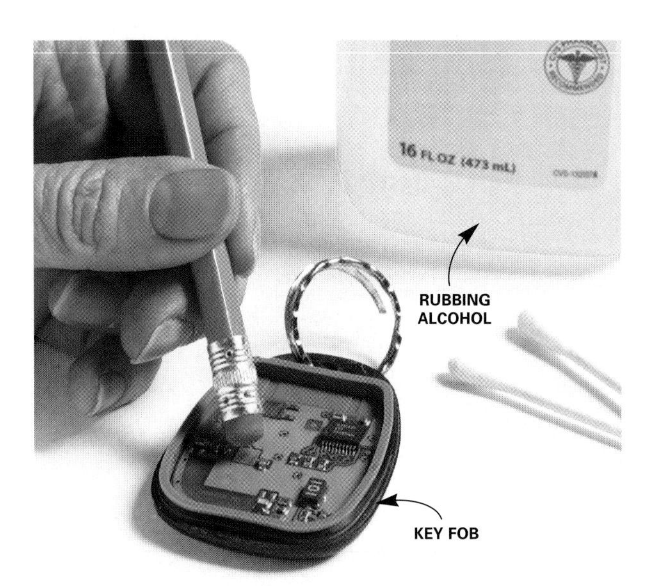

QUICK KEY-FOB FIX

If your key fob or TV remote stops working, try this fix before shelling out the dough for an expensive replacement. Take the cover off the fob and use a clean pencil eraser to remove the gummy stuff where the buttons touch the circuit board. Then use a cotton swab dipped in rubbing alcohol to clean the same area. Reassemble the fob or remote and it should work like new!

EASY NAILING IN AWKWARD SPOTS

Nailing small fasteners in hard-to-reach spots can be really frustrating, especially for people with large hands. I came up with this solution. Poke the fastener through a foam brush. You can hold the brush handle while you hammer the nail home and then just pull the foam end free through the nail head. Easy, cheap and effective!

HC&R Hodgepodge

BROKEN STARTER ROPE

You tug one last time to get the lawn mower started, and suddenly the rope breaks and the end goes spinning into the hole. Don't blow a gasket. If you have even a tinge of mechanical aptitude, replacing a starter rope is pretty easy. If the spring breaks—a rare event, according to our repair expert—the fix is a lot harder, and we recommend you take the mower to a repair center.

The first step is to remove the rewind assembly from the lawn mower, and how you do this varies. It's usually held on by three or more screws. Remove the screws and lift off the rewind (Photo 1). Some mowers have a shroud covering the top of the mower. On these you'll have to search for and remove the screws that hold the shroud in place. If your rewind unit is held on by rivets instead of screws, see "No Screws?" on p. 228.

After you remove the rewind unit, flip it over and look inside to find the knotted end of the broken rope. Grab it with needle-nose pliers and pull it out. You'll thread the new rope through this hole. You'll find replacement starter ropes at home centers, hardware stores and small-engine repair centers.

Before you install the new rope, you have to rewind the spring by twisting the rope pulley in the same direction it goes when you pull on the rope. You'll know when you're turning the pulley in the right direction because it will get harder to turn. Keep turning the pulley until you feel resistance and it won't turn easily. Then let it unwind about

1 Remove the rewind unit. Remove the screws that hold the rewind to the engine and lift it off. Use a nut driver to remove hex head screws.

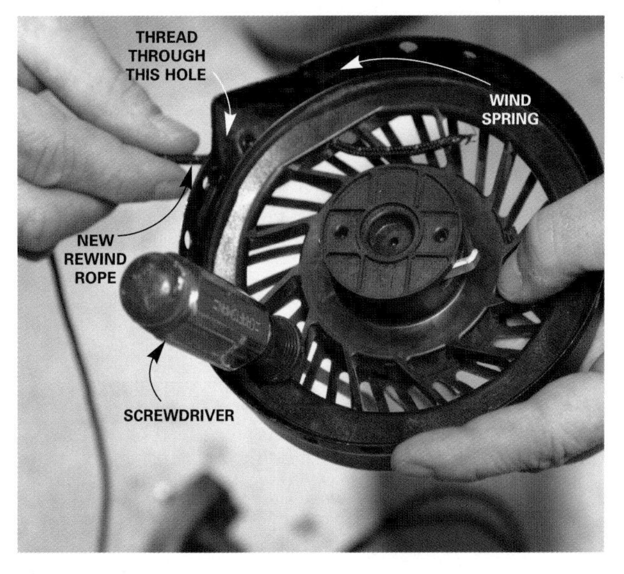

2 Replace the rope. First, remove the broken piece of rope by unwinding it, grabbing the knot and pulling it out. Then rewind the spring and hold it in place with a screwdriver.

HC&R Hodgepodge

one-half to one revolution until the hole in the pulley lines up with the hole in the rewind housing. Wedge a screwdriver against the pulley to keep the spring from unwinding while you thread the rope through the holes (**Photo 2**). **Tip:** With leather gloves on, melt the end of the rope with a match. While the plastic is hot, give it a quick twist to create a pointed end so it's easier to thread in.

Push the end of the rope through both holes and tie a knot (**Photo 3**). Heat the knot a little bit with a match and pull it tight to keep it from coming undone. Remove the screwdriver while you keep pressure on the pulley with your finger, and gradually let the rope wind onto the wheel. You may have extra rope to cut off after everything's back together. Mount the rewind unit and reinstall any shrouding or other parts you had to remove. Put the handle on the rope and tie a knot. Position the knot so that there's a little tension on the rope when you release the handle. If the rope on your lawn mower extends up the handle, make sure to place the rope handle in its final position before tensioning the rope slightly and tying the knot.

3 Tie a knot. Tie a knot in the end of the rope. Let the pulley wind the rope back into the rewind. Reinstall the rewind unit and any other parts you've removed.

No screws?

Rivets hold this rewind unit to the metal shroud. To access the rewind unit, remove the bolts that hold the shroud to the engine. If the rivets are loose, drill them out and replace them with bolts and locknuts.

GreatGoofs®

Nailed it!

For a remodeling job, I ordered $800 of prefinished cherry for a countertop. I was pinning a 3/4-in. cherry strip to the underside of the countertop with 1-1/2-in. brad nails, angling them slightly so they wouldn't break through the piano-grade finish—scary! In the middle of the project, one of my carpenters asked to borrow my gun for a few minutes.

When he returned the gun, I finished nailing on the trim. But when I tried to lift the piece up, I realized there was a definite problem—the countertop had been nailed through the drop cloth into the floor. What my knucklehead carpenter didn't tell me was that when he took my gun, he exchanged my nails for ones that were about an inch longer. I had to spend $200 to hire a furniture restorer to fix all the splintered nail holes. I still get mad at that idiot every time I think about it.

IN THIS CHAPTER

BRINGIN' IT HOME
IN YOUR PICKUP

Follow these tips for a safe ride home.

by **Rick Muscoplat**

According to AAA's Foundation for Traffic Safety, poorly secured loads are responsible for more than 25,000 crashes and approximately 90 fatalities in this country each year. And on top of that, there are all those nonfatal injuries to drivers behind you and damage to their vehicle. Guess who's responsible if something falls off your truck and injures somebody? Yup, you.

We checked with experts to find the best ways to secure loads on a pickup. Then we drove our pickup to the nearest Menards home center and loaded it with common DIY materials to show you how to properly secure them. You may think our tie-down methods are over the top, but securing a load to your vehicle isn't just about making sure it all gets home. It's about getting it all home without harming anybody.

You can use these methods when you're moving furniture and other household goods too. These loads are just as likely to fly off your vehicle and cause injury, and you'll be just as liable.

Hauling is dangerous!

- **In California, 155 people were killed in a two-year period by objects spilled onto roads.**
- **In Georgia, 66 percent of road debris is the result of junk flying off vehicles.**
- **In California, an estimated 140,000 cu. yds. of road debris is the result of improperly secured loads.**

Use ratchet straps

Rule No. 1 in safely securing your load is to buy a set (four minimum) of heavy-duty 15-ft. ratchet straps (minimum 1,000-lb. load limit/3,000-lb. break strength). Sure, rope and bungee cords work fine if you drive slow and don't hit any bumps or get into an accident. But in the real world, you have to be prepared to swerve or come to an emergency stop, without ejecting your cargo. That's precisely when rope, bungees and twine fail.

Stay away from wimpy straps. Buy heavy-duty ratchet straps (1-1/4 in. or wider) and store them in a box in your cab to protect them from moisture and sunlight.

Wrap flimsy materials

Just about every home improvement job involves hauling 10-ft. lengths of some type of flimsy material. But things like drip edges, flashing, plastic conduit or siding will all flop around and get damaged on the way home. So while you're at the store, buy a roll of stretch cling film (about $9 a roll). Wrap both ends. If lumber is part of the load, wrap the fragile bundle with it for added support.

Bundle long boards

If you're hauling a large load of long lumber, don't rest it on a raised gate—it just can't handle that kind of weight. Start by laying out two or more ratchet straps along the bottom of the bed and load the longest and heaviest lumber over the straps. Then stack shorter lengths on top. Secure the cab end, the middle and the trailing end with the straps.

Next, anchor the bundle to the truck bed with two ratchet straps. Crisscross the ratchet straps across the load, attaching one end to the cab end anchor rings and the other end to the farthest bundle strap.

Support and protect drywall

If you have a 6-ft. bed, you'll have to haul a large load of sheet goods with the tailgate down. We're showing you an extreme example by loading 4 x 12-ft. drywall in a 6-ft. bed. Start by laying out two ratchet straps across the truck bed. Then lay out at least two 12-ft. 2x4s to help support the overhang (check the load limit of your truck and the weight of each sheet). The 2x4s will also protect the drywall from any water, rocks or crud on your truck bed. We scrounged up some cardboard corners to protect the edges of our drywall (check the trash bins in the store or lumberyard). Then tighten the bottom straps to secure the bundle. Next, run two straps from the truck bed anchor rings around the back edge of the sheets and down to the bumper.

Use a cargo net for bulky loads

There will come a day when you haul bundles of light materials like insulation. Don't just throw it in the bed and hope it stays put. It needs to be secured too. The best way to do that is with a cargo net. Buy one at a home center or online (such as the Allied No. 84067 CargoLoc Adjustable Truck Net; $20 at amazon.com). Then snap the retainer clips into the anchor points on your bed.

Tailgate can be up for light 8- to 10-ft. loads

Light loads can rest on the tailgate. But they still have to be secured. Don't fool yourself into thinking they'll stay put because the longest portion is inside the bed. Use ratchet straps on the bundle in two places and secure each end to the anchor rings on the bed.

Red-flag it

After you've secured your load, make sure you attach a red flag on the end. It's required by law. Most home centers provide them for free. Just make sure you staple the heck out of it to prevent it from ripping off while you're tooling down the highway.

TOP 6 ATV AND MOTORCYCLE REPAIRS

Save money by doing these fixes yourself.

by **Rick Muscoplat**

What common bike and ATV repairs are genuinely DIY-friendly? We asked Josh Fischer, the owner of Unlimited Motor Sports Repair, for advice.

After only a little arm twisting, Josh agreed to divulge the most common repairs and maintenance tasks he does in his shop that you could do yourself. You won't have to hassle with getting your bike or ATV to and from the shop or buy any expensive tools. And best of all, each repair will save you money—sometimes big money—by helping you avoid much more expensive fixes in the future.

Tire pressure matters!

Many ATV owners have lost their low-pressure tire gauge and use an auto tire gauge instead. Big mistake! It won't give you an accurate reading. And according to Josh, most customers overfill their tires, sometimes by as much as 20 to 30 lbs. That reduces traction and increases the "bounce" factor that could throw you from the machine. In 2006, ATV accidents in the United States resulted in an estimated 882 deaths and 146,600 visits to the emergency room. Don't be the next statistic. Inflate your tires to the proper pressure.

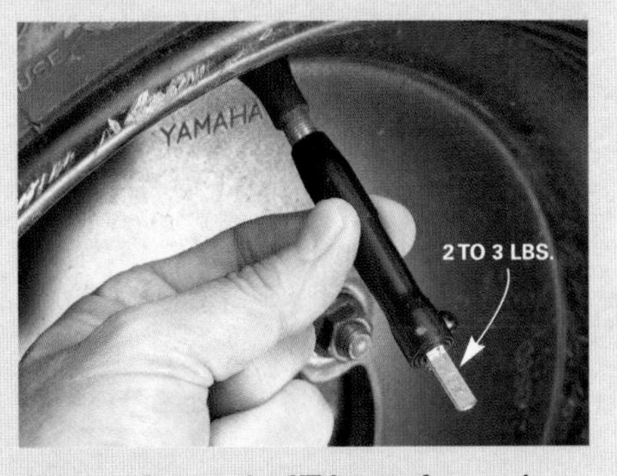

Fill your tires to the ATV manufacturer's recommended pressure (it's printed on a label stuck to the machine and in your owner's manual), never to the maximum pressure shown on the tire sidewall.

AUTO & GARAGE

2 Replace your ATV's CV boots and save $100s

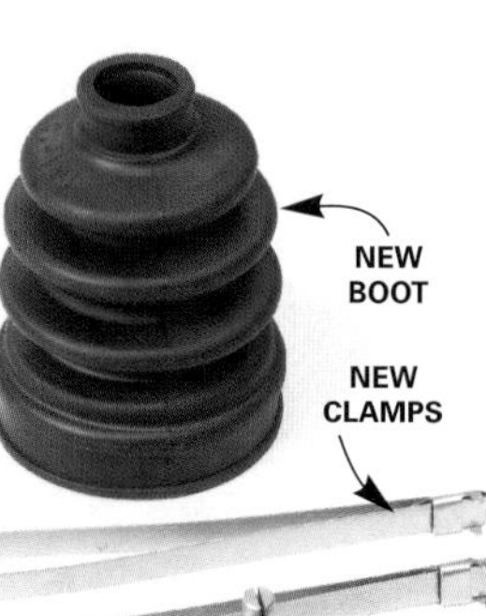

Constant velocity (CV) boots keep the lubricating grease inside the joint and the dirt out—until they crack. Then you have to replace them—and fast! Once they're open to the environment, the grease attracts dirt, which grinds up the metal parts in no time. Instead of replacing an $18 boot, you'll be buying the entire joint at $125 a pop.

It's easy to check the condition of the CV boots. Just look for fresh grease around the pleats. If you see any, the boot is toast.

Replacing a CV boot is fairly simple maintenance, but you'll have to remove the axle shaft from the machine. To do that, you'll have to jack up the machine and support it with jack stands (see your service manual for jacking and support locations). Then remove the wheel and the axle nut.

Next, remove the axle from the differential. Most axle styles pop out with a crowbar, but some require a special procedure, so refer to your service manual. Service manuals cost about $80 and are worth the investment if you plan to do your own work (check the dealer or online for prices and availability).

You can buy individual CV boots ($18 each), but as long as you have the axle shaft out of the machine, it's best to replace both of them at once. You'll also need a band installation tool. Buy one from your local dealer, or get banding tool No. WE145020 for $3 from erlandsonperformance.com (218-829-6036). Once the axle is out, follow the boot replacement procedure shown.

1 Cut the retaining bands with side cutters and slice the old boot lengthwise with a utility knife to remove it. Clean the joint in degreaser until you can see the retaining clip. Compress or expand the C-clip (depending on the style), and pop the joint off the axle.

2 Soak the disassembled joint in degreaser, scrub the parts with a toothbrush, rinse with clean degreaser and wipe the parts dry. Slide the boot over the axle shaft and crimp the band clamp. Then fill the joint with new grease.

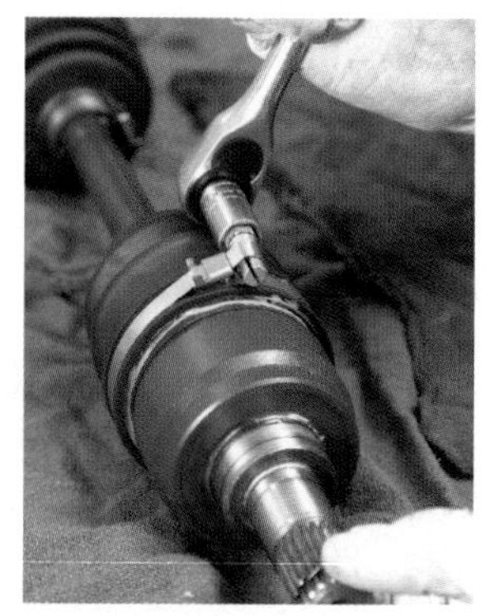

3 Slip the large end of the boot over the joint. Burp the air out of the boot and crimp the remaining band. Tighten just enough to prevent the boot from rotating.

3 Lube clutch and brake cables

Josh replaces a lot of cables that could last much longer with periodic lubrication. And, with replacements costing $20 and up, regular lubrication is just plain smart. Lubricate the cables twice per season. It's easy to do, but you'll need this special lubrication tool for an effective job. Buy it (and a can of spray cable lube) at your dealer or at Motorcycle-Superstore.com (877-668-6872). The Motion Pro Cable Luber is $10.

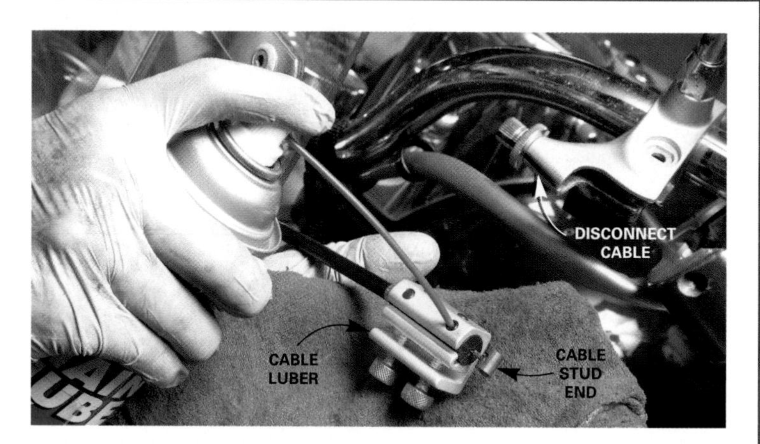

Disconnect the stud end of the cable from the lever. Then attach the cable luber. Insert the spray straw into the opening on the luber and inject the lube under pressure to force it into the cable.

4 Clean and maintain your ATV air filter

Most of you operate your ATVs in dirty conditions. That's fine; they're designed for that. But you have to keep the air filter clean. According to Josh, just about every machine he works on has a seriously clogged filter. A dirty filter lowers your gas mileage and causes poor engine performance. Cleaning the filter is messy, but anybody can do it.

Buy an air filter cleaning kit ($20) from your dealer. It contains a bottle of cleaning solution and a spray can of filter oil. You'll also need a plastic cleaning tub, rags, a bucket of soapy water and chemical-resistant gloves.

1 Remove the foam filter and wipe any debris from the outside. Then dunk the filter in the cleaning solution for the recommended time. Squeeze out the excess solution. Rinse the filter with water and let it dry.

2 Pour fresh oil on the cleaned filter element. Then squeeze the foam to spread the oil into the pores. Reinstall it on the carburetor.

5 Clean and lubricate your motorcycle chain

Cleaning and lubing your motorcycle chain takes only a few minutes and can dramatically increase the life of the chain. Many bike owners do it wrong. Lube needs to be applied to the part of the chain that meshes with the cogs. If you apply it to the outside of the chain, centrifugal force will throw it off before it can penetrate to the chain's innards. Josh recommends the Grunge Brush ($11 from amazon.com) to scrub the crud off the chain (**see photo**).

1 Dunk the brush in degreaser and slide it up and down the chain. Rotate the chain and repeat until you've cleaned the entire chain. Rinse with clean degreaser and sponge it dry with a rag.

2 Spray the sprocket side of the chain links, not the outside. Then take the bike for a spin. Centrifugal force will spin the lube deep into the links for complete lubrication.

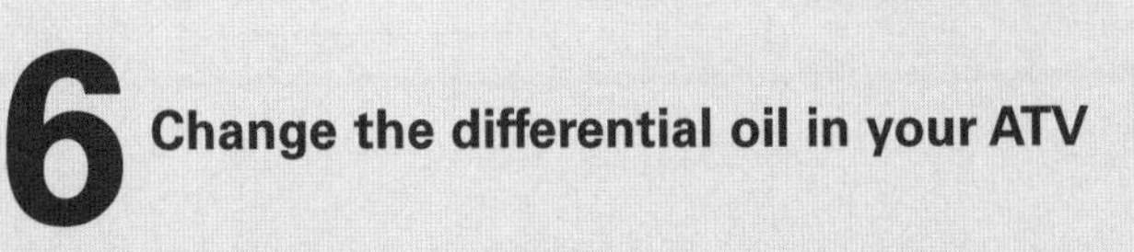

6 Change the differential oil in your ATV

This simple drain-and-refill procedure should be done regularly. But many owners neglect it, resulting in huge repair bills. Refer to your owner's manual for recommended change intervals and the proper type of lube oil.

Car&Garage

REPLACE YOUR BENT ANTENNA

Need to fix a bent or broken antenna? That problem goes back as far as car radios and marauding teenagers. The two most common styles are "pillar mounts," which slide in and out of the top of door pillars, and "fixed masts," nonretractable ones that are mounted on fenders. Both styles are easy to fix yourself. Start the repair by buying a replacement unit (less than $20) from an auto parts store or antennamastsRus.com (920-686-0644).

New pillar-mount antennas come with the coaxial cables already attached. So after you unscrew and pull out the old unit, cut the old cable and use it to fish the new cable through the pillar to the radio. (Splicing old and new cables together isn't recommended; you may get radio interference.) But be careful! If the splice comes apart inside the pillar, you'll have to remove the pillar trim to fish the new cable. Form a hook in the old cable, loop a picture-hanging wire through it and then wrap it with tape for added insurance. You'll have to remove the car radio to hook up the new cable. For about $5, you can buy removal instructions from carstereoremoval.com.

Fixed-mast antennas are much easier to replace. Buy a universal kit ($15) from any auto parts store. Just unscrew the bent mast with an adjustable wrench and install the new mast. You may have to install an adapter (included in the kit) to match the thread size.

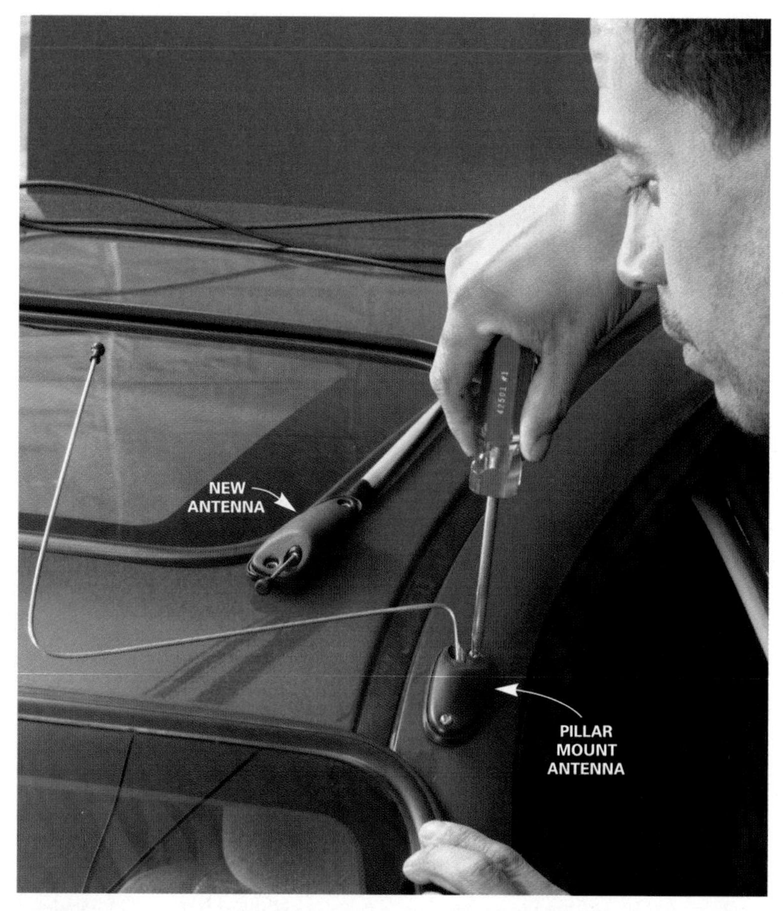

PILLAR MOUNT
Fish the new cable through the door pillar by using the old one to pull it through. You'll have to securely splice together the new cable to the old one while you do this.

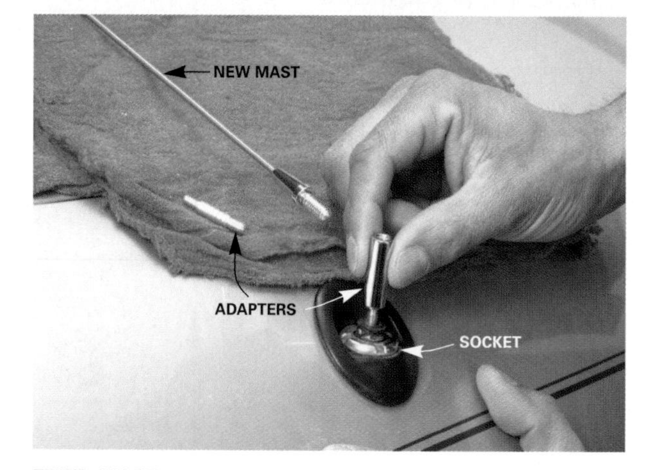

FIXED MAST
Replace the old base stud with the matching one from the kit. Then screw in the new mast.

FORD ECOBOOST ENGINE

Fuel injection and computer control are so yesterday. Ford's new EcoBoost engine technology kicks the technology ball so far down the road that it's playing in a different ballpark. To get up to 20 percent better fuel economy and 15 percent lower emissions, Ford couples gasoline direct injection (DI) with totally redesigned turbochargers (the V-6 engine has two of them).

Ordinary fuel injectors spray the gas behind the intake valves at about 50 psi. But DI injectors inject fuel directly into the combustion chamber at much higher pressures (220 to 2,150 psi). That higher pressure cools the incoming air and reduces the likelihood of knock. To reduce heat further and assist vaporization, the computer varies the injector spray pattern during the entire compression stroke.

DUAL OVERHEAD CAMS

TURBO

FORD MOTOR CO.

These new turbochargers bear no resemblance to their predecessors. These high-tech babies run at ultra-high speeds (up to 200,000 rpm) to give quick response and eliminate "turbo-lag." To keep them cool during these incredible revolutions, Ford has engineered liquid-cooled bearings.

The EcoBoost engine, which is made at the famous Cleveland engine plant, will be available on 90 percent of Ford vehicles by 2013. This truly is an innovation in engine technology. For more information on the EcoBoost engine, visit thefordstory.com. Then enter "A V-6 Engine Like No Other" in the search bar.

Ford's new 4-cylinder EcoBoost Engine

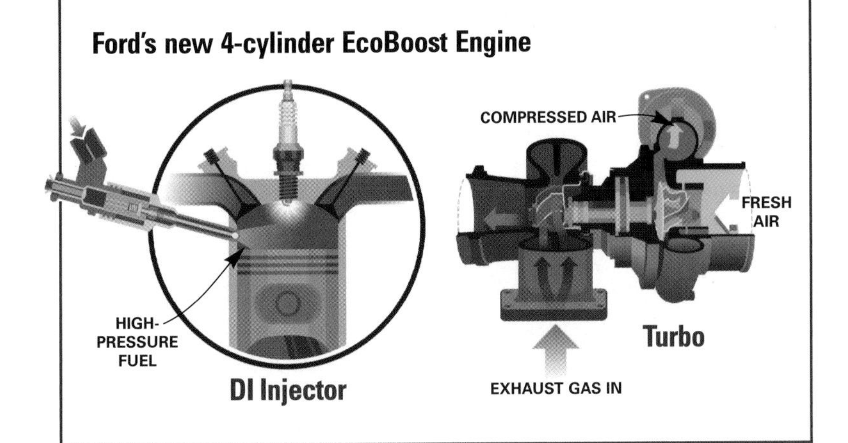

EXORCISE ELECTRICAL GREMLINS

Do the needles on your gauges jump around, sweep from side to side or just plain refuse to budge? How about your other electrical accessories—do they work intermittently or so strangely that you swear they're possessed? If so, it's time to clean your ground cables.

The pros always start by cleaning the ground cables. Carmakers use the steel body as the return "ground" electrical path, so when the cables corrode (and they *will* corrode), the stray current can cause all sorts of strange behavior.

A rotary tool with a wire brush works great. But you can also use sandpaper. The key is to get shiny metal on all the connections. Use a shop manual to find the locations of the other ground connections in your vehicle.

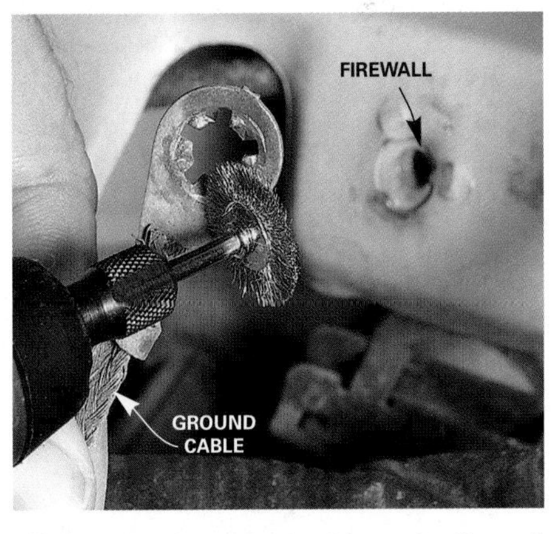

1 Remove the ground cable at the firewall or fender and clean both the steel and the ring with a wire brush.

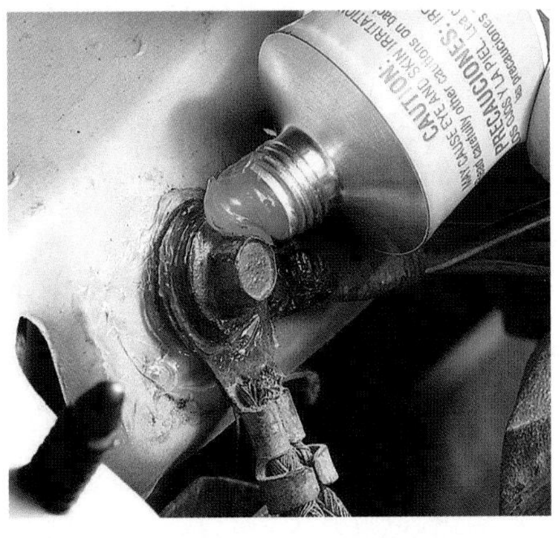

2 Coat the bare steel with dielectric grease and reassemble the connection. Then smear a dab of grease around the entire connection.

AUTO & GARAGE

Car&Garage

SMARTER TOWING

PHOTO FROM CHEVROLET

The 2011 Chevrolet Silverado with the Duramax 6.6L diesel can haul and tow more weight than any other vehicle in its class. Cram in up to 6,335 lbs. of your old LPs or tow up to 16,000 lbs. of your mother-in-law's furniture. To bring all that weight to a safe stop, Chevy added intelligent exhaust braking. Exhaust braking has been around forever; truckers call it a "Jake brake." But it's always been so noisy that some states ban its use at night. Chevy figured out a quieter way to use the exhaust pressure. Plus, the braking system is smart. When used with cruise control, it'll automatically slow the vehicle on downhill grades. You don't even have to touch the pedal. Exhaust braking prolongs brake pad life and prevents brake overheating.

To safely tow more weight, the 2500HD and 3500HD models offer an intelligent trailer anti-sway feature. When the system detects trailer sway, it either applies the trailer's electric brakes or reduces engine speed, depending on the amount of sway and other driving conditions.

GARMIN

BRAINIER NAVIGATION

Even if you're not map impaired, you need this cool GPS from Garmin. It taps into traffic reports and reroutes you around traffic jams. That'll save you time. Want to pick up food on the way? This baby will pull up all the restaurants along your route and sort them by cuisine. Get the Bluetooth model and you can use it as a speakerphone.

Garmin nüvi No. 1390T; $202 from amazon.com. (No. 1350T is shown.)

THE PROS AND CONS OF EXTENDED WARRANTIES

I'm buying a new car for the first time in 12 years. Should I buy an extended warranty, or are new cars more reliable?

New cars are more reliable than your old clunker. But they're also loaded with computers and sensors. A moderately equipped vehicle can have as many as 10 separate computers controlling nearly everything that has moving parts or electronics. When one of those computers fails, the repair can easily exceed $1,000. Even if the computer only needs a software update, you'll still have to pay upward of $200 to fix the problem.

You can buy non-factory warranties, but factory-extended warranties are the best because they cover more components. But they're also more expensive. Just be aware that the dealer's prices on factory-extended warranties are negotiable—so haggle.

KEEP YOUR MEMORY

Any time you disconnect the battery cables, you lose all your radio, power seat and clock settings. The engine computer can also "forget" a few things (it will "relearn" on its own after about 10 starts). So if you don't want to reset them all, invest in a 12-volt EZR-MSBD28 memory saver cable ($23 from usatoolwarehouse.com).

Connect one end to the OBDII computer port and the other end to a portable jump start box or any other 12-volt power supply (battery or battery maintainer). Isolate the positive terminal and cable while you work on it to prevent it from shorting on a metal part.

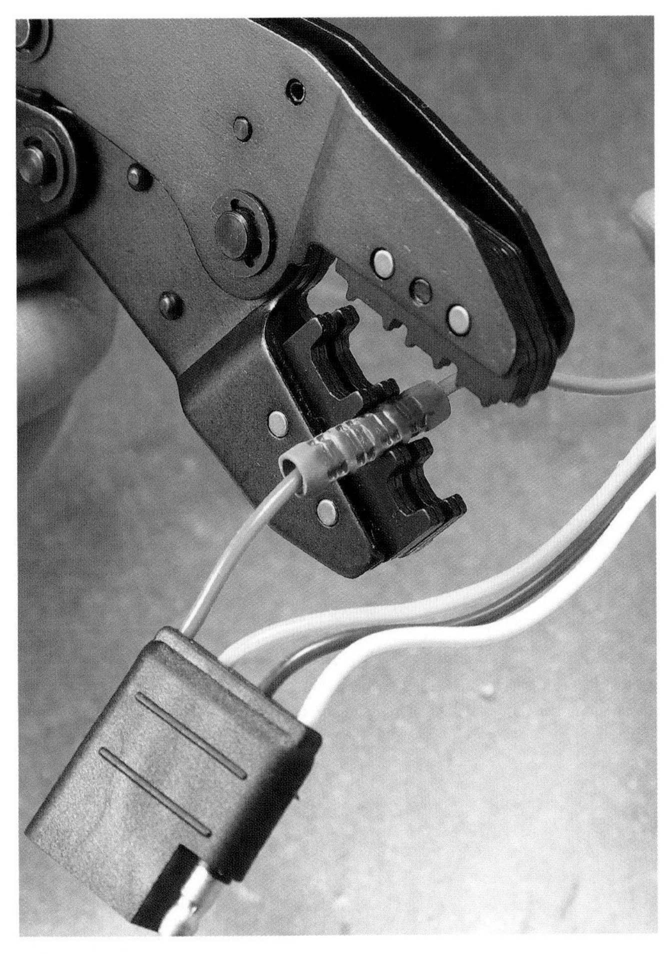

1 **Strip the insulation so only the bare wire is inside the connector. Then make a single 5/16-in. crimp on each side of the butt connector.**

SPLICE AUTOMOTIVE WIRES IN SECONDS

Crimp-on wire connectors work well if they're crimped properly (a 5/16-in.-wide crimp) and sealed (usually with heat-shrinkable tubing). But most cheap crimping tools only make a 1/8-in. crimp, so you'd have to make four of them for a simple butt connection.

Invest $21 in a professional crimping tool (OTC No. 4497 from sjdiscounttools.com). Then buy a roll of electrical moisture sealant (3M No. 06147; $20 from amazon.com). Then just follow the steps in **Photos 1 and 2**.

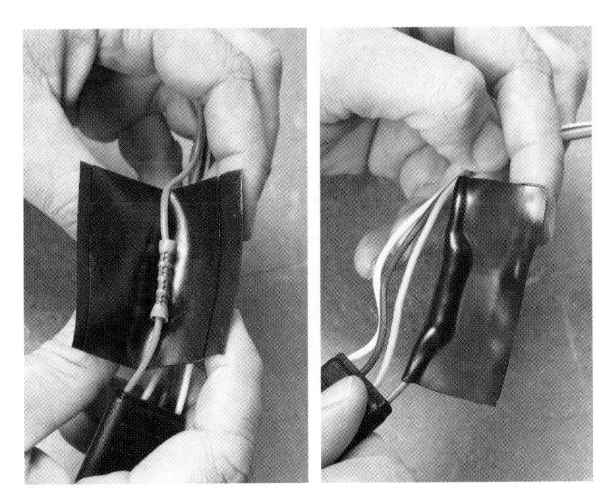

2 **Cut a section of moisture sealant to cover the entire connector and a 1/2-in. overlap on each end. Then double it over and squeeze it together with your fingertips.**

BET YOU DIDN'T KNOW THIS!

Your air bag light is on and you've decided not to fix the problem. But did you know that the computer keeps track of how many times you start the car with a nonfunctional air bag? If your passenger is injured because the air bag didn't deploy, think about how much fun the lawyers could have with that information after an accident.

PHONE APP HELPERS

Find car pool buddies on your iPhone

Install "carticipate" on your iPhone and enter your destination and time parameters. The app matches you with other car poolers. You can get more information at carticipate.com. The app is also available at facebook.com.

Find the best gas prices online or by phone

You've got two new tools to help you find the best gas prices. Go to gasbuddytogo.com or add the "Gas Detective" Android app to your phone. One source is 101bestandroidapps.com.

REPLACING HEADLIGHTS

Replacing a headlight bulb is easy. You can replace both of yours (always replace them as a set) in about 30 minutes and save about $30 labor. The best part is that the entire procedure is almost always right there in your owner's manual.

In some late-model vehicles, you have to remove the entire headlight assembly from the vehicle to get clear access to the bulb (**Photo 1**). Remove the old bulb and install the new one (**Photos 2 and 3**). Then put the headlight assembly back in and secure it.

The hardest part of the job is choosing a new bulb. You can spend more time shopping for the bulbs than it takes to install them. The choices are mind-boggling. Every bulb manufacturer has its own confusing names for each style, making comparisons difficult. But it boils down to four upgrade categories—brightness level, life span, light color and energy consumption (photo below right). Here's the scoop:

- Bright bulbs draw the same power as factory bulbs but give off 30 to 80 percent more light. You'll sacrifice bulb life, but if you live in a rural area or do a lot of highway driving, these may be your best choice.
- If the factory brightness works for you and you do a lot of night driving, choose a "long-life" bulb. It lasts three times longer than a standard bulb.
- If you're into "cool," choose a "blue" bulb if you want to imitate the look of the high-intensity discharge (HID) lamps in luxury vehicles.
- Or, if you're an aging boomer, choose a bulb that projects different colors of light at different sections of the road.

Finally, if you want to milk your fuel budget for every last nickel, buy an "eco-friendly" bulb. They can save four gallons of gas over the life of the bulb and they last twice as long.

- **GE: gelighting.com/na/home_lighting/products/nighthawk**
- **Philips: lighting.philips.com/us_en/automotive**
- **Sylvania: sylvania.com/BusinessProducts/AutomotiveLighting**

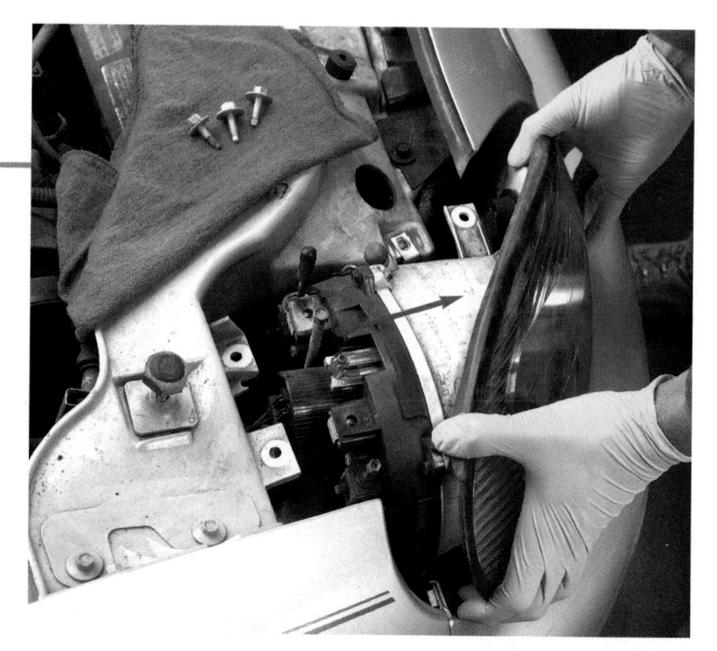

1 Unbolt the headlight to save your knuckles. Eliminate the hassle of trying to fish the bulb out from under the hood. Remove the headlight assembly retaining bolts and pull the whole unit forward.

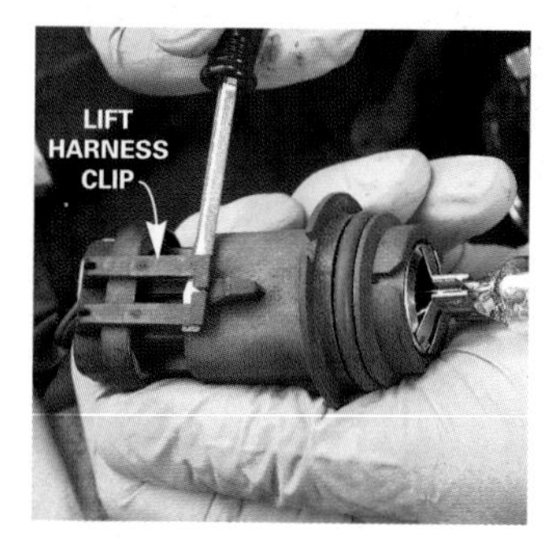

2 Out with the old. Disconnect the wiring harness from the bulb and twist the bulb a quarter turn. Then pull it straight out.

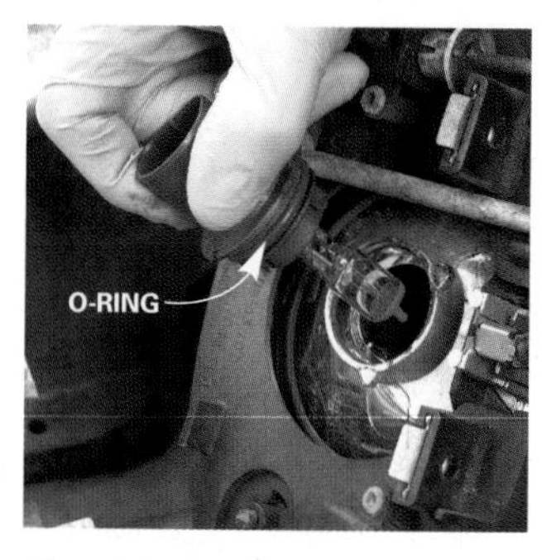

3 In with the new. Push the new bulb straight in (don't touch the glass with your fingers) until you feel the silicone O-ring seat. Then twist the bulb (or retaining ring) to lock it in place. Reconnect the wiring harness.

Pick your passion
Browse the manufacturers' Web sites before you go to the store. The options are mind-numbing (prices are per set from oereplacement.com).

FIX A LEAKING SUNROOF

You've got water on your seats right below the sunroof, and you're about to take matters into your own hands. We're warning you: *Put down the caulk gun and step away from the vehicle.* Usually it's simply a drain tube that's clogged with debris. Then the water can't drain and it overflows into the cabin. And that's a simple DIY repair that you can do in about 20 minutes.

Open your sunroof and look for the drain holes in both front corners. Those tubes run through the door pillars and drain through to the rocker panels. You may be tempted to run a coat hanger down the tubes or blast them with compressed air. Don't! You might poke the wire right through the tubing or disconnect it from the drain hole. Then you'd have to remove the entire headliner to reconnect it—a big job. Instead, use a shop vacuum and small-diameter vinyl tubing to suck out the clog (**Photo 1**).

If that doesn't do the trick, try running a very small flexible "plumbing" snake down the tube to break up the clog. (Actually, it's a speedometer cable found at any auto parts store for about $8.)

If cleaning the tubes doesn't work, don't try to disassemble the mechanism or bend the sheet metal to get a better fit. That's a job for a top-notch body shop. If the car isn't worth the cost of the repair, we rescind our earlier warning. Go for the silicone and live without the wind in your hair.

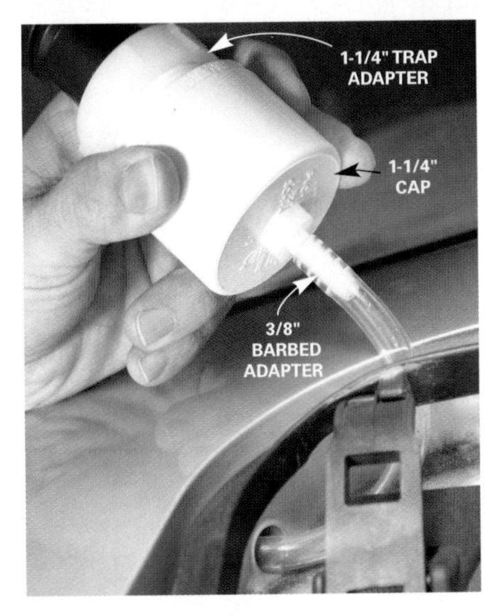

1 Make a hose reducer with ordinary PVC plumbing parts and attach a vinyl hose to the end. Then vacuum the crud out of the water channel and the drain tube.

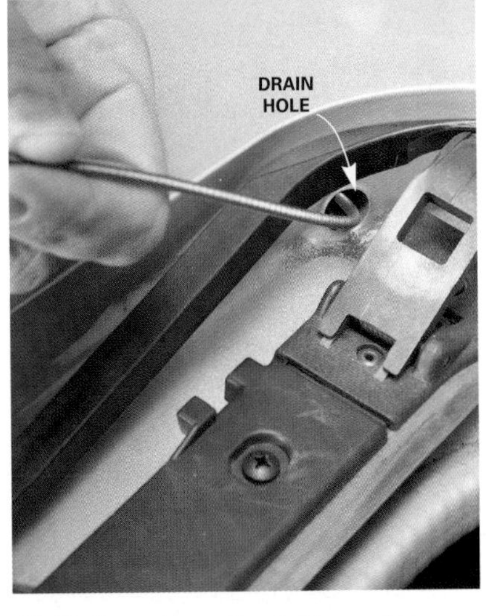

2 Snake out a really stubborn clog with a speedometer cable. Twist the cable as you feed it down the tube.

REPAIR A DIM HEADLIGHT

If your car has a headlight that puts out about as much light as a flashlight with weak batteries, we've got a fix for you. Most DIYers think they've got a bad headlight switch or a bad connection in the power feed. But most dim headlights are caused by a corroded ground wire. Just trace the wiring harness from the back of each headlight assembly and see where it connects to the vehicle body. Clean it as described at right.

Disassemble the connection, clean it with a wire brush and reassemble it. Coat the parts with dielectric grease to slow down corrosion.

STARTING PROBLEMS

Every morning I have to pump the gas pedal to keep my car running. My mechanic says you should never have to touch the gas pedal and he's replaced a bunch of parts and billed me $250. It still does the same thing. A friend says it must be a sensor. Can you help?

The computer in every fuel-injected car must know two things before it can figure out the correct cold-start air/fuel mixture: the engine coolant temperature and the outside air temperature. Your symptoms are a dead ringer for a bad engine coolant temperature sensor (ECT). The computer is calculating an air/fuel mixture that is too lean. That's why pumping the gas pedal keeps your engine running.

You can have a bad sensor even without a "check engine" light or trouble code. I could tell you how to test it, but they're so cheap (about $15) and easy to replace, that it makes more sense to just replace it. Ask the auto parts store clerk to find the right sensor for you (you may have two—one for the computer and one for the temp gauge on your dash) and to show you where it installs on your engine.

ENGINE COOLANT TEMPERATURE SENSOR (ECT)

Bad sensor causes cold starting problems
See the crack? This sensor didn't set off a trouble code or "check engine" light. But the owner had to pump the pedal to keep the engine running.

POWER STEERING DILEMMA

A week ago I topped off the power steering reservoir and lost all power assist a few days later. The mechanic says I used the wrong fluid and burned up the pump. The bottle said it "met all O.E. requirements," so I figured it was safe for my car. What gives?

Contrary to what it says on the bottle's label, there's really no such thing as a universal power steering fluid. Each carmaker specifies its own fluid and you must use that. In fact, a major power steering pump rebuilder recently issued a service bulletin warning shop owners that using the wrong fluid can destroy a freshly rebuilt pump in as little as 20 minutes.

If your owner's manual lists a type of power steering fluid that's carried by your local auto parts store (like Chrysler's ATF+4 or Mercon V), buy it there. But if the store doesn't have the exact fluid listed, buy it directly from the dealer. Don't be fooled by statements such as "Meets all O.E. requirements." No single fluid meets all O.E. requirements.

PRO UPGRADES FOR YOUR **GARAGE WORKSHOP**

Low cost—high impact!

by **Rick Muscoplat**

Fixing mechanical contraptions is hard enough without having to mop up the oil, grease and gas that spilled on your workbench or spending half your time looking for tools. We've put together five great garage improvements that'll save you cleanup time and keep your tools in order—all without breaking the bank.

The always-clean workshop

This sheet metal workbench cover is the first upgrade I made to my garage, and it's one of the wisest investments I've ever made. (Well, it beats my two wedding licenses anyway.) It's easy to clean (just squeegee the oil into the gutter and drain bucket), and it's heavy duty enough to handle heavy car parts. All it takes is some measuring and sketching and a trip to a sheet metal shop or a local HVAC shop and steel yard. The whole thing assembles in less than an hour and costs less than $300.

Skip the steel decking if you wish, but it does prevent the top from denting and provides a more solid work surface. I paid $180 for the top and $92 for the 11-gauge (1/8-in.) steel plate (cut to size and then whacked into thirds for easy transport).

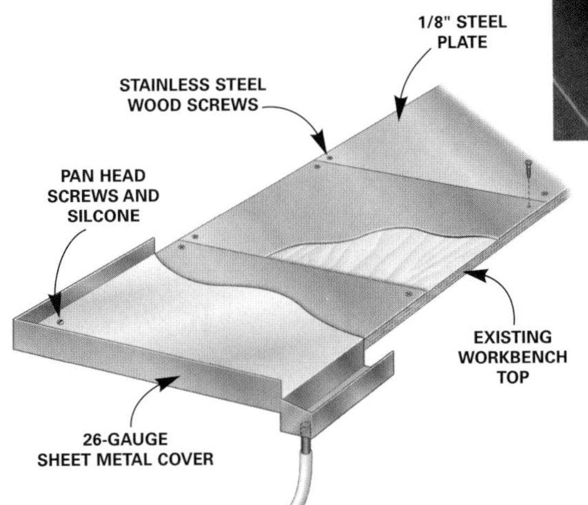

Drill, countersink and screw the steel plate to any wood top. Then screw down the cover with a few pan head screws covered with a dollop of silicone. Clamp a vinyl tube onto the drainpipe and route it into a bucket.

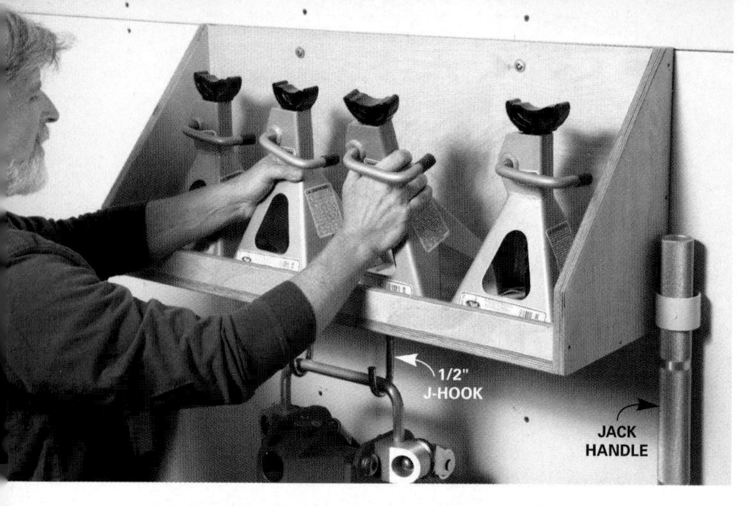

Jack and jack-stand holder

Haven't you tripped over your jack stands enough? Build this brain-dead–simple storage rack and get them off the floor. If you have a lightweight floor jack, add mounting hooks under the holder. Screw a 2-in. PVC coupler onto the side of the rack and a 2-in. cap on the wall near the floor for the handle.

Grease gun holster

A grease gun is big and, uh, greasy. So don't slime up your drawers or cabinets with it. Slice up a few sections of 1-in. and 3-in. PVC pipe and screw them to a plywood backer to make this slick grease gun holder. Then slap up a 2-in. coupler and cap to hold a backup tube of grease.

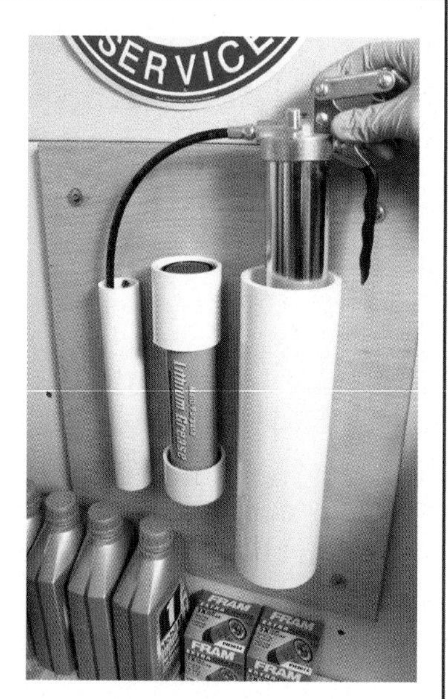

PVC drawer organizers

When you're right in the middle of a project, you don't need to waste time pawing through drawers looking for tools. So keep frequently used tools neatly stacked in your workbench drawer using this handy setup.

Cut 1- or 2-in. PVC pipe to length. Glue on end caps and then slit each pipe in half on a band saw. Screw them to the drawer bottoms and load them up!

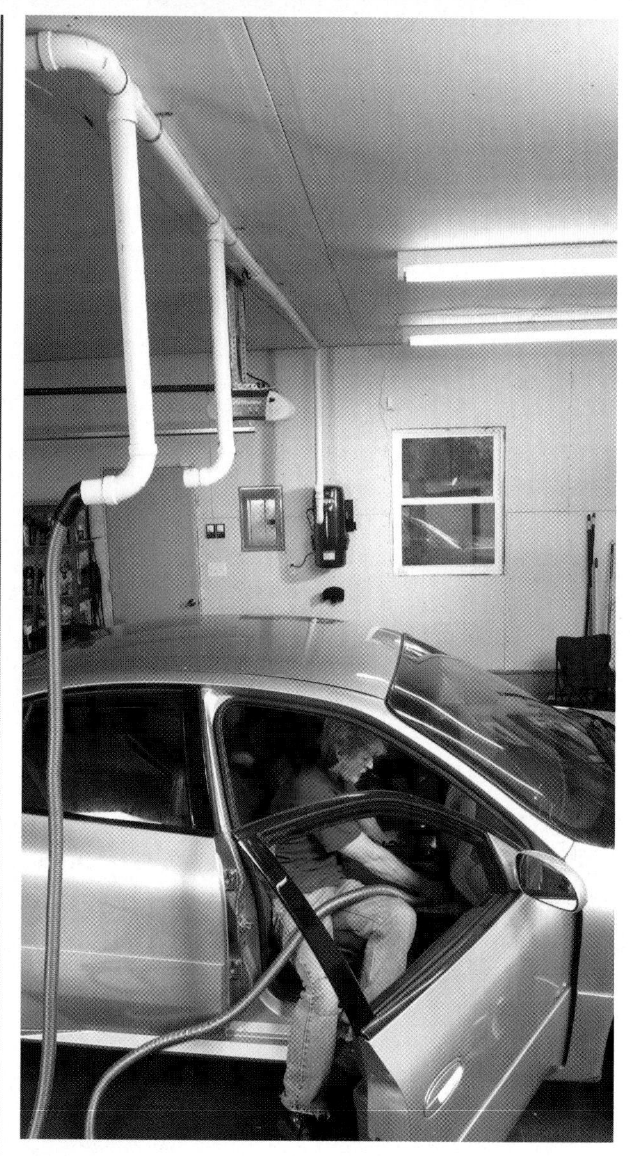

Install 2-in. sanitary tees on the ceiling and drop a pipe near each car door. Install a long 90-degree bend and a stubout to connect the hose. Cap off the stubout with a standard 2-in. pipe cap when not in use.

Central vac for the garage

OK, I admit it. This setup is overkill. But once I got the vacuum (Bissell Garage Pro Wet/Dry Vacuum, 18P0; $190 from amazon.com) mounted to the wall, it just made sense to run inexpensive 2-in. PVC all over the place. That way I didn't have to drag the 35-ft. hose all over the garage. Buy adapters to connect standard plumbing PVC to the vacuum (central vacuum fittings are 2-in. O.D., while plumbing fittings are 2-in. I.D.).

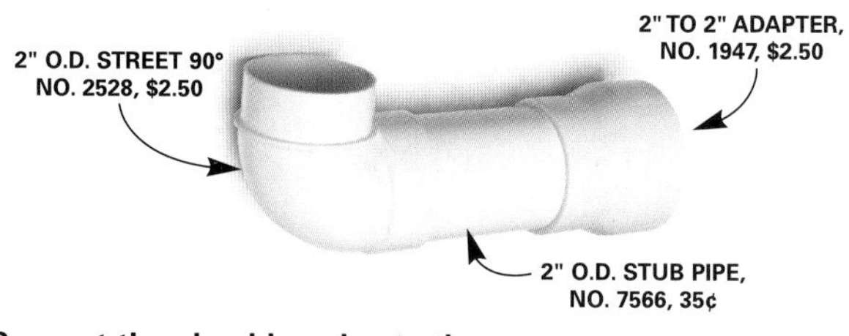

Connect the plumbing pipe to the power unit with adapter fittings. These are from centralvacuumstores.com.

GLOVEBOX EMERGENCY GUIDE

How to handle roadside trouble

by Rick Muscoplat

© KADMY DREAMSTIME.COM

When you're dealing with roadside emergencies, it's always better to have a plan of attack than a panic attack. A few simple preparations, including an inexpensive emergency kit, will get you through most breakdowns and accidents. You're already familiar with the standard kit you hear about every fall, which includes a blanket, candy bars, a candle and all that other stuff. That kit is a good idea. But there are a few additional items you should stock in every vehicle you own, along with this guide. By the way, seriously consider joining a roadside assistance plan. Even seasoned mechanics aren't too proud to belong to one. One tow or a jump start on a freezing day and the $80 annual fee will pay for itself.

Photocopy this guide and put a copy in each of your vehicles. Tell family members to refer to it in an emergency. But first, build the emergency kit shown below and store it in your glove box.

CHEAP CELL PHONE

LED FLAMELESS FLARE

Build this emergency kit

- **Your car's owner's manual.** If you don't have one, get one from your dealer. It'll show you how to change a tire, explain what all the warning lights mean, list part numbers for lightbulbs, and provide the fluid types and capacities so you can refill with the right stuff.
- **This LED Flameless Flare** ($7 at vat19.com) lasts much longer than an ordinary flaming road flare. Attach the magnetic base to your vehicle and set it to flashing mode to warn other drivers.
- **Spiral notebook and mechanical pencil** (writes in any position or weather and needs no sharpening). Use to record accident information, police report numbers, phone numbers, etc.
- **A cheap prepaid cell phone and a car charger.** Even if you already own a cell phone, get one to keep in your glove box. This Virgin Mobile setup (phone and charger) cost less than $25 at Walmart and can be reloaded with minutes from the side of the road.

What to do if you're in an accident

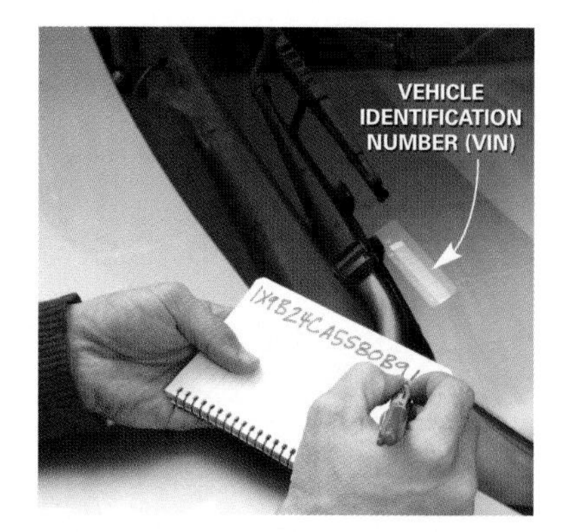

Get the other driver's license number, insurance company name and policy number, the vehicle's plate number and its VIN (vehicle identification number, located in the lower corner of the windshield).

1. Check for injuries. If anyone is injured, call 911 immediately. Do not move injured occupants unless you see fire, suspect the risk of fire, or are instructed to do so by 911 operators.
2. Find out your location. Note the street address, highway mile marker, destination sign or nearest billboard. Emergency personnel and your insurance company need this information.
3. Note the weather conditions, skid marks and the damage to the other vehicle. Sketch the accident scene.
4. Locate any witnesses and get their account of the accident and their name, address and phone numbers.
5. Don't admit to any fault.
6. Get a copy of the police report or find out how to obtain a copy.
7. Don't make any "deals" to pay out-of-pocket in order to avoid notifying your insurance company. Your policy *requires* you to report the accident *even if you choose not to file a claim.*
8. Contact a towing service (above right) to move your vehicle to a repair shop, and make arrangements to get home.
9. Call your insurance company to report the accident and file a claim.

How to get unstuck

Place the gearshift in "1" or "low." Press the accelerator and allow the spinning wheels to move the vehicle forward a bit (do not exceed 15 mph on the speedometer). Then release the gas and let the vehicle roll backward. Immediately apply the gas to roll forward again. Continue this procedure to build enough momentum to rock your vehicle out of the rut.

Do NOT shift the transmission back and forth between "D" and "R." That can destroy your transmission and result in a repair bill of at least $1,500. If you cannot rock the vehicle out using the procedure above, call a towing service—it's cheaper than a new transmission.

Get help online

Find a towing service.
If you have Internet access on your cell phone, enter towing.com and then your location. Or call a friend who has computer access and ask him or her to enter your location information at towing.com.

Find a local mechanic.
Use your cell phone's Internet function or call a friend with Internet access. Then enter iatn.net and click on the "Having car trouble?" tab. Or enter cartalk.com and search for "mechanics files."

© MY LIGHTSCAPES DREAMSTIME.COM

When it's safe to change a tire

Changing a tire is fairly straightforward. You'll find all the instructions on a decal near the jack and in the owner's manual. But in some situations, *you should not change your own tire.*

If you have a flat tire on a highway or narrow residential street *and the flat tire is on the driver's side of the vehicle,* call for roadside assistance. Even if you pull off onto a paved shoulder, the risk of being struck by another vehicle is extremely high—especially at night.

If the highway has a narrow or unpaved shoulder and there's a nearby exit, you can drive the vehicle to the exit and call for help once you're off the main road. *Turn on your hazard flashers and drive slowly.* Be warned that *you will most likely destroy the tire and possibly the wheel by driving to the exit.* But that's smarter than changing a flat tire on a busy shoulder.

Tip

Break the lug nuts loose before you jack up the vehicle. Once the spare is in place, spin on the lug nuts and tighten them partially. Then lower the vehicle and perform a final tightening. Drive to the nearest service station and check the air pressure in the spare (it's often low).

Jump-start a dead battery

DON'T SKIP THIS WARNING:
Connecting the jumper cables in the wrong order or attaching the spring clamps in the wrong location ***can damage expensive electrical components and even cause an explosion.*** **Your owner's manual leads you through the procedure step by step. Follow it to the letter! If you don't understand the procedure,** ***call a tow truck.*** **Automotive batteries can vent explosive hydrogen gas when they are discharged. Do not smoke when jump-starting, and don't use jumper cables with cracked or missing insulation.**

1 Turn off the ignition and all electrical accessories in both vehicles.

2 Connect the positive jumper clamp (marked "+" or colored red) to the remote terminals on the good vehicle. They're located away from the battery. If you cannot find the remote terminals, connect the positive ("+") jumper clamp to the positive ("+") battery terminals. Then do the same on the dead vehicle.

3 Connect the negative jumper clamp (marked "–" or colored black) to the remote negative terminal on the dead vehicle. Then connect the clamp to the good vehicle. If the vehicles don't have remote terminals, connect the negative jumper clamp to an unpainted metal surface at least 18 in. away from the battery.

4 Start the good vehicle and let it charge up the dead battery for at least five minutes. Then try to start the dead vehicle with the cables still in place. If it doesn't start, call for service.

Warning lights—what they mean

Oil light on. The engine has low oil pressure. Check the oil level and add oil if you have some with you. Otherwise, have the vehicle towed to a repair shop. Driving a vehicle with low oil pressure can cause catastrophic engine damage.

BRAKES

Brake light on. Check the operation of the brake pedal. If it feels spongy or goes to the floor, stop driving and have the vehicle towed to a repair shop. If the pedal feels firm and the brakes stop the vehicle, check the brake fluid level in the reservoir. If it's low, add more brake fluid. If the light stays on after you've added fluid but the pedal is still firm, have the vehicle serviced as soon as possible.

AIRBAG

Airbag/SRS light on. The airbags have shut down and will not work if you get into an accident. Get the vehicle serviced soon.

TRACTION CONTROL

Traction control/stability control light on. There's a problem with the system. You can still drive the vehicle, but exercise extra caution on slippery roads and in turns. Have the system serviced soon.

SERVICE ENGINE SOON

"Check engine" light on. If the engine's running smoothly and the transmission is shifting properly, you can continue to drive the vehicle until you can get it checked by a mechanic. If it's flashing, pull over at the nearest safe spot. Have the vehicle towed to a repair shop immediately. Driving with a flashing "check engine" light can destroy expensive ($1,200 and up) emissions components.

CHARGING SYSTEM

Charging system light on. There's a major failure with the charging system. Drive immediately to the nearest repair shop.

ABS

ABS light on. There's a fault in the anti-lock brake system. You can drive the vehicle and operate the brakes. But exercise more caution on slippery roads. Get the problem checked out soon.

HOT

High temperature. Pull over at the nearest safe spot and turn off the engine. DO NOT open the radiator or the coolant reservoir. Have the vehicle immediately towed to a repair shop. Driving an overheated vehicle can cause serious engine damage costing thousands of dollars to repair.

INSTALL A GARAGE DOOR OPENER

THAT'S JOHN RENO, GARAGE DOOR EXPERT

We'll tell you what's missing and what matters in the instruction manual!

by **Brett Martin**

Garage door openers are designed for easy installation. But the instruction manuals tend to be so full of legalese that most of us don't read them (I confess to just looking at a couple of illustrations). In this story, we'll clarify the instructions that are most important and pass along some pro advice that you won't find in the manual.

Make sure the door parts are working

If your garage door is opening slowly or making a lot of noise, the problem may not be your opener. So before you buy a new one, check for broken or wobbly rollers and brackets. Visit familyhandyman.com and search for "garage door tune up" to see how to replace them. But don't replace the bottom roller bracket yourself—the cable attached to it is under extreme tension. You'll need to call a pro (about $90 for the service call).

If you're replacing the rollers, get nylon rollers ($8 for a two-pack at home centers). They operate quieter than steel rollers and cost only a few bucks more.

Next, check the torsion spring (mounted on the header above the door opening) to see if it's broken.

When one breaks, you'll see a gap in the coils (**Photo 1**). You'll need a pro to replace a broken spring, a repair that will cost about $155 in parts and labor for a single door and $185 for a double door.

Finally, check to make sure the door is balanced. Close the door and pull the emergency release cord (always close the door first so it can't come crashing down!). Lift the door about halfway up and let go (**Photo 2**). The door shouldn't move. If it slides up or down, the torsion spring needs to be adjusted (or maybe even replaced).

Adjusting the torsion spring is dangerous, so don't attempt it yourself (you could get seriously hurt). Call a pro to adjust it, and expect to pay about $90.

Set the opener on a ladder for easier installation

Follow the manufacturer's instructions to assemble the opener and mount the rail to the header bracket above the door. Then set the opener on a ladder where you're going to install it. The ladder (usually an 8-footer) holds the opener in position while you measure for your lengths of angle iron (**Photo 3**). If necessary, put boards under the opener to raise it.

Have the door open when you install the opener (clamp locking pliers onto the roller track below a roller to keep the door from closing). It's easier to align the opener with the center of the door when the door is open.

Buy heavy-duty angle iron

Garage door openers come with everything you need for installation. But the mounting straps that are included are often so flimsy that you can bend them with your hands. So buy slotted angle iron at a hardware store ($15 for 4 ft. of 14-gauge). Cut it to size with a hacksaw.

Angle iron provides a stronger installation and reduces vibration, which helps extend the opener's life span. In an unfinished garage, attach the angle iron directly to the face of a joist with 1-in. lag screws. For finished ceilings, attach angle iron along the bottom of a joist with 3-in. lag screws. Hang the opener using two more lengths of angle iron and nuts and bolts (**Photo 4**). Use lock washers or thread-locking adhesive to keep vibration from loosening the nuts.

Replace all the components

Don't be tempted to reuse the old photoelectric eyes and wall button (opener button). The new photo eyes and wall button are designed to work with your new opener.

If the wires that run from your opener to the photo eyes and to the wall button are exposed, replace them, too. Those wires have probably been in your garage for 10 years or more, and they may be nicked or worn. Newer openers are extremely sensitive and won't work if a wire is damaged. It only takes about 15 minutes to run the new

1 Check for a broken spring. If you have two garage doors and they get similar use, have the springs above both doors replaced when one breaks. The other one would probably break within a year.

2 Check the door balance. Open your door halfway and let go. If the door moves up or down on its own, the torsion spring is out of adjustment, which causes your opener to work harder and wear out faster.

Choosing a new opener

Garage door openers are available at home centers, starting at $140. When buying an opener, choose a 1/3 hp or 1/2 hp opener for a single garage door (1/3 hp can be hard to find at some home centers). Go with 1/2 hp for a double door and 3/4 hp for a door that has a wood or faux wood overlay (they can be heavy!). Openers have a set opening speed, so installing an opener with a higher horsepower won't open your door any faster.

Openers are available with a chain drive, screw drive or belt drive. Chain drives (a long chain pulls the door open and closed) are the least expensive, but they're loud. Screw drives (a long threaded rod drives a mechanism that opens and closes the door) are priced in the mid-range. They require the least maintenance, but they're not as quiet as belt drives. Belt drives (a rubber belt opens and closes the door) are the quietest, making them the best choice if you have living space above the garage. They're also the most expensive (about $50 more than a chain drive).

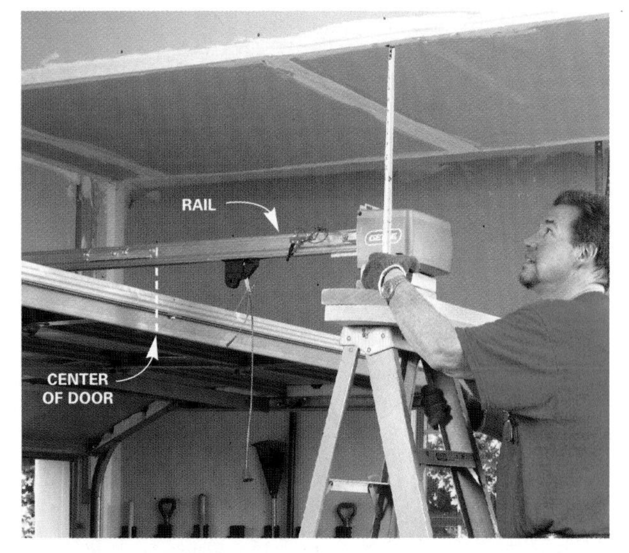

3 **Position the opener. Place the opener on a ladder and use scrap lumber to get it at the height you need. Align the opener's rail with the center of the garage door.**

4 **Hang the opener with angle iron. Don't use the flimsy strap that comes with some openers. Solid mounting means less vibration and a longer life. If the opener is more than 6 in. from the ceiling, attach an angle brace to eliminate sway.**

Fix a reversing door

The most common problem with garage door openers is the door reversing when it's closing, even when there's nothing obvious obscuring the photoelectric eyes. If your closing force is adjusted correctly, then the problem is almost always the photoelectric eyes. The eyes are very sensitive—even cobwebs can interfere with them.

First make sure the eyes are still in alignment (something may have knocked them out of whack). Then make sure the eyes are clean and the path between them is clear. Finally, look for loose wires in the eyes and the opener.

wire, so it's time well spent. If the wires are protected inside the wall, you don't need to run new wire.

Check the door's opening force

Your instructions probably don't cover checking the opening force. If your door encounters more than about 5 lbs. of resistance when it's opening, you want it to stop. This is an important safety feature. The "resistance" could be your finger caught in the track.

To check the opening force, rest your foot on the door handle near the floor and open the door using the remote control. When the door lifts against your foot, it should stop with very little pressure (Photo 5). If the door continues to open, adjust the force (see the next step).

Fine-tune the opening and closing force

The opener's instructions probably tell you to place a 2x4 on the floor under the center of the door, then close it.

5 **Check the opening force. Rest your foot on the door and open it with a remote control. The light pressure from your foot should cause the door to stop. If it doesn't, adjust the opening force.**

When the door contacts the wood, it should stop and then reverse. Proper closing force ensures that if something is in the door's path, the door won't crush it.

The locations of the opening and closing force adjustment screws vary. Our unit has two screws on the front. When adjusting the opening or closing force, turn the screw only about 1/8 in., then recheck the force (Photo 6).

If the door starts to open and then stops on its own, increase the opening force. Likewise, if it stops on its own while closing, increase the closing force. You might have to make several small adjustments to get the force exactly how it should be.

Use bulbs that handle vibration

Garage door openers vibrate, so you'll need special lightbulbs that can handle it. Look for "rough service" or "garage door" on the label (**Photo 7**). The bulbs cost $4 for a two-pack at home centers.

Be sure to use the wattage specified in your manual. If you use a higher wattage, the heat could melt the plastic cover over the bulbs or even damage the circuit board inside the opener.

This is one place where LED or CFL bulbs aren't the best choice. LEDs have a low light output, and CFLs aren't designed to handle the vibration. And since the lights are on only briefly, the energy saved with these bulbs would be negligible.

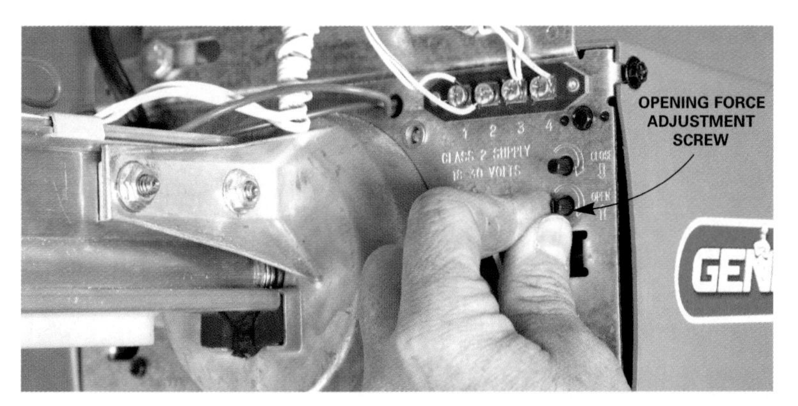

6 Adjust the opening and closing force. Make minor adjustments to the opening and closing force screws, then retest the force. A 1/8-in. turn is sometimes all you need.

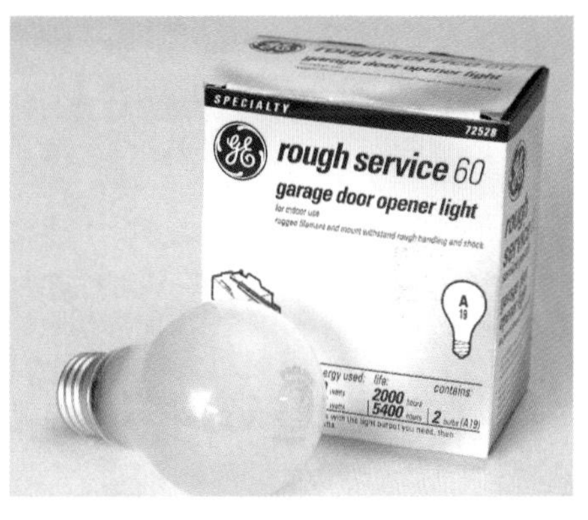

7 Install tough bulbs. Use "rough service" bulbs and don't exceed the wattage listed on the opener. Bulbs that are too hot can damage the opener.

GreatGoofs®

It's never where you left it

We live on a busy road and our driveway's very steep. One snowy evening when I came home from work, the driveway was just too slick to climb with my pickup. No matter how many runs I took at it, I could only make it halfway up the driveway to the garage before I lost traction.

Frustrated, I decided to just lock my pickup where it was and call it a night. After a blissfully ignorant night's sleep, I grabbed my morning coffee, walked outside and mentally prepared to get back to the old grind. But my truck was gone! I looked around in a panic before spotting it—the truck had slid down the driveway, across the sidewalk and was blocking half the street. Miraculously, no one had broadsided it during the night.

Oil change gone wrong

I was feeling like a sucker for paying those quick-change oil joints 25 bucks or more when I'm so capable of changing the oil myself. It was time to get my hands dirty. Ten minutes to save $15? No problemo! I rounded up everything I needed and went to work. I pulled the plug and watched the black gold start to flow. While the oil drained, I headed to the kitchen for a cup of joe. When I came back out, my garage floor looked like Kuwait after Saddam blew up the oil wells. I didn't know it, but my old oil pan had a crack in the bottom. Ever try cleaning 5 qts. of dirty oil off a concrete floor? Well, it takes longer than 10 minutes!

FIBERGLASS **FACE-LIFT**

Fix boats, personal watercraft, even truck toppers. Do it yourself and save thousands!

by **Rick Muscoplat**

Even the best boat captain has had a docking turn into a scuff-and-chip event. But you don't have to pay astronomical marina fees to get your boat fixed. You can do it yourself with advice from expert fiberglass repair specialist Chris Hassis. He's fixed boo-boos on fiberglass personal watercraft, snowmobiles and pickup toppers, and even luxury yachts. You'll need the right tools and materials—and lots of patience. But he'll show you how to save a ton of money and make your boat look like new. We were astounded at this refurbished boat's rebirth. The boat now looks every bit as good as it did in the showroom.

Most hired-out repairs of any type are roughly 50 percent labor and 50 percent materials. Not so with this fix—hull repairs are all about labor. The repairs on this boat would cost roughly $3,000 at a shop. But the materials only cost $250 and the buffer $150! So roll up your sleeves. Your repairs might not be perfect, but your boat will look unbelievably better than it did before. Just don't try to rush or skimp on the materials. And know that this job is much bigger than it looks.

All fiberglass boats have a thick structural core of fiberglass strands impregnated with polyester resin. But the part you actually see is the gel coat. That's the thin layer of pigmented resin that gives the boat its sheen and color. Most light scratches are in the gel coat layer. They can be sanded out and the area built back up with new gel coat. But if they penetrate the core, they need to be filled. You can tell that the scratch is into the core if you see fiberglass fibers (**Photo 2**).

Remove graphics

No boat spiff-up is complete without new license numbers, transom names and pinstripes. Just do an Internet search for "boat graphics" and you'll find thousands of options to choose from. Find stripes by searching for "boat pinstripes." Remove the old ones by warming them with a heat gun (**Photo 1**). But be careful—if you overheat the surface, you can burn the gel coat. If yours are painted on, sand them off with 1,200-grit sandpaper.

Fixing gouges and deep scratches

To fix gouges and deep scratches, you'll need "chop" (powdered fiberglass) filler, gel coat and gel coat reducer. Jot down your boat's model and serial numbers and contact the

Order of events

- **Wash and rinse the boat. That will show you all the dings that need fixing. Mark them with masking tape so you won't forget any.**
- **If you're replacing pinstripes, license decals or other graphics, remove them next.**
- **Fill any deep gouges and spend your time sanding out scratches while the filler sets up.**
- **Apply gel coat to the filled gouges and finish to the scratches and then final-sand the filled gouges.**
- **Buff all the repaired areas and then the rest of the boat.**
- **Apply any graphics to finish up.**

1 **Remove old numbers and pinstripes.** Set the heat gun to a low setting and peel off the old decals and numbers. Use adhesive remover to get rid of any residue.

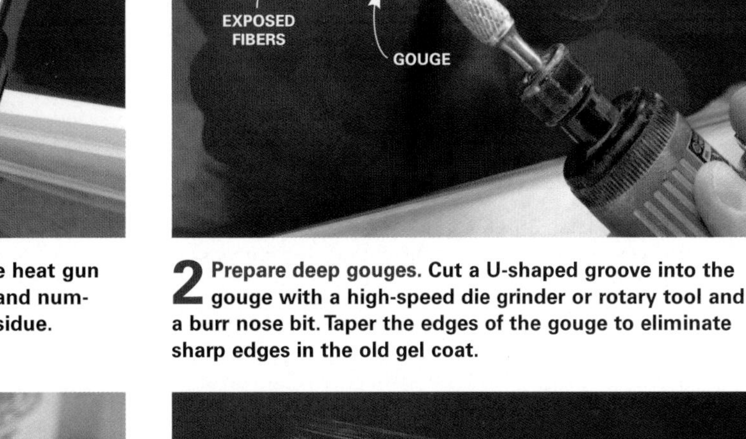

2 **Prepare deep gouges.** Cut a U-shaped groove into the gouge with a high-speed die grinder or rotary tool and a burr nose bit. Taper the edges of the gouge to eliminate sharp edges in the old gel coat.

3 **Prepare the filler.** Stir in enough chop to get the mixture to the consistency of peanut butter. Then add hardener (follow the manufacturer's ratio) and stir, stir, stir.

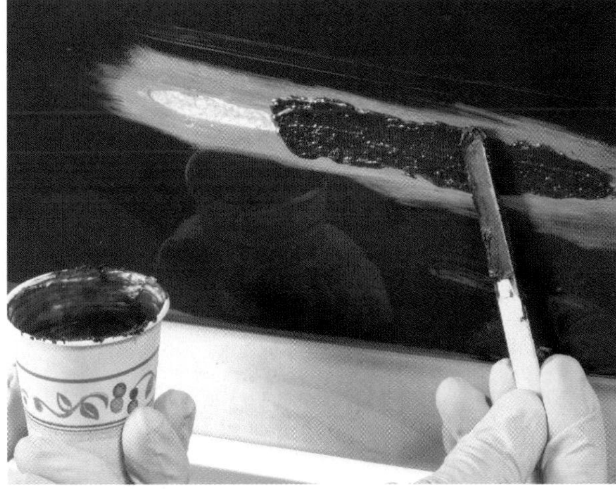

4 **Fill in the gouge.** Scoop the gel coat putty into the gouge. Then press it into the fibers with a craft stick. Add more putty until you're about 1/32 in. above the surface. Clean up any goofs with acetone.

manufacturer to order gel coat (about $100 per qt.) to match your boat's color. It may not be an exact match, but it'll be a lot closer than mixing colors from scratch. Then order some gel coat reducer. (Patch-Aid is one brand; $49 per qt. Search "patch-aid" online for retailers.) Use the gel coat reducer to thin the mixture enough to go through the spray gun. For gouge repair, you'll mix chop filler (Chris uses Cab-O-Sil, which is available for $8 per qt. from epoxy5050.com) with the gel coat to create a thick paste. Then pick up paper cups, stir sticks, acetone (for cleanup) and rags. You'll also need a disposable spray gun (Preval is one brand; $7 online or at paint and art supply stores). To finish the job, you'll need a professional-type buffer. The variable-speed feature is important, and so is the high power of a professional buffer. So don't skimp on one or think you can get by with a $29 wax polisher. Use a wool buffing pad (such as a Dewalt DW4988 pad; $20), and buffing compound (3M Imperial Compound and Finishing Material is what Chris uses). Get the 3M product from amazon.com, westmarine.com or a marine supplier.

5 **Sand the patch.** Knock down the excess putty with 80-grit sandpaper and a rubber sanding block. Then switch to 240-grit.

Grind out gouged areas with a V-shaped grinder bit (Champion SF1; $15 from heavydutystore.com; Photo 2). Sand out the light scratches, starting with 80-grit and ending with 240-grit.

Mixing gel coat is a messy and stinky process—so wear chemical-resistant gloves, safety goggles and a

6 **Mix new gel coat. Add the hardener after you've mixed in the reducer. Follow the manufacturer's recommended ratio of hardener to gel coat.**

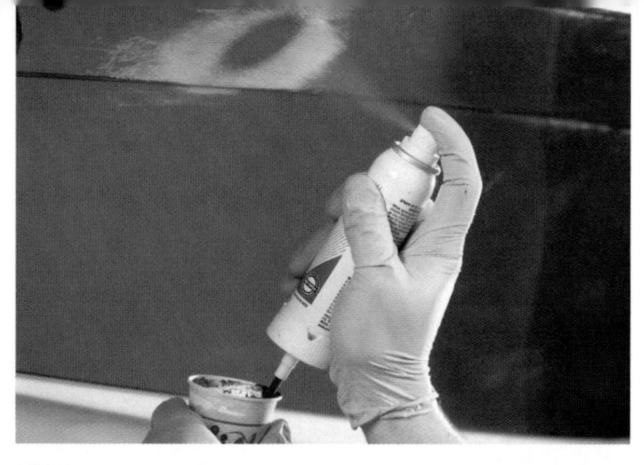

7 **Spray on the final coat. Pulse the sprayer to get short bursts of gel coat. Feather the spray along the edges to reduce sanding.**

respirator. Start with a small amount of gel coat and stir in the chop and hardener to make a putty that's the consistency of peanut butter (**Photo 3**). Once you add the hardener, you've only got a 10- to 20-minute "open" time, so mix small batches and work on one gouge at a time. Thorough mixing is critical to proper curing. Spend a full minute stirring. If you don't, you'll end up with patches of sticky resin that can take days to harden.

PRECHARGED SPRAYER

Overfill gouges so the filler mounds slightly. You'll sand it flush after it cures. Curing can take one to two hours—depending on humidity levels. So test it by touch. If it's sticky, it's not fully cured. Once it's fully hardened, sand it with 80-grit sandpaper (**Photo 5**).

Now you're ready to mix a fresh batch of gel coat (without the chop) and spray the scratched and patched areas (**Photos 6 and 7**). Chris recommends using a disposable spray gun and paper cups. Unthinned gel coat won't go through the sprayer. Add the recommended amount of reducer (read label directions) and hardener and mix the ingredients. Spray the patched areas with short bursts. Spraying gel coat isn't like spraying paint. It splatters on and has to be sanded and buffed to get to a smooth gloss. So don't be disappointed that the finish isn't paintlike right away.

Final-sand, buff and wax

Wait for the gel coat to cure. Sand the repairs with 600-grit and then 800-grit sandpaper. For the perfect finish, sand with 1,200-grit wet/dry paper then buff (**Photo 8**). Apply buffing compound directly to the pad. Work on a 2 x 2-ft. area and use light to medium pressure at a fairly low speed. Reduce pressure as the compound starts to dry. Wipe off the haze as you go. Apply the graphics and then wax.

BUFFING COMPOUND

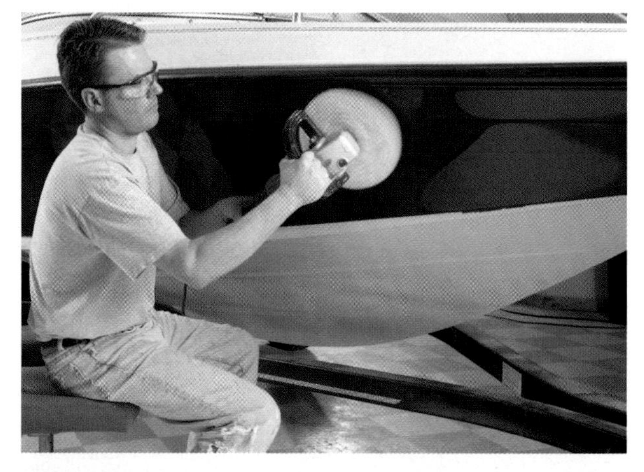

8 **Buff to a great shine. Take a seat and heft the buffer into position. Start slowly and buff small sections at a time.**

9 **Apply new decals. Position the new boat numbers and tape the sheet in place. Then lift the sheet up, remove the backer and press each number individually. Don't try to apply them all at once—they'll wrinkle.**

Color-matching gel coats

Sometimes you can't get your hands on factory gel coat (your boat is too old or the manufacturer is out of business). Then you have two options. You can order an off-the-shelf color that's close to yours and decide that "close enough is good enough." The other option is to custom mix, but be aware that this is no easy task. Buy a color chip chart for off-the-shelf colors (from a local marine supplier, or get the No. 01900 color chart from rayplex.com for $12). Mix your own color with a kit (No. 33114; $38) from rayplex.com (905-579-1433).

FIX A FLAT ON A BIKE

The first step is to release the brake and loosen the axle nut so you can remove the wheel from the bike. Most bikes have a quick-release mechanism on the brake and a quick-release lever on the axle. If you're not sure how to remove the wheels on your bike, check the manual or visit your local bike store and ask someone on staff to show you how. Do this before you have a flat so you'll be prepared. For a guaranteed trouble-free fix, buy a new tube rather than patching the old one (see "Valve Types" below).

After removing the wheel from the bike, the next step is to take one edge, or bead, of the tire off the rim so you can remove the damaged tube (Photo 1). Pull out the tube. Then remove the tire completely from the rim, put it around your neck like a necklace and turn it inside out while running your fingers along the inside to feel for sharp objects. Be careful, though—there could be bits of glass lodged in the tire. After checking the tire, put one bead back on the rim, leaving the other side loose so you can install the new (or patched) tube (Photo 2).

Photo 3 shows how to push the second tire bead back onto the rim after the tube is in place. When the tire is completely installed, check all around on both sides to make sure the tube isn't pinched between the tire and rim. To do this, push against the bead and look into the space between the tire and rim to be sure it's clear.

Now you're ready to fully inflate the tire. But there's one last thing to watch for. Occasionally the bead may not seat properly on the rim, so stop before the tire is inflated to full pressure and rotate the wheel while you inspect the area where the tire and rim meet. If you see a spot where the bead isn't seated in the rim, let a little air out and work the bead into the rim with your fingers. Then inflate the tire to the pressure listed on the side. Reinstall the wheel and spin it to make sure it's centered between the brakes and rotates freely. If you've done an emergency repair using the CO2 cartridge, you may not have enough pressure. When you get home or to a bike store or gas station, fill the tire.

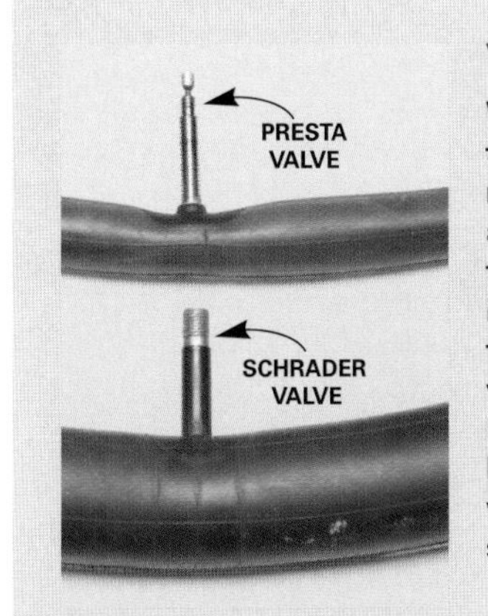

Valve types

When you go to buy a new tube, take the old tube with you and match the valve. Presta valves have a nut on a threaded shaft that seals the air in and must be loosened to inflate the tube. You need a pump that's compatible with a Presta valve to inflate these tubes. If you have Presta valves on your bike, keep a Presta-to-Schrader adapter with you so you can use a gas-station air pump to inflate your tire.

1 Remove the tire. Pry under the bead of the tire with one of the tire levers and hook it to a spoke. Move over about 4 to 6 in. and insert the other tire lever. Pry it down and then slide it along the rim to release the tire.

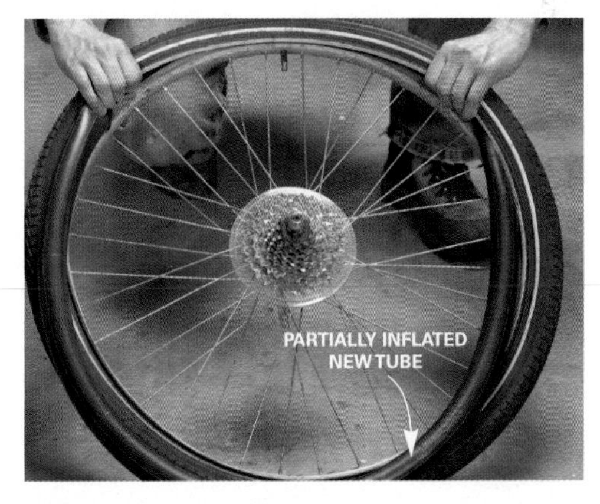

2 Install a new inner tube. Partially inflate the new or patched tube and insert the valve stem into the hole in the rim. Then work the tube into the tire.

3 Reinstall the tire. Press the tire back over the rim, being careful not to pinch the tube. If it's too tight to push the last section by hand, use the tire levers to pry the tire onto the rim.

BUILD YOUR **DREAM GARAGE**

Nine great ways to make it a better space

by **Jeff Gorton**

For most of us, a garage is a lot more than a place to park. We use it to build big projects, we load it up with everything from Hot Wheels to Harleys, and sometimes we party or just hang out with the guys there. And for all these purposes, you want more than the basic four walls and a roof. You want to make your garage a better place to work and play. So we teamed up with our field editors to show you our favorite garage features. Whether you're planning your dream garage or just looking to improve your old one, check them out!

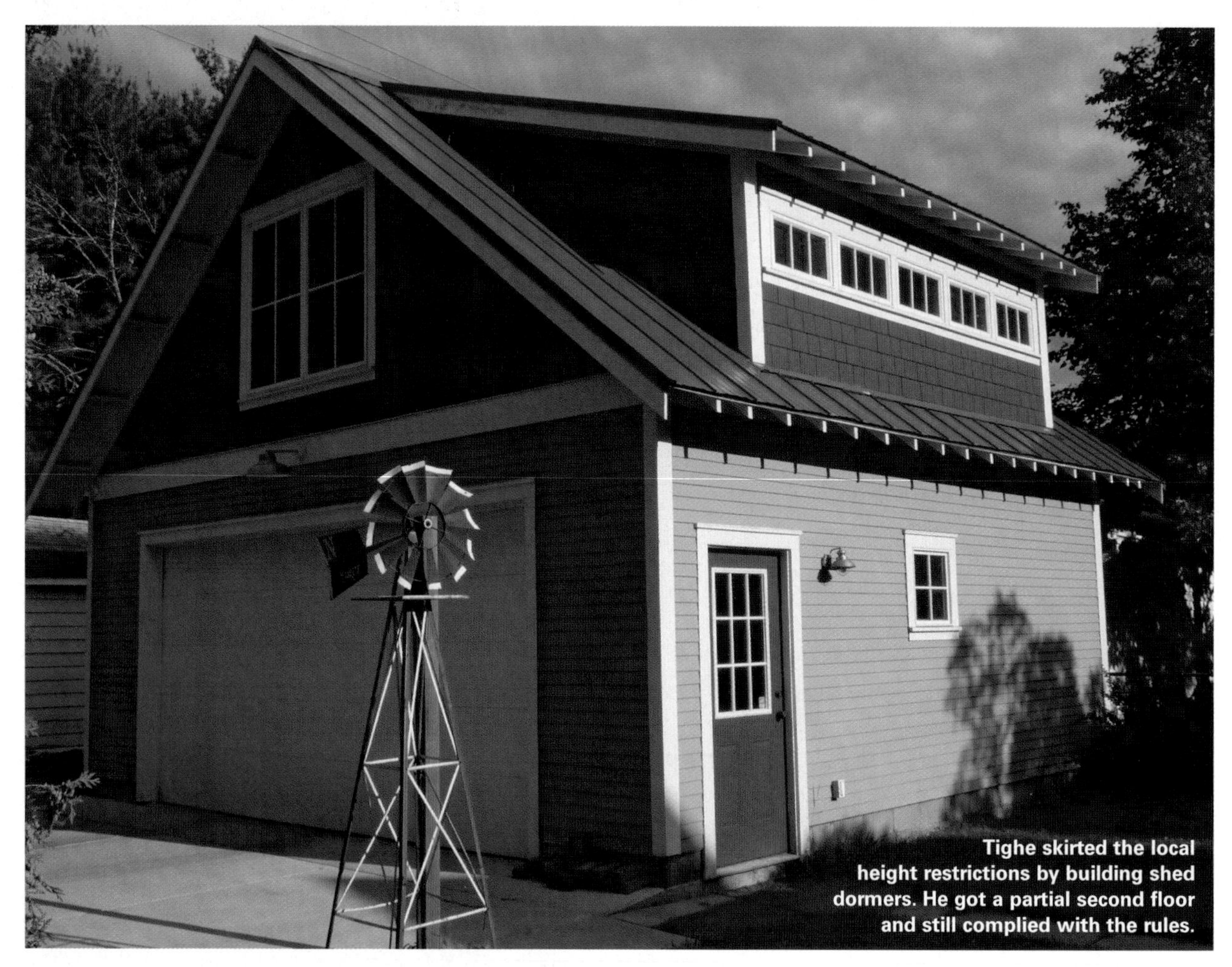

Tighe skirted the local height restrictions by building shed dormers. He got a partial second floor and still complied with the rules.

Shed dormers add second-floor headroom

Tighe Belden knew he wanted space on the second floor for an office, but local building codes restricting the height of the roof were throwing a wrench into his plans. His solution was to add shed dormers. By carefully planning the size of the dormers, he was able to meet code requirements and still get plenty of headroom on the second floor. Incorporating shed dormers in your plan allows you to gain some of the benefits of a second floor—more headroom and extra windows—without the added hassle of a full second floor. Unfortunately, you can't just throw up trusses, though. Consult an architect or structural engineer to help work out the framing details. You'll probably end up hand-framing the roof, but don't worry. It's not that hard, and you'll gain a real sense of satisfaction from building it yourself.

Joe Jensen installed an 8-ft. door on his new garage so he can drive in with a load on top without worrying about taking out the garage door.

Tall doors prevent Great Goofs

Every month we receive at least one Great Goof letter from a reader who strapped something to his roof and wrecked the garage door. So when our set builder, Joe, built this new extra-large double garage, he wanted to be able to drive in with a load on top of the van. This meant installing an 8-ft.-tall garage door rather than the more common 7-ft. size.

If you decide to install an 8-ft. door, you'll have to build the walls at least 9 ft. tall to accommodate it. But tall walls are better anyway. They allow you more room to maneuver 4 x 8-ft. sheets of plywood and 8-ft.-long boards without hitting the ceiling or breaking lightbulbs.

Don't forget the AC

Many of our field editors suggested adding garage air conditioning. A through-the-wall AC unit is a good choice since it doesn't block a window and you can put it wherever you want.

Air conditioning in a garage may seem like a luxury, but there are a lot of advantages. Our field editors like the fact that AC reduces humidity, which helps keep their tools dry and rust free. Use the dimensions provided with the unit to build the opening in the wall. Add a header over the opening, just like you would if you were putting in a window. Also add a separate 20-amp circuit for power to the AC.

Vern Johnson planned ahead and framed the opening for the air conditioner sleeve and added a dedicated outlet while he was building the garage.

Weekend mechanics love warm floors

Tom Kapikian was looking for a DIY-friendly heating system for his new garage. He was tired of crawling around on a cold concrete floor to work on his car and wanted a system that was quiet and efficient. He decided to install a PEX radiant in-floor heating system and loves the results.

PEX tubing carries warm water through the slab, where it releases heat, warming the floor and garage. Since the floor is warm, you can keep the heat set at a lower level and still feel comfortable. Materials for a DIY in-floor heat system cost about $2 to $3 per square foot. A professionally installed system costs about twice this much. And you don't need a boiler. You can use a conventional water heater or an on-demand water heater as a heat source.

To insulate the tubing and prevent heat loss through the slab, you install sheets of rigid insulation board under the tubing and around the edges of the slab. And of course you'll want to insulate the garage walls, ceiling and overhead door and pay close attention to sealing air leaks around all the doors and windows too. For information on installing and purchasing in-floor heat supplies, go to pexsupply.com.

"I'd rather run tubing in a circle and do a little plumbing than piece together air ducts in wall cavities."

Tom designed his dream garage to include a PEX in-floor heating system.

Make your garage a drive-through

When Kristin and her family decided to build a new garage, they had a list of cool ideas to incorporate. These included lots of outlets, slat wall rather than pegboard on the walls, and a 220-outlet just in case. But the neatest idea was the second garage door in back so they could park the boat trailer out of sight in the backyard. Plus, there are other benefits to a big back door. For dusty woodworking operations, you can't beat the flow-through ventilation provided by two big garage doors. And if you're planning a backyard get-together, you can open the back garage door and turn your garage into party central.

Kristin Green wanted to park the boat and trailer out of sight behind the garage, and a back door made it possible.

Ken Collier's old house doesn't have much storage space, so when he built the new garage, he used storage trusses to make sure every foot of the attic was put to good use.

Storage trusses are cheap

In addition to the normal garage stuff, Ken has tons of camping gear to store, so when it came time to build a new garage, he wanted to make good use of all the space. He discovered that substituting storage trusses for standard roof trusses would open up the attic space without breaking the budget. Upgrading to storage trusses on a 24 x 24-ft. garage would only raise the price about $200. Storage trusses have a wide-open area in the center, about 12 ft. wide for a truss with a 24-ft. span, and a 2x6 floor frame that's designed to support the extra weight. If you need more storage space in your garage, storage trusses are a no-brainer.

Attic trusses are pricey, but they add tons of space

Ben learned a lot about what features his new garage should have by talking to friends and relatives. One of the best decisions Ben made was to upgrade to attic trusses.

Attic trusses cost about 2-1/2 times what a standard truss costs, raising the price on a standard-size garage about $1,600. But that's a bargain considering you'll have a full-size room ready to wire, insulate and finish. Attic trusses for a 24-ft.-wide garage with a steep roof pitch would provide a room about 16 ft. wide. There will be plenty of space for an office or workout area.

"Attic trusses were a lot more money and a little more work but definitely worth it."

Ben Westby used attic trusses to get a second-floor room on his garage. Ben and his nephew helper, Garret, are enjoying the view from the big, wide open space.

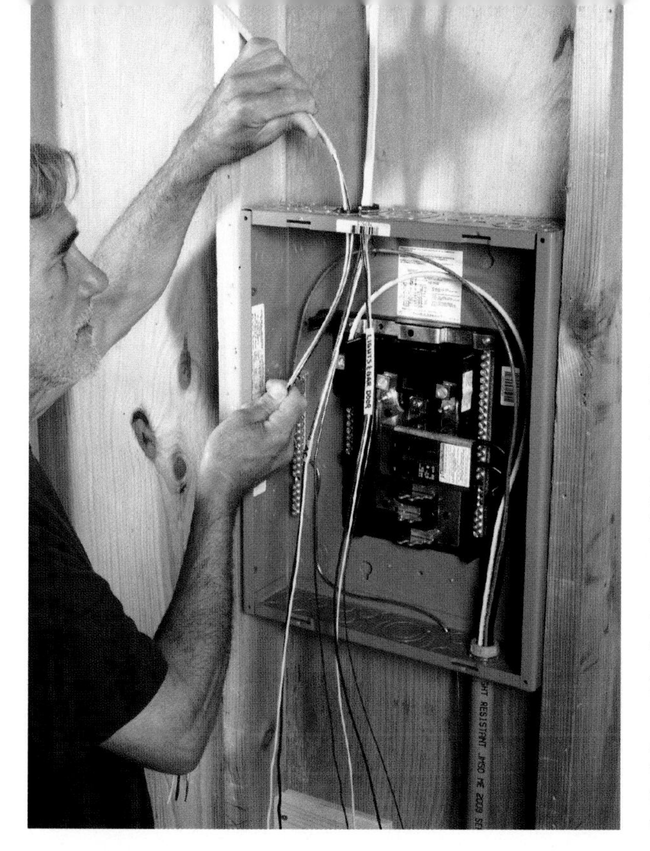

Put in a subpanel now—or regret it later!

Lots of field editors told us that their biggest garage mistake was not installing a subpanel. Lots of others said including a subpanel was the best move they made. The reasons are pretty simple: more power and more convenience.

If you want to use your garage for a shop or plan to install air conditioning or other power-hungry appliances or tools, you'll have all the power you need. And it's more convenient to have the circuit breakers in the garage. If you pop a breaker, you don't have to run to the main panel to reset it. Plus, you can easily add more circuits without having to run wires all the way to the main panel.

It'll cost you a few hundred dollars more for the load center, circuit breakers and heavy-gauge wire that runs to the main panel. But for convenience and future flexibility, it's hard to beat a separate panel in the garage.

A subpanel is just like your main circuit breaker panel but with special wiring. The neutral bar must be isolated from the ground and the main breaker secured with a special tie-down mechanism. This box has room for 12 circuit breakers.

The simplest way to the attic

Many of our field editors suggested adding a pull-down attic ladder as one of the cheapest, easiest garage upgrades. You're more likely to take advantage of the storage space in your garage if there's an easy way to get up there. Most attic ladders fit between 24-in. on-center trusses so you can install them without any structural changes. Search online for "attic ladder" to see what's available. Prices start at about $150 for wood ladders or about $250 for sturdier aluminum models.

This heavy-duty aluminum pull-down ladder sells for about $450. It's a little spendy but worth it for the extra strength and longevity.

HandyHints®

Easier car cleaning

Cleaning out my car with a vacuum cleaner always took forever, and the vacuum didn't do such a great job of getting into all the nooks and crannies. Here's a much better solution: Use a leaf blower instead. I open all four doors, take out the floor mats and hit the power switch. The leaf blower cleans faster than a vacuum, and it blows out every speck of dirt and dust.

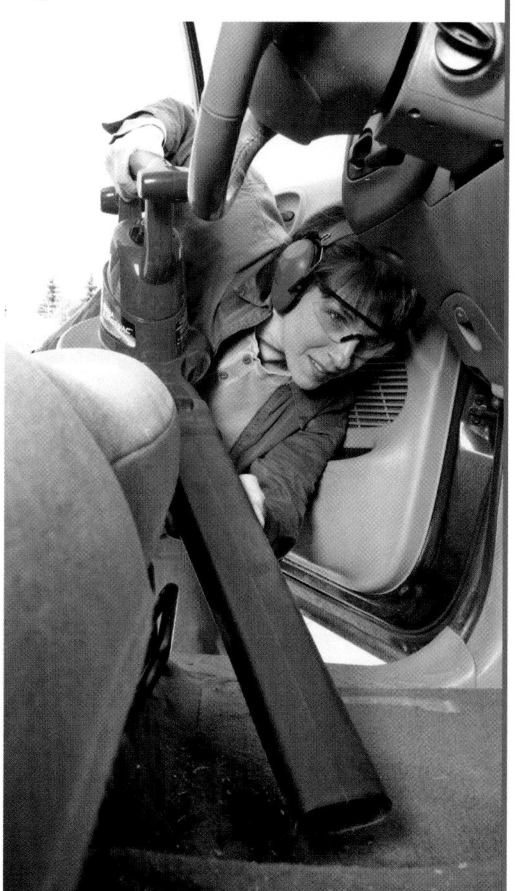

AUTO & GARAGE

Question&Comment

DIY CONCRETE CRACK REPAIR

My garage floor has several large cracks. I've tried filling them with that crack-repair-in-a-tube stuff. But they always come back. How can I fix them for good?

Concrete cracks are caused by sideways expansion, poor drainage conditions or settling soil beneath the concrete. If your concrete is the same height on both sides of the crack, you can fix it yourself. But you have to enlarge the crack (Photo 1). Then power-wash the area and squeegee off the excess water before applying the filler. Fill with a polymer-modified cement such as Quikrete concrete resurfacer No. 1131 (about $25 for a 40-lb. bag at home centers).

Our crack was wide and deep, so we chiseled out the entire opening and refilled it (Photos 2 and 3).

However, if one side of the crack is lower, call an expert to diagnose and fix the underlying soil/drainage problem. Then either replace the sunken portion or call a mud-jacking company to raise it.

1 Cut a chiseling groove. Using a diamond blade on your circular saw, cut a 1/2-in.-deep groove along each side of the crack. Wear an N-95 respirator and turn on a fan to blow the concrete dust out of the garage. Chip out the cracked portion with a maul and cold chisel.

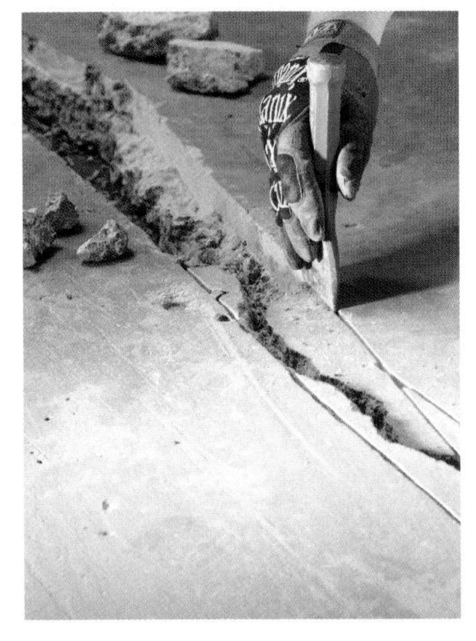

2 Knock out the old stuff. Chip out the cracked portion with a maul and cold chisel. Remove the chipped pieces and vacuum out the crack before power washing.

3 Fill groove with concrete. Add latex modifier to regular concrete mix and pack it into the channel. Fill to within 1/2 in. of the original height. Let it set up for a few days, then fill with resurfacer.

4 Spread the resurfacer. Pour concrete resurfacing mixture into the crack and smooth it out with a rubber floor squeegee. Feather the edges to get the best appearance.

Hints & Tips for Storage & Organizing

SPECIAL SECTION

TEMPORARY VALET ROD

We often need temporary clothes-hanging space around the house, so we keep an extra shower tension bar handy. We put it between the jambs in the laundry room door on heavy laundry days. And other times I use it in our bedroom closet to pack for trips or stick it in the closet opening in the guest room/den so overnight guests can hang up their clothes. It's a quick and easy way to gain an extra closet!

SEE-THROUGH SCREW STORAGE

A lot of people store their screws in an old coffee can. You can't immediately see what's inside, and when you reach in for screws, the points prick your fingers and you're likely to bring up dirt and dust along with the screws. Use a clear water bottle instead. The screws stay clean and you can shake them out one at a time.

SCREW SIZE

HOSE HIDE-A-KEY

Every thief knows that people often hide their spare house key under a doormat or inside a fake rock. Here's a better idea. File down the head of the key (make sure it still works easily in the lock) and then hide it inside the cap of a soaker hose. Brass keys don't rust, and a thief isn't likely to unscrew your hose cap to search for your key.

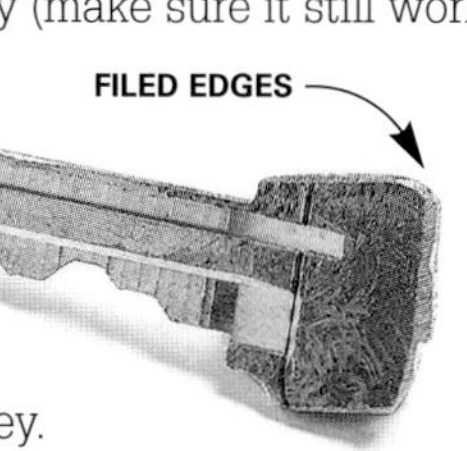

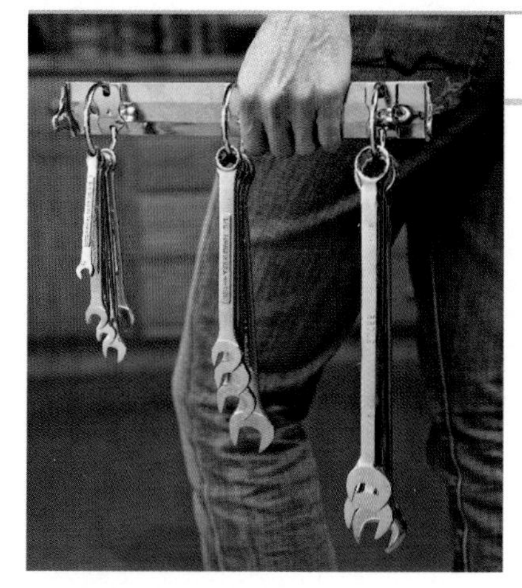

PORTABLE THREE-RING WRENCH BINDER

Here's a way to carry your wrenches around with you so you're sure to have the one you need when and where you need it. Use a three-ring binder assembly from an old notebook as a portable wrench organizer. The three rings hold a ton of wrenches, and it's a snap to get them on and off. The binder works great to keep the wrenches handy when you're working in your shop, too. Just drill out the rivets and hang it on some nails to keep everything you need close by.

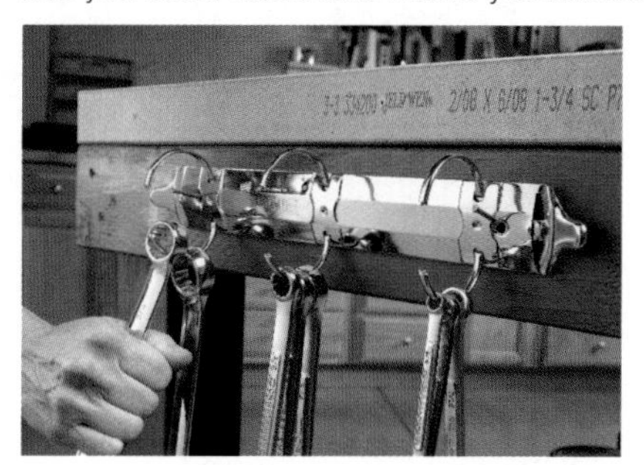

Hints & Tips for Storage & Organizing

LOW-COST STORAGE TUBES

Storing fishing rods, drill bits, blueprints, maps, cross-country skis and other long, skinny items is a challenge. You can buy special plastic storage tubes, but they're not cheap. Why not make your own for a fraction of the cost? Use PVC pipe, caps, female adapters and cleanout plugs. You can find the parts at any hardware store or home center. Cut the pipe to length with a handsaw or miter saw. Glue an end cap to one end and a female adapter to the other with PVC cement. Twist in a threaded cleanout plug for a cap. If sealing isn't important, you can drill holes in the pipe to make it lighter weight.

BILL ZUEHLKE

A WALL OF STORAGE FOR JOE'S GARAGE

Joe had a lot of stuff in his garage and nowhere to put all of it. Sound familiar?! Go to familyhandyman.com and type "garage storage wall" into the search box. You'll get the complete how-to for building the storage wall shown here.

CABINET DOOR BAG BINDER

Here's a handy way to keep paper bags organized and out of the way. Screw cup hooks to the inside of a cabinet door and stretch two screen-door springs ($2 at home centers) between them.

WIRE SHELVING "CORRAL"

For years we stored our gift wrap propped against the wall in the hall closet. Of course, some of the rolls would fall over and get lost behind other things or end up wrinkled or torn. Last summer I added wire shelves to the closet and had some shelving left over. Using the plastic shelf clips, I screwed a small section to the closet wall and made a wrapping paper "corral."

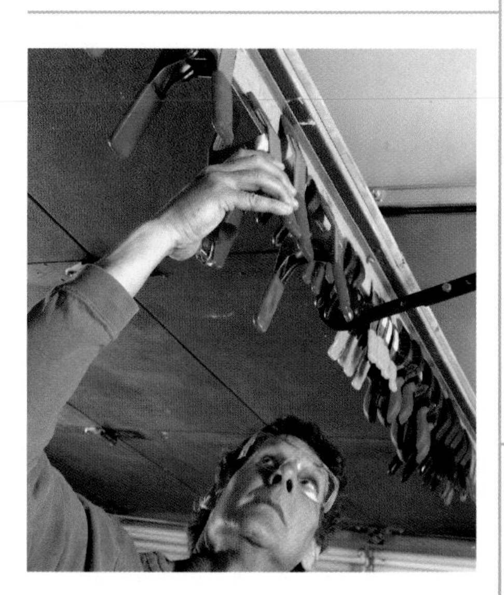

OVERHEAD SPRING CLAMPS

If you have a shop in the garage, try this tip from reader Dan Amstutz. Clip all of your spring clamps on the top garage door brace. The clamps are always right at hand whether you're working with the door shut or al fresco (that's with the door open, for those of you who don't speak Garage Italiano).

MOVABLE MUDROOM STORAGE HOOKS

You know that old saying, "If I wanted you to hang your stuff on the floor, I would have put hooks there"? That fit my kids and their backpacks to a "T." Every day after school, they dropped their packs on the floor near the back door, and I tripped over them constantly. We tried regular hooks on the wall, but the kids found it hard to slip the narrow fabric loops over them. Then I installed a towel bar near the door and hung S-hooks from it. The hooks move around, so it's easy to fit several packs on it at once. It's perfect for hanging up wet hats, scarves and mittens, too. Bring your towel bar along when you buy the S-hooks so you get the right size. I found mine at the hardware store, but the pot rack S-hooks at cooking stores work great too.

ELECTRICAL BOX TOOL HOLDERS

Does all the little stuff lying around your shop drive you crazy? Junction boxes can do a lot more than hold switches and wiring—they can also help you stay organized! They're inexpensive (50¢ to $2) and they come in different sizes and shapes. Nail or screw them wherever you need handy holders for small tools, tape measures, bottles of glue—almost anything little.

BILL ZUEHLKE

CONVENIENT CORD LABELS

You crawl underneath your desk to unplug something, only to find six different cords—and you have no clue which is the one you're after. Here's a simple idea. Label each cord with a piece of tape. It makes finding the one you need a snap.

Hints & Tips for Storage & Organizing

FLAT COOKWARE ORGANIZER

I found it frustrating to dig through a cabinet jam-packed with baking sheets, cake pans, pizza pans and cutting boards all stacked on top of one another. It was always a chore to find the one I needed. I transformed the cabinet by removing the shelf and screwing in short sections of wire shelving to create vertical dividers. Now I can easily see where everything is located, and I slide out just what I'm looking for.

PVC CURLING IRON HOLSTERS

I hated the messy look of my curling irons lying on the vanity or the toilet tank. They were always in the way, and the cords kept falling into the sink or onto the floor. I solved the problem with PVC pipe. I used hook-and-loop tape to attach 5-in. lengths of 2-in.-diameter pipe to the vanity door to hold my curling irons. I did the same thing with 3-in. pieces of 1-1/2-in.-diameter pipe to hold the cords. Just measure your curling irons to see how long your "holsters" need to be. Let your curling irons cool before you stow them away.

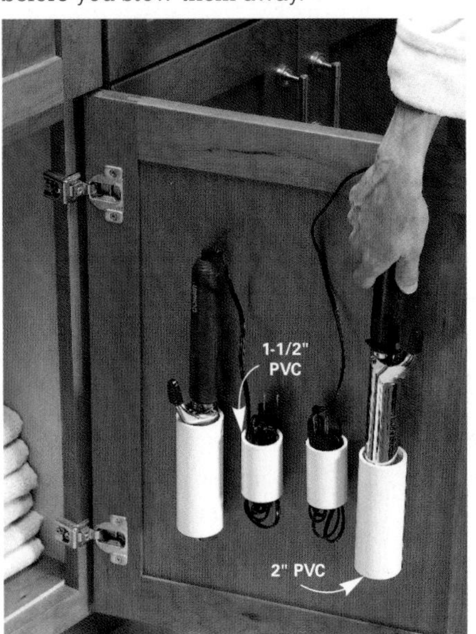

SPOOL CENTER

I used to keep all my tape, twine and ribbon spools in a drawer. Not only did it look messy, but it wasted a lot of space and made it hard to find things. Last winter I came up with this great organizing idea. I screwed a paper towel holder to the window trim in my craft room and stuck rolls of the things I use most often on the holder. Now I know right where everything is, and I can pull off the amount I need without the spool jumping out of my hand and rolling across the floor.

OUTLET BOX SAFE

I love the idea of foiling a crook, and I saw fake wall outlet "safes" online for $10 plus shipping. I made my own for less than $5. All I did was cut a hole in my drywall and install a 3-1/2-in.-deep "remodeler" outlet box. I screwed on a coax cable cover for a convenient little handle. Now I have a secret place to stash cash and jewelry where no thieves would ever think to look. (Unless they read *The Family Handyman* magazine.)

PORTABLE PLASTIC BAG DISPENSER

Like a lot of other people, I reuse plastic shopping bags whenever I can. I use them in the small trash cans around my house and grab one to take along each time I walk the dog. Here's a convenient way to store bags and do a little recycling while you're at it—stuff them into empty tissue boxes. Set the boxes inside a bathroom cabinet, on a laundry room shelf or near the front door.

HIDDEN TOOTHBRUSH ORGANIZER

We like to keep our toothbrushes out of sight. Until recently, we kept them in our medicine cabinet stacked on a shelf and they often fell out when we opened the door. Then I came up with the bright idea of cutting notches in the cabinet shelves. I used a rotary tool along with a wood-cutting bit and sanding drum.

BILL ZUEHLKE

MUFFIN TIN SMALL-PARTS ORGANIZER

Right in the middle of several shop projects? Maybe you're breaking down a small engine and repairing a broken power tool, and you don't want all those small parts to get mixed up. Try using separate muffin tins to store the hardware for each project. The parts won't roll all over, and you can keep them in order and find what you want fast.

QUICK-GRIP ELECTRIC TOOTHBRUSH HOLDER

Most toothbrush holders aren't big enough for electric toothbrushes. They end up falling out of the holder or taking up too much room on the vanity. Here's a clever storage idea: Make a holder for them using large grip-type clips (the kind you normally use for brooms or garden tools, available at hardware stores and home centers for $3.50 a pair). Mount the clips on your medicine chest or on a piece of wood that you can hang on the wall. The clips work great to keep your toothbrushes secure!

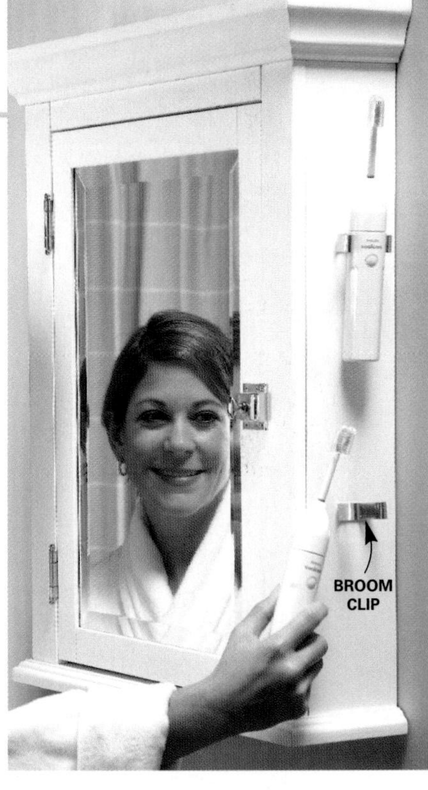

SPACE-SAVING CLOTHES-HANGING CHAIN

We have a tiny laundry room, so every square foot counts. Because there's no room for a clothesline, I use a ceiling hook to hang a plastic chain above the laundry tub. I can hang things to drip dry without getting water on the floor. I don't have to set up a folding drying rack in the bathroom anymore!

OUR BEST
FOLDING WORKBENCH

Build this solid, roll-around bench in a day with simple hardware and only two sheets of plywood. Once you've built it, you'll wonder how you lived without it.

by **David Radtke**

Here's a workspace that's huge and accessible from all sides yet folds up and stows away easily. If you don't have room for a full-size permanent workbench but really need space to spread things out, this workbench is it. It opens to a solid 4 x 7-ft. surface with both wings up, yet closes and rolls into a small 4-ft. x 18-in. spot in a corner of the room. It's a perfect

work space for the garage or basement. It's also a great surface for making repairs, working on hobbies, cutting sewing patterns, wrapping gifts, folding laundry, doing stained glass crafts or even just holding a mechanic's parts.

This project has no complex wood joints. Just straight cuts, careful measuring and some nailing and screwing.

Assembly is as simple as glue and nails

Take a look at the Cutting List and cut all your pieces from 3/4-in.-thick hardwood plywood. I used birch plywood from a home center, but any flat plywood sheet will do. Avoid construction-grade plywoods because they'll often have bows or

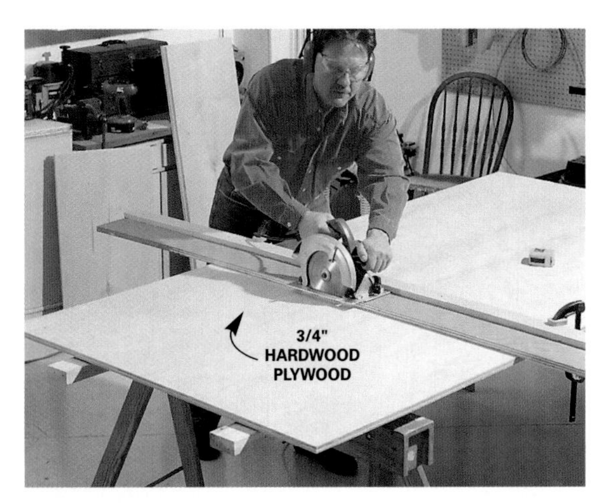

1 Cut all the pieces to size from two sheets of 3/4-in. birch plywood. Use a 40-tooth carbide blade or a 150-tooth plywood blade for a smooth cut. A straightedge cutting guide clamped to the plywood will give you factory-straight cuts.

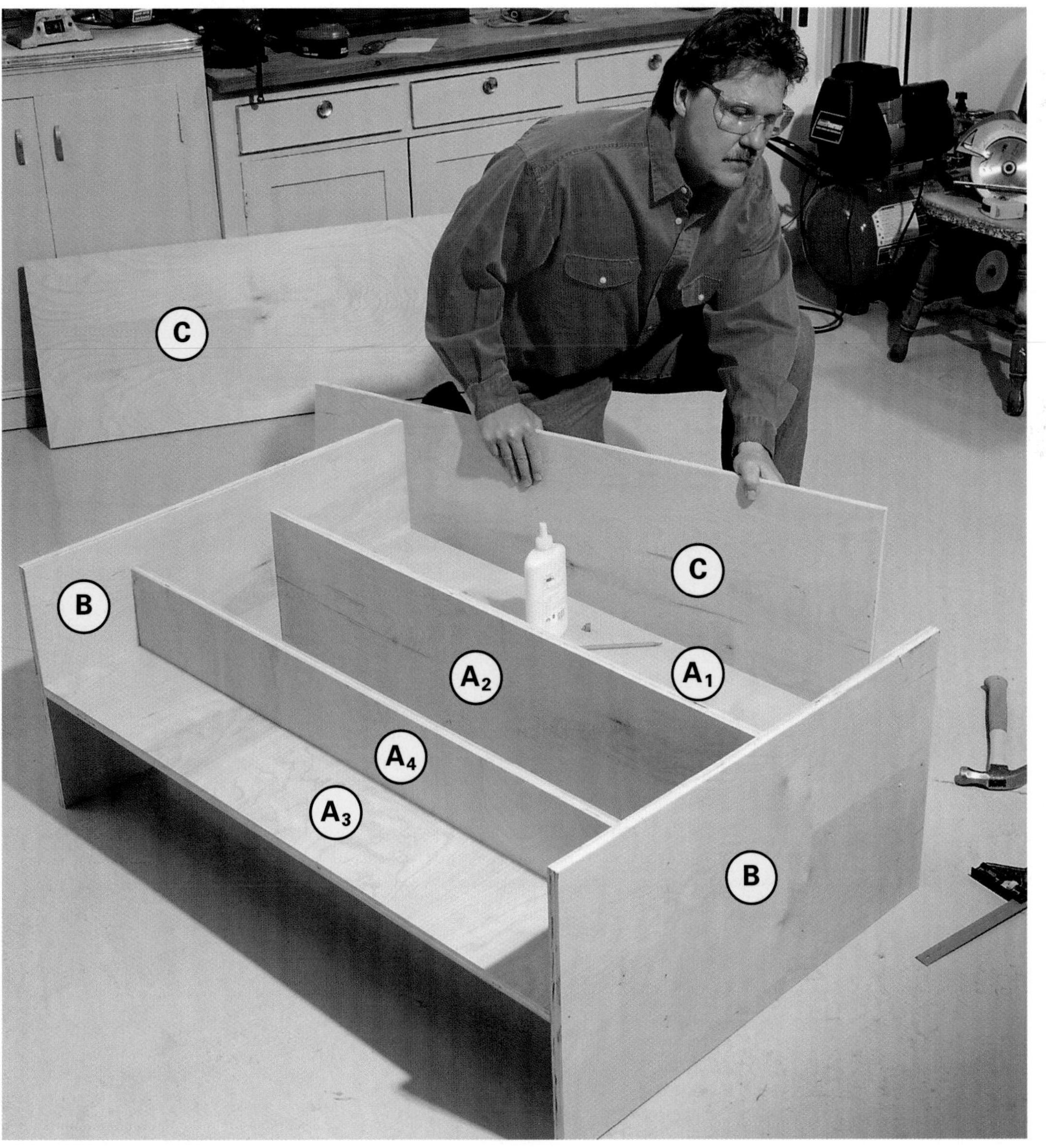

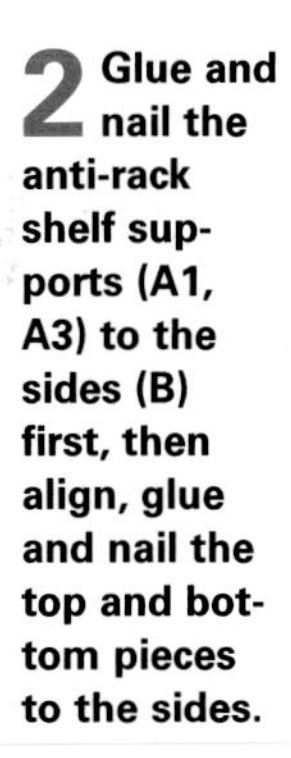

2 Glue and nail the anti-rack shelf supports (A1, A3) to the sides (B) first, then align, glue and nail the top and bottom pieces to the sides.

Figure A
Folding workbench details

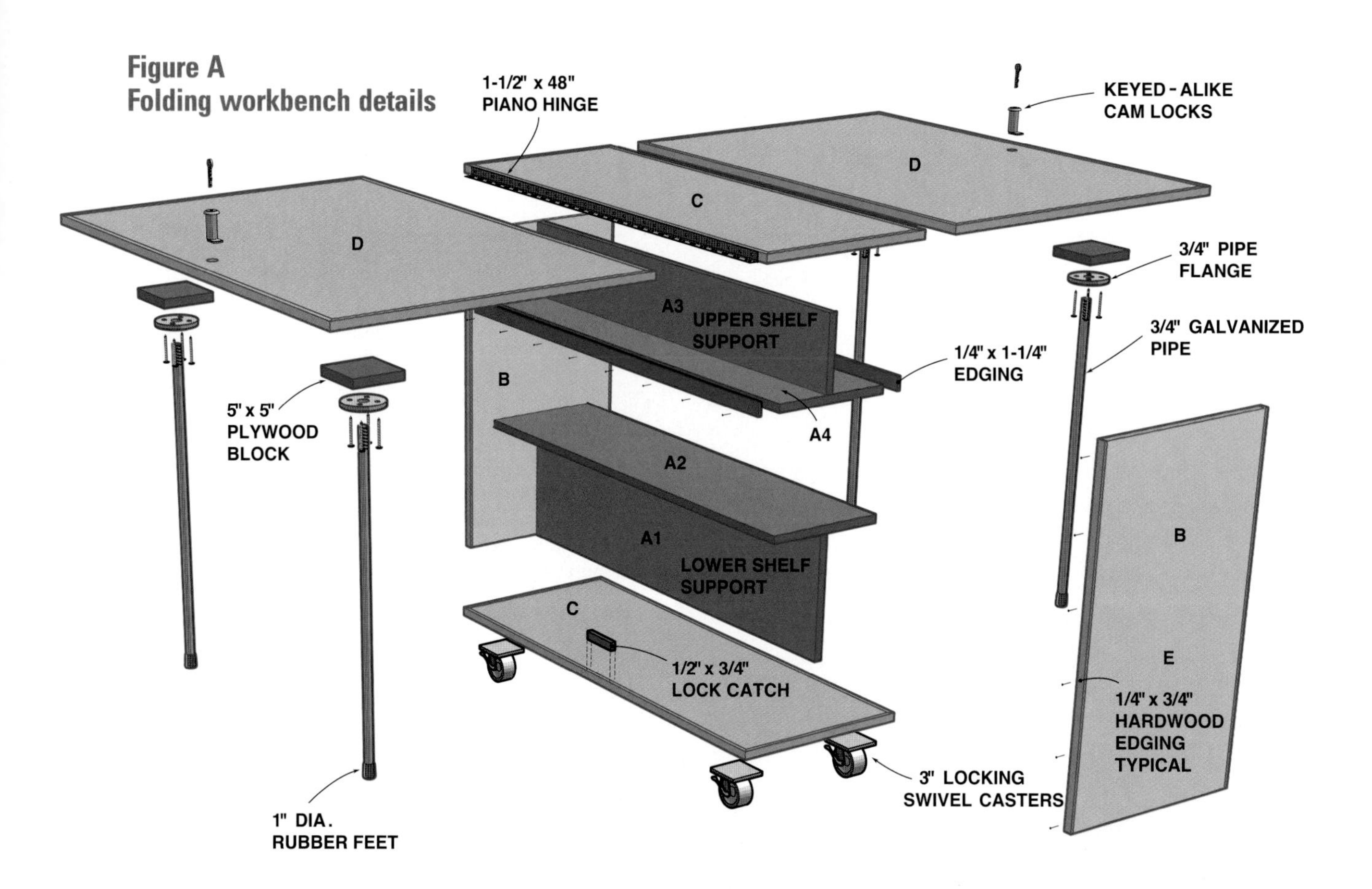

SHOPPING LIST

ITEM	QTY.
3/4" x 4' x 8' hardwood plywood	2
3/4" x 6" x 8' hardwood boards*	2
3" locking casters	4
1" brad nails	1 pkg.
6d finish nails	1/4 lb.
3/4" pipe flanges	4
3/4" x 36" galv. pipe (one end threaded)	4
Wood glue	1 pint
1-in. rubber feet	4
1/4" x 1-1/4" lag screws and washers	8
1/4" x 1-1/4" carriage bolts and washers	8
1-1/2" x 48" piano hinges	2
Cam locks (see Buyer's Guide)	2

*Rip on table saw to make edging.

CUTTING LIST

KEY	PCS.	SIZE & DESCRIPTION
A1	1	3/4" x 12" x 46-3/8" lower shelf support
A2	1	3/4" x 12" x 46-3/8" lower shelf
A3	1	3/4" x 7-1/4" x 46-3/8" upper shelf support
A4	1	3/4" x 12" x 46-3/8" upper shelf
B	2	3/4" x 17-1/2" x 31-7/8" sides
C	2	3/4" x 17-1/2" x 47-7/8" top and bottom
D	2	3/4" x 31-7/8" x 47-7/8" tilt panels
E	62 ln.ft.	1/4" x 3/4" hardwood edging (strips cut from boards)

warps that'll make precise fitting impossible. I strongly recommend you use a guide (**Photo 1**) to cut the plywood. You'll have tighter-fitting joints and better glue bonds.

Once all the plywood pieces are cut, rip the 1/4-in.-wide edge banding from 3/4-in.-thick boards. If you don't have a table saw, ask a full-service lumberyard to do it for you.

Assemble the upper and lower shelves as shown in **Figure A** and **Photo 2** with carpenter's glue and 6d finish nails. **Note:** Don't alter the design of the shelves for this workbench. The large shelf supports (A1 and A3) on the bottom and top of the shelves keep the bench from racking out of square. Glue and nail the sides to the shelf ends, then let the assembly sit for an hour to let the glue dry before attaching the casters as shown in **Photo 3**.

Small, 1-in. brads work great for attaching the hardwood edging

The thin hardwood edging is a necessary component of the bench; without it, the hinge screws would not hold as well and the plywood could delaminate along the edges.

To apply the edging, start a few brads into each piece of wood edging, put glue on the plywood and tack each piece into position (Photo 4). Once the edging is tacked in place, nail it every 6 in. with the brads. When the glue is dry, sand the sharp corners of the edging.

Piano hinges are a pain in the neck—all those tiny screws. But they're the key to why this bench is so great!

All those screws give continuous support along the joint for a sturdy worktop. Be sure to align one hinge blade with the top (C) and the other with the top of panel D. Use a hinge center punch like the one shown or a Vix bit, a special drill bit that's self centering; see Buyer's Guide, p. 270. Screw the hinges securely in place with the screws provided.

Glue and screw the blocks to the underside of each panel (D) to support the 3/4-in. pipe flanges and pipe legs. I bought 3-ft. lengths of pipe, threaded on one side, and found that I needed to cut (with a hacksaw) about 1 in. off this length. This allowed room for the flanges and the rubber feet.

The locks serve a dual purpose. First, they keep little hands from getting into things and getting pinched, and second, they'll keep everything inside from tipping out if the bench is jarred. To install them, drill the holes for the lock (Photo 7) and glue a wooden catch to the bottom of the shelf as shown in Figure A. Measure the shaft of the lock once it's installed to get the correct thickness for the block. We used a 1/2-in.-thick block for ours.

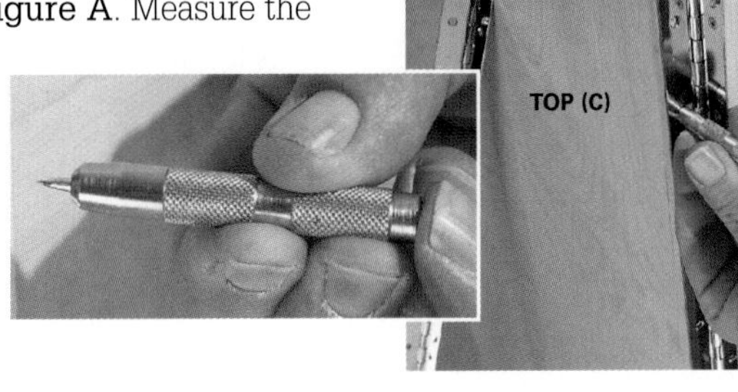

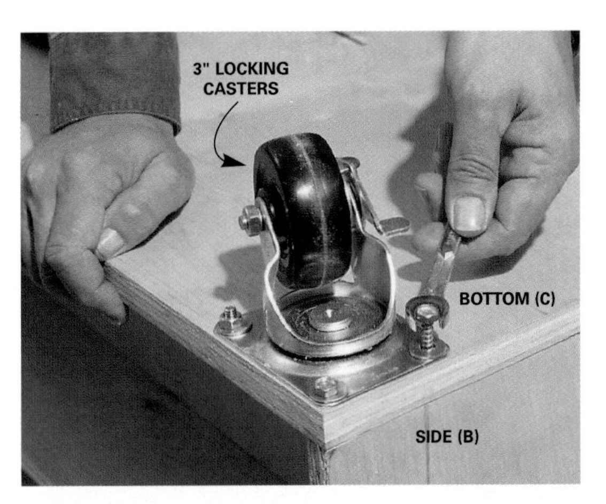

3 **Flip the assembly upside down and align the caster bases with the outer edges of the bottom. Use 1-1/4-in.-long lag screws (drill a 3/16-in. pilot hole) on the outer edge and 1-1/4-in. carriage bolts (drill a 1/4-in. pilot hole) with nuts and washers for the inner fasteners.**

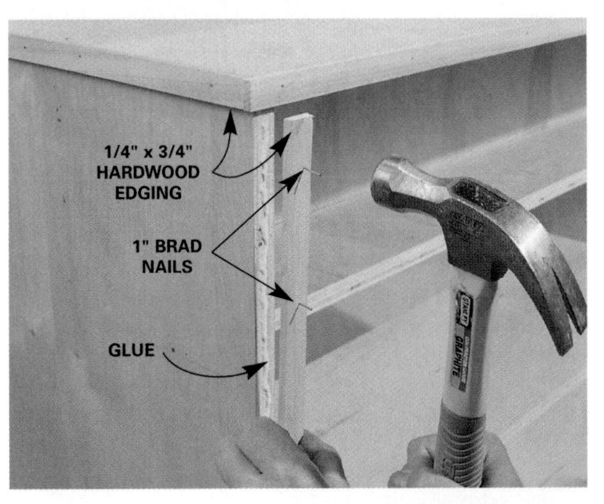

4 **Flip the bench onto the casters and begin gluing and nailing the 3/4-in. by 1/4-in. hardwood edging to the exposed plywood edges.**

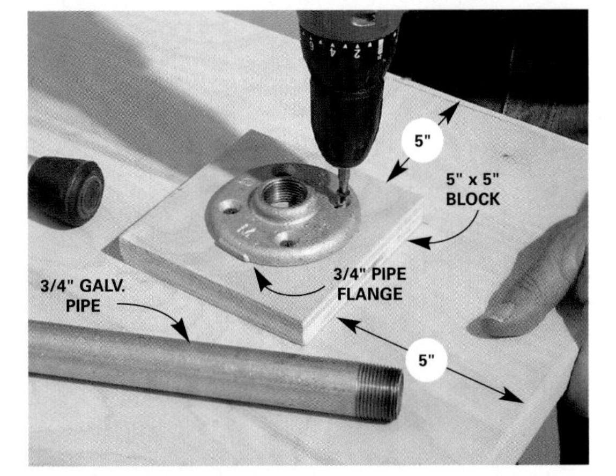

5 **Screw the 3/4-in. pipe flanges onto 5-in. square reinforcing blocks cut from scrap plywood. Glue and screw the blocks to the underside of the front panels as shown in Figure A.**

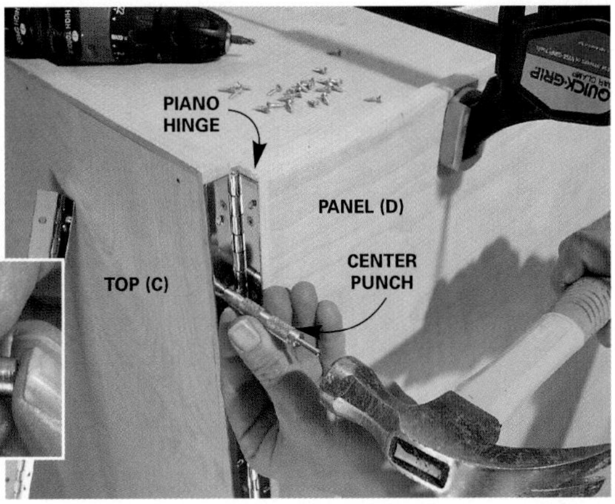

6 **Tip the bench onto its side. Align each tip-up panel (D) with the bench frame so your 1-1/2-in. piano hinge fits as shown. Align your screw holes perfectly with a center punch or a Vix bit (see Buyer's Guide, p. 270).**

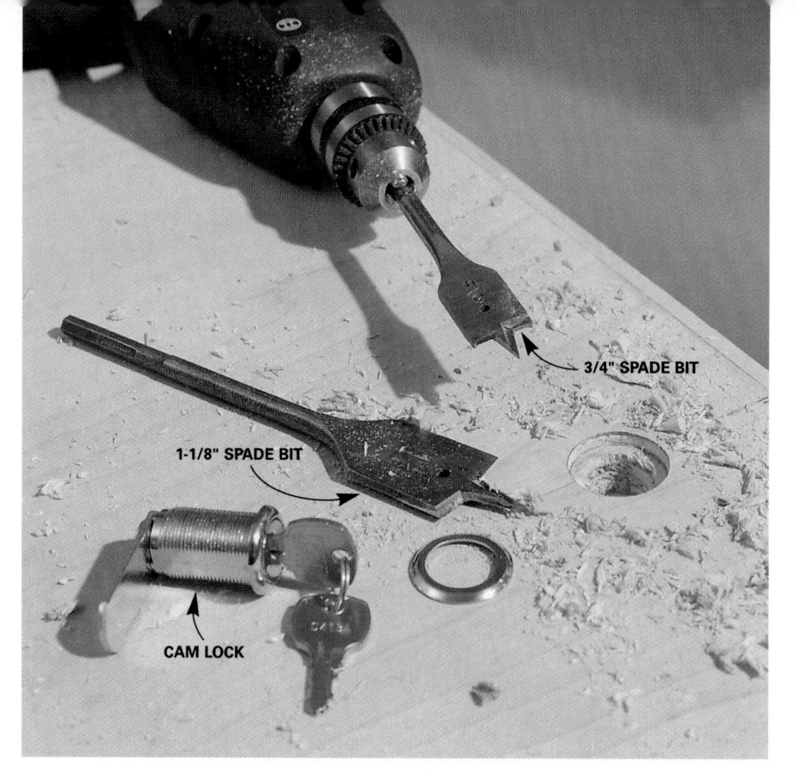

7 **Drill the holes for the cam locks into each panel (D); see Figure A for exact placement. The larger 1-1/8-in.-dia. recess is only 1/4 in. deep and allows the lock to be hidden below the surface. The second 3/4-in.-dia. hole goes through to the other side and supports the lock shaft. Follow the directions on the package for mounting.**

8 **Twist the 3/4-in. threaded pipe onto the pipe flanges for a rock-solid workbench. Be sure to lock the casters in place when using the bench.**

We finished our bench with a tough urethane varnish, but a durable oil enamel can add color and personality

Remove the hardware to make painting or varnishing a whole lot easier. Label the panels in a hidden spot so you get the right on the right side when you assemble. Small variations from one panel to the next can show up on your hinge placement and locks.

Sand the entire bench with 150-grit sandpaper and use a power sander to knock down any high spots on the hardwood edging. Vacuum the dust, wipe the bench down with a tack cloth and apply your finish. Wait a few days after the last coat of finish to let it cure before you put your first scratches on the workbench.

Buyer's Guide

You can buy keyed-alike cam locks No. 98998 and Vix bit No. 91995 at Rockler Hardware (800-279-4441; rockler.com).

You can buy a hinge center punch No. 23K05.01 at Lee Valley Tools (800-871-8158; leevalley.com).

PRO TIPS FOR PERFECT TRIM

All the basics–start to finish–plus a clever way to get those miters tight.

by **Jeff Timm**

Installing trim is one of the most rewarding home improvement projects you can do. No matter what style you choose, you'll take pride in the finished product .as long as you get all those joints tight.

Fortunately, installing trim isn't all that difficult. With a few basic carpentry tools and a little bit of patience, you can complete a room in less than a weekend.

In this story, we'll show you the basic steps for installing a wide trim around a door and window, complete with mitered comers. We'll also show you how to put in a built-up baseboard made from a combination of three types of moldings. The key to a good job is two joint techniques: mitering and coping. We'll help you master these techniques for tight and professional-looking joints.

1. TRIM A **DOOR**

1 Mark a reveal line 3/16 in. from the edge of the jamb with a combination square. Use a sharp pencil and position the marks in the corners and about every foot along the jamb edge.

Key tools

■ Use a POWER MITER SAW for clean angle cuts

A power miter saw (**Photo 2**) vastly simplifies the job because it allows you to make incredibly accurate cuts in a matter of seconds. Even professionals admit they couldn't do the same quality of work without one. If you don't have a power miter saw, you can rent one at most rental stores for about $50 a day.

TIP: If you're renting a miter saw, cut several scrap pieces to get the feel of the tool before cutting your trim.

CAUTION: This saw is powerful and loud. Be sure to keep your hands well away from the blade and wear hearing protection and safety glasses when using it.

■ Buy a GOOD-QUALITY BLADE for your miter saw

The more teeth a blade has, the crisper the cut. Choose a blade with a minimum of 40 teeth (about $30). I prefer a blade with 80 teeth (about $70). It leaves a cut that's as smooth as glass, making it well worth the investment.

■ You'll also need a COPING SAW

This saw (**Photo 18**, p. 279) has a narrow blade and tiny teeth that allow you to cut tight curves; it costs less than $10 and is available at any hardware store.

TIP: Avoid that annoying trip to the hardware store in the middle of your project—pick up a couple of spare blades in case you break one.

The only other tools you'll need are basic carpentry tools: a sharp pencil, a tape measure and a combination square. A wood file also is a must for fine-tuning joints (**Photo 20**). Use a round file, called a rattail file, for fitting tight curved profiles, and a combination flat/half round for all other trim (**Photo 19**).

In this project, we predrilled our nail holes. If you have more than one room to trim, consider using an air-powered finish nailer to speed up the process. It rents for about $75 a day.

CAUTION: Air nailers are dangerous if used improperly. If you rent one, follow all safety precautions.

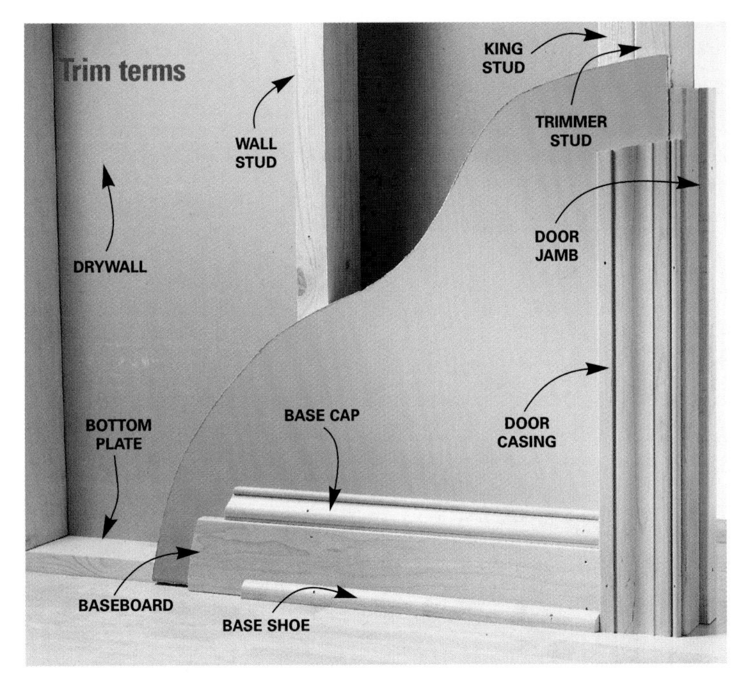

Reduce legwork: Set up your saw in the room you're trimming

If sawdust isn't a problem, cut your trim in the room where you plan to install it (**Photo 13**). Set up the miter saw in the middle of the floor with plenty of room on either side. Cover the floor with a tarp to prevent scuff marks and scratches. Use blocks the same height as the miter saw table to support long lengths of trim.

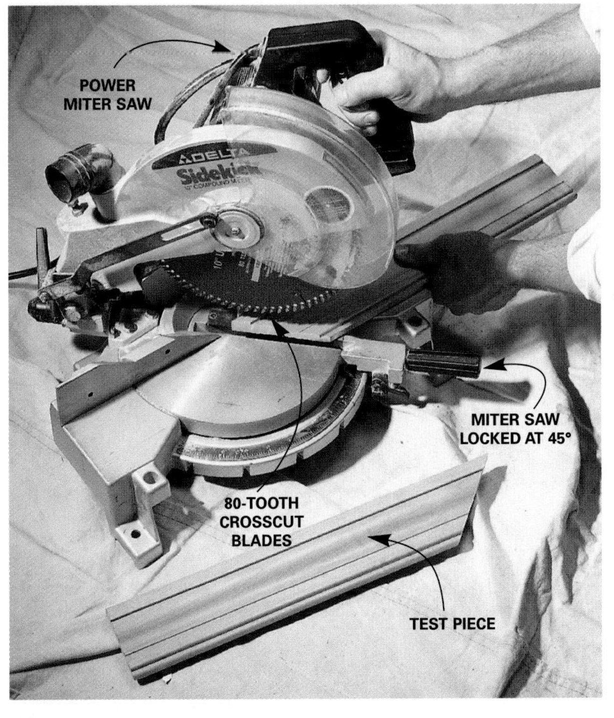

2 Cut two 12-in.-long test pieces of casing at opposite 45-degree angles on the power miter box to check the fit of your casing on the door jamb.

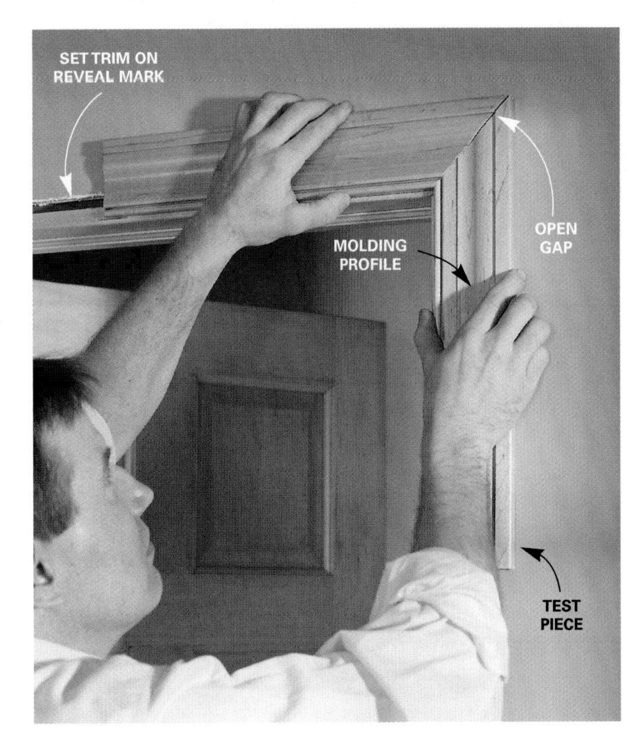

3 Hold the test pieces on the reveal marks to check the fit of the miter in the corner. If the joint is even slightly open at the top or bottom of the miter, adjust the angle on the miter saw slightly, recut both pieces and check the fit again. Take your time—you may be surprised how tight you can get the joint to fit.

Start with the casing around the doors and windows. The first few times you install casing, we suggest drawing light lines (called "reveal lines") 3/16 in. from the edge of the jamb to align the casing to the door jamb and windows (Photo 1). With experience, you'll skip this step and simply "eyeball" the reveal when you put up the trim.

Prefinishing saves a ton of time

Once you get your trim home, sand and stain or paint the trim before you install it. To be perfectly honest, this part of the project isn't much fun. But it's a lot easier to finish trim before installation, working on sawhorses, than afterward, lying on the floor with sandpaper and a staining rag. Plus you can do a better job of sanding and finishing the pieces. After you've installed the pieces, be prepared to touch them up a bit. Do all the finish work in a well-ventilated area.

We applied a Salem maple stain to our trim and three coats of low-sheen varnish to protect it.

CAUTION: Dispose of any staining rags carefully to avoid spontaneous combustion: Open up the oil-soaked rags and hang them up until they're completely dry. Then dispose of them in the trash.

The test-piece technique simplifies the toughest part—getting the miters tight

Check the miters at the corners with two 12-in. sections of casing cut at exactly 45 degrees (Photo 3). Even though the corners should be a perfect 90 degrees, often they're not. In addition, if the jamb sticks out or is set back slightly from the wall, a 45-degree miter cut won't fit tight. By holding the test pieces at the corner you can see exactly how your casings will fit. If you see a gap, adjust the saw slightly and cut both pieces at the new angle (Photo 3).

TIP: Make small adjustments. Even one-quarter of a degree makes a big difference.

If the angle of the miter is accurate but a gap still appears along the face, the pieces are probably tipping back against the wall. Cut or file the back side of the miter (back cut). This allows the joint to fit tight on the face of the miter. Don't worry about taking too much off the back; it won't be visible.

4 Cut the side casing about 1/2 in. overlong and hold it in place on the door jamb along your reveal marks. Use a sharp pencil to transfer the top reveal mark from the head jamb to the side casing. Then cut the miter at the angle you established with your test pieces.

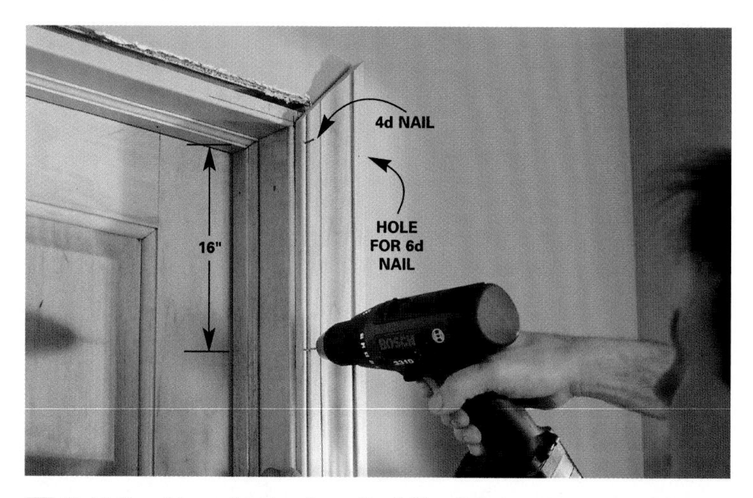

5 Hold the side casing in place. Predrill nail holes every 12 to 16 in., using a drill bit about 1/32 in. smaller than the nail size. Stay 1 in. away from the ends to avoid splitting. Drive 4d finishing nails into the jamb and 6d finishing nails into the wall.

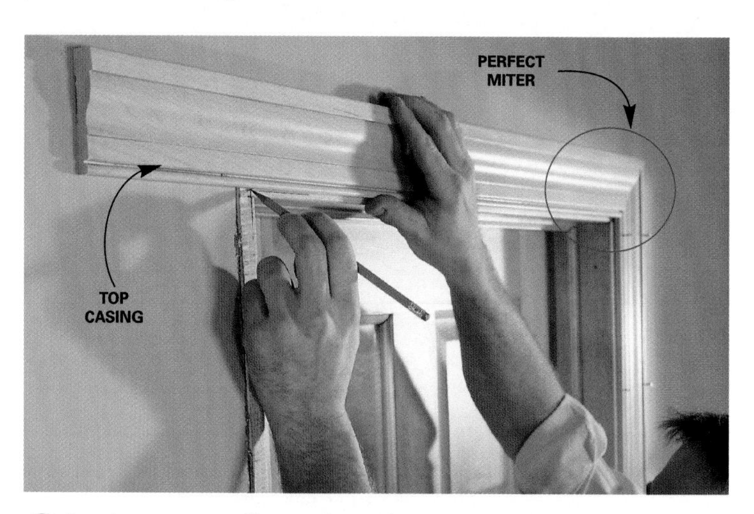

6 Cut the corresponding angle on the top casing, leaving the opposite side at least 1 in. overlong. Check your miter at the second corner with your test pieces, and adjust if necessary to fit tight. Then mark the opposite corner on the top casing, cut it and tack it up.

Mark and cut the first side casing at the angle you established with your test pieces (**Photo 4**). Always cut the pieces a little long and check the fit; the power miter saw gives you the ability to cut very slight amounts off with a high degree of accuracy. When the inside angle of the miter lines up with the reveal mark on the top of the jamb, tack the casing in place.

Don't split that perfect miter—predrill nail holes

With maple, oak and other dense wood, predrilling your nail holes in the casing is a must (**Photo 5**). Even with a softwood like pine, I prefer to predrill to avoid splitting a perfectly fit piece. Use a 1/16-in. bit for 4d nails, 3/32-in. for 6d nails and 1/8-in. for 8d nails.

TIP: Use a nail with the head snipped off as a substitute for a drill bit. The same size nail you're driving works best.

Tack the casing into the jamb first, then to the wall. Wait until you've fit all the casings before you drive the nails in completely in case something doesn't fit right and you have to remove the trim to recut it. We used 4d nails for the jamb and 6d nails for walls. If you're using thicker casing, increase your nail size one increment, using 6d nails in the jamb and 8d nails in the wall. Your nails should penetrate the studs and the jamb at least 3/4 in.

TIP: On wood with a strong grain pattern, place your nails in the dark portion of the grain to make them less noticeable.

With your first corner fit perfectly, set the top casing aside and check the second corner with your test pieces the same way you did the first. Once you have established the angle of the miter, hold your top casing in place and transfer the reveal mark from the side jamb to your top casing (**Photo 6**). Cut the miter, check your fit and tack in place.

TIP: Match your pieces of wood so the grain pattern and color are similar at the joints.

Then mark and cut the second side casing, leaving an extra 1/32 in. for fitting purposes (**Photo 7**). Slide the casing into place parallel to your reveal marks and check your fit. If the miter is tight and the length is a little long, trim a hair off the bottom at a 90-degree angle until you get a perfect fit.

7 Cut the second side casing about 1 in. overlong. Then hold the casing backward and parallel to the door jamb. Make a mark where the edge of the side casing intersects the upper edge of the top casing. Cut the side casing about 1/32 in. overlong. Slide the casing into place. Check your fit, and then trim it to its final length. Once the miter fits, nail the casing in place.

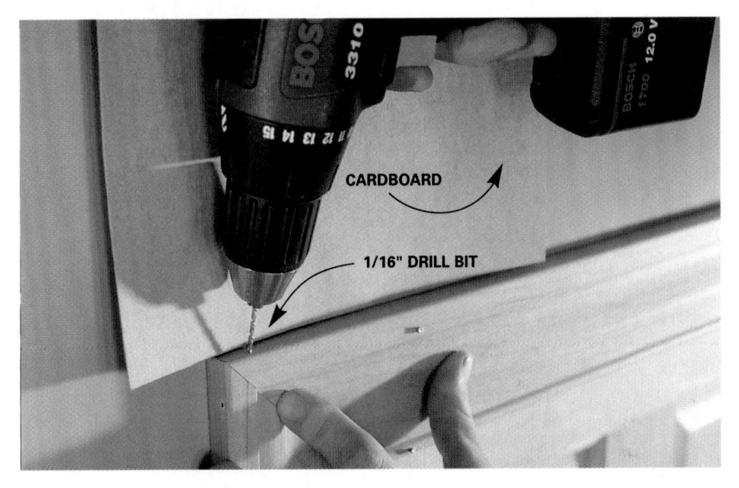

8 Align the miters and predrill a 1/16-in. hole for 3d finish nails, one from the top and one from the side. Hold a piece of cardboard against the wall to prevent marring the wall while drilling.

9 Drive the nails into the casing gradually, alternating between the two nails so the miter doesn't slide out of alignment. Use cardboard again between the wall and the hammer to avoid marring the wall.

This pinning technique will hold the miters tight

When your miters fit perfectly, "pin" the corners (**Photos 8 and 9**) to help align the two casings and keep the joint tight. Use your finger to press the casings flush with each other. You may have to slip a small shim behind one of the casings to align them. Next predrill the corners for 3d finishing nails, one from the top and one from the side (**Photo 8**). If your casing is less than 1/2 in. thick, you'll have to predrill the corners before tacking the casing up.

Finally, work around the door, driving the nailheads slightly below the surface with a hammer and a nail set (**Photo 10**). Nail sets are sold in various sizes; choose one that matches the size of the nailhead you're using. Set the nails deep enough to hold nail putty: A good rule of thumb is half the diameter of the nailhead.

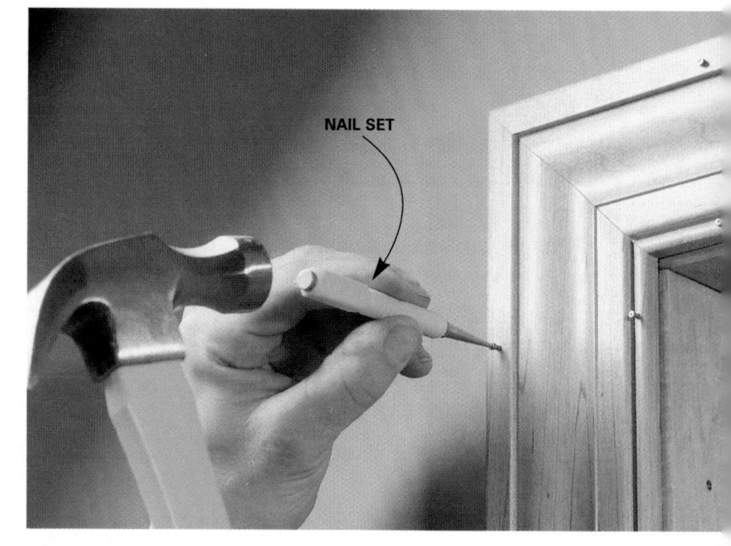

10 **Tap the nails just below the surface with a hammer and a nail set.**

2. CASE A **WINDOW**

11 **Trim a window using the same techniques as we showed for a door. However, cut and tack the top casing first. Then fit the sides and finish with the bottom.**

The trick to 'picture-frame' window trimming is fitting that fourth piece

There are two basic ways to trim a window. One way is to "picture frame" the window, so that all four corners are mitered to 90 degrees. This method is common on most newer homes, especially with casement windows. The second way is to install a stool and apron. Basically, this is a small ledge (a stool) at the bottom of the window with a piece of casing (an apron) under it. This method is normally found in older homes and

continued on p. 278

12 **Fit one miter on the bottom, then overlap the opposite miter and mark it. Cut the miter 1/8 in. overlong, slide the casing into place and trim it down gradually while checking the fit.**

3. INSTALL A **BASEBOARD**

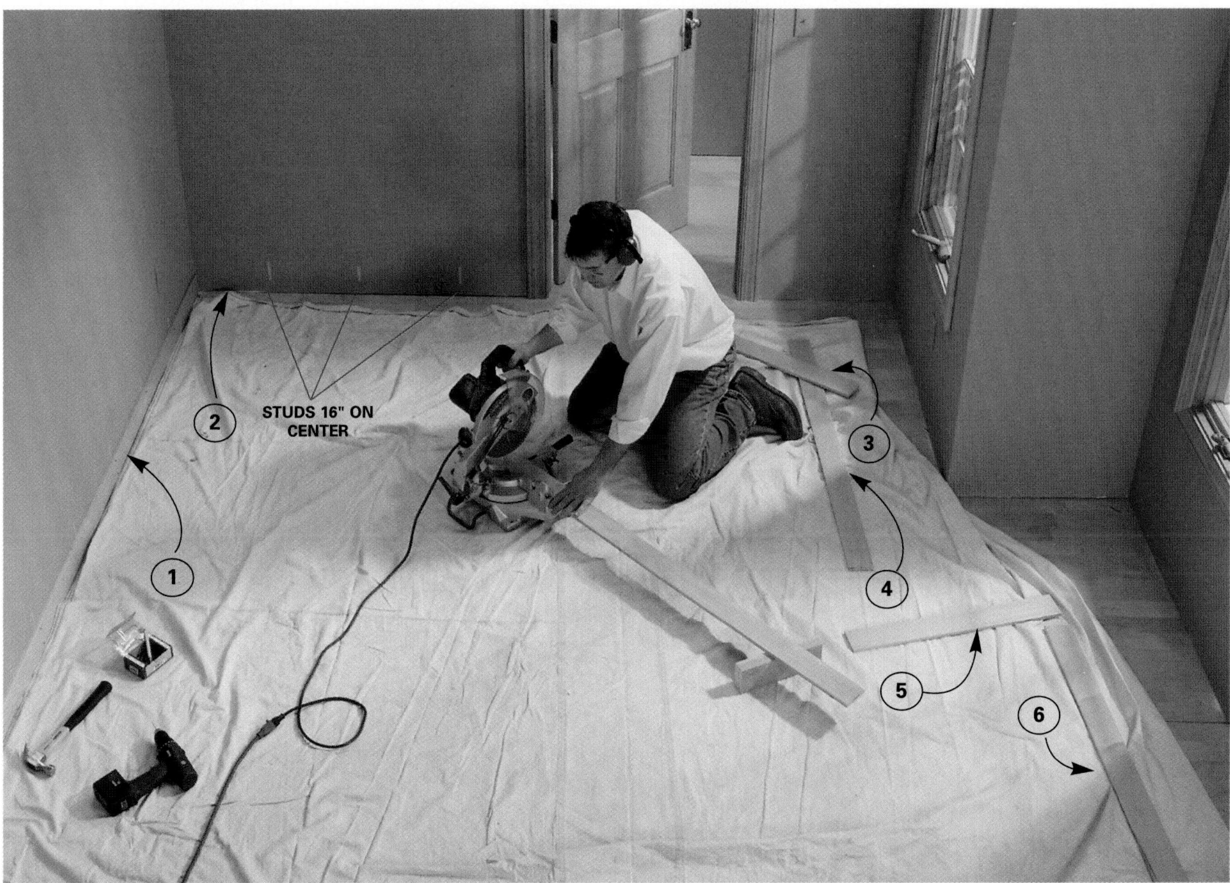

13 **Rough-cut all the baseboards about 2 in. overlong and lay them in place around the perimeter of the floor. Start with the longest wall, cut the first piece to length and nail it into the studs with 6d finishing nails. Remember to predrill your holes. Continue around the room, cutting the inside corners off at 90 degrees and butting them together.**

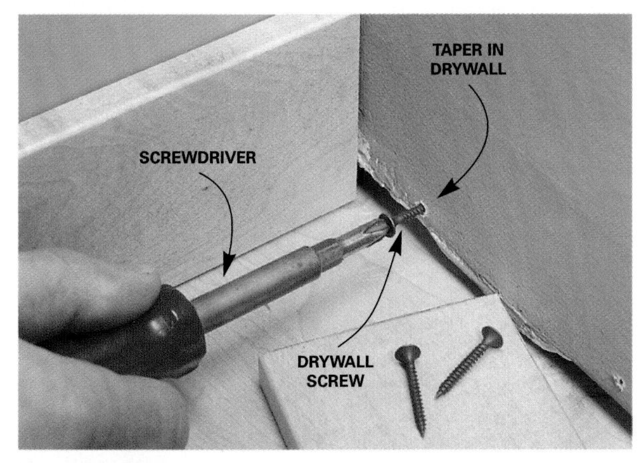

Screw tip

If the drywall tapers in at the bottom of the wall or stops short of the floor, simply drive a screw at the bottom of the wall and turn it in until the head of the screw is at the same plane as the main wall. The head will prevent the baseboard from tipping in.

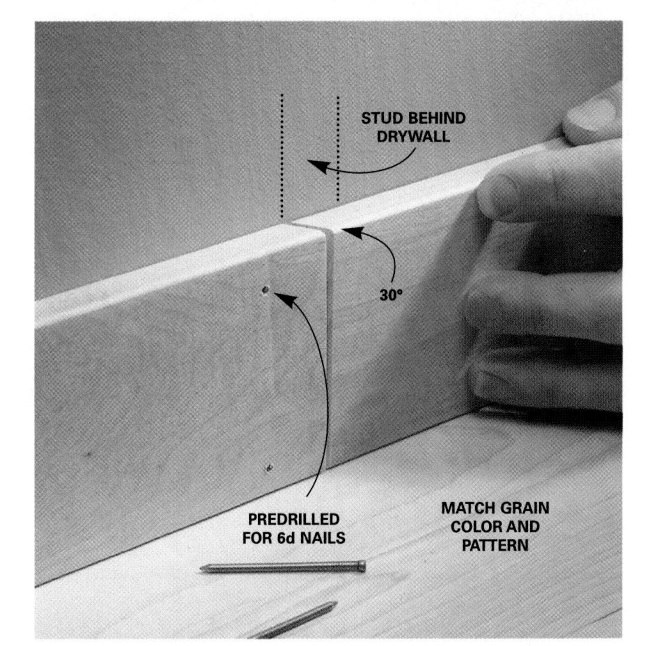

Splice tip

If possible, purchase your trim in lengths long enough to cover an entire wall. If you have to splice two pieces on a wall, use a "scarf joint." Cut a 30-degree angle on each piece; if the joint opens slightly, this angle will hide the crack. Select pieces with similar grain color and pattern so the joint is less visible. Always locate a splice over a wall stud.

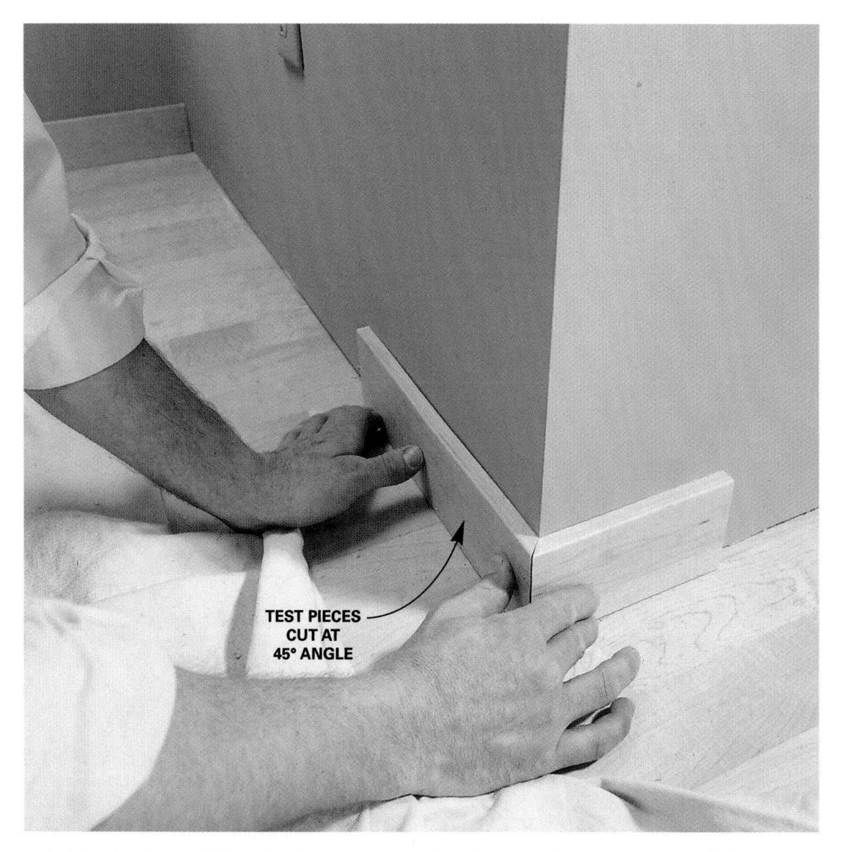

14 **Miter two 1-ft. test pieces about a foot long and press them tightly against the outside corners to determine the correct angle. Adjust the miter saw to get a tight fit.**

continued from p. 276

is more often used on double-hung windows.

Trim a window using the same techniques as with a door. Mark your reveal lines, use test pieces to check your corners, and transfer the reveal lines to the casings for cutting and nailing. When you "picture frame" a window, however, install the top casing first (**Photo 11**), then the two sides, and finally, the bottom. Fitting the bottom is the toughest part, because you have to fit both corners at once (**Photo 12**). But if you use your test pieces and *always cut the casing a little long*, you shouldn't have any problem. Cutting the piece long allows you to adjust the miters if you have to. Once the miters are tight, gradually trim a small amount off with your miter saw until you have the proper length.

Trim out a window with a stool in the same order as you would a door, but with a few added steps. Install the

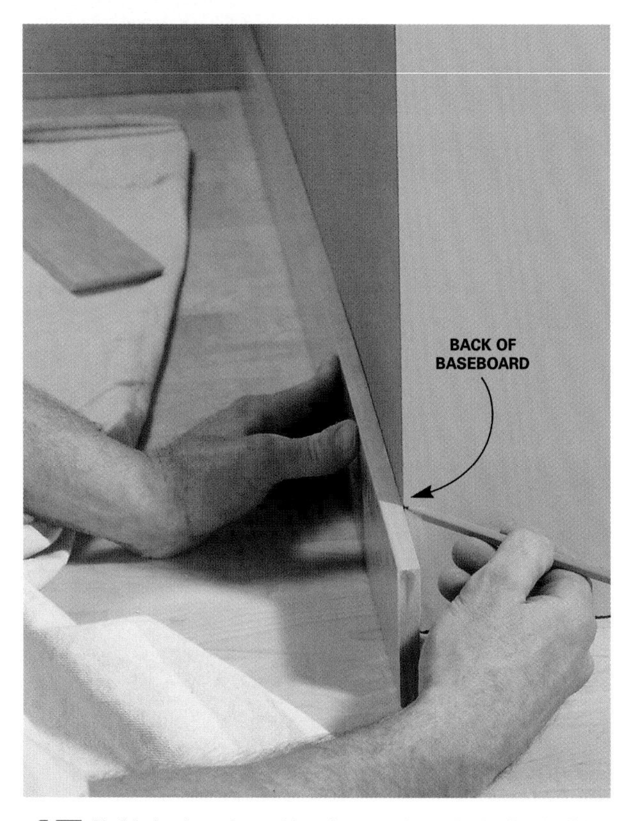

15 **Hold the baseboard in place and mark the back side at the corner. Now cut the piece to length at the predetermined angle for an exact fit.**

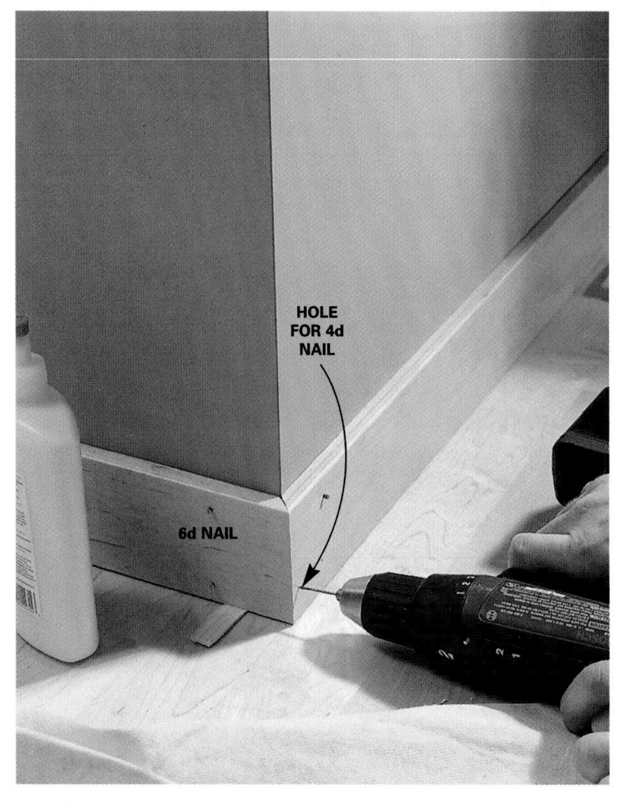

16 **Cut the second piece to length at the same angle. Predrill, glue and nail the outside corner.**

stool first, then one side, the top and the other side. Install the apron under the stool last.

Installing a three-piece baseboard is well worth the extra effort

Begin by using a stud finder to locate the studs, and mark their location on the wall with a narrow piece of painter's tape (**Photo 13**). You can pull the tape off without leaving a mark. Rough-cut the baseboard about 2 in. overlong and lay the pieces along the wall. Install the longest section first and work away from the ends until you reach an opening or door. This ensures that the last cut will be a simple 90-degree cut.

In general, measure and cut each piece about 1/16 in. overlong to ensure a tight fit. If you don't have a piece of baseboard long enough to cover the entire wall, splice two pieces with a "scarf joint" (**see "splice tip" photo, p. 277**). Bow the casing slightly to fit

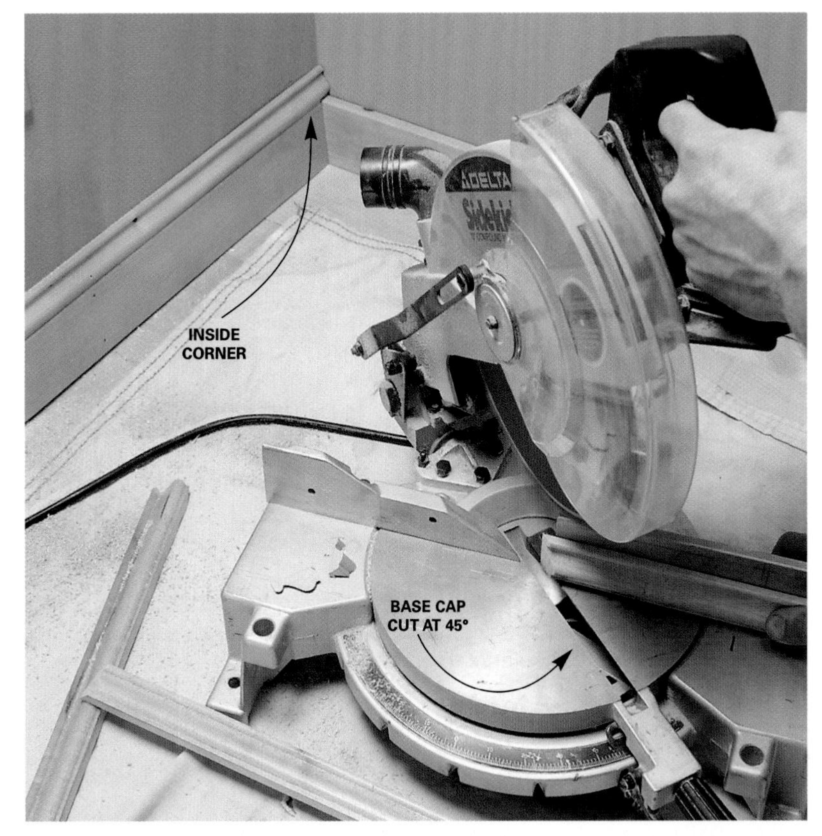

17 **Run the base cap in the same order as the baseboard. To cope the inside corner of the base cap for a tight fit, first cut one end at a 45-degree angle as if you were cutting an inside miter.**

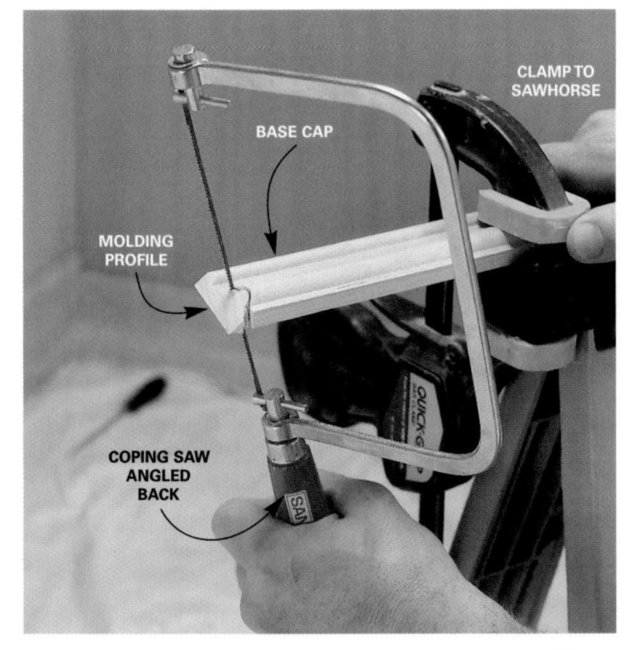

18 **Use a coping saw to cut along the profile left by the miter. Angle your coping saw back slightly (back cut) to get a tighter fit on the face of the profile.**

19 **Check the fit against the adjoining base cap in the corner.**

SPECIAL BONUS SECTION

between the walls and press it into place. This ensures a nice, tight fit. But don't force the piece in. Trim a bit off and try the fit again.

Continue around the room butting the inside corners at 90 degrees. When you come to an outside corner, use test pieces to find exact angles (Photo 14).

TIP: If you're adding a base cap, as we are, overcut the miter slightly, leaving the back side slightly open (Photo 16). The front side will be tight and the cap will cover the gap.

Nail the pieces in place using 6d finishing nails. You can also put a small amount of glue at the miters and cross-nail them with 4d finishing nails. But remember to predrill to avoid splitting the ends (Photo 16).

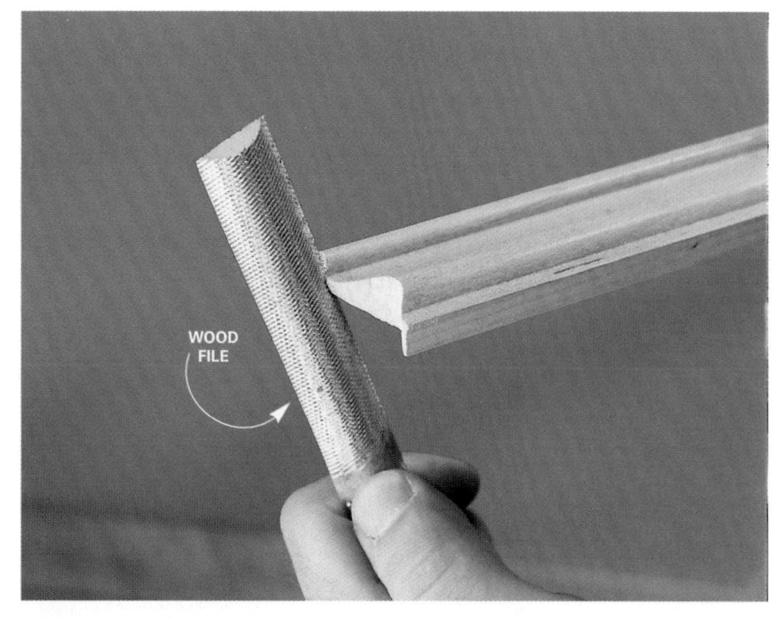

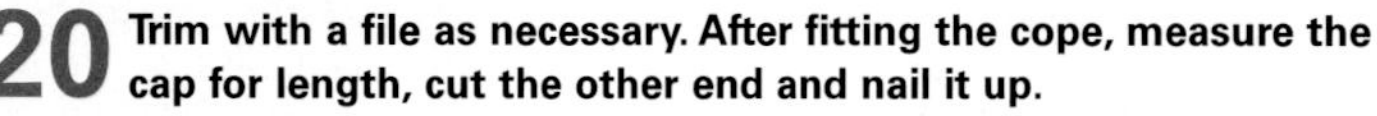
20 **Trim with a file as necessary. After fitting the cope, measure the cap for length, cut the other end and nail it up.**

The coping technique simplifies the cap installation

Install the base cap pieces in the same order as the baseboard. However, because base cap has a curved profile, you can't butt the inside corners. Instead, make a "coped joint" by cutting off one piece square and cutting the adjoining piece to match the profile of the molding (Photo 19). Just follow the steps in Photos 17 – 20 and you'll find it's easier than it looks. (Actually, coping is kind of fun once you get the hang of it.) Practice a few times on scrap pieces to get used to it.

Install the base shoe last. Base shoe is usually used on hard-surface floors to conceal any irregularities or gaps between the floor and the baseboard. Even if your baseboards fit perfectly tight to the floor, you can install the shoe to add another dimension to your trim. Install the shoe the same as the cap, mitering outside corners and coping inside corners (Photo 21). Be sure to nail the shoe into the baseboard, not the floor, so it won't pull away from the baseboard when the flooring expands and contracts. Finally, set all your nails and fill them with putty. We couldn't find a putty color to exactly match the stain we chose, so we mixed two shades together (Photo 22).

TIP: With light-colored wood, always mix the color on the light side; darker putty stands out.

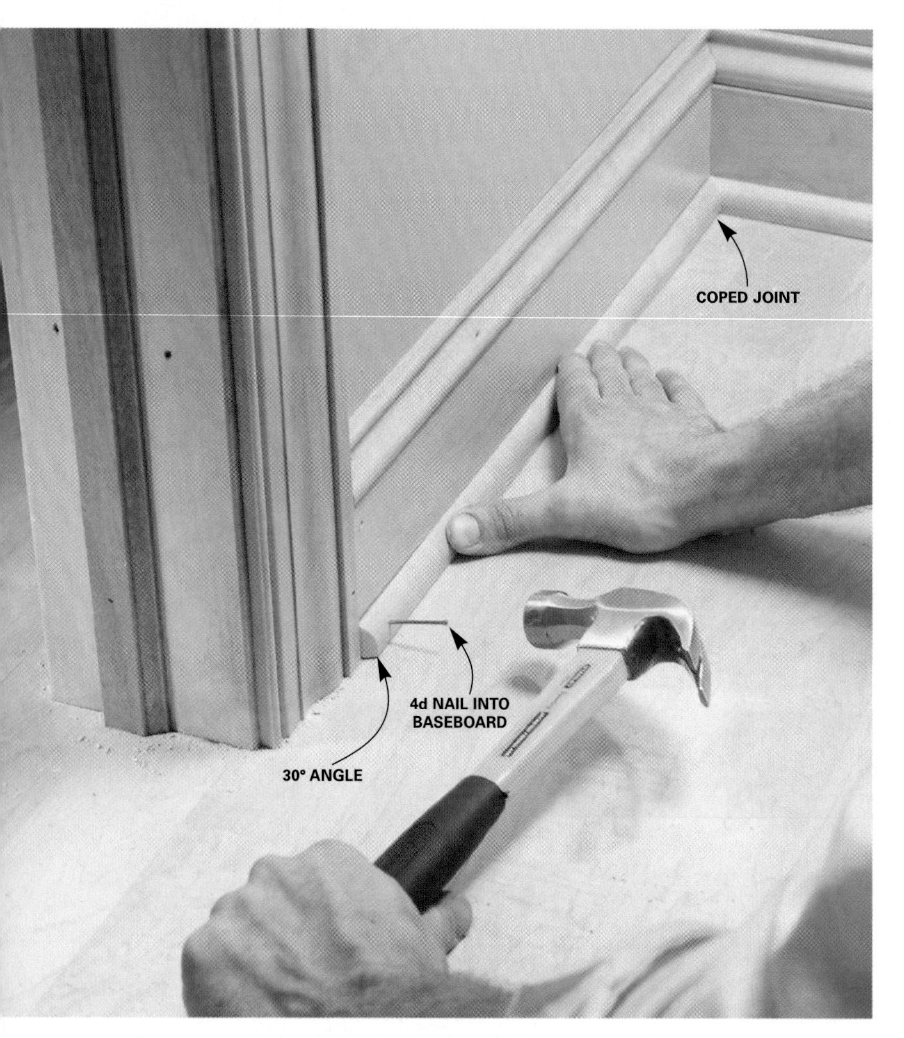

21 **Install base shoe the same as the base cap, coping inside corners and mitering outside corners. Where the shoe meets the door casing, cut at a 30-degree angle the portion that sticks out. Predrill and nail the base shoe to the baseboard with 4d finishing nails.**

22 Set the nails and fill the holes with colored putty to match the wood stain. We mixed two shades of putty together to get a good color match. Press the putty into the holes with your finger and wipe the excess off with a cloth.

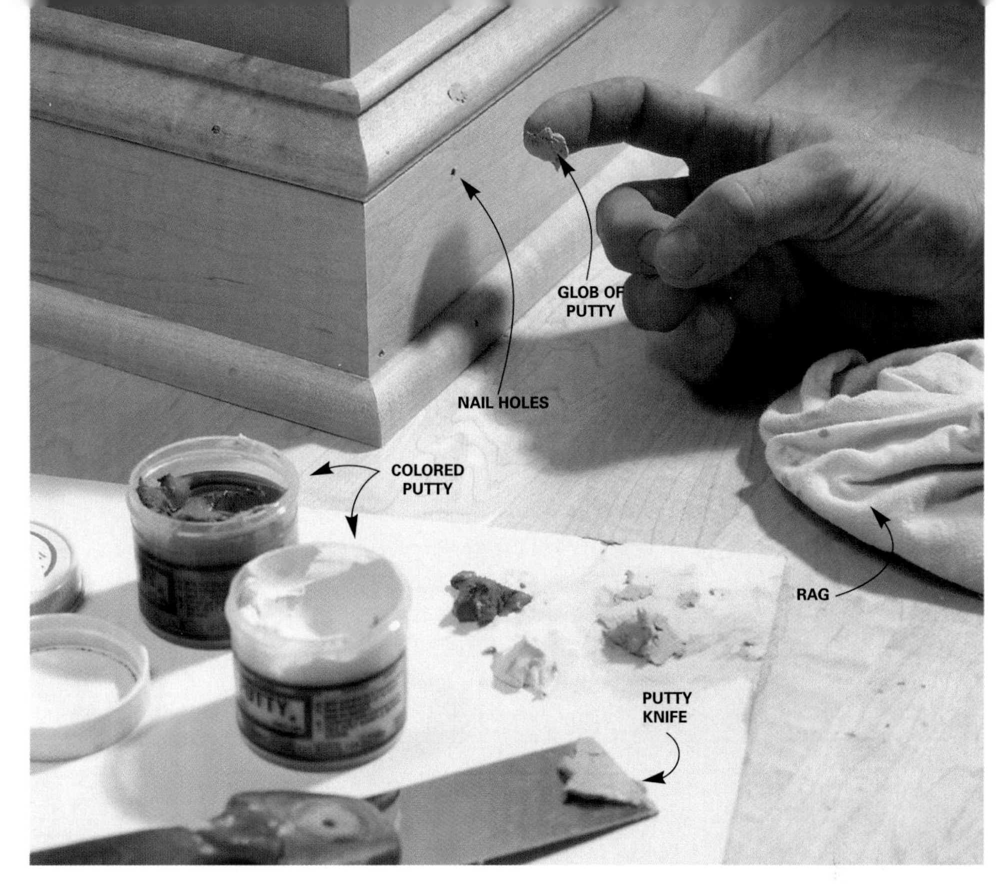

How to shop for trim

Stock trim is available in a wide range of styles from most lumberyards and home centers.

We chose a relatively wide (3-1/4 in.) beaded casing to go around our doors and windows. It's 11/16 in. thick and costs $2.40 per ft. We used three components to create the base: a 1/2-in. x 3-1/4 in. "hook strip," a 9/16-in. x 1-3/8 in. base cap, and a 7/16-in. x 3/4-in. base shoe (see "Trim Terms," p. 273). The three together cost $2.70 per ft. Combine other standard trim types to create wider and more detailed shapes.

If you don't find a trim style you like or you're trying to match a molding in an older house, look online or in the yellow pages under "Millwork." Millwork shops can custom-produce almost any type of trim from most species of wood. Custom work, however, comes at a price; be prepared to pay as much as three times the cost of stock moldings, plus setup charges of as much as $200. In addition, you may have to wait four to eight weeks.

Most trim is made of solid wood or medium-density fiberboard with a wood veneer. Oak, pine, birch, maple and poplar are the most common types available. We chose maple for our project.

Sometimes you can find trim made of various types of plastic, most often prefinished in white, brown or simulated wood. This trim is far more stable than wood but cuts much the same, if not easier. What it lacks, however, is the warmth and varied grain pattern you can only find in real wood.

Purchase your trim in lengths long enough to cover each wall. If you can't purchase the trim in long enough lengths, don't worry. On p. 277, we show you how to splice two pieces to cover the length of a long wall.

Water, Water Everywhere
Great Goofs®

Safe, but sorry

I decided to buy a floor safe to protect my wife's jewelry. The locksmith wanted $200 to install it in my concrete floor—which was more than the safe cost! To do the job myself, I rented the biggest jackhammer known to mankind and bought some concrete mix for the patchwork. I fired up the jackhammer and it broke through the basement slab just fine. Then it hammered through the main water line, sending water shooting up like a geyser.

The project took some extra time and an emergency visit from my plumber, but you know what? That $200 locksmith would have caused the same disaster!

Unplanned shower

Last year my fiancée and I started our first home improvement project together, aptly, a shower. We installed a new control valve along with new tile. Although my fiancée was still grouting the tile, I decided it was safe to turn on the main water supply valve because we'd finished the plumbing. A second later, a scream echoed through the house. I ran to the bathroom and saw that the shower was blasting on my fiancée. We'd left the valve in the open position and she couldn't turn it off because we hadn't installed the handles. Anyway, a year after this first shower, we're happily married!

Toilet blues

My wife came home with one of those $10 chlorination gadgets for the toilet that "self-cleans" the bowl after flushing. Installation seemed simple enough, but within minutes I had broken the fill valve assembly at the base.

I quickly turned off the water supply at the wall and tried to loosen the coupling nut that secures the valve so I could replace the part. It was corroded and wouldn't budge. I decided to pull the toilet for better access to the stuck nut. I removed the flange nuts and lifted the toilet with all my might…and learned that the caulking bead around the toilet base can be exceptionally strong. The bowl base broke into three pieces and water spilled everywhere.

My wife and I decided that I should quit while I was behind and call a real plumber. The $350 bill was an expensive end to a simple task, but there is no cleaner toilet than a brand new one.

A shower in a tub

My handy husband was tearing out our old fiberglass tub/shower combination to remodel our bathroom. He proudly brought out his trusty reciprocating saw and went to work. All of a sudden, the steady buzz of the blade cutting through fiberglass was replaced by his favorite naughty word, followed by a cry for help. He'd sawed straight through a water pipe and water was spraying everywhere. Our remodeled bathroom is extra deluxe now that it has some brand new pipes.

Tidal wave

While folding laundry one rainy Saturday, I noticed water seeping from the bottom of a basement window. Figuring the window was unable to shut properly because the seal was dirty, I got a small rag and started to open the window to wipe it out.

What I didn't realize was that the entire window well was full of water. When I turned the latch, the whole laundry room was hit with a tidal wave that completely soaked me and everything in it.

I went upstairs to change and told my wife the laundry was still a little damp.

Water works

In an attempt to bring our lawn up to par with our neighbors', I installed an underground sprinkler system. A few months went by and the results were terrific—our lawn was green and weed free.

A neighbor suggested we'd get even better results if we had our lawn professionally aerated. So of course I called up a lawn service and had it done.

The next morning, I peered out the window to see streams of water spurting up from random spots in the lawn. Apparently I hadn't buried the underground tubing deep enough and the machine that aerated the lawn punctured the lines.

Now I can impress my neighbors with my pipe-patching skills.

F is for flub—and flood

I couldn't get the valves that fed my washing machine to stop leaking, so I replaced the entire faucet assembly. The installation went fine. I reconnected the washer hoses, double-checked for leaks and washed my first load of clothes. Satisfied with my leak-free connections, I went upstairs.

Everything worked perfectly—until I returned to the laundry room and found myself standing in a pool of soapy water. Unfortunately, I'd forgotten to put the drain line back into the laundry tub and an entire washer's worth of dirty water had poured onto my floor. Talk about washed up!

INDEX

Visit ***familyhandyman.com*** *for hundreds of home improvement articles.*

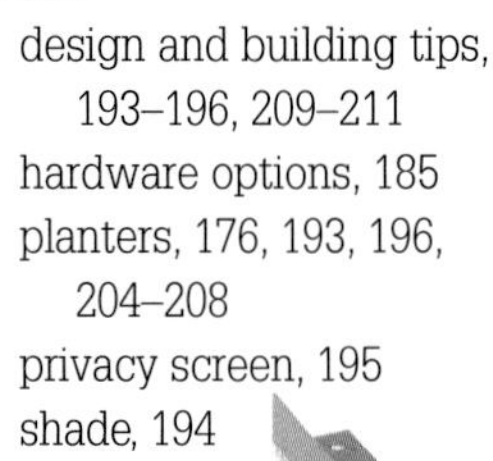

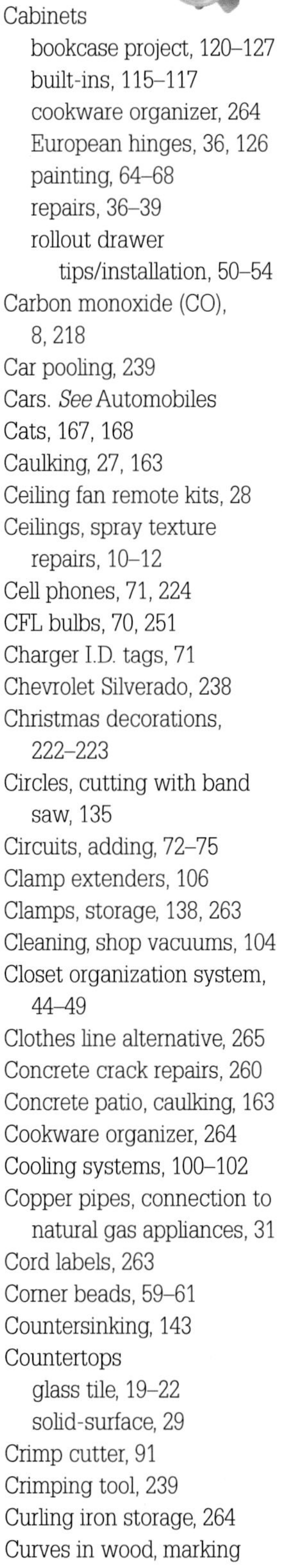

F

G

H

I

J

K

L

M

N

O

P

R

S

ACKNOWLEDGMENTS

FOR THE FAMILY HANDYMAN

Editor in Chief	Ken Collier
Senior Editors	Travis Larson
	Gary Wentz
Associate Editors	Elisa Bernick
	Mary Flanagan
	Jeff Gorton
Senior Copy Editor	Donna Bierbach
Art Directors	Vern Johnson
	Becky Pfluger
	Marcia Roepke
Photographer	Tom Fenenga
Production Artist	Mary Schwender
Office Administrative Manager	Alice Garrett
Financial Assistant	Steven Charbonneau
Admin. Editorial Assistant	Roxie Filipkowski
Production Manager	Judy Rodriguez

CONTRIBUTING EDITORS

Spike Carlsen
Tom Dvorak
Duane Johnson
Brett Martin
Dave Munkittrick
Rick Muscoplat
David Radtke
Jeff Timm

CONTRIBUTING ART DIRECTORS

Roberta Peters
David Simpson
Bob Ungar

CONTRIBUTING PHOTOGRAPHERS

Tate Carlson
Mike Krivit, Krivit Photography
Ramon Moreno
Shawn Nielsen
Bill Zuehlke

ILLUSTRATORS

Steve Björkman
Gabe De Matteis
Mario Ferro
John Hartman
Don Mannes
Paul Perreault
Frank Rohrbach III

OTHER CONSULTANTS

Charles Avoles, plumbing
Al Hildenbrand, electrical
Joe Jensen, Jon Jensen, carpentry
Dave MacDonald, structural engineer
William Nunn, painting
Dean Sorem, tile
Costas Stavrou, appliance repair
John Williamson, electrical
Les Zell, plumbing

For information about advertising in *The Family Handyman* magazine, call (646) 293-6333

To subscribe to *The Family Handyman* magazine:

- By phone: (800) 285-4961
- By Internet: FHMservice@rd.com
- By mail: The Family Handyman, Subscriber Service Dept., P.O. Box 6099, Harlan, IA 51593-1599

We welcome your ideas and opinions.
Write: The Editor, The Family Handyman
2915 Commers Drive, Suite 700
Eagan, MN 55121
Fax: (651) 994-2250
E-mail: editors@thefamilyhandyman.com

In loving memory
Sara Koehler
Design Director,
The Family Handyman
2004–2009

Photocopies of articles are available for $3.00 each. Call (800) 285-4961 from 8 a.m. to 5 p.m. Central, Monday through Friday or send an e-mail to FHMservice@rd.com. Visa, MasterCard and Discover accepted.